Contents

KU-647-675

List of Tables and Figures

Acknowledgements

Most important to me during the process of writing this and juggling it with too many other interests has been my family. I feel unending gratitude to them – to Adam, Eric, Gerda, Joshua, Tony, Max, Anna, Lucia, Hannah, Sofia, and Abraham and to my parents, Miriam and Sidney. I think that over many years we've worked out ways both to support one another and to encourage each other to take chances and to walk our own walk. I am also grateful to my generous and supportive advisor and compañera, Cecilia Zapata; to my long-time friends and thought-provokers, Dale Farran and Pat Fischer; to my newer friend Trude Bennett, for her creative critiques; to John Hatch for inspiration and for providing a role model; to Gordon H. DeFriese, a boss and a friend who has encouraged me and provided me with what I needed to complete this work; to Milton Kotelchuck, who helped me to begin this project; to Steve Wing for his advice; and to 'my' librarians, Lynn Whitener and Janice Pope. Much thanks also to Louise Murray of Zed Books for her vital support and assistance. She and Zed play an important role in the international women's movement. I am grateful to have an editor and publisher whose values reflect the content of my book.

I have also had the great luck to be connected with a university that has an extraordinary library and so have had available a wide range of books and journals. I only hope that the new communications age helps to distribute these resources more equitably throughout the world. With regard to the communications age, I am greatly indebted to a San Francisco-based computer network, Peacenet, and to the Institute for Global Communications, which for many years have been providing users in many countries with a means of communicating with each other and have made available to all of us news about women and about their organizing activities. Through news releases from the Inter-Press Service, an international, non-profit, news cooperative, and many other smaller news services, I have been able to follow much that is not considered newsworthy by the popular news sources. It was this service, as much as anything, that convinced me that an international woman's movement, based on empowerment, is being developed in many different locations simultaneously.

I want to acknowledge my large intellectual debt to the writers who have helped me to understand the issues and the questions raised in this book. Leonard Sagan first introduced me to the world of psycho-social and cultural determinants of health. Sylvia Tesh, who asks wonderful questions, brilliantly clarified the theories of health and the relationship of our society to those theories. Richard Wilkinson and Robert Evans have provided support for my beliefs about inequality and justice. Mildred Blaxter has done more and better research and thinking about health than seems possible in one lifetime. William Dressler, like Blaxter, has spent years building on his own research into cultural and social determinants of health, while demonstrating how to combine quantitative and qualitative research methods to understand significant and complex states of health. Nancy Krieger and Diane Rowley have and continue to put together the key and elusive concepts of race, class, gender, and health in a coherent and enlightening way. Anton Antonovsky has developed an important concept – the sense of coherence – and Howard Kaplan has clarified the murky realm of psychoneuroimmunology. Nina Wallerstein and Lee Staples grapple with and illuminate the challenging concept of empowerment. Sara Evans, a feminist historian, opened up the field of history for me, who had long resisted it. John Caldwell has formalized his long-term re-search about the importance of maternal education into an important field – health transition theory, which focuses on the social, cultural, and behavioral determinants of health. Margaret Wheatley is, to my knowledge, the first to draw connections between the new sciences and organization theory.

Above all, I want to express my gratitude to John Cassel, post-humously. His quantitative skills, social sensitivity, clear thinking, and courageous innovations have made me and so many others aware of the effects of social organization on health.

Finally, I want to thank the many women who have talked to me about their lives. I particularly thank them for recognizing what we as women have in common and for focusing on our similarities, helping to lessen the distance between the researcher and the subject.

Preface

> Inequalities are poorly studied from a detached point of view; the task of
> the committed researcher is to make arguments persuasive enough to
> convince the uncommitted and mobilize those prepared for action
> (Papanek 1990: 165).

In September 1995, I attended the NGO Forum at the Fourth World
Conference on Women in Beijing. I went looking for reassurance that
what I have written about – an international movement of women
compelled by needs, discrimination, and injustice, guided by feminist
ideals, and developing innovative and participatory strategies for
making women's lives better – is alive and well. I returned most reas-
sured, and even more aware of the importance of the concept of
empowerment, and of its protean nature. While acknowledging the
macroeconomic, geopolitical, and cultural forces that so strongly determine all of our lives, women at the conference were righteously
angry, painfully honest, and infinitely creative; they were sad and joyful. Above all, they were looking to a better future, determined to
influence their own and their children's lives through concerted and
participatory actions whose means would reflect their ends. This experience has reinforced my desire to spread the word about what women
are accomplishing, and how their activities are helping us to expand
our understanding of such basic concepts as health and development.

Several personal experiences led me to consider possible links between empowerment and women's health. In the mid-1980s, during
the period of Sandinista leadership, I went to Nicaragua for a short
time to teach statistical programming. I was very moved by the energy
and dedication of the three young women in my class, by their descriptions of their lives before the revolution, and how the education they
received as a result of the revolution gave them previously unimagined

opportunities. Inspired by them, I began to do research on the effects of education on women in developing countries. The literature was startling because so many researchers were just then coming to the conclusion that education was not only important but one of the most important factors in explaining why some women's children were healthier than others and why health-related behavior differed among certain groups of women. These findings were based on multivariate analyses that include many other potential predictors, both individual and societal (Caldwell 1986; Cleland and van Ginneken 1988; Cochrane *et al.* 1980).

The positive effect of maternal education on children's health is nearly universal. Moreover, after more than fifteen years of evidence about the importance of maternal education to child health – fifteen years during which child health became the major focus of the field of international health – there is still little understanding of the phenomenon. Research identified the importance of education, but discussion about the pathways from education to health were observational and theoretical. People hazarded guesses about what might be occurring. While quantitative studies were able to flag maternal education as a key variable and show an effect on child health that is independent of socioeconomic status, they have not been able to explicate it.

The situation was strikingly similar to another area of my work: the analyses of race, class, and health. This research led me repeatedly to the following question: why is the higher rate of poor birth outcomes (and adult health outcomes) for African-Americans as compared to whites and to some other minorities in the United States so obdurate, regardless of the mother's level of education (Alexander and Cornely 1987; Collins and David 1990; Schoendorf *et al.* 1992)? Quantitative analyses consistently identify this problem, but multivariate analyses using any and all of the measured medical, social, economic, and geographic factors expected to explain the differences fail to account for a large part of those differences (Krieger *et al.* 1993).

I looked to the political science literature on modernity to see what might be known about changes related to education. Many carefully executed studies described some character traits and behaviors that accompanied modernity. These were attributed to schooling, as well as to work situations and urbanization, but looked only at men. Where were women? Why were they ignored by the academicians? Fortunately, I discovered an increasingly extensive and powerful literature on women and development that clarified why women were not included in the early studies of modernity and why they were so often left out of the processes of development, acculturation, and modernization.

Literature abounded about women's activities and strategies, given their exclusion from formal policies. Unlike the education and modernization literature, however, most of this literature was non-academic.

Wanting to see more of what women were doing, I traveled to Costa Rica and interviewed some women who were part of a housing movement, and had devoted years to obtaining land and building their houses. They showed strength, independence, energy, apparent good health, control over their lives, and happiness. During my interviews with them, I discovered how their participation in the housing movement had transformed their lives. As poor women, they had previously lived lives with which we are all too familiar: isolated, battered, giving birth to many children at an early age, receiving no or poor medical care, little education, and little independence. I went to Honduras and saw much the same thing. The amazing thing was to hear the women talk about their transformations; one woman described others as being 'like socks that got turned inside out.' All the women talked extensively about their friendships and the support they got from other women in their group. I remembered my own history, and how the women's movement changed my own life and consciousness. I remembered how each positive experience increased my ability to make decisions and to take control of my personal circumstances. What seemed to be going on in Costa Rica and elsewhere was what we commonly call empowerment, and I felt connected through my own experiences with what I was seeing and reading about.

Empowerment is a strategy that has as a primary goal an equitable redistribution of power and resources. Because of an increasing amount of evidence indicating that third world women have been using empowerment processes effectively to improve their own conditions, empowerment seemed to be a potentially important strategy to improve women's health. That strategy includes group organizing, the use of consciousness-raising techniques to raise women's awareness of the importance of gender discrimination in their personal lives, a recognition of women's three major roles – productive, reproductive, and community work, a rejection of top-down strategies as the only way to accomplish social change, and a belief in the importance of women organizing by and for themselves.

In the late 1980s empowerment became a popular topic, both in academic and non-academic literature, including television advertisements and political sound bites. Others began to study empowerment and to link it to health. Having returned to school to study international maternal and child health, I decided to write my dissertation on empowerment and women's health, and began to design a traditional research project. I started pulling the many strands of information and intuition into a coherent conceptual model that would justify such a project. This meant linking thoughts and knowledge about health and illness, empowerment and modernization, and development and strategies for survival.

Through my participation over many years in a large and varied number of research projects, however, I had grown increasingly concerned with design limitations, with the many compromises that were imposed by the quality of data, and with the oversimplifications imposed by available analytic techniques. Money, time, and implementation and analysis problems all too often seemed to determine both questions and answers. The immediacy and importance of improving the health of women living in difficult circumstances, in conjunction with the inability of traditional methodologies to unravel social issues such as maternal education and birth outcomes, indicated to me a need for less traditional methodologies. Like many other feminist researchers, I also felt a need to do work 'consistent with the values and commitments we express in the rest of our lives' (Longino 1989).

I concentrated, then, on making sense of what I thought I knew by constructing a more appropriate framework for understanding the potential role of empowerment in improving women's health. I wanted to look at women's development, empowerment, and health from a woman's perspective: 'to see things one did not see before and also to see the familiar rather differently' (Nielsen 1990: 20). Finally, having ideological tendencies, I have also been motivated by an adherence to what Julian Rappaport (1986: 70) has called an empowerment ideology. That ideology requires two things of its proponents: first to learn more about 'how people are already handling their own problems in living,' and then to share that information with others who lack control over the circumstances of their lives.

Women are speaking in one voice, in many voices, in a different voice. Listen to them. Listen to the Women. They are arriving over the wise distances on their dancing feet. Women speaking from the edges of all our societies are challenging the dominant paradigms of politics and knowledge. (Soethe 1993)

There is a women's resistance that is not 'feminist,' 'socialist,' 'radical,' or 'liberal' because it does not come out of an understanding of one or another social theory, and it is not informed by experience in conventional politics. It is a resistance that exists outside the parameters of those politics and outside the purview of any of the traditional definitions of progress and social change. Women's resistance as I am defining it here is shaped by the dailiness of women's lives. It comes out of the sexual division of labor that assigns to women responsibility for sustaining the lives of their children and, in a broader sense, their families, including husbands, relatives, elders, and community. This responsibility is knowingly accepted, albeit under enormous social pressure. Women's resistance also comes out of women's subordinated status to men, institutionalized in society and lived through every day in countless personal ways. Women's resistance is not necessarily or intrinsically oppositional; it is not necessarily or intrinsically contesting for power. It does, however, have a profound impact on the fabric of social life because of its steady, cumulative effects. It is central to the making of history, and ... it is the bedrock of social change. Too often we have not seen this kind of resistance or appreciated its cumulative effects because we have been looking for social movements as these have been traditionally defined, and we have looked for the historical moments when these movements have reached their apex, making sweeping social changes. To see women's resistance is also to see the accumulated effects of daily, arduous, creative, sometimes ingenious labors, performed over time, sometimes over generations. (Aptheker 1989: 173)

I

Introduction

In the search for solutions, we should not overlook the fact that women everywhere are actively involved in working against social, cultural, racial, economic and political discrimination. It seems therefore just as important to ask the question of 'how do women stay healthy in difficult circumstances and how can we strengthen those processes' as the question 'what makes them sick?' (Richters 1992: 749)

Empowerment is a strategy designed to redistribute power and resources. It is a group activity dedicated to increasing political and social consciousness, grounded in a belief in the essential need for self-determination, and designed around a continuing cycle of reflection and action. This book is primarily concerned with the health of women who live in difficult circumstances and the role that empowerment activities may have in maintaining and improving their health. The women in question usually live in third world countries or in areas of the industrialized world where similar conditions of deprivation prevail. They face many difficult circumstances, including cultural norms that often denigrate women and accord them very low status, lack of legal safeguards and rights to property, lack of political power or access to those with power, and lack of educational opportunities and health care services. They are frequently excluded from wage employment and access to credit and technology because of their gender. Women's daily lives are often difficult, burdened by unwanted and dangerous child-bearing; lack of proper nutrition; high levels of responsibility for their families; extremely long work-days that include productive, re-productive, and community responsibilities; poor and dangerous living conditions; and exposure to violence – both social and domestic. More than half of the world's refugees and displaced persons are women. These difficult circumstances faced by many women negatively affect their health and well-being, and produce some common needs. In response to these needs, many women are creating mechanisms designed to reduce their burdens and disadvantages, including new types of organizations. These organizations often see empowerment of the participants as vital to their success.

In this book I will explore, from a woman's perspective, four distinct areas of literature and thought: scientific inquiry, development, empowerment, and health. My real interest, however, is in the relationships between different areas: between the theories and policies of international development and women's situations, between the theories and research about health and women's situations, between scientific inquiry itself and theories of development and health, and the role of empowerment in improving both women's situations and their health.

With the aim of linking inquiry, development, empowerment, and health, I look at each of the separate domains broadly – from historical, theoretical, and practical perspectives. I then attempt, in the context of women's health and empowerment, to establish connections between what are often seen as isolated pieces of information or knowledge. There is a worldwide surfeit of information, resulting from developments in communications and transportation. Currently information is gathered from almost everywhere on earth and distributed around the world by means of computers, satellites, telephones, fax machines, newspapers, magazines and journals, books, television, radios, videos and movies. At the same time there is an explosion of specialized knowledge due to the formalization of scientific inquiry, requirements for original research, simplification and multiplication of publishing techniques, and pressures for academics to publish books and articles regularly. Perhaps as a response to this surfeit and fragmentation of information, 'we persevere in looking at small questions instead of large ones and our view of the forest is forever obscured by the trees' (Bevan 1991: 475). I hope to further the understanding of health through synthesis and through the use of a wide-angle lens – capturing as large a picture as possible while still preserving enough detail to be convincing to the reader. We need to step back and look very broadly at women and their situations within these historical, theoretical, and practical frameworks. We must accept the complexity and the extensivity of the web of factors that are relevant to health. After that, we should be able to see linkages, connections, associations, and interactions that were previously hidden from us.

This book focuses on 'what to think about' more than 'what to do.' Thus one intent is to construct theory – to present systematically organized knowledge 'devised to analyze ... or otherwise explain the nature or behavior of a specified set of phenomena' (Morris 1973: 1335) – that will explicate the posited relationship between empowerment and health. However, I also link knowledge to practice, believing that practice produces knowledge and vice versa, and that the two cannot be disentangled. I attempt to synthesize information across academic disciplines, grounding the constructed theory in empirical evidence gathered from the activities of those women who are the subjects of my inquiries. My methods have been eclectic: identifying major writings, often review articles or textbooks, and then following up on references to other works that seemed relevant, scouring computer bulletin boards for 'news from the field,' and reading a wide variety of newsletters and other informal publications. Existent research, theory, and policy have been reviewed and synthesized from a woman's perspective – 'a form of attention, a lens that brings into focus particular questions' (Keller 1985: 6).

I hope to inform and to stimulate discussion and political action among multiple audiences, as well as to provide educational information. The primary intended audiences are policy-makers, funders, practitioners, researchers, students, activists, and participants in the fields of women's studies, public health and biomedical medicine, and development. These are not disjoint groups, as individuals often have multiple roles within them.

I would particularly like this book to be read by those who formulate health and development policy through definition and funding. This includes a wide variety of organizations: global, multinational, regional, national, and local; these may be public, private, or, increasingly, joint public–private. Within these organizations are individuals with a variety of personal and public goals and responsibilities, and a wide variety of attitudes towards gender issues. While it is difficult to address this group as a single entity, they are among the most important players in the areas of women's health and development.

Both because of strong links between development and health (Rodriguez-García and Goldman 1994) and because health activities are often carried out in the development realm, this study is also directly addressed to development practitioners. They were among the first to observe the effectiveness of empowerment strategies, although they have generally limited their use to the area of income generation.

The field of international health is undergoing redefinition, and I hope that this book will contribute to its reconceptualization. International health has generally meant the health of people living in developing countries. However, the term is increasingly used to address global health issues. These issues include a focus on interdependence rather than dependence, a recognition of diversity within the third world and between developed countries, an understanding that health exists in an international and national political context and that international development policies are closely related to health, and a vision of health as an interdisciplinary and intersectoral concern (Pan American Health Organization 1992). This book – although it is frequently dependent on research done under the older international health paradigm, which restricts the domain and the context of research – is itself situated firmly in a context of global health. From within this context, my framework stresses the global economic and political context of women's situations and focuses on underdevelopment wherever it may be located. I also attempt to represent the diversity that exists among third world women and to locate health in a broad, multi-disciplinary context.

An increased awareness of biological and cultural gender differences is leading workers in many fields – including health, development, and scientific inquiry – to the consideration of theory, research, and practice specifically concerned with women (Charlton 1984; Koblinsky *et al.* 1993b; Tavris 1992; Tuana 1989). The field of women's studies and feminist approaches within traditional disciplines investigate gender and its repercussions by comparing women to men as well as concentrating on women alone – looking at the differences and similarities among them. I use both these strategies in this book. I compare women's situations and health to those of men in order to establish gender differences. By restricting the proposed framework to women, however, I seek answers to the research questions that arise from observations of women, and are particularly relevant to women's needs. While men may live in poverty, have similar needs to women, and suffer from many of the same health problems, I will show in this gender study that women's situations are related to particular forms of gender discrimination, that empowerment is a strategy adopted primarily by women, and that women's health is directly and indirectly affected by gender-determined policies and conditions. None the less, much of the information presented is relevant to the study of health irrespective of gender.

Finally, I wish this book to contribute to the growing body of feminist research: research about women designed to assist them in their struggle for their share of health, resources, and power, and to provide a venue for their voices and presence. Information from and about women has been essential to the development of the framework I will present. I want the women who are the subjects of this study and those who actively support their activities to know that they are not alone, and that what they do is often heroic and worthy of study and recognition. Their successes and their failures can and should inform others in similar circumstances, or in positions where they can be helpful. This book is designed to provide these women with a framework that will help them to evaluate their strategies, to see both the importance of their health and its relationship to their lives in their entirety, to show connections and to encourage solidarity between many groups working towards the same goals, and to help to protect groups from political oppression, if necessary, by documenting and publicizing their efforts.

I apologize up front to specialists in the specific areas I so briefly review. I have deliberately sacrificed depth for breadth. This undoubtedly reflects my own personal affinity and style, but also the complexity of the concepts and the multiplicity of the factors affecting health. I am *not* attempting to provide readers with an in-depth understanding of each of the areas and factors that I discuss. What I do wish to accomplish is to bring to the reader's attention the many associations and connections between what are often treated as narrow areas of specialization. I would feel successful if specialists in each of the areas recognized linkages they had previously ignored, and continued their work with a desire to follow up some strands that might lead outside their domain.

I also regret that certain parts of the world are only minimally included. I have not in the course of my research followed women's activities in the countries that formerly belonged to the USSR, the countries of the Middle East, and China. Therefore, the women about whom I am writing are primarily from Latin America, sub-Saharan Africa, and Asia (minus China).

A Theoretical Framework

Towards the end of this book there is a chapter on theories and practice of scientific inquiry as they relate to the concepts of women's situations, empowerment, and health. However, I want to include a brief introduction to that material at this point. I said in the Preface that I do not think that traditional research theory and methods can clarify the relationships between these dimensions at this time, and that conceptual work is now called for. I have found many common strands in the ways in which a variety of researchers are beginning to look at complex problems and the world itself. They are drawn in their search for patterns and meaning to look for connections, interactions, instability, and disorder, instead of focusing on linear approximations of relationships among fairly discrete factors. They are sometimes moved by an explicit desire that their work should contribute to increasing social justice as opposed to objectively contributing to 'knowledge.'

Among these scientists and researchers are the proponents of the 'New Sciences,' which include chaos and complexity theory and dialecticism. These scientists, who come from many different disciplines including physics, biology, meteorology, economics, and psychology, see the world as a kaleidoscope with no fixed structure; they recognize the far-reaching effects of local occurrences; and they see parts and whole as fluid and totally interdependent. Feminist researchers in many fields have similar perspectives, and often stress the importance of actor and observer in the search for understanding and meaning. They are particularly concerned with relationships between power and knowledge, and argue that through the historical exclusion of women from science, our collective 'knowledge' is flawed and partial. In this they are accompanied by many postmodernists whose credo is that traditional linear Western thought is insufficient for understanding the complex contexts within which we live and carry out our work.

These critiques of logical positivism, the scientific model that has dominated Western society for more than three centuries, do not form a coherent, well-formulated replacement for that model. Much of the work is too new, and there has as yet been little cross-fertilization between the hard and the soft sciences. The emerging theoretical frameworks, however, indicate that we will never have a straightforward replacement model since they are based on change, context and particularities, and conflict. We shall have to ask our questions knowing that we can see only so many configurations of the glass bits in our kaleidoscope. We shall have to consider carefully our role as 'change-makers' in an already dynamic and interactive environment.

I see empowerment as a construct poorly suited to traditional analytic approaches because of its variability and its complex and interactive relationship to a multiplicity of factors that affect women's lives and women's health. I critique development and its effects on women's lives from a post-rationalist perspective, using arguments from the new sciences and feminism. I see health, in particular, as complex, dynamic, and holistic, a whole whose parts are neither independent nor linearly related. Finally, I encourage innovative forms of research into problems and successful strategies important to women's lives and women's health. Research is an important bridge between theory and practice. However, research itself has been constricted by the framework of positivism. As we look at what is and what should or could be from new and multiple perspectives, we can anticipate new techniques to aid us.

The task I undertake is one of synthesis, focusing on context, connections, and relationships. I see the context of this study as dynamic, dialectical, unpredictable, and one in which power relationships, particularly gender relationships, are vital and integral. This book is a feminist work in so far as women are the primary subjects, and its intent is to increase understanding of their lives and to help to make those lives a little better. It adheres to feminist precepts of knowledge and objectivity, and the role of the researcher. From postmodernism comes the imperative to listen to many voices, particularly to the voices of those who are in marginal positions with regard to power and to the dominant forms of expression.

A Glossary of Terms

The concepts discussed in this book – such as empowerment, health, development, and scientific inquiry – are often used with imprecision; they are concepts about which individuals may have strong feelings and preconceived explanatory models. The following section presents some working definitions that I have used.

Empowerment

While empowerment means many things to many people, the following definition formulated by Nina Wallerstein and Edward Bernstein (1988: 380), has guided my discussion:

> [Empowerment is] a social action process that promotes participation of people, organizations, and communities in gaining control over their lives in their community and larger society. With this perspective, empowerment is not characterized as achieving power to dominate others, but rather power to act with others to effect change.

I give particular emphasis to participation in groups as a means of promoting change at the three levels presented by Wallerstein and Bernstein: individual, organizational, and community. Empowerment is seen as a multi-level group process designed to lead to positive individual and social change. Empowerment also commonly denotes outcomes of empowering activities, such as achieving power, improved self-esteem, or increased control over personal income.

Empowerment is a word that seems to exist only in English, although the concept is broadly understood worldwide. Since the word can imply the *giving* of power, some writers use the phrase 'self-empowerment' – the consensus being that to give empowerment is an oxymoron. I will use the more commonly employed term *empowerment* in this book, for the sake of simplicity.

Conscientization and consciousness-raising

An important facet of the empowerment process as formulated by Paulo Freire – and as explored in Chapter 3 below – is conscientization, or the development of a critical consciousness. It has been defined as 'learning to perceive social, political, and economic contradictions, and to take action against the oppressive elements of reality' (Freire 1990: 19, translator's note). Archer and Costello (1990: 75–6) describe it as a time when individuals begin to see themselves in relation to the world and the world in relation to themselves, becoming aware of their ability to influence events.

Definitions of consciousness-raising – an important factor in the evolution of the women's movement in the USA in the 1970s – describe a very similar process. Ruth Hubbard (1990: 17) describes it as 'recognizing one's individual experience of oppression and understanding its significance within the wider setting that generates the oppression and defines its social function(s).' Paula Eastman (1973: 163) incorporates the important role of the group: '[C]onsciousness-raising attempts to bring women's own creative world, intelligence, and insights into group thinking; thus the group becomes a centralized force for bringing together women's personal and political lives.' I will use the two terms, 'conscientization' and 'consciousness-raising', in their respective historical contexts in this study, but consider that both serve the same function in the empowerment process.

Health

HEALTH n. 1. The state of an organism with respect to functioning, disease, and abnormality at any given time. 2. The state of an organism functioning normally without disease or abnormality. 3. Optimal functioning with freedom from disease and abnormality. 4. Broadly, any state of optimal functioning, well being, or progress. (Morris 1973: 607)

These dictionary definitions indicate that we use the term 'health' in several ways: as a descriptor – 'the state of an organism at any given time,' as a normative term – 'the state of an organism functioning normally,' and as a description of the ideal – 'optimal functioning.'

Several major models of health have been used by those attempting to operationalize and measure the concept. Some see a single line with death at the negative end and some measure of normal or perfect health at the positive end. Others see the positive side of the line as infinite, headed in the direction of an unreachable optimal health. Many see health as multidimensional, requiring multiple lines representing different components of a concept of health that is not itself directly measurable but is, rather, a whole composed of measurable parts. Finally, Antonovsky (1979; 1987) posits that negative health and positive health are in fact distinct concepts.

According to Rene Dubos (1965: 346, 351), '[t]he concept of perfect and positive health is a utopian creation of the human mind.... The nearest approach to health is a physical and mental state fairly free of discomfort and pain, which permits the person concerned to function as effectively and as long as possible in the environment where chance or choice has placed him.'

Utopian though they be, however, definitions of positive health do exist: 'Health is not simply the absence of disease; it is something positive, a joyful attitude towards life and a cheerful acceptance of the responsibilities that life puts on the individual' (Sigerist 1941: 100). R.G. Evans *et al.* (1994) prefer to define *health* as an absence of illness, and *well-being*, which they see as the objective of *all* human activities, as what I am calling positive health.

In this book I will use the word *health* descriptively, normatively, and as an ideal state, but it will often be set in opposition to illness, emphasizing either normal or optimal functioning. Health will be presented as multidimensional, with distinctions drawn between positive and negative health; as a concept that is culturally determined, and therefore dynamic; as a Dubosian state where we function as effectively and as long as possible in the environment where chance or choice has placed us; and as a component of well-being – that positive and joyful attitude towards life.

Determinants, factors, predictors, contributors

Traditionally, the discussion about factors related to health is framed in terms of *determinants*. This may be an unfortunate term because it connotes an implicit causality. The framework presented here is based on a *tangled web* metaphor that focuses on interactions and synergy rather than on reductionism and direct effects. However, there is no readily available vocabulary to support the web concept; therefore several phrases will be used interchangeably in this study. These include *factors related to* and *associated with health, predictors of health, contributors to health,* and *determinants of health.*

Development or international development

The word *development,* generally used in place of *international development,* is less than descriptive of a very complex and controversial historical process. 'Development … is a user-friendly term having virtually as many potential meanings as potential users' (J.K. Black 1991: 15). If one is looking for a normative definition of development to apply to entities such as nations or specific population subgroups, one strategy is to define *underdevelopment,* and then to consider (positive) development as a process designed to counter underdevelopment. Underdevelopment can be defined in terms of vulnerability and poverty – as a condition of political and economic vulnerability that leads to exploitation and as a condition of inequitable poverty that leads to deprivation and disadvantage. It is an initial state, while development is 'both as change process and as terminal state' (Goulet 1985: xvi). Development strategies can be evaluated according to their efficacy in reducing both poverty and vulnerability. It is, of course, an oversimplification to assign all the blame for poverty and vulnerability to the theories and policies of development. It is impossible to isolate the effects of development, or to attribute women's situations to development alone. Poverty and vulnerability existed long before this century and before the colonialist era that paved the way for international development. However, all too often and all too obviously, as I will discuss, development policies have contributed to the difficulties that women now face.

The vocabulary of development is also difficult. *Developing, underdeveloped, non-industrialized, non-Western, third world, low income, the south, colonized and dominated* (Gottschalk and Teymour 1993: 112) are just some of the phrases used to discuss countries that are not considered developed. All terms are offensive to some; none fully captures the status of those countries. There is no attempt in this study for consistency, since none of the existing terms is adequate. In general, the terms *women's development* or *development for women* will be used to describe women's relationship to development policies and activities. The more commonly used terms *women in development* (WID) and *women and development* (WAD) identify specific approaches to women's development, and are reserved for use in discussions of those approaches.

Adjustment or structural adjustment

Development policies and conditions in developing countries have been greatly affected by multinational economic policies fostered by the World Bank and the International Monetary Fund. These monetary policies are usually described as 'adjustment' or 'structural adjustment' policies. The following definition from UNICEF is succinct:

> ADJUSTMENT: The process of responding to (often severe) imbalances in the economy, particularly deficits in a country's balance of payment, usually by adopting measures which expand exports, reduce imports, or otherwise attract foreign exchange to a country. Often, measures to curb a government deficit by increasing government revenue or reducing expenditure are also involved. These actions involve changes in the structure of the economy. (Cornia *et al.* 1987a: viii)

It is important to understand that the often severe deficits in a country's balance of payments result in large part from undisciplined lending practices by the private banking institutions during the 1970s. The expenditures that are being reduced are most often in social programs such as education and health, in subsidies for food supports and other necessities, and in distributional economic programs such as credit availability and government employment.

Women's situations

The *American Heritage Dictionary* (Morris 1973: 1211) defines *situation* as 'position or status with regard to conditions and attendant circumstances.' I have chosen *women's situations* as an encompassing term that can be used to describe the complex mix of information about where women are located, how they fare, their histories, the conditions among which they live, and the circumstances that shape their lives, while accentuating the placement of women at the center of the discussion.

Third world women

Chandra Mohanty (1991: 52–6) rightly warns against treating '"third world women" as a singular monolithic subject' – a perspective that views them as an 'already constituted, coherent group with identical interests and desires, regardless of class, ethnic or racial location, or contradictions' caught in a world defined only by power and oppression relationships. 'This average third world woman leads an essentially truncated life based on her feminine gender (read: sexually constrained) and her being "third world" (read: ignorant, poor, uneducated, tradition-bound, domestic, family-oriented, victimized, etc.).'

None the less, I have found it necessary to generalize about third world women. Where possible, however, I have taken into account differences based on class, ethnicity, race, age, geographic setting, and purely individual traits. I have also tried to emphasize the diversity, creativity, resilience, strength, and energy of so many third world women rather than negative stereotypical traits.

Feminism

I use the terms *feminist* and *feminism* frequently in this book. Many third world and minority women have rejected those terms, identifying them with what they see as a Western movement that is often male-hating, competitive, restricted to analyses of gender, and insensitive to racial, ethnic, and class differences. However, there is much evidence of an evolving third world feminism both linked to and independent of the West. Authors such as Chandra Mohanty demonstrate an increasing acceptance of the terms in literature from developing countries. Kumari Jayawardena (1986: 2) provides the working definition adopted in this study:

> [T]he word [feminism] has now been expanded to mean an awareness of women's oppression and exploitation within the family, at work and in society, and conscious action by women (and men) to change this situation.... In this study the word 'feminism' is used in [this] larger sense, embracing movements for equality within the current system and significant struggles that have attempted to change the system.

The Organization of this Book

The organization of this book is somewhat arbitrary. In a published work, one chapter must follow another, and links from one thought to another may be difficult to establish when they are presented in spatially distant sections. But this book is about connections and relationships. I have ordered and reordered the chapters and sections, but cannot conquer the problem of conformity between linear form and non-linear content. Therefore the reader should not feel constrained by the organization. I have tried to write each section so that it can serve as an entry point. Development and empowerment are discussed in the first part, health in the second, and scientific inquiry in the third. The final chapters contain my conclusions and recommendations.

Caveat

I posit that empowerment is a key strand in the web of factors that affect health. I hope that I will add to the understanding of the concept and suggest effective strategies for encouragement and support of efforts towards empowerment. None the less, it must be recognized that empowerment is a complex and somewhat fragile concept whose role is neither straightforward nor static. As I will discuss, it can have negative effects, is easily cooptable, will improve health only for some women in some situations, and will be very difficult to evaluate and research. However, an important message from those who are developing new scientific paradigms is that there is *no* single, magical factor. These emerging paradigms question the reassuring assumptions of positivism concerning solvability, the feasibility of universal solutions, and the irreversibility of progress. They suggest that 'You go for viability, something that's workable, rather than what's "optimal"' (Waldrop [1992: 333], quoting B. Arthur). Viable work designed to assist women in their battle for good health must be sensitive to local conditions, to complexity, to the importances of relations and interactions at many different levels, to the constancy of change, and to the right that we each have of self-determination.

PART I

Development and Empowerment

2

Women's Situations and Development

Women are embracing the concept of empowerment because of their situations – their disempowerment and their unmet needs. As women have increasingly discovered their commonalities, through improved means of communications and through international conferences such as the 1995 NGO conference in Beijing, they have attempted to understand the global and local political, economic, and cultural forces that shape these situations. While there are many factors that play a role in gender-based stratification, an examination of international development during the past half-century provides insight into some of these factors. The changes in the world since the end of World War II have been profound; in the third world, many of these changes – positive and negative – have occurred under the rubric of development. Recently, however, the assumptions underlying the theory and practice of development (Charlton 1984), the feasibility of reducing vulnerability and poverty through development activities (Small 1990), and the practices themselves (Hancock 1989), are being questioned.

Traditional Development Theory

Since the end of the Second World War, several competing theories of international development have dominated the field and influenced development practice (So 1990). The first and perhaps most important of these is modernization, based on liberal positivist economic theories and developed principally in the United States. (This theory is closely related to positivist approaches to scientific inquiry, which I will discuss in Chapter 8.) It envisioned a progressive continuum of economic development and growth that would bring social and political benefits to all citizens of all countries.

The major attacks on modernization theory came from political scientists (*dependistas*) in developing countries, particularly from Latin Americans. On the basis of their personal experiences, they found the belief that their countries were slowly but inevitably evolving into developed countries simply incredible. Dependency theorists posited that non-developed countries were dependent because of their economic relationship with developed countries – one in which their natural resources and the products of their cheap labor were supplied to the Western capitalist countries, which also garnered the profits.

Dependency theory, however, was unable to explain some of the new international economic patterns that were appearing, and variations in growth in both developed and underdeveloped countries. Immanuel Wallerstein led those who looked for a more inclusive theory. In his world system theory, nation-states were seen as elements of a world system, driven by economics. Politicians were dominated by an international 'economic elite.'

The 1980s and 1990s have been described as a period of impasse in development theory, owing to an increasing awareness of the negative effects of economic growth on some countries, on some people in all countries, and on the environment; an increasing awareness of diversity; and the effectiveness of postmodernism in undermining 'the great narratives' (Schuurman 1993). Some theorists have even forecast the end of the 'age of development' (Sachs 1993). A current trend among development thinkers is to particularize and to look at more subtle effects of development, manifestations of repression, and conflicting interests at all levels. In particular, culture and social structure are gaining special importance as factors that can explain differing patterns of development (Gereffi 1989).

Development theory and women

The assumptions of the modernization theorists, who had in some sense a global perspective, are particularly important to an understanding of the effects of development on women. They saw one road along which all nations traveled, regardless of where they started. Since all aspects of a society were synergistically modernized, the end was universally desirable, and the process was inevitable, there was little reason for them to consider differential impact. Jane Jaquette (1982: 269) notes that the modernists, when they did take women into account, thought of them as the rearguard – the most underdeveloped of the underdeveloped: 'Women's relative "backwardness," like that of rural peasants, is explained as the stubborn and irrational persistence of traditional attitudes.' That is to say: women were 'responsible' for their own exclusion from the benefits of development; the processes of development were not to blame.

In a study of 6,000 men, Inkeles and Smith (1974: 290–91) described 'modern man' – the man who adapted to progress and westernization. He was an 'informed participant citizen,' had a 'marked sense of personal efficacy,' was 'independent and autonomous' in personal decision-making, and 'relatively *open-minded* and *cognitively flexible.*' Modern man has much in common with what we think of as empowered woman. Among the components of empowerment described in the next chapter are better information, active participation, self-esteem and self-confidence, autonomy and independence in decision-making, and flexibility and openness to new experiences – all also components of modernity as defined by Inkeles and others. The differences, however, are informative. Modern man is usually in concert with modern society. They are both changing in the same direction, and change in one leads to and reinforces change in the other. Women, as we shall see, are often hindered by modern society, and must wrest their power through concerted action; power has not trickled down to them, nor have they been absorbed into the supposed unidirectional flow of development. Secondly, man was modernized through his contact with modern institutions: formal schooling, factories, cities. Women are also sometimes both modernized and empowered in these settings, but women's communal activities, which can lead to empowerment, often take place in the most traditional of settings or under the most deprived conditions. Women are often reacting to rather than flowing with the times.

The dependency movement made clear how developed societies were dependent on and benefited from the underdevelopment of the third world. It thus brought attention to oppressed groups and to the importance of power relations between nations. Although the *dependistas* did not address the effects of dependency on subpopulations, they did establish a framework within which such a discussion could take place. Others (Fanon 1963; Solomon 1976) were clarifying the pervasive psychological and political effects of economic domination through the imposition of definitions of 'what is possible, what is right, what is rational, what is real' (Fishman 1990: 255). Empowerment can be seen as one strategy to counteract this internalization of oppression. Barbara Solomon saw US black empowerment strategies, aimed first at individual and then at social change, as a solution to the maldistribution of power. Both indigenous and first world feminists saw the effects of oppression on the psyche and on the distribution of power in a similar fashion, and began to encourage empowerment strategies as a means of countering the negative effects of both development and patriarchy.

World system theory moved development theory away from positivist assumptions, providing an opening for women. Wallerstein questioned the basic tenets of Western thought, providing a useful framework for looking at the effects of development on women. His recognition of the non-linearity of history; his vision of the world as a web of the political, the economic, and the social that is impossible to disentangle; his emphasis on the importance of both a broad *and* an individual perspective; his recognition of the contribution of non-wage labor to the international economy; and his analyses based on the world rather than the nation-state as the primary unit of analysis all play a role in feminist analyses of development.

Traditional Development Practice

The process of development assistance has to tackle the problems of ignorance, backwardness, helplessness, and resistance to change – not amongst the rural poor but amongst development agencies themselves. (Almond 1990: vii)

Almost any social or economic change in underdeveloped countries since 1950 can be accounted for as an effect of development. There have been 'successes' and 'failures,' heroes and goats. It is none the less true that, as modernization proceeds, many people – men and women – who live in poverty suffer disproportionately and perhaps unnecessarily. Since its inception following World War II, international development has been a top-down activity, with international aid agencies at the top, regional and national political and economic elites usually forming the next layer. These elites are undergirded by international development workers, who in turn are dependent on indigenous staff. Based on the modernization theory that social advances follow economic growth and economic gains trickle down to all, an enormous industry devoted to the economic modernization of underdeveloped countries has come into being.

The basic thrust of development practice involves industrialization; urbanization; increased division of labor and modification of traditional roles; a changing role for agriculture – from providing subsistence and local supplies to the production of exportable crops; larger landholdings; modernization of the infrastructure, including water, sanitation, roads and transportation, health care facilities, and energy sources; and increased institutional support for these changes through formal education and media communication.

Clearly, such efforts must deeply affect the organization of society and cultural patterns. Even if development activities were always well designed and implemented, negative – or at least unanticipated – effects are to be expected. But because of poor design and implementation – top-down decision-making, belief in a fallacious trickle-down theory, the desires of donor countries to '"domesticate" the process so that [their] strategic, ideological, and economic interests will not be threatened' (Goulet 1985: 68), and the well-documented and unfortunate propensity of development bureaucrats to live in luxury and to entrench themselves in a costly and out-of-touch bureaucracy (Hancock 1989) – the impact of development activities often negatively affects many of those who are (or should be) its beneficiaries.

Much has been written on the 'errors' of development. Here are two typical examples. In 1990, a group of Nicaraguan war veterans were trained to make ceramic electrical insulators for 65 cents, thus enabling them to earn a living in a country with extremely high unemployment. When the US Agency for International Development (USAID) later gave the Nicaraguan government foreign aid, it was in part contingent on the country's agreement to purchase cheaper insulators made in the USA. The war veterans were then put out of business. Thus US business became a major beneficiary of US aid, and local unemployment and dependency were increased as a result of aid policies (Editors 1991).

On a larger scale, a carefully designed 'sustainable, low-tech, community-oriented' project to develop Lake Victoria's fishing industry by stocking back-yard ponds with Nile perch went awry. The perch escaped into the lake, killing off the local fish and thereby allowing the algae to gain control and extract the lake's oxygen. The perch required smoking, leading to the cutting down of all the trees. The project thus produced 'a desert, eroded soil and deforestation in the most fertile area on earth; 180 [fish] species rendered extinct and the number rising; 10,000 square miles, the largest fresh-water lake in the world, stone dead; and the world's climate doing who knows what' (Editors 1990: 24). Unfortunately, many development efforts have had untoward negative impacts on some part of the population. Unsurprisingly, the people thus affected are usually vulnerable, poor, and powerless to affect top-down policies and activities.

Structural adjustment

> For most countries in Africa and Latin America at this time, adjustment policy is the dominating economic preoccupation for setting the frame and constraints within which all other economic and development issues have to be considered. (Cornia *et al.* 1987b: 5)

Development practices must be seen in terms of structural adjustment policies – policies that have not been shown to protect the vulnerable nor effectively to reduce the dependency of third world countries. Adjustment policies are in general mandated by organizations such as the World Bank and the International Monetary Fund, to which third world countries must go to obtain loans and funds for development projects. Structural adjustment packages usually include monetary devaluations to encourage exports and discourage imports; reduced government social expenditures through privatization and withdrawal of subsidies for food, health care, education, and other basic needs; trade liberalization; and sales of government-owned banks and businesses (Kanji *et al.* 1991). Increased inflation, higher prices for imported goods, lower wages, reduced or removed subsidies for basic goods, and increased unemployment constitute the local and national environment within which development activities are carried out.

Often, the effects of these policies have been devastating to the poor, have greatly affected the middle class, and have had little or no positive impact on the wealthy. For example, Ghana decreased its health care expenditures by 47 percent in the 1980s (Chossudovsky 1992). The nutritional status of children declined in eight of ten countries practicing structural adjustment in sub-Saharan Africa. The infant and child mortality rate either turned upward or the previous rate of improvement decelerated in many countries. In Mali, there was an increase in both the infant and child mortality rates of 25.6 percent from 1980 to 1985. In Uganda the infant mortality rate increased by 11.3 percent and the child mortality rate by 16.7 percent in that time period; in Kenya infant mortality increased by 4.6 percent and child mortality by 6.7 percent (Kanji *et al.* 1991). Nor have the policies accomplished what was expected in terms of affecting the balances of trade. As of 1992, 'the net transfer of resources from the South [southern hemisphere] to the North [northern hemisphere] is almost 50 billion dollars a year' (Forum on Women and Politics 1992).

UNICEF first drew attention to the negative effects of structural adjustment, particularly on children, in its 1987 book *Adjustment with a Human Face: Protecting the Vulnerable and Promoting Growth* (Cornia *et al.* 1987a). Since that time, both national governments and international organizations such as the UN and the World Bank itself have begun to attempt to mitigate these negative effects, developing modified structural adjustment policies that call for targeting the poorest of the poor. However, Kanji *et al.* (1991: 991) doubt the efficacy of this strategy:

> Within the adjustment context, costs for social reproduction have been further shifted onto women making their burden intolerable, with dire consequences for their own and their children's health. To then call for 'targeting' women and children implies addressing the needs of approx [*sic*] 75% of the population – a patently absurd use of the word targeting. Small wonder that World Bank officials have shown irritation at the inability of experts to reduce the 'vulnerable population' to 'targetable' proportions.

These authors recommend diversification of production, development of indigenous technologies, regional self-sufficiency in food, increased spending in the agricultural and social sectors, and environmental protection, but state that such changes will occur only through a fundamental democratization of political and social structures.

Traditional development practice and women

> Two-thirds of the world's labor. One-tenth of the world's capital. One-one hundredth of the world's property. (Ferguson 1990: 291)

> A survey that claimed women in Sri Lanka work much harder than their menfolk has triggered scathing rebuttals from the country's male strongholds. 'Women,' one newspaper editorial writer sneered, '[appear to] work harder than their husbands [only] if domestic chores and employment are both taken into account'. (Gourlay 1992)

It remains problematic to group together men and women – or different ethnic groups or races – when one is analyzing either the level of development or the effects of development strategies. Differential effects are thereby masked, much as average income levels mask groups living in absolute poverty. Women are frequently treated as subsidiary members of male-headed households in measures of development; this ignores their own major contributions to the family, the variety of complicated family structures that exist in both the first and third worlds, and the frequently inequitable distribution of resources within the family.

However, women have generally been disregarded in development practice, as they have in theory. The litany of the underdevelopment of women and the adverse effects of development on women is now central to the field of women's development. Women are disproportionately represented among the poor and are disproportionately responsible for family survival, particularly that of young children. While it is not easy to distinguish between the specific effects of development on women and the long-term effects of poverty and patriarchy, the lives of poor women are often incredibly difficult compared to the lives either of non-poor women or of men. This is not to say that men's lives are easy, or that many men do not suffer as a result of some development practices and from devastating poverty. However, many of the problems that women face are directly and undeniably related to the fact that they are women.

Specifically, women are disadvantaged or disproportionately responsible in the areas of education, family, health, work, exposure to poverty, displacement, and environmental hazards (Buvinic and Lycette 1988; Charlton 1984; Tinker 1976). According to Ferguson (1990: 296), '[i]t has become commonplace to note that development hurts women, that it cuts women off from access to the land, creates more work for women to do, and increases women's dependency on men.' In rural areas, where women often do most of the subsistence farming, only men are provided with machinery, training, land ownership, and credit. Women lose power and resources at the same time as their workload increases – they assist their husbands and do their own subsistence farming on land that is farther from home and of poorer quality. Men both earn and control the disposition of cash. Men follow jobs and leave rural areas. They often establish new families in the cities, provide little financial support to the rural family, and on their rare return visits impregnate their wives. Rural women also suffer disproportionately from environmental degradation, going farther and farther to get water and fuel. Urban women receive less education and training than men, and are usually forced into the informal economy – increasing their workload, providing them with jobs that are often dangerous, and giving them no job security or possibility for advancement. They are also frequently denied credit and property rights. Women in urban areas are often isolated and apart from family and kinship networks. Such circumstances have major impacts on women's health and well-being.

Structural adjustment policies have had particularly negative effects on women and children. According to Lourdes Beneria (1992), based on her interviews with Mexican women, there are many reasons for this. Household budgets, for which women are responsible, have been cut deeply. Women must constantly decide how to spend their meager resources – medicine or shoes, school books or milk. These situations are intensified by anxiety over the future. Women must also spend more time on domestic chores: cooking, sewing, repairing, travel to cheaper stores. In this work they are assisted by girls, not by boys.

Beneria points out that women also have less time to devote to social life, owing to increased domestic work and work in the informal sector that they have taken on. Men go out to bars or sporting events for diversion; women tend to create their own by entertaining and being entertained by family, and they have less and less time available for such activities. Finally, women have taken on more community work, such as communal kitchens or milk programs, the management of which is complex and time-consuming. Beneria has put forward some suggestions that could be put into effect immediately to reduce this burden on women: the establishment of local stores and markets; financial help for community kitchens; credit for women; training programs for women; the establishment of neighborhood day care, health clinics, and nutritional programs; and support for women's networks and organizations.

Vandana Shiva (1989: 2) maintains that women have not suffered from lack of participation in development but, rather, from 'their enforced but asymmetric participation in it, by which they bore the costs but were excluded from the benefits.' Given that most programs to date have not treated women equitably, and that this has been recognized since the 1970s, Kathy Ferguson (1990: 293) provides some depressing information. In 1986, USAID devoted 4 percent of its budget to projects benefiting women; the UN 3.5 percent; its Food and Agricultural Organization 1 percent; the Ford Foundation 3.5 percent of its international budget; and the Inter-American Foundation, whose focus is on grass-roots activities, only 13 percent.

This is not, of course, the whole picture. There have been positive changes in the situations of some women as a result of development. Middle-class women often benefit from the employment opportunities that result from development. Valentine Moghadam (1990: 21) states:

> As development increases, and as women are drawn in greater numbers into paid employment and public life, their subjugation *as women* is undermined and gender roles and constructs change. Thus development has long-term emancipatory effects (although these are largely unintended).

The overall picture of women's relative status, however, is not positive, as reflected in data presented below in Chapter 5. Women do not form a homogeneous group. Age is a particularly strong determinant of women's position, with women's status improving as they grow older in many traditional cultures. These older women may be more negatively affected by changes in social structure than younger women (Foner 1989; Heisel 1989). Such interactions between gender, class, race, age, residence, and ethnic group must be given attention to avoid duplicating the mistakes made by those who ignore gender issues – mistakes that lead to harmful effects on subgroups whose unique needs are not taken into account.

Thus neither development theory nor practice has included woman's perspectives. These perspectives, inductively derived from observations of women's lives and activities, will be considered in the next section.

Development Theory for Women

There have been many different players, and many and varied responses to the effects of development and structural adjustment on women, since the 1970s. Attempts have been made to include women, in the development process since that time. There has been a historical progression of approaches to the problem, some imposed by donors, advocates, and practitioners (who may or may not be feminists), and others that have come from national women's groups, activists, and from the grass roots. All the while, scholars – often activists themselves – have evaluated and reported on these activities. In traditional development, theory appeared to drive practice. In feminist development, the two are so intertwined that they evolve simultaneously.

Ester Boserup's (1970) pragmatic work in the 1970s initiated a bifurcation between generalized development theory and development theory focused on women. The latter has the three distinct streams just described: one coming from the modified practices of development organizations, another from feminist scholarship, and the third from the initiatives of women themselves.

United Nations activities and conferences have been vital to those concerned with feminist development. In 1946, the UN established a Commission on the Status of Women that lay dormant for almost thirty years, until the 1970s. The 1970s were a time of growing feminism, growing awareness of women's situation *vis-à-vis* development, and increasing activism. In response, the UN reactivated the Commission and declared 1976 to 1985 to be the UN Decade for Women. They held the first International Women's Conference in Mexico City in 1975, the second in Copenhagen in 1980, a decade-closing conference in Nairobi in 1985, and a fourth in Beijing, China, in 1995. These conferences, particularly the Non-Governmental Forums, have progressively defined women's concerns, and confronted national and international powers with their issues. They have brought together scholars and activists (Stamp 1990). Above all, they have energized and mobilized the participants:

Part fair, part revival meeting, part open university, these meetings were a marketplace for ideas and handicrafts, a showcase for songs and movies and debates, a gigantic international party where women from every country in the world could meet women with similar interests to form friendships, networks, and organizations. (Tinker 1990: 32)

The women who were and are the subjects of this field of development have been major contributors throughout. They, in conjunction with the activists, created strategies at the grass-roots level. As a result of the interactions among the three sets of contributors – advocates and practitioners, scholars, participants and grass-roots activists – women are no longer invisible and no longer unheard. They have claimed their voices. Biographies, anthropological studies, sociological studies, oral histories, interviews, videos, poetry, fiction, participatory research and learning activities, international meetings, international computer networks, and sympathetic journalism now present them and their stories – their difficulties, their strategies, and their wisdom. 'Oppressed people resist by identifying themselves as subjects, by defining their reality, shaping their new identity, naming their history, telling their story,' according to bell hooks (1989: 43). If one particular activity above all others deserves credit for the strength of the international women's movement, it would be this giving voice and face to women. It serves as the glue that holds together the different parties, and as the principal source of energy. One of the major tenets of feminism – the personal is political – has given the field these testimonies, from which it has gathered its honesty and its strength.

Although traditional development theory moved from a belief in concordant interests and inevitable progress to an understanding that – at least between nations or regions of the world – competition, a need for domination, and differential levels of development represented reality better, the view was from above. The actors were those with power: nations, elites, financiers and multinational corporations. Feminist development theory grew out of observations of and activities by those out of power. From Boserup on, the viewpoint was from below.

Eva Rathgeber (1990) has attempted to relate women's development activities to traditional development theory. She traces a historical progression from Women in Development (WID) to Women and Development (WAD) to Gender and Development (GAD). She sees WID as closely linked to modernization theory and focusing on technological fixes. WID practitioners accepted 'existing social structures' and 'overlooked the impact and influence of class, race, and culture.' They saw increased income and participation in economic development as the solution to women's problems. Rathgeber relates WAD to dependency theory – both see the international structure of the world economy as the central problem. While class problems are important, the intersection of race, class, ethnicity, and gender is not. GAD, the latest rubric, will be discussed shortly in relation to empowerment.

Caroline Moser has traced the evolution of practice in the field of development for women through five approaches – from traditional to what can be called feminist. She formulates development for women as *gender planning*, which, in identifying that 'women and men play different roles in third world society and therefore often have different needs, provides the conceptual framework and the methodological tools for incorporating gender into planning' (Moser 1989: 1799). 'The goal of gender planning is the emancipation of women from their subordination, and their achievement of equality, equity and empowerment' (Moser 1993: 1). She categorizes two sets of women's needs: *strategic* – needs related to a restructured society – and *practical* – needs that are related to survival or basic needs but that take gender into account. The five different historical approaches to gender planning that she identifies are welfare, equity, anti-poverty, efficiency, and empowerment. Of those, equity and empowerment are aimed at meeting strategic needs, while the other three deal solely with practical needs.

The *welfare approach* is the 'oldest and still the most popular social development policy for the third world in general, and women in particular' (1989: 1807). Women are classified as targets because of their identification as a 'vulnerable group,' outside of the economy. They are given assistance because they are mothers, recognized only in their reproductive role. They are passive recipients of welfare – seen as the problem, not the solution. Programs following this model include food distribution programs, nutrition education, and population control projects. The *equity approach* recognizes that 'women are active participants in the development process, who through both their productive and reproductive roles provide a critical, if often unacknowledged contribution to economic growth' (1989: 1810). The subordination of women is identified as the central problem. In general, the equity approach does not challenge the fundamental economic structure of society but does advocate a redistribution of power and resources. The *anti-poverty approach* focuses on women's poverty and the failure of modernization to redistribute (or distribute) income. It is also known as the 'basic needs' approach, and views underdevelopment as the central problem. Efforts are concentrated on enabling women to become income generators, generally through small-scale enterprises. However, these efforts do not take account of women's special needs, and still see women's participation as less important than men's. The fourth approach to gender planning is the *efficiency approach*, which Moser describes as the currently dominant WID approach. Women are treated as elastic resources in this approach, seen as the solution to problems of a worsening international economy. Economic development is the goal, and it is assumed that women's status will improve as a concomitant of their increased role in economic development: 'In reality this approach often simply means a shifting of costs from the paid to the unpaid economy, particularly through the use of women's unpaid time' (1989: 1813). Examples include soup kitchens, food distribution programs, health promoters, water and sewer projects, and self-help housing projects.

Moser describes *empowerment*, a GAD strategy, as the fifth approach to gender planning. She sees it as addressing both practical and strategic needs: organizing around practical needs with a consciousness of both economic and gender oppression, and expanding to meet strategic needs. The approach is indigenous to third world activists and feminists, although (as we shall see in Chapter 3) it also has other roots:

> It emphasizes the fact that women experience oppression differently according to their race, class, colonial history and current position in the international economic order.... While it acknowledges the importance for women to increase their power, it seeks to identify power less in terms of domination over others (with its implicit assumption that a gain for women implies a loss for men), and more in terms of the capacity of women to increase their own self-reliance and internal strength. This is identified as the right to determine choices in life and to influence the direction of change, through the ability to gain control over crucial material and nonmaterial resources. (Moser 1989: 1815)

The principal differences between empowerment and the other approaches are a rejection of top-down strategies, the inclusion of consciousness-raising, a recognition of women's triple roles – production, reproduction, and community – and a belief in the importance of women organizing by and for themselves. Moser sees women's organizations as the key to the empowerment strategy. However, empowerment groups remain underfunded and undersupported, in part because governments and aid agencies often find the empowerment approach threatening. In the main, such groups have been outside the development stream, although there is pressure to incorporate empowerment into development, and to go beyond the empowerment of individuals – to 'the creation and strengthening of whole movements of poor women around livelihood and political issues' (McKee 1989: 1006).

Jan Knippers Black (1991a) describes empowerment as a strategy rather than a theory, suggesting that it is thus protected from excessive objectification and quantification. This, however, may be a mixed

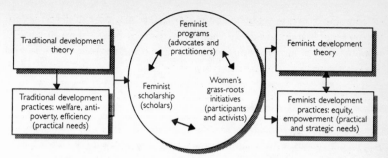

Figure 2.1 The evolution of feminist development theory and practice

blessing. It is difficult to attract support without a clear definition of empowerment, while it is all too easy to use the word empowerment to describe and justify dependency on women for activities that are or should be the responsibility of others – governments, families, social and health agencies.

Rathgeber (1990) classifies the empowerment (and equity) approach as Gender and Development. She states that although it is difficult to find examples of development projects that have been designed from a GAD perspective, 'one might speculate that such projects would be designed to empower women and to give them an equal voice by recognizing the full spectrum of their knowledge, experience, and activities, including both productive and reproductive labor' (Rathgeber 1990: 499).

Figure 2.1 depicts my discussion of the evolution of feminist development theory and practice. Whether or not the feminist perspective will be incorporated into mainstream analyses of development is yet to be seen. If women are to be effectively incorporated into development theory and practice, gender-specific data on participation and on access to resources – at the local, regional, national, and global level – must continue to be collected and disseminated. It is data that provide the evidence and ammunition for policy change. Boserup's work, the many careful studies of women's roles and women's cultures that followed her lead, and the collection and presentation of national data by gender (Grant 1993; New Internationalist 1985; Seager and Olson 1986; Sivard 1985; United Nations 1991b; World Bank 1993) have successfully raised the consciousness of the development community. Now that data must be used to educate women about their own situation and help them to organize to gain power for themselves and for their visions of society, which, as we shall see, repudiate domination and support diversity and social justice.

New visions of development

> By sticking to the concrete details of daily life, women are helping us find new directions as we work our way through the greatest crisis since the Conquest. The breakdown of the technocratic, bureaucratic, patriarchal models ... typically associated with men is allowing women – but not just women – to rethink society overall. (Pacific News Service 1991)

While the practice of women's development was evolving, informed by a growing feminist consciousness, a base of knowledge was accreting that led to the design of 'alternative visions' of development – away from concepts of linear, universal progress principally defined by economic growth and towards peace, equity, and social justice. These visions are not generally discussed in the context of traditional development. The new visions of development are not just for women; nor have only women contributed to their definitions. They do, however, derive much of their power from their insistence that development that does not benefit women as well as men, that does not delight in diversity, and that does not work to reduce oppression is not in fact development. A social transformation is called for bringing stability, peace, equality, the satisfactions of basic needs for all, and harmony with nature. Above all, development should lead to self-determination and increased human capacity – 'a process by which a populace acquires a greater mastery over its own destiny' (Goulet 1985: 155).

Some new visions *are* explicitly feminist, calling for: human relations based on 'women's values of nurturance and solidarity,' shared and communal child care, women's participation in decision-making and priority setting, valuing the work of women, and an equitable division of labor between men and women (Moghadam 1990; Sen and Grown 1987). Gita Sen and Caren Grown (1987: 79) stress that how we get there is as important as where we are going: 'At its deepest women's development is not an effort to play "catch up" with the competitive, aggressive "dog-eat-dog" spirit of the dominant system. It is, rather, an attempt to convert men and the system to the sense of responsibility, nurturance, openness, and rejection of hierarchy that are part of our vision.' Such visions are still far from reality. However, many women share them and consciously or unconsciously try to act in concert with such visions.

Development Practice By and For Women

Women's progress is forever our aim.
Women's progress must be our pursuit.
Our husbands, listen tentatively and carefully.
Women's progress must be our pursuit.
Good health and well-being for everyone in the family
It depends – it depends! on women's progress.

(Kneerim 1989)[1]

As I have argued, circumstances are grim throughout the third world, and women are particularly vulnerable in times of hardship. While there is great variety in both their situations and their activities, and women respond to their self-defined needs in ways that reflect their different cultures and historical circumstances, certain global trends are having similar effects on women everywhere. Major changes in family composition are increasing the number of women who have complete responsibility for their children – indeed, as a result of war and migration for work, there is a growing number of entire communities without men in permanent residence (Mencher and Okongwu 1993). Subsistence agriculture has become increasingly difficult. The growing importance of cash economies and the pervasiveness of consumerism cause a need for cash. Massive un- and underemployment contributes to the deteriorating self-images of many men, and leads to concomitant increases in alcoholism and family violence. Women have needs for food, housing, cash, education, health care, child care, social support, protection from violence, and, above all, for power within their families, communities, and political units. Without economic and decision-making power, one is dependent on others for the resources one needs; when resources are scarce, dependency is a sure route to deprivation.

At the same time, the rise of feminism in its many different forms has led to an increased consciousness of the inequities women suffer, and women's isolation has been reduced through the development and prevalence of new means of communication. The earlier discussion on development as it relates to women focused on scholarship and professional practice. At least as important have been the activities of women themselves, often encouraged and aided by external groups. In response to their increasing needs and as a result of their increasing consciousness and reduced isolation, women – who have little or no 'leisure' time – are finding time to come together to create new organizations. While women have long banded together out of need, there is something unique about their present activities – a universality and intensity that might be described as an international social movement. In part this universality is due to the recent global historical shifts discussed above, which have had direct negative effects on many women. Women take on the extra burden of organizing because they cannot meet all their needs and those of their families by themselves:

> [M]any women are on their own and the rest can't make ends meet on just their husbands' salaries. We share the same problems and we look for ways to resolve the situation.... We're limited by the fact that we have no power. We speak, but we're not heard.... It's hard to grow, and if you're alone it's really tough. But together, it's possible – our experience proves it. (Urribarri 1991)

A Brazilian leader says: 'We have to have confidence in ourselves, hope and also patience with ourselves. Meeting other women and other groups gives us courage because we can see that there are others who think like we do and share our dreams' (Caipora Women's Group 1993: 99).

The organizations they form or join are varied: organized around receiving credit, establishing savings, or income generation; meeting basic needs such as health care, housing, food, child care, water and sanitation; violence prevention; non-formal education for health or literacy; job-training; advocacy and policy reform; radio or print-based communications networks for women; environmental protection; human rights; and consciousness-raising. While health is always important to women, it is seen as one of a number of concerns – not necessarily distinct from those other needs. The organizations may be part of a larger movement – sponsored by progressive political movements, lending institutions, unions, non-governmental organizations, governmental agencies, women's groups, neighborhood organizations – or purely local: unsponsored grass-roots groups. What seems to be common is the *process* – a cycle of identification of problems, coming together to solve them, and then continuing to work on those problems while identifying others. Groups are flexible and responsive to local conditions, and to the individual needs of women and their families. As Charlton (1984) has stated, women have both reshaped their traditional roles and adapted to new roles in their efforts to meet their needs.

Of growing importance are regional and international networks and funders of organizations, such as DAWN (Development Alternative with Women for a New Era), WEDO (Women's Environment and Development Organization), FEMNET (African Women's Communication and Development Network), the US-based Global Fund for Women, GROOTS (Grass Roots Organizing Together in Sisterhood), IWTC

(International Women's Tribune Centre), and ISIS International (Women's International Resource Centre). These supporting organizations provide technical and financial support, a forum, and validation for local organizations. Increasingly such networks are relying on worldwide computer networks such as the Association for Progressive Communications and the Internet. This form of communication, having been developed partly in preparation for the UN Conference on Human Rights held in June 1993, and integral to the planning for the 1994 Conference on Population and Development held in Cairo and the 1995 Fourth World Conference on Women in Beijing, is likely to have a great impact on many organizations for women.

Women's social networks have long provided assistance to individuals, with women providing child care, money, services, and information to one another on an exchange basis. When they realize that they have common interests and needs, women use these already developed networks and the interactive style to meet community needs as well. Muller and Plantenga (1990: 18) point out that it is not easy to draw a line between home and neighborhood for women: 'The public water tap, the bathhouse, the school, the health office, the local market, the bus stop and whatever other neighbourhood facilities there might be all serve as meeting places.' Women are increasingly moving beyond home and neighborhood into social and political movements. The organizations they form are recognized by governments, non-governmental organizations, and churches, and women are seeing themselves as having important roles (Safa 1990).

Women's projects

Information about organizations for women is generally anecdotal or part of an in-depth study or a descriptive collection.[2] While it is not possible to present a representative sample of women's projects in a few pages, so great is the variety of organizational functions and style, I shall describe several briefly.

Africa

'Despite urbanization, we live in communal fashion.' [Khosi Xaba] laughs when she recalls U.S. women telling her about self-help groups. 'You don't have to tell us to come together – we are. Our life-style of communal living is a strength. It's getting a bit scratched at the edges, but it hasn't been destroyed. The hard lives we live give us strength.' (Editors 1993)

Sub-Saharan African women have a long history of collective action. Colonialism undermined women's status in those parts of Africa where women's groups had provided for self-government and political power for women. Perhaps that history, in combination with women's participation in revolutionary activity and their later formation into political support organizations and the fact that conditions in sub-Saharan Africa are particularly bad and deteriorating, helps to explain the wide variety of women's activities in Africa. These include microenterprise work groups, occupational associations, and religious organizations (Wipper 1984). Women's organizations in sub-Saharan Africa have been particularly effective in fighting against environmental degradation, and in obtaining and maintaining water and sanitation equipment in rural areas.

In the village of Kang'ombe in western Kenya, women have organized around health with the support of UNICEF and the Aga Khan Health Service (Munyakho 1992). The Wasare Women's Group was formed in 1987 to 'tackle endemic diseases such as malaria and diarrhoea.' Their first project was to raise money to drill a well. They have since set up a pharmacy, the profits from which they are using to expand their programs. They have established a community fund to provide medicines for those unable to pay. As part of their expansion, they have encouraged kitchen gardens, nutritional programs, and income-generating projects such as beekeeping. The African-led Bamako Initiative, dedicated to the promotion of the local provision of primary health care in Africa, has since joined in the sponsorship of the women's programs. The Wasare group provides an example of local initiative, with the cooperation of a regional NGO, a multi-governmental program, and international health organizations. The incentive grew out of women's concern with disease and their problems around water.

In Lusaka, Zambia, a group called Push, sponsored by the World Food Programme, is building roads (Anyadike 1991). 'Wielding pickaxes and shovels in flying dust, a group of women of all ages, some with babies strapped to their backs, are building a dirt road.' The program was not designed for women, but 'it is overwhelmingly women that are taking part. "Men have always refused to get involved," Vicky Mumba of WFP said. "They wanted cash, while the women are more concerned with the kitchen, with feeding their kids. So it ended up being a women's programme."' The local group sets its own priorities and is also working on garbage disposal, sanitation, and food distribution. As in many African programs, once women organize, a cohesive and active program to meet their varied needs evolves.

Asia

In Asia, as in project Push in Africa, women sometimes transform groups originally established by and for men. The Bhagavatula Charitable Trust (BCT) started out training local men as 'animators' or organizers for a savings and loan project (Vindhya and Kalpana 1989). After two failures, some women asked to participate. Because they were older than the men and illiterate (the men had a primary school education), they asked for a separate training program.

The women expanded the project's activities. They became politically active in the village governing organization; they earned some income that helped them 'to make some space for themselves in which the men are not the central figures'; they opened and controlled the management of a village shop; they restored the electricity supply by taxing themselves the overdue amount (after waiting one month for the village men to pay the debt); they collectively provided support to a 'low-caste' family, being 'more concerned about injustice than about caste loyalty.' The women's sense of 'doing good work for their village' has enabled them to challenge the status quo:

> According to Suri Babu, one of the Community Organizers of BCT, the programme with women was more successful because: (a) women transmit new ideas from one to another, whereas men generally keep these ideas to themselves; (b) women accept new ideas more easily, while men are resistant to change; (c) women are more reliable and can be expected to ensure implementation of their plans, while men get sub-divided because of their loyalties and affiliations to some political party or other. (Vindhya and Kalpana 1989: 188)

Asia has also been the location of very large programs for women; among the most successful has been the Self Employed Women's Association (SEWA), located in Ahmedabad, the sixth largest city in India (Bhatt 1989). Almost 95 percent of working women in India are self-employed, and SEWA, a trade union for these women, has more than 40,000 members. Its members practice many different trades and the organization deals with many issues, reflecting the variety of its membership. The organization began as the Women's Wing of the Textile Labor Association, and has been led since the late 1960s by Ela Bhatt.

> It functions as a union through what it terms 'struggle' on behalf of workers; and it functions as a cooperative that offers a wide variety of developmental services to its members. It aims to increase the visibility of its members as workers, to increase their income, and to increase their control over income and property. The goals for self-employed women are 'economic regeneration and social uplift.' (Sebstad 1984: 8)

On the basis of an acceptable form of organizing in India – trade unionization – women are developing parallel organizations that focus on their particular needs. With Gandhi as their source of inspiration, they are able to use strategies and forms of action that have long been accepted in their culture. Owing to SEWA's size and potential political power, the women can organize to address practical needs such as credit and child care, and strategic needs such as laws and policies that respond to their demands for justice and status.

The first completely grass-roots rural movement in India is much less formal, organized around closing down all the liquor shops in Andhra Pradesh – by raiding them and pouring out all the liquor, by hijacking delivery trucks, by burning shops down, by humiliating shop owners, and by shaving the heads of drunken men (Moore and Anderson 1993). The movement was catalyzed by a story used in a literacy program that described 'a young heroine who mobilized the women in her village to force the local liquor shop to close.' In the story, as in the entire region, men spent their income on alcohol, and frequently came home drunk and violent. As of early 1993, more than 6,000 shops had been closed. The government has since removed the story from the literacy program.

Latin America

In Latin America, women have also moved into the public arena, leading human rights movements and becoming more visible and active in politics. The partition of life into a public (male)/private (female) dichotomy seems to be a useful concept for understanding gender in Latin America.[3] The assumption is that women are denied equality because of their relegation to the domestic or private sphere. That sphere is devalued, and women are thereby subordinated to men.

Helen Safa (1990: 355) describes how Latin American women have tried to unify the spheres: they have moved into the public domain by 'redefining and transforming their domestic role from one of private nurturance to one of collective, public protest,' while 'insisting upon distinct forms of incorporation that reaffirm their identity as women, and particularly as wives and mothers.' Safa focuses on the 'collectivization of private tasks,' such as community kitchens and community child care, which takes advantage of the domestic role to 'give them strength and legitimacy.' Women are 'redefining the meaning associated with domesticity to include participation and struggle rather than obedience and passivity' (1990: 362). Safa acknowledges that as women move into domains formerly occupied only by men, they will encounter more opposition. However, 'the issue is not simply one of women's incorporation into a male-defined world but of transforming this world to do away with the hierarchies of class, gender, race, and ethnicity that have so long subordinated much of the Latin American population, men as well as women' (1990: 367).

The Agrupación de Mujeres Peteneras Ixchel (AMPI) in Guatemala (Guy 1992) provides a specific example of an organization that moved from the private to the public sphere. AMPI was founded in 1979, and survived due to the will and energies of one of its founders, who grew up in the rural Peten area. A group of young women who originally formed a cohort that played together as children began to hold more organized discussions during which they addressed family problems such as 'fathers who beat their wives, single mothers forced to beg to feed their children, and illegitimate children shunned by their fathers and the community.' They wanted to make changes in their lives and to protect their threatened environment, so they formalized their group as AMPI. When one member moved to Guatemala City and there made contact with feminist/activist women, she gained the skills she needed to raise funds and to establish workshops on health, self-esteem and self-determination, popular culture, and the history of women in the Peten. The group is now working towards the establishment of an educational center where women and children 'can learn about and practice various skills (e.g., beekeeping, gardening, sewing, bread baking, animal husbandry, etc.) and develop their mental capabilities, literacy skills, creativity, and self esteem.'

The philosophy underlying the AMPI programs reflects the mixture of Indian and mestizo cultures in the Peten. Women are unused to decision-making and to participating in development activities. Therefore they are more comfortable in women-only groups. They begin to value the skills they have, and to resent the limitations their society has placed on them and on their female children. The women have a strong sense of responsibility for the environment and for their cultural heritage. Ethnic pride is fostered, and they learn the importance of their role as 'primary gatekeepers and transmitters of folk beliefs, customs, and practices,' and that 'women are fundamental to the recollection and reintegration of traditional knowledge.' In the Peten, the creation of an educational center is a public act.

When women move their activities into the public sphere, they do more than become political activists. They attempt to maintain control and ownership of their organizations, transforming themselves and their communities according to strategies and visions that they develop. Perhaps the most famous women's organization is Las Madres de Plaza de Mayo, the Mothers of the Plaza de Mayo, in Buenos Aires, Argentina. This extraordinary (and ordinary) group of women came together informally in 1977 and formally in 1979 to protest the disappearances of their children and grandchildren. The fourteen original members of the organization met as each visited and haunted public offices searching for information about their missing children. They were housewives who had left the privacy of their homes because of their great pain and need. They were fortunate to find a natural leader among the members, Azucena Villaflor de Vicenti. She suggested that the women 'go public,' gathering in the Plaza de Mayo. Harassed by police for sitting or standing in groups, they decided to march silently. According to Marysa Navarro (1989: 251), '[b]y walking around the pyramid as mothers of children who had disappeared, they transformed their private, personal statement into a public and political act.' They held weekly marches, circulated petitions, contacted other human rights organizations and international leaders, and held demonstrations. Two nuns and Azucena Villaflor were themselves disappeared in 1977. The group found another natural leader in Hebé Bonafina. Membership in the group grew to 2,500 by 1982. The women showed incredible courage and perseverance, and an unexpected militancy. Navarro suggests several reasons for their success: they felt compelled to act because, '[s]uddenly deprived of their children, their lives as wives and mothers had lost meaning'; since they were housewives, they could devote time to their activities and not lose their jobs; they were somewhat protected by their society because of their status as mothers; and their activities were completely unexpected because of their previous relegation to the 'private' realm.

> Finally, motherhood also gave the Madres an additional advantage. Since most of the mothers lacked political experience, they were unburdened by ideological constraints or obedience to party directives or the need to replicate proven tactics. They were therefore free to use new symbols, devise appropriate tactics, and adopt actions, such as the Thursday marches, that had not been tried before in Argentina. In the terrorist state created by the military, motherhood in fact protected them and gave them a freedom and a power not available to traditional political actors, especially if they were male. (Navarro 1989: 258)

One last important example of women's organizing is the national networks of feminist organizations that were created in Nicaragua in 1992 (Alemán and Miranda 1993; Cuadra *et al.* 1992). During the Sandinista period, from 1979 until 1990, women were organized through the Luisa Amanda Espinoza Nicaraguan Women's Association

(AMNLAE), a branch of the governing FSLN party. The hierarchical structure of AMNLAE paralleled that of the FSLN and, as so often happens after a revolution, many 'women's issues' were placed on the back burner both to maintain harmony within the party and because they were not a priority of many of the men who held the positions of power. Following the 1990 elections, which led to a reduction in social involvement on the part of the government, AMNLAE proposed a reorganization of the women's movement. An extremely (and unexpectedly) successful meeting was held in January 1992, with some 800 attendees. During the 1980s, the Sandinistas had encouraged grassroots organizing and many groups from that era attended, although in the end AMNLAE itself did not actively participate. The participants sought to maintain their ideological and organizational autonomy, and so formed a loose group of networks addressing violence, health, sexuality, the economy, education, and the environment.

At this time some networks are stronger than others. Both the health and the violence groups have conducted sustained activities, some in conjunction with the Ministry of Health, while retaining their autonomy. Other groups, such as those concerned about the economy, have had a more difficult time, facing class issues and a bottomed-out economy. While non-hierarchical forms of organizing are still vitally important to members, there is an expressed need for more coordination and for assistance in moving from protest to proposals. There is some discussion about the need for 'an organizational structure to facilitate joint actions in response to state policies or decide common positions with respect to mixed institutions' (Alemán and Miranda 1993).

Nicaragua may be in the forefront of such activities because of the ten years during which grass-roots organizing was encouraged, and because the Sandinista government did endorse, if not implement, many feminist goals. It is also a relatively underpopulated country (fewer than four million, with over one-third living in the capital and the majority of the population clustered in the southwest), which allows women and groups to know about one another easily. We will surely see the development of other such national networks as governments continue to encourage grass-roots organizing among women as part of the neo-liberal economic strategy to make the satisfaction of basic needs the business of people, not government (Alemán and Miranda 1993).

Summary

The projects just described included groups organized around health, road-building, savings and loans, workers' rights, opposition to liquor, cultural and environmental preservation, human rights, and increased independence. They were independent or sponsored, organized around strong leaders or non-hierarchical, small or large, rural or urban. There are many other documented women's organizations: food kitchens in Peru, organized miners' wives in Bolivia, environmental groups in Africa and in India, women's banks and credit groups in Bangladesh, video cooperatives in Africa and in Asia, a black women's health organization in the USA, and white women's adult education and job training programs in the Appalachian region of the USA. Women in the Philippines who survive by selling the junk that they and their children scavenge from a dump have organized a garbage miners' association. Rural Zimbabwean women have formed radio clubs, producing and receiving programs to facilitate the development of self-reliance projects. Not all are success stories, although traditional measures of organizational success – longevity, self-sufficiency, and power – may not take account of important effects on individuals and communities that can continue long after the demise of the organization.[4]

Activities are also being organized in the Islamic world, although the conflict in those countries between feminists/activists and traditionalists is particularly complex and often virulent. Also, although I have not discussed women's organizing in wartime, the examples of Palestinian, Eritrean, and Somalian women indicate, tragically, that war opens options for women. Thus women throughout the developing world are going beyond their traditional gender roles to create new spaces that foster personal and communal achievements.

Personal transformations

The organizations that women are now creating reflect both their increasing needs, by stressing direct forms of action, and their increasing awareness of their condition, by incorporating into their activities a process of conscientization. As a result, dramatic transformations occur in many of the participants. This process has often been described as empowerment. A facilitator from the Unidad de Servicios de Apoyo para la Participación de la Mujer Hondureña (Unidad de Servicios 1991) described it thus: 'I never believed that what the theory said was real. That women can turn inside out like you turn a sock inside out. But it is true; there are such changes.... Women's personalities are transformed and they are converted into a person who no longer has contradictions and they don't fight among themselves.'

A woman from the Philippines described her life as a laundress, beaten by her husband, desperately poor and with too many children.

She became active in SAMAKANA, a national federation of poor urban women, and in the liberation theology movement:

> Before, I thought I was the poorest, most exploited person in the world. But through interacting with others, I saw that there are others even more oppressed and exploited. Even if you are poor, you must understand your situation; otherwise you would want to commit suicide because it would seem that there is no other hope.
>
> Before, I thought I was alone in the world, but now I've found that other people do want to help. One finds that one is not isolated. The one thing that gives me energy is my knowledge that I can help others....
>
> There have also been a lot of changes within me.... My organization [SAMAKANA] has helped me in many ways. All that I've achieved and learned, even the upbringing of my children, has been made possible by my organization. (NCAHRN 1991: 22)

Women living in the community of Guarari, Costa Rica, who participated in a land takeover and the construction of self-built communities described their transformations to me (Stein 1989). These women lived in a section for female-headed families, and were in the process of completing the construction of a women's center in 1989. They described the isolation they had previously experienced, and the confidence and knowledge they gained from being part of a group. Several of the women had had severe problems with nerves, drugs, or alcohol; many had had difficult marriages and suffered from abuse. Each one of them seemed to have taken control of her life since participating in the housing project. Janet talked about moving from a barrio where 'no one communicated; problems belonged to the individual, not to the community.' In Guarari, 'we all live each other's problems and try to help one another.... It's a commitment; here one learns at the very least not to be such an egoist.' To quote Sonia: 'Before, my life was totally different. By knowing such people, one changes definitively, psychologically and socially. And another thing you learn is how to talk with those who cause you problems without being afraid, to share a meal, drink coffee, make jokes.' Xenia proudly described the skills she learned: carpentry, masonry, and roofing.

Critiques of women's organizations

Women have come together to improve their situation and to get their fair share of resources. Their organizations are ubiquitous, flexible, and designed to meet needs that are locally determined by means that are culturally suitable. While the similarities and the sheer number of projects justify calling them part of a social movement, it is not yet known whether resources and power are being or will in fact be transferred to women. A key to the long-term effectiveness of this new movement will be the strength, effectiveness, and durability of the organizations themselves.

Sen and Grown (1987) identify some common and difficult problems that women's organizations must grapple with. Many groups 'have been wary of viewing large public policy issues as within their domain.' They 'have not developed enduring and effective channels for acquiring representation.' They 'avoid clear assignment of responsibilities or delegation of authority for fear of mirroring existing hierarchies or established power structures.' They 'tend to look with suspicion upon any political force or body that is not of [their] own making,' based on experiences of attempted and successful cooptation. They have not worked out ways of power-sharing within organizations. Organizations must be broadened and democratized, must explicitly reject personal aggrandizement, and must show 'respect for the many voices of our movement.' Their recipe for resolving such problems includes 'resources (finance, knowledge, technology), skills training, and leadership formation on the one side; and democratic processes, dialogue, participation in policy and decision making, and techniques for conflict resolution on the other' (Sen and Grown 1987: 89).

Some insights into successful organization are presented in *Leadership and the New Science: Learning about Organization from an Orderly Universe* (Wheatley 1994). The author suggests that the models being formulated by the new scientists correspond to the reality within which we now exist. She applies quantum mechanics, field theory, chaos theory, and complexity theory to organizations, which she sees as little different from other organisms struggling to function in and understand a new world using outmoded frameworks (see Chapter 8 below). Successful organizations, she argues, will be those that focus on communication and collaboration, connections and relations, autonomy, and participative decision-making. They will respond intuitively and dynamically to 'new and interesting' information, trusting that the ethos of the organization is strong enough to serve to organize that information. 'We need to be able to trust that something as simple as a clear core of values and vision, kept in motion through continuing dialogue, can lead to order' (Wheatley 1994). Margaret Wheatley emphasizes the mysterious relationship between parts and wholes, neither existing without the other, the existence of patterns and order within chaos, and the strength of the self-organizing principle of complexity theory. She sees the search for meaning as the root of self-organization.

Empowerment may be closely related to these concepts. Successful empowerment projects may naturally be more 'organic,' more in tune with this 'new' reality. They are governed by vision and by continuing dialogue, open to new information and flexible, participatory, non-hierarchical, encourage autonomy, and more than the sum of the participating individuals. They are dedicated to helping people to make sense of their lives and their situations. They are rooted in the local situation, aware of history and responsive to 'local perturbations.'

Given the plethora of women's organizations and their importance in women's lives, it is time to study these women's organizations in greater depth – both to particularize and to generalize. Such work can enable us to understand better the relationships between structure, process, and outcomes in empowerment (see Seitz [1992] and Sultana [1988]).

Summary

While one must look carefully at the relationship between development and women's situations due to differential and particular effects, the information on women's situations is clear: women are disadvantaged in terms of education, employment, income, access to programs and services, health care, and the benefits of modernization projects such as credit, training, and jobs. They are greatly affected by negative effects of development on the environment, nutrition, and exposure to toxicities. They bear a disproportionate burden with regard to refugee status, the exodus of men in search of jobs, and changing gender roles. Development theories – particularly modernization, based as it is on positivist economic theory – have guided current development policy: top-down, trickle-down, and usually ignoring differential effects.

There is a developing consensus among scholars, advocates, practitioners, activists, and third world women that if society is to be restructured to reflect a feminist vision of development – a vision not only of equity but of a transformed society – a movement composed of empowered women, households, and organizations is required. It is necessary to 'transform ... women's survival tactics into viable political strategies' (Batt 1992: 13). In this chapter I have described the complexity of the field of women's development, and noted that the goal of the empowerment of participants and their community is more and more frequently a unifying theme in discussions about strategies and goals. We have seen that women's organizing as a means for survival is taking on a particular form, incorporating the process of empowerment. As the number of empowerment groups increases, and regional and international networks of these local organizations emerge, an international women's empowerment movement is fast developing.

Notes

1. This is the song of *Maendeleo ya Wanawake*, the Kenyan national women's organization.

2. Anecdotal information is available through non-traditional news sources such as the *Institute for Global Communications*, 18 De Boom Street, San Francisco, CA 94107, (415) 442–0220; items reviewed by *Third World Resources*, a quarterly review of resources from and about the third world, 464 19th St., Oakland, CA 94612–2297; the international section of *Ms.* magazine, P.O. Box 57132, Boulder, CO 80322–7132; the North American Congress on Latin America's (NACLA) *Report on the Americas*, 475 Riverside Drive, Suite 454, New York, NY 10015; the *New Internationalist*, P.O. Box 1143, Lewiston, New York 14092–9984; and newsletters of organizations such as the *National Central America Health Rights Network*, P.O. Box 202, New York, NY 10276; the *InterAmerican Foundation*, 1515 Wilson Blvd., Rosslyn, VA 22209; the *Christian Medical Commission*, CMC/WCC, P.O. Box 2100, CH-1211 Geneva 2, Switzerland; the *Women's International Public Health Network*, 7100 Oak Forest Lane, Bethesda, Maryland 20817; the *Hesperian Foundation*, P.O. Box 1692, Palo Alto, CA 94302; *Women's World Banking*, 8 West 40th St., New York, NY 10018; *The Global Fund for Women*, 2480 Sand Hill Road, Suite 100, Menlo Park, CA 94025; the *Bernard van Leer Foundation*, P.O. Box 82334, 2508 EH, The Hague, The Netherlands; and the *International Women's Tribune Center*, 777 United Nations Plaza, New York, NY 10017. In-depth studies include project evaluations and reviews such as Wahid (1993) and dissertation research projects such as Sultana (1988) and Seitz (1992). Descriptive collections include Fisher (1993), Isis International and Development Alternatives With Women for a New Era (1988), Leonard (1989), M.F. Levy (1988), Wignaraja (1990), Yudelman (1987), Karl (1995), Küppers (1994), and Women's Feature Service (1993).

3. It has proved less useful in Africa. Stamp (1990) stresses the danger of generalization and the importance of acknowledging the historical particularities that distinguish African women's situations from those of other third world women. She questions as Western bias the acceptance of a global public/private dichotomy – defining the public realm in Africa as the extended family, which also determines political organization. She also questions the priority of the economic realm over other aspects of human life; the assumption that 'family' and 'household' have the same meanings in different cultures; the assumption 'that women have been universally oppressed'; and the inapplicability of 'unitary concepts such as "position" and "role" given the multifaceted nature of power, decision-making and authority ... which undermines the concept of a simplistic dominance/submission dichotomy.'

4. Albert Hirschman (1984), one of the few economists studying grass-roots development, was struck by how much of what he observed during a study of several grass-roots projects funded by the Inter American Foundation was contrary to intuition and to popular assumptions. Among his 'wrong-way-round' observations is that participants in failed radical communal activities often find renewed social energy and participate in other communal activities – their isolation and distrust having been reduced. He also noted that grass-roots development will often induce the desire for education, rather than education necessarily preceding development – that in fact there is no 'natural order' to successful development – and that experience in cooperatives often leads to 'constructive involvement in public affairs and to public advocacy.'

3

Empowerment

Efforts are being made in many places to mobilize women – especially very poor women – so that they can more effectively act in their own interests vis-à-vis employers, landowners, moneylenders and other power-ful interests ... implicitly and explicitly, these efforts stress the impor-tance of women's 'empowerment' – that is learning through collective action that they can successfully challenge individuals and institutions opposed to their self-interests. (Papanek 1990: 168)

The Women's Empowerment Movement

Taken together, the many projects, organizations, networks, and confer-ences described in the previous chapter can be seen as a women's movement centered around empowerment. This movement is occurring in many different communities. The women who participate act as a group, through political action, to obtain economic and other resources. They are pragmatic – learning from both their failures and their successes – and hopeful and confident (Allen and Barr 1990: 14–16).

Sara Evans (1979: 219–20) presents five 'essential preconditions for an insurgent collective identity,' derived from her study of the US women's movement. They include:

(1) *social spaces* within which members of an oppressed group can develop an independent sense of worth in contrast to their received definitions as second-class or inferior citizens;
(2) *role models* of people breaking out of patterns of passivity;
(3) *an ideology* that can explain the sources of oppression, justify revolt, and provide a vision of a qualitatively different future;
(4) *a threat* to the newfound sense of self that forces a confrontation with the inherited cultural definitions – in other words, it becomes impossible for

45

the individual to 'make it on her own' and escape the boundaries of the oppressed group; and finally

(5) *a communication or friendship network* through which a new interpretation can spread, activating the insurgent consciousness into a social movement. [emphasis added]

The social spaces are there for the women's empowerment movement – in part due to the absence of men, in part due to women's efforts to create such spaces for themselves. There is an ever-increasing number of role models, and the communications networks help to expose women to those role models. There is an ideology that is an amalgam of empowerment and feminist theories and the responses of women to the negative impacts of development. There is very little opportunity for individual women to make it on their own. Finally, there are vibrant communication and friendship networks that reach everywhere. From Nepal to Cochibamba to New York City women are organizing as women, to meet their own needs and the needs of their families.

There are several excellent guides to organizing women and communities in general, which have been used to train leaders, facilitators, and community and health workers (Hope and Timmel 1990; Kindervatter 1986, 1987a, 1987b; Programa Educativa para la Mujer 1990; Vella 1989; Werner and Bower 1982, 1984). These materials are particularly focused on conscientization – on helping women who have been taught not to (or have not been taught to) think about their feelings, who have suppressed their anger, who have often accepted an unjust situation.

The formalization of this process, through the production of educational materials, is speeding up its dissemination. The ever-increasing capability and actuality of networking, the group experiences that so many women had at the UN conferences for women, and the plethora of videos and books that report on successful projects have 'internationalized' many of the techniques described. It is, of course, possible that such formalization may also stifle some of the creativity and spontaneity of the process. As in any movement, pragmatism and creativity must struggle against the rigidity that often accompanies institutionalization. In order to know how these tensions will be resolved, it is necessary to watch and wait to see how the movement develops as it gains momentum.

Empowerment is not a cure-all

While empowerment may be the answer to some problems, it cannot solve all problems and will itself create new ones. As I mentioned above, younger and older women may be pitted against one another in situations where power has traditionally accompanied aging. As younger women take control and have more opportunities available to them, older women are likely to lose power. Younger women may become geographically, emotionally, and culturally distanced from their families, their mothers. Of course this can happen for many other reasons as well, and it is possible that community activities can bring different generations together. However, change is often most threatening to those who have lived the longest with the conditions that are to be changed.

Women may be even busier than before, facing a *triple* day, that now includes group activities as well as productive and reproductive ones. Jeanine Anderson (1989: 238) describes an infant who died while her mother was 'exceptionally active in her shanty settlement's projects and organizations.' Her point is that because women are socialized to take care of day-to-day business in the neighborhood, they shoulder an enormous and unfair burden that may negatively affect their children. She maintains that until they are able to 'deal with the larger society beyond the confines of the shantytown' they will not get the information, experience, and resources they need. Some organizations do provide support such as child care during the group's activities, and – through group purchasing, group marketing, communal food preparation – make other tasks easier for women. Also, women may be energized by their group activities. However, activities must be scheduled at the convenience of the women, and additional burdens should be minimized as much as possible. If conscientization and empowerment are not part of the group process, there may in fact be little or no long-term gain to compensate for the time loss from women's participation in community activities.

Another potential problem is that women's expectations may be raised unrealistically. Monawar Sultana (1988: 318) notes that '[w]omen's new power and autonomy do not allow them to deal with the broader processes of modernization that are increasingly marginalizing poor women from access to land, other productive resources, and political power.' That is to say: as women build their new selves and their new communities, macro policies are working much more quickly to make their situations even more difficult and more untenable. Structural adjustment policies may make survival so difficult that women no longer have time to participate in empowering activities. Communal kitchens in Peru are often unable to obtain any food. Also, as Nancy Scheper-Hughes (1992: 509) painfully learned from her experiences in northeast Brazil, 'one cannot underestimate the savagery of hunger and scarcity or the brutality of police terror in diminishing all possibilities for collective action.' Can empowerment survive severe deprivation?

It is inevitable that not all projects will endure – because of opposition, a dearth of resources, poor organization, a lack of results. However, Albert Hirschman (1984) found that people who participated in grass-roots activities that failed often joined other, perhaps less radical, projects later: they wanted to recover the earlier experience. Thus the failure or demise of one project need not mean that members will not look for another opportunity to solve their problems cooperatively.

Peggy Antrobus (1989: 189) warns us of the danger of cooptation, another threat facing this movement. She notes that those who have drawn attention to the importance of women in development may have made governments aware that women can be counted on to cope even if they are neglected. She describes the 'super-exploitation' of women by governments who are abdicating their responsibilities for education, public health, care of the elderly, and the provision of basic foods:

> [Cooptation] is nothing short of taking advantage of women's willingness to struggle against enormous odds. It irritates me when people speak of empowerment without thinking through the implications of this in terms of the challenge to their own privileged position. My impression is that most people who speak of the empowerment of people, and especially of women, have no intention of giving up their privileged position. (Allen and Barr 1990: 11, quoting Antrobus)

Little is yet known about the political repercussions that take place as groups of women question the status quo and seek to take control of resources for themselves and their families. One can assume that when power is seriously threatened, it will respond. Susan George (1977: 289) provides a word of warning, noting that when power is at stake, those who are being challenged will find out (and use) all they can about the strategies of the oppressed. She suggests that we should 'study the rich and powerful, not the poor and powerless.' In this context, researchers should be observing how those in power respond to women's empowerment, and bringing information to the women about these responses. It may well be that organizing has not yet reached that critical point at which the opposition counterattacks. The most visibly troubling projects to those in power are human rights organizations in countries like China, Argentina, Chile, Peru, Guatemala, and El Salvador. Observing how government and the military respond to these organizations can indicate where and how the organizations are vulnerable. The Arab Women's Solidarity Association (AWSA), founded in 1982, was shut down by the Egyptian government in 1991. Nawal El Sadaawi, AWSA's founder, sees progress in Egypt none the less, and is continuing to work towards a pan-Arab women's organization. The enormous variety of women's empowerment strategies is in their favor. When one technique fails, they try another. It is also to be hoped that the emergent networks and pan-organizations will be able to provide needed support for and visibility to groups that face suppression.

Finally, all too frequently, the situation from which women are trying to escape involves excessive drinking by their husbands or partners, violence against them in the home, and lack of support. A crisis can develop in a family when a man forbids a woman to participate in women's groups, or when she frees herself from his domination and finds emotional support and other sources of income. The couple separate, and the woman may be left alone with her children. Although many women report being much happier on their own, the increasing prevalence of female-headed households is a troublesome phenomenon. Such households tend to be poorer, children lack fathers, and men are distanced from their families.

Thus negative outcomes of empowerment activities must be anticipated, including division between generations, overwhelming demands on women, unmet expectations, cooptation, political oppression and suppression, and family disruption. While these problems are intrinsic, and to some extent unavoidable, awareness can help to mitigate them. For example, strategies to reduce family disruption and to ease women's work burdens are being developed by some projects. None the less, it will be important to measure, evaluate, and, most of all, understand the health effects of negative as well as positive outcomes of empowerment, and to investigate their interactions.

Men and the empowerment of women

Potential family disruption and the role of men in an international women's movement are rarely addressed in the literature. Relations between men and women are determined by economic, cultural, and social forces, and, as rapid change has been occurring, many cultures have not adopted family and child-raising patterns that enable the family to remain a strong unit. While the patriarchal system gives men control within the family, few poor men in poor countries have much control outside it. Unemployment is increasingly common – estimated at 30 percent worldwide (InterPress Service 1994). Alcoholism is endemic and practically epidemic (Human Resources Development 1993), and violence levels are frighteningly high (Heise 1993). One fairly common explanation for these destructive gender behaviors traces them back to child-rearing practices:

> In developing countries, one often sees little boys scampering in a game, swimming in a river, laughing and leaping in freedom – playing. And, nearby, one often sees little girls staggering under the weight of their younger siblings (often almost as big as they are), fetching heavy loads of water or fuel, or laboring in the fields with their mothers – working. Many development workers have observed that when these children grow up, it is often the hardworking, disciplined girls who are better equipped to take on the responsibilities of family survival, since they have already been practicing these arts for so long. These specialists note that when boys, who had always been catered to and favored, become men, they often find the hard knocks of poverty, alienation, and frustration too much to bear. For many, the bottle offers an irresistible escape. Alcoholism, when combined with the inevitable frustrations of poverty and unemployment, leads many men to acts of violence against their families. (Helmore 1985)

It is also true that men and women are often competing for employment and for economic opportunities. What is occurring may be a zero-sum trap, with female gains balanced by male losses – a far cry from feminist visions of society. Whether this is a necessary stage in a process of righting past wrongs or whether it is remediable remains to be seen. Social, cultural, historical, and economic forces are powerful and intertwined.

Whatever the cause, men and women often have different reactions to poverty and difficult circumstances. Men have not in general been drawn into empowerment projects. At this historical moment, given the decline of Marxism and socialism, there are few competing visionary ideologies. There is evidence, however, that some men are benefiting from participation in evangelical movements – they change their lifestyles, since drinking, smoking, and extramarital sex are usually forbidden; they dress better; they develop pride and self-confidence (Moríz 1991). Elizabeth Brusco (1986) suggests that by undermining the 'machismo' ethic and reorienting men and their resources to the household, evangelical movements enhance women's status and the resources available to them. It is not clear why evangelical movements have been successful in attracting men while empowerment projects have not. Many of the groups that have developed into women's empowerment groups were begun by men and had men as members. Certainly, revolutions and social movements have primarily been led by men, with both men and women participating at most levels below top leadership. As we shall see, men have played an important role in the evolution of the concept of empowerment. However, women have been much more responsive than men to the techniques and strategies used for empowerment. The slow process of participation, self-emancipation, group action, and reflection has been more attractive to women than to men. Some suggested explanations include: women have a history of working together and sharing (Safa 1990); women 'hang in there' longer than men (Vindhya and Kalpana 1989); men participate in organizations whose relationships to those in power is more direct, such as the local political party; men's position in the family has been undermined by unemployment and changing roles, so they feel less responsibility towards it; cultural patterns lead men to use their resources for their own social activities (Bruce 1989; T.L. Whitehead 1986); and the recognition of gender oppression gives women an added incentive to organize.

What is important in the context of this book about women is men's role in women's increasing burden for family survival, the attitudes of husbands and fathers about women's participation in empowerment projects, and men's support or opposition to the feminist goal of a more equitable society. While much of the literature on women in development mentions 'bringing the men along' in order to facilitate women's participation, little has been written on how to do that. It is an issue on many levels. Men are the political leaders, they usually hold the tangible power in the community, and they consider themselves head of the household. It may, however, be possible for (some) women to organize without further disintegration of the family and alienation of their male relatives and associates. Special efforts to help men understand what their wives are doing have been effective in Honduras (Unidad de Servicios de Apoyo 1991). Men often do recognize the importance of additional income and resources for their families and communities, and assist local women's groups (Small 1990). When this does not happen, however, women are prepared to support one another in taking control of their own lives. As the issues for women become more clearly drawn, one can hope to see more discussion about relations between men and women.

Thus, while empowerment can have negative effects, it appears to be a popular, hopeful, and effective strategy for women, but one that is not attracting men. In keeping with feminist visions of an equitable and non-hierarchical society, it is important that men also have the opportunity for hope and for empowerment.

The Roots of Empowerment

An exploration of the roots of empowerment will contribute to an understanding of its importance to third world women. While the intellectualization of the concept of empowerment – as it relates to this study and as will be discussed later in this chapter – occurred primarily in developed countries, its roots are global. In both the first and the third world, the phenomenon is firmly rooted in opposition to oppression, traceable back to anti-colonialism and Marxist theory. Aspects of empowerment have been important in revolutionary situations in Latin American, Asia, and Africa, in movements for less radical social change throughout the third world, in the civil rights and women's movements in the USA, and in the international women's movement today. What seems to be similar in these disparate settings is the opening of '"social spaces" within which members of an oppressed group can develop an independent sense of worth in contrast to their received definitions as second-class or inferior citizens' (S. Evans 1979: 219). These spaces provide participants with occasion to envision opportunity and to experience hopefulness. Specific historical circumstances lead to such an opening of society. As Paulo Freire, one of the founders of the empowerment movement, said: 'my experience in the sixties in Brazil did not happen in the air. They happened in some historical space, in a context with some special historical, political, social, cultural elements in the atmosphere' (Horton *et al.* 1990: 92).

Today one sees a desire among many women for self-determination and control stemming from an enhanced understanding of their oppression as women, an increased burden on them for the survival of their families, and a historical opening – a period of attention to women's issues, and of possible change and democratization. Figure 3.1 below pictorially summarizes some of the historical roots of the women's empowerment movement.

Anti-colonialism in India, Africa, and China influenced the civil rights movement in the USA, which in turn helped to catalyze the second phase of the feminist movement in industrialized countries as well as other participatory forms of organization. In Latin America, where anti-imperialism was more relevant than anti-colonialism in the second half of the twentieth century, an anti-dependency movement developed which, along with liberation theology, greatly influenced popular forms of organizing that stressed participation. Both anti-colonialism and anti-dependency led to the evolution of empowerment theory and practice among women in the non-industrialized world. This latter movement, discussed in Chapter 2, is represented in Figure 3.1 by the large circle at the bottom of the diagram. The present discussion concentrates on the earlier precursors of women's empowerment activities, as represented by the top three circles.

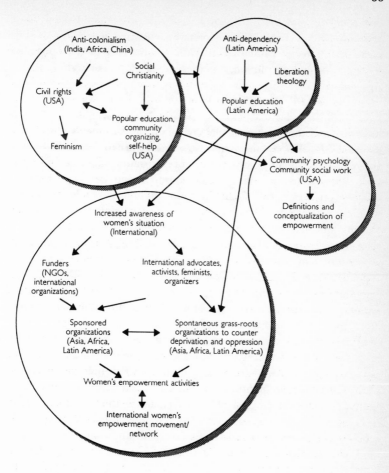

Figure 3.1 Roots of the women's empowerment movement

Anti-colonialism

In the nineteenth century, countries in Western Europe expanded the domain of their commerce and their political control to countries in Asia and Africa, soon to followed by the United States in Latin America. Whether this was primarily an inevitable outcome of capitalism's need for markets and raw materials (Harrison 1981), or an inevitable stage in the historical pattern of strong powers dominating weaker ones (Isbister 1991), or both, the effect was the creation of what is known today as the third world. The roots of empowerment lie in the multifaceted efforts of many of those who experienced domination to achieve self-determination and to free themselves from external control – through revolution, other less violent forms of resistance, and nationalism.

Opposition to colonialism in India, China, and Africa affected both those women who participated in freedom movements in those countries and those active in the civil rights and women's movements in the USA. Among the major strategies learned from these anti-colonialists were alternative forms of resistance, the use of group processes to develop political consciousness, and the importance of pride in one's ethnicity. Gandhi's *Satyagraha* movement in India used alternatives to violent revolution such as non-violent demonstrations and the application of moral pressure to free the country from British rule. Mao Tse-tung, uniting China against foreign and Kuomintang domination, instituted group processes – albeit harsh ones – to create a political consciousness among the Chinese people. Black Africans were either given or fought for freedom from the British, the Spanish, the Germans, the French, the Portuguese, and the Afrikaners. Out of their struggles came a sense of identity and negritude – pride in blackness. Steven Biko combined negritude and Frantz Fanon's ideas on the internalization of oppression into a concept of black consciousness (Isbister 1991). These strategies – non-violence, the use of group processes to increase political consciousness, and ethnic or racial pride – directly affected the civil rights movement in the USA and can be seen as precursors of the women's empowerment movement. In particular, Gandhi, Fanon, and Biko were all important influences on the civil rights movement in the United States.

Highlander and the US civil rights movement

Changes in consciousness were the building blocks of the civil rights movement:

> On its own terms, the movement made vivid once again the lesson which weaves through the black freedom struggle from its inception: There can be no democracy without dignity and self-respect, and such values are the measure of a people's own determination to resist oppression. For people who have been rendered invisible by the dominant culture, gaining such a transformative sense of themselves requires more than exhortation or experiences of being oppressed. A new sense of self is sustained and augmented in particular sorts of public places where people can discover 'who they are' and to what they aspire on their own terms, and where they can begin to think about what democracy means. (Evans and Boyte 1986: 68)

The Highlander School in Tennessee was such a place; it has played an important role in the history of both the civil rights and the empowerment movements in the USA (Branch 1988; Horton *et al.* 1990). It was founded and led by Myles Horton, who – after studying religion with Reinhold Niebuhr, working with Jane Addams in the settlement house movement in Chicago, and traveling to Denmark to study the Danish folk high school movement – returned to his native Tennessee in 1932 to open the Highlander Folk School. The school, which provided training for people fighting for racial and economic justice, became an intellectual home for civil rights leaders, including Martin Luther King, Jr.

One of the most important programs fostered by Highlander and by Horton was the Citizenship Schools. These schools were originally designed to provide literacy training for uneducated southern blacks, but Bernice Robinson, who had never finished high school herself, molded them into the core of a movement for social change. In Horton's words (1990: 72): 'It wasn't a literacy class. It was a community organization.' It provided an opportunity for the development of critical consciousness. Robinson did not teach; she learned with the class. The idea spread quickly, with Highlander training leaders who then worked throughout the south. The localness of the program, the roles of the leaders as participants, the process of group conscientization, and the goal of community organization were all important precursors to the women's movement and to later conceptualizations of empowerment.

Empowerment was a concept well understood by the civil rights movement, as evidenced by Highlander's activities and formulated by Barbara Solomon (1976) in her book *Black Empowerment*. The experiences of the 1960s and 1970s serve both as a historical parallel to women's activities today, providing examples of problems and solutions, and as models that women active in that movement, or affected by those who were active, took to heart and used to deal with their own problems.

The civil rights movement spawned many examples of successful self-help programs and community organizations. It also experienced some of the barriers to empowerment: dependency, cooptation, and intransigence. Groups grew dependent upon outside financing that could be withdrawn when interests changed or when the recipients became uppity or threatening. Cooptation, particularly among the leadership, was not uncommon. Power could be illusory, since some democratization plus many legal and social improvements did not necessarily translate into equity and a redistribution of power. Nicholas

Lemann (1991) asserts that wresting power from the powerful means more than getting local control. Unless connections are made and maintained between the ghetto and the larger world where resources reside, no meaningful shift in resources and power will result.

US feminism and consciousness-raising

Although feminism has roots in earlier times, the present feminist movements in the USA had their beginnings in the civil rights movement. Sara Evans (1979) traces links between African-American and white southern women in the USA who were early participants in the civil rights movement in the south. The civil rights movement had both charismatic leaders, like Martin Luther King, and 'mamas' – a term used by the movement to describe strong, enduring, and creative local leaders who had been involved in organizing activities for many years. Among the best known of those 'mamas' were Rosa Parks, who initiated the Montgomery bus boycott, and Ella Baker, an untiring organizer who focused her attention and the attention of the civil rights movement on the development of local leadership. The white women – mostly young, southern, religious, and often rejected by their families and their communities – had these extraordinary women as role models.

As the civil rights movement began to exclude white participation and as northern organizing grew in strength – beginning with civil rights and later in opposition to the Vietnam war and in support of student rights – these white women led the northern movement's efforts to expand community organizing into northern cities. Subject to less overt oppression, both the urban poor and the students who worked as organizers in the north needed to increase their awareness of the structural and social roots of what they were used to seeing as personal problems. They developed processes that involved 'talking together, discovering common problems, and thereby understanding the need for collective action' (Evans 1979: 134). According to Evans, men who participated as organizers were much less successful than women – both because they set up situations where they competed with members of the community, and because the energetic and effective men in the community were busy working, and thus did not participate as readily as did the women. Again, women in the community provided role models for the young women organizers.

The white women who participated in both the civil rights movement and the new left movement slowly came to realize that they were facing an oppression based on their gender that paralleled racial oppression. After attempts to break into leadership positions and to sensitize male leaders to sexism failed, they began to organize themselves – as women. Their primary technique was the informal group process of consciousness-raising. Small groups found spaces in their own homes where they 'could examine the nature of their own oppression and share the growing knowledge that they were not alone' (Evans 1979: 215). Such groups were easy to form and supportive, reducing women's isolation and resocializing them – 'transforming their individual subjective reality' (Eastman 1973: 155).

This group technique was an extremely effective basis for a political movement. While the US women's movement has been and can rightfully be criticized for failing to include class and race as issues, and therefore for failing to expand the movement much beyond the white middle class, it is also true that many of the women who write about women in development and empowerment come from that movement. There is thus a clear link between US feminism and women's empowerment activities internationally. Those whose roots are in the USA or the European women's movements experienced empowerment in the sense of self-knowledge and of discovering the historical, social, political, and economic roots of systemic gender-based problems through group processes. Their personal experiences prepared them to recognize and value the new international women's movement. Peggy Antrobus (1989: 190), a major intellectual force in the women's empowerment movement, describes her personal transformation:

> I ... speak from the perspective of a Third World feminist with the privilege and role power associated with the middle class, a university education, and an important position, namely one of the 'elite.' But more important, I speak as someone whose 'real' authority emerged mainly from the personal power of a developing and deepening feminist consciousness, which naturally led me to challenge those institutions – personal, professional, and political – in which my role power is embedded.

Despite the narrowness of the US women's movement, some of the women who participated in consciousness-raising were able to respond empathetically to women and situations very different from their own. While the survival needs of women in the third world are very different from the situation of first (and third) world middle-class feminists, the two groups have been able to find enough in common to work together and to help one another. Among those commonalities are the need to develop many different, creative survival strategies, an emphasis on process as well as outcome, and an understanding of the complexities of power. As I argued in Chapter 2, there is an important synergy among scholars, advocates, practitioners, and participants who compose the women's empowerment movement. Thus anti-colonialism, the civil rights movement, and feminism not only share the aim of overcoming domination and oppression, they also are linked historically by a movement of ideas and people from one to the other.

US community mental health, social work, and community organizing

The 'helping' professions of community mental health and social work were also deeply affected by the civil rights movement in the USA. A recognition that structural and racist conditions were in large part responsible for the powerlessness and the 'negative valuation' of blackness among blacks (Solomon 1976: 12), an understanding of the importance of replacing 'doing for' by 'doing with,' a reappraisal of the role of the professional as an instrument of the powerful and supporter of the status quo, and a questioning of the 'scientific basis' of practice all contributed to professional ferment and attempts to intellectualize the concept of empowerment. Julian Rappaport (1981: 3) began to develop a theory of empowerment specifically to counter a 'doing for' movement among community psychologists fostering prevention. Doing for only led to those traits which, Rappaport feels, represent the absence of empowerment: 'powerlessness, real or imagined; learned helplessness; alienation; loss of a sense of control over one's own life.'

Other community activities, most notably urban community organizing and social action, also contributed to ideas about empowerment (Kindervatter 1979). More aware of and concerned with issues of actual power and resources, these community activists avoided some of the conflicts that afflict those trained in the 'helping' professions – a training that leads one to be more comfortable with individuals than with groups, techniques that are individually oriented, and a lack of good examples of how to get power away from those who have it.

The US self-help tradition

Barbara Simon (1990: 29) also credits the modern self-help movement of the past twenty years in the USA – which has traditionally been less dominated by professionals than have the fields of mental health and social work – with contributing to the empowerment movement:

> This legacy of commitment to a model of the exchange among equals of assistance, caring, resources, and information, when grafted to the precept

of self-determination articulated by anti-poverty activists, black power advocates, student power leaders, and other grass roots political actors of the
1960s, became the conceptual basis for the contemporary empowerment
movement.

There has been a strong interaction between US feminism and the
US tradition of self-help: 'Drawing on the broader context of the
women's movement, self-help groups seek to restore women's sense of
autonomy over their own lives, to restore their self-reliance, and lessen
their dependency on institutions that define the lives of women' (Katz
and Bender 1990: 35). In particular, women formed groups that focused
on their health and their problematic treatment by the medical
establishment. These self-help groups emphasize voluntariness, peer
structure, orientation towards meeting needs and bringing about
change, provision of an 'enhanced sense of personal identity,' and
'goodness' – 'broadly beneficial ... both to the welfare of member/
participants, and to the wider society, in terms of principles of social
justice, morality, and concern for one's fellow humans.' The attitudes
and behaviors of these groups include a non-competitive, cooperative
orientation, a non-hierarchical structure, local definition of problems,
an evolving process, shared or circulating leadership, an emphasis on
control over one's own life, small beginnings, and a critical stance
towards professionalism (Katz and Bender 1990). In all these aspects,
self-help groups parallel empowerment groups. What they may lack,
however, is a basic commitment to social change and social justice,
although as self-help groups move towards advocacy, 'the potential for
social and political change is great' (Rappaport 1986: 76).

Thus several interlinked movements have exposed a large number
of women to the concepts and process of empowerment in the USA
over the past thirty years. These women have often been theoreticians
for the women's empowerment movement, but, most importantly, they
have used their own visibility to increase the visibility of those women
in third world countries who have been developing their own empowerment strategies.

Non-formal education in Latin America

Non-formal education in the third (and first) world developed as a
response to a belief in the importance of education and literacy, and
to a lack of opportunity for formal education (Kindervatter 1979). The
work of Paulo Freire (1970, 1974, 1990), a Brazilian educator, has inextricably linked non-formal education with empowerment, and with
efforts aimed at social and political change.

While the links between the current women's empowerment move-ment and anti-colonialism, civil rights, and the women's movement need elaboration, evidence of its links to Paulo Freire is more direct. From their beginnings in Latin America through their transport to the many countries to which Freire has traveled and consulted – among them Bolivia, Cuba, Nicaragua, Guinea-Bissau, Tanzania, and the USA – his theories about the revolutionary implications of non-formal edu-cation for adults have had a major impact. Freire defined a process of popular non-formal education in which a sensitized leader works with a group of oppressed people to raise their consciousness of their social and political situation. In his theory, conscientization is not an end in itself. The end is the transformation of society.

This transformation occurs through a cycle he calls *praxis*: from listening, dialogue, discussion, self-reflection, and critical thought to action and back. The key elements are the small group process, the ending of silence and of the internalization of oppression, and group action to change the social situation that the group has come to realize has been oppressing them. The cycle requires that the group members critically reflect on their actions and design new actions based on those reflections, a longitudinal process that is greatly distorted by cross-sectional perspectives. The process is perhaps easier to define than to effect. The role of the leader is difficult and can become manipulative; the process can be slow; the choice of action can be controversial; and the transformation of society is an illusive goal. The process may result in improvement in the lot of individuals without any real group transformation.

Nevertheless, the power of Freire's ideas is reflected by the large number of adherents they have attracted and the many references to them in the literature of empowerment and development. The non-formal education movement is a major force in the organizing of poor women. Illiteracy and ignorance of the dominant language have a great deal to do with the exclusion of women from the benefits of develop-ment. Freire's pedagogic techniques have been effectively used to train women to read, write, and learn the dominant language. His intuition that this process, properly conducted, can lead to power has had a major influence on the field of women's development.

Freire was strongly influenced by theories of Marxism and depend-ency, communicating with and learning from other radicals. A particu-larly important influence on his thinking was Antonio Gramsci, an Italian who, while he was a Marxist who acknowledged that economic organization is pivotal, also recognized that class domination relies on 'persuading the ruled to accept the system of beliefs of the ruling class and to share their social, cultural and moral values' (Joll 1977: 8). Gramsci believed in the power of traditional education to coopt intellectuals and provide a means for those in power to maintain a cultural hegemony. The antidote to this was in reflection and action, tenets that came to play a major role in Freire's theories.

One of the most serendipitous associations of modern history has been the friendship of Paulo Freire and Myles Horton, the founder of the Highlander Center – one from a poor family in the poorest region in Brazil, the other from rural Tennessee in the impoverished Appalachian region of the USA. Both men became well educated, but never rejected their pasts. Both were strongly influenced by their parents, by their wives, and by idealistic religious philosophy. Each was totally dedicated to two basic ideas: (1) freedom for all; (2) the ability and right of all to 'achieve that freedom through self-emancipation' and through participation in popular education practice that 'simultaneously creates a new society and involves the people themselves in the creation of their own knowledge' (Horton *et al.* 1990: xxx).

Thus the roots of empowerment spread far, and intertwine. They are linked by their grounding in ideals of freedom, self-emancipation, equity, democratic participation, self-control, and responsibility for self and others. They evolved in response to a variety of situations where domination, lack of power, hierarchical relationships, and deprivation were imposed by those with power on those without it.

The Conceptualization of Empowerment

The word *empowerment* represents a concept for which there are neither synonyms nor a consistent definition. Julian Rappaport (1984: 2) writes: '[t]he *idea* is more important than the thing itself. We do not know what empowerment is, but like obscenity, we know it when we see it.' He points out that it is difficult to frame positive definitions of empowerment, because 'it has components that are both psychological and political' (Rappaport 1986: 69), and because 'it takes on a different form in different people and contexts' (Rappaport 1984: 2).

As indicated in Chapter 1, the following definition from Wallerstein and Bernstein (1988: 380) has been adopted for this study:

> [Empowerment is] a social action process that promotes participation of people, organizations, and communities in gaining control over their lives in their community and larger society. With this perspective, empowerment is not characterized as achieving power to dominate others, but rather power to act with others to effect change.

HAROLD BRIDGES LIBRARY
S. MARTIN'S COLLEGE
LANCASTER

This definition emphasizes empowerment as an ongoing process and as an outcome – achieving power so as to effect change. Barbara Israel *et al.* (1994: 153) have specifically emphasized process and outcome activities at the three different levels of empowerment: individual, organizational, and community, linking them through Freire's concept of conscientization. However, the interactions between the levels are highly fluid. Lee Staples (1990), also linking process and outcome, describes empowerment as a dialectic or a spiral. Individuals, through their participation in group activities, gain skills and resources that lead to personal development. Their self-concept improves and they develop personal interaction skills. As individuals develop skills, the group functions more effectively. It gains strength as a group through a broader membership, increasingly effective leaders, more resources, allies, opportunities, and strategies, and the development of skills for effectively using power. New goals are set, and new opportunities arise for personal development. Personal and political transformations continue to take place.

Suzanne Kindervatter (1979: 245) describes 'eight broad character-istics and a certain pattern of events' that are common to empower-ment groups. These include small group structure, a facilitator instead of a teacher, participant leadership, transfer of responsibility to partici-pants, democratic and non-hierarchical processes and relationships, an integration of reflection and action, the promotion of self-reliance, and improvements in social, economic, and/or political standing.

The strength and cohesiveness of the group is a key component in the process of empowerment. Robert Hess (1984: 230) discusses 'that moment when the power of individuals in the group becomes totally synchronous, yielding a renewable and expanding power greater than the group itself.' Barbara Solomon (1976: 390) stresses the creation of a 'true collectivity in which the good of the whole is the highest value held by the individual.' However, the transformation of a group of individuals into a 'true collectivity' is a large challenge. There are, for example, some very thorny issues revolving around submission to leadership and to group norms. Willing participants in a cult may well belong to a collective, achieve self-confidence, garner such resources as they need, and internalize an ethic and a world-view that governs their behavior, but are not considered to be empowered because they lack independence of thought and what Paulo Freire calls 'critical consciousness.' Self-help groups, while serving their members and empowering individuals, often lack the orientation to structural social change that characterizes empowerment projects.

Even when a group is clearly oriented towards change and group empowerment, social change may or may not occur. To have an impact on the larger society requires allies, political skill, prestige, and power. There are no simple rules to take a group from internal change to external effectiveness. Irma Serrano-García (1984) reports on an intervention in Puerto Rico where people *did* gain greater control over their lives, but did not develop 'an alternate ideology' – which had been the goal of the interveners. Serrano described the results as 'the illusion of empowerment.' However, judgments taking into account the local situation and opportunities are perhaps best made by participants. If they do not see a change in ideology as in their best interest, either the case has not been made well enough or they are correct. At the very least, if means are to accord with ends, an ideology of empowerment cannot be imposed. The power to make decisions and to control one's own life is the key to empowerment: 'By its very nature, the process of empowerment is uncertain: although it is possible to initiate the journey in a structured way (using particular techniques and methods, for example), the ultimate destination is always unknown' (Edwards 1993: 86).

Participation and empowerment

Participation is a major component of empowerment. Research in participation and empowerment links them bidirectionally – empowered individuals may be more likely to participate in organizations, and participation promotes empowerment (Zimmerman 1990a; Zimmerman and Rappaport 1988). Marc Zimmerman (1990b: 75) suggests that participation in voluntary organizations leads to something he calls 'learned hopefulness,' the converse of a learned hopelessness model. Groups provide individuals with experiences in which they have control. This in turn provides them with a perception of that control. That perception leads to a causal attribution of successful control to oneself, which in turn leads to future expectations of control and to characteristics of hopefulness. In addition, Staples emphasizes the practical knowledge, concrete skills, and genuine opportunities gained from group participation.

Participation in empowering activities can come about purposively or accidentally. It is impelled by a crisis or an accumulated sense of need. Activities can be purely economic, purely educational, sociopolitical, community-level, or any combination. The sponsoring organizations can be new or existing grass-roots groups (with or without outside sponsorship and leadership), overtly political groups, economic development entities, unions, or either governmental or nongovernmental organizations. Participants are often brought into these activities by a neighbor, a friend, a family member, a co-worker, or a community organizer. Kindervatter (1979: 80) reports on one study which found that the major factors determining participation were immediate material and social benefits, anticipated future benefits, and symbolic benefits such as increased status.

Group organization and empowerment

Little is known about the relationship between group structure, individual commitment, and empowerment. The format that I have most often identified in developing countries is frequent meetings – at least weekly, with slowly evolving involvement on the part of women. Often within two years the group members become active, empowered women, sharing responsibilities and with a strong social support and friendship network. What is important is that the organization should fit – that it should reflect the needs and aspirations of the participants, and is designed so that the participants are comfortable within the structure. However, women will vary as to their degree of participation. Membership will not be constant. Participants may drop out because they move, because of time pressure, because their husbands object to their participation, because they lose interest, or because they become individually empowered and go on to seek individual advancement.

Leadership issues can be complex in organizations that stress active participation. Participant leadership and democratic and non-hierarchical structures depend upon leaders who can share decision-making and power. An overly strong leader of a small group at the outset can prevent a non-hierarchical leadership model from coming into effect. '[P]articipation without redistribution of power is an empty and frustrating process for the powerless' (Arnstein 1969: 218). None the less, large organizations, such as the Self-Employed Women's Association (SEWA) in Ahmedabad, India – a trade union with more than 40,000 members – prosper in part because of charismatic leadership at the top. The effectiveness of charismatic leaders at negotiating for power in the political sphere *is* important, but must be balanced by opportunities for meaningful participation at the local level.

Empowerment, then, is a subtle concept – both psychological and political, with a form determined locally. It describes both a process and an outcome. As a process it is cyclical or spiral, with alternating activities of reflection and action, based on small group participation and democratic, usually non-hierarchical, structures, and dedicated to helping people to gain control of their lives and to improve their social, economic, and political situations. Its meaning as an outcome is less well-defined, but related to effective uses of power and access to resources. Since active participation is basic to empowerment and self-determination, the format of empowerment activities and the structure of empowerment organizations must encourage it, while simultaneously attempting to effect change in the political, social, cultural, and economic environment.

Components of empowerment

A complex concept can be studied by partitioning it into measurable components. Empowerment is particularly complex because it is multi-dimensional and takes place in multiple domains: home, community, organizations, political realm, and so on. It is locally defined and embedded in social, cultural, and political contexts. It has personal, group, and political components, although discussions about the measurement of empowerment have been primarily focused on the personal psychological level.

The concept of empowerment has been broken down in different ways into personal factors – attitudes, traits, skills – which together enable one to exert control over aspects of one's own life and to participate effectively in group efforts for social change (Gutiérrez 1990; Wedeen and Weiss 1993; Zimmerman and Rappaport 1988). There has to date been no effort to coordinate or compare these different schemata. They are briefly reviewed here, but not synthesized, since each seems so independently derived and theoretical. It is probable that, in practice, different research situations will elicit different schemata.

Marc Zimmerman (1988) has done extensive statistical work to measure and define empowerment in the USA, using psychological constructs in a community psychology framework. He defines the following dimensions of empowerment: *personality*, which includes locus of control, chance control, belief in powerful others, and control ideology; *cognition*, including general self-efficacy, a sense of mastery, perceived competence, and internal and external political efficacy; and *motivation*, including desire for control and civic duty (Zimmerman and Rappaport 1988: 729). He defines psychological empowerment as 'the connection between a sense of personal competence, a desire for, and a willingness to take action in, the public domain' (Zimmerman and Rappaport 1988: 746) – a construct that 'assumes a proactive approach to life, a psychological sense of efficacy and control, socio-political activity, and organizational involvement' (Rappaport (1986: 71), quoting Zimmerman). Although Zimmerman's unit of analysis is the individual, he places psychological empowerment in a 'contextually oriented' eco-logical and cultural setting (Zimmerman 1990a: 173). Zimmerman's approach is grounded in US culture, and grows out of attempts to link psychology to community. While aspects of his work may have inter-national implications, these have not yet been explored in that context.

Lorraine Gutiérrez (1990: 150) takes a slightly different approach, also based in psychology, describing the process of empowerment by emphasizing the simultaneity and synergism of four psychological changes: *increasing self-efficacy,*[1] *developing group consciousness, reducing self-blame,* and *assuming personal responsibility* for change. Gutiérrez groups psychological constructs of control, mastery, initiative, and ability to act as components of self-efficacy. She see the development of a group consciousness – 'a sense of shared fate' – as the development of a 'critical perspective on society' that allows individuals to 'focus their energies on the causes of their problems, rather than on changing their internal subjective states.' A reduction in self-blame follows raised consciousness while the assumption of personal responsibility is linked to a transition from passive subject to active participant.

Others have developed schemata from an international context and a more sociological perspective. Laura Wedeen and Eugene Weiss (1993: 6) provide another list of personal factors. They define self-esteem, self-confidence, a sense of freedom, aspirations, and identification as *ways of feeling*; human control over life, knowledge of environment, critical consciousness, and problem-solving as *ways of thinking*; and autonomy, assertiveness, and joint action as *ways of behaving*. Lily Kak and Suresh Narasimhan (1992) define three different categories: *self enhancement*, measured by economic status, knowledge and skills, autonomy/independence, self-esteem and well-being (confidence, happiness, less depressed, less frustrated); *family relations* with husband, with parents-in-law, through aspirations for daughters' education and future, and with regard to increased decision-making (children's education, children's medical care, household expenses, and children's educational expendi-tures); and *community relations*, measured by mobility, relations with neighbors, respect from community, and community attitudes towards family planning. These schemata are difficult to critique out of context, but sound reasonable, although perhaps excessively oriented to the level of the individual.

For the purposes of this book, I collected the components of individual-level empowerment from literature and very loosely organ-ized them into two groups: individual *internal/psychological* and indi-vidual *situational/social* (see Chapter 11, Figure 11.1 below). The first group includes factors such as a sense of control, competence, coherence, confidence, self-esteem, entitlement, responsibility, participation, solidarity, and community. Other psychologically based factors are flexibility, initiative, and future orientation. Situational components can include control over resources; interpersonal, work, and organizational skills; decision-making powers; self-sufficiency, mobility, and 'savvy' or an ability to 'get around' in society; increased status, financial and social support, autonomy, information, income; improvements in living conditions such as child care, school attendance of children, and housing improvements. Such a simple organization allows for flexibility, since both situation and culture will have a major role in determining the relative importance and relevance of specific factors.

An inductive approach is well suited to looking at empowerment. Sidney Schuler and Sayed Hashemi (1993), working inductively through interviews with participants and organizers in Bangladesh, have listed six potentially measurable individual aspects of empowerment that include participation in groups. They are a sense of self and vision of a future, mobility and visibility, economic security, status and decision-making power in the household, an ability to interact effectively in public spheres, and participation in non-family groups. They have also developed specific, localized indicators for each construct. These categories, which the researchers describe as manifestations of empowerment, represent a broader framework – one that focuses on the integral relationship between participation and empowerment – than do the preceding lists of traits. As the women's empowerment movement is a network of groups, not of individuals, taking this relationship into account is vital.

The components of empowerment just presented probably do not include all that are thought to be important to those who reflect on the concept, nor are all necessarily important. The factors will vary, at least in importance, from individual to individual and from culture to culture. Changes as a result of empowerment may occur in some dimensions and some domains, and not in others. It will not be the case that the 'unempowered' have none of these traits, or that the empowered have all of them. Nor can each factor be treated independently; in the process of empowerment, changes interact and the whole is more than its parts. For example, while *initiative* may be important, it may relate to empowerment only if it is accompanied by other traits such as mobility or control over resources. It may lead over time to other changes that are more important, such as participating in organizing activities. It may be that the trait is more important to those who have never exercised it and begin tentatively to take some initiative than to those who have always taken some initiative.

Empowerment can also be analyzed at the group level, although little attention has been paid to its components at that level. The Reproductive Health and Population officers of the Ford Foundation (1992: 9) propose a set of group indicators that could be used to measure groups' empowerment, including the ability to name problems, to identify actions leading to solutions, to understand and get what is needed from others, and to establish links with other groups. They also recommend looking at internal governance, and at changes in outcomes that reflect the project's goals.

In this book, group factors are divided into organizational and situational, paralleling the individual groupings of internal and situational. Organizational components include membership, leadership, external relationships, prestige, and network membership. Situational factors include community-level ones such as access to services, programs and facilities, environmental conditions, and self-help or support activities. Thus a successful empowerment program may have increased membership and strengthened relationships with local political leaders, and may have obtained a new health facility and improved the sanitation in the community.

There is much further work to be done in the investigation of the components and the levels of empowerment, including comparisons between and integration of the above typologies, the development and testing of measurement strategies, further inductive investigations into the concept in developing countries, and efforts to link components to outcomes. It will be important, however, to recognize and preserve variation: 'Classification and simplification can aid understanding, but if interpreted too literally, they exert a confining or diversionary hold on imagination as interest in the classificatory "map" replaces interest in the "territory"' (Morgan 1983: 41).

Measurement of empowerment

While scales for many of the individual-level traits that constitute empowerment do exist, these scales often consist of a long battery of questions said to be statistically valid and reliable (to measure what they say they measure, and to do so consistently). However, many of these questions make no sense in a third world context – often they were developed and tested on a population of US college students. Even if one could rephrase them, the result would be a long series of questions to capture information on several of these traits. Long, structured interviews with busy women who have many children around them and no opportunity for quiet concentration are far from an ideal way to learn about a complicated process. What will be needed is a process that Wedeen and Weiss (1993) call 'indigenization' – contextualizing research approaches and empowerment concepts such as self-esteem in the local setting. Two recent publications (Israel *et al.* 1994; Schuler and Hashemi 1993) contain items developed in a local framework, designed to be administered to participating individuals, but attempting to capture empowerment at multiple levels.

Difficult as it may be to measure psychological transformation, it is even more difficult to capture what Staples (1990: 13) calls 'the capacity for effective action.' That capacity relates to changes in power and in resources as well as individual capabilities, including practical knowledge, solid information, real competencies, concrete skills, material resources, genuine opportunities and tangible results. Staples notes that 'soft', individual perceptions are easier to quantify through a series of attitude questions than are the 'harder' changes in actual 'capacity for effective action.' While measurement strategies have been developed in disparate fields such as education and employment testing that may contribute to research in this area, it will also be necessary to develop creative ways to measure women's activities. Of interest will be items such as the degree of responsibility that they have assumed, reports and fliers produced, meetings attended, and contacts with professionals. Participatory-action research (see Chapter 11 below) is particularly suited to looking at changes in participants' situations.

Empowerment is defined here as 'a social action process' – a group activity. It is the effects of that group activity on individual women and their health, on the groups themselves, and on their families, communities, and societies that is my major interest. The issue of measurement of group outcomes, however, is one that bedevils much of current social science. A multidisciplinary approach, bringing together those familiar with group behavior, organizational behavior, women's organizations, political effectiveness, and non-formal learning may lead to the development of useful measures of group process and group success. Sources of information should be members and their leadership as well as outside groups – allies and political opponents – in a position to evaluate group effectiveness.

Even thornier, however, is the multi-level aspect of empowerment since, as Rappaport notes (1987), all levels interact, and the impact of one level of analysis on the others is assumed to be important. While fairly sophisticated analytic methods of studying the causes of individual actions and their effects on individuals exist, it is less obvious how to combine levels – individual, household, family, group, community. While some consideration of these issues has resulted from the work of the new scientists, applications to social science are not yet available. By keeping up with these innovative scientists and drawing parallels between their domains and those of social science, however, researchers may be able to borrow and shape new techniques as they develop.

Finally, just a few words about those proponents who wish to research empowerment: 'Empowerment theory is self-consciously a world view theory – it explicitly presents the researcher's values, goals, attitudes, beliefs, and intentions' (Rappaport 1987: 142). Concern for and placing a value on empowerment locates researchers in a political process. If they have increased empowerment as an espoused and explicit goal, they must use their work and their results to contribute to the building of the empowerment movement. (This will be discussed further in Chapter 11.)

Summary

In this chapter and in Chapter 2 I have traced the evolution of an international women's empowerment movement. Empowerment is a popular and very hopeful strategy used by women whose basic needs are unmet. It can have negative effects, including distance between generations of women, an increase in what is already an intolerable workload, an inability to counter negative macroeconomic trends, an opportunity for cooptation and for political repression, and broken homes. At this time, empowerment seems to be an effective strategy for women, but one that is not attracting men.

As part of an effort to understand empowerment, it is useful to trace the widespread roots that support women's present empowerment activities – roots in anti-colonialist and anti-imperialist activities, in the US civil rights movement, feminist, self-help, and community services movements, and in the non-formal education movement spearheaded by Paulo Freire in Latin America. Besides having common goals of overcoming domination and oppression, these predecessors are all linked historically by a movement of ideas and people from one to the other.

I have described empowerment as a complex psychological and political concept that represents both a cyclical small group process and an outcome that is intended to help people to gain control of their lives and to improve their social, economic, and political situations. Active participation is essential to this process, but little is known about the relationship between participation and empowerment.

There is little consensus on what the components of empowerment are, or how to measure them, although the psychological components are more familiar and more thoroughly explored than the group and political components. Before deciding on a specific list of components, it is important to gather more information from people actually involved in the process in different locations. Studies of empowerment face the difficulty of measuring aspects that are not self-perceptions or individual-level variables, logistic problems of data collection, and the unusual relationship between researcher and process being studied. At this time, it may be most useful to work towards a gradual understanding of what is still a developing concept, within an adaptable framework that can reflect the great variety of strategies that exist.

Note

1. Self-efficacy is a belief in one's ability 'to produce and to regulate events in [one's life]' (Bandura 1982: 122).

PART II

Health

4

Health: Meaning, Methods, and Trends

Before we can begin to examine the relationships between empowerment and health, we need to explore the murky domain of health
the four chapters in Part II are devoted to this subject. In this chapter
I begin with theoretical and measurement considerations and delve
briefly into health through history. Chapter 5 contains data about
women's health. The remaining two chapters look one by one at
selected factors affecting health, in order to locate empowerment in
the context of our knowledge about improving health.

Theories of Health

Both individuals and societies invest heavily in health. Health is valued
both for itself and because it enables individuals to take advantage of
opportunities that improve life in general. Because of its centrality to
life itself, theories of health have been formulated or implicit in many
cultures throughout history. My discussion is limited to Western thought
over the past two centuries, during which time Western conceptualizations of health and medicine, closely linked to modernization and
development, have greatly influenced thinking and policy throughout
the world.

Unicausal theories

Sylvia Tesh (1988) traces several unicausal theories of health – contagion, germ, personal behavior, and miasma – from the nineteenth
century to the twentieth. Most importantly, she emphasizes the relation-

ship between theories of health and the politics of health – different theories assign responsibility for health to different groups. Contagion theory, which posited that all illnesses were passed from one individual to another, developed naturally out of civilization's history of devastation by infectious diseases. It placed responsibility for population health on governments and other political entities, which were expected to protect their populations through quarantines and border closings. This theory, however, did not explain why some isolated people became ill while some who came into close contact with the ill did not. The demise of contagion theory, however, was due less to these anomalies than to economic pressures to reduce disruption to travel and trade, and a historical reduction in centralized political control. Governments began to cede responsibility for health. Thus politics also influences theory. Contagion theory was a forerunner of germ theory, which currently dominates thinking about disease causality. The remarkable discoveries of science and the apparent ability to control infectious disease through scientific methods in this century have led to germ theory's dominant role in the realms of health and disease. Germ theory, like contagion theory, posits *a* specific, potentially controllable cause. The power to control illness, however, has passed from governments to scientists and physicians.

A different set of theories places responsibility for health at the individual level. In the nineteenth century, this was known as the personal behavior theory. Tesh (1988: 24) notes that it 'was a homage to middle-class life. It extolled temperate behavior, controlled emotions, minimal physical labor, and the possession of enough money to allow for economic choices.' It also 'advanced the central political idea of modern times: the belief in individual freedom and autonomy.' The personal behavior/lifestyles theory is the twentieth-century version, focusing on individual health habits and behaviors as determinants of health. Here primary responsibility rests with the individual.

Finally, the miasma theory – holding that the odor of decaying organic material was responsible for illness – led to the public health movement in Europe and the USA in the nineteenth century. This theory held government accountable not just for containment but also for prevention of disease. Public health programs were justified on the grounds that they were essential to the economic success of an industrial society. The miasma theory provided political justification for important governmental activities. The twentieth-century version of the miasma theory is that disease is environmentally caused, and must be controlled at a societal level.

Multicausal theories

In general, however, current Western theories of health are more often multicausal: based on multiple factors that contribute to health both independently and through interaction. Different models are distinguishable by the types of factors they contain and the mathematical structures used to represent the relationships among those factors.

The factors come from all the twentieth-century theories: germs, personal behavior, and the environment, as well as innate individual characteristics. The selection of variables to be included in a given model often reflects a researcher's causal orientation. There is some distinction by discipline, with epidemiological models usually measuring the effect of a specific exposure (risk factor) and sociological models concerned with sets of factors whose relative import emerges from the analyses. The field of social epidemiology attempts to bridge the two. While it is concerned with risk factors, those risk factors are often more sociological than biomedical. In addition, social epidemiologists balance the import of exposures and susceptibilities/resistance on both the individual and social levels. While this perspective is 'not yet synthesized into one well-defined paradigm,' it 'posits that the occurrence of disease at both the individual and population level results from a dynamic interplay between exposure and susceptibility within a historical and social environment' (Krieger *et al.* 1993: 99).

Meredith Turshen (1989: 23) points out that in most multifactoral models all the factors are treated in the same way – 'Multifactorialists can discuss income, race, and class only as personal characteristics; they have no way to look at group characteristics or at social structures and conceptual systems.' As we shall see in Chapter 9, although there are analytic techniques that distinguish between individual and contextual variables, they are at this time so complex to use and to interpret that Turshen is essentially correct.

Suggesting that the determinants of positive and negative health may differ, Anton Antonovsky (1979: 55) has developed a theory of salutogenesis (origins of health) in contrast to pathogenesis (origins of disease). He has also focused on susceptibility and resistance rather than risk and exposure:

> Given the ubiquity of pathogens – microbiological, chemical, physical, psychological, social, and cultural – it seems to me self-evident that everyone should succumb to this bombardment and constantly be dying.... How can it be explained that a given individual, in this miserable world of ours, has not broken down?

Societies continue to put most of their resources into the prevention, stabilization, and cure of what might be called negative health (disease, illness, disability) – because it is what has been done historically, and because it may be instinctive to respond to pain and discomfort. Antonovsky suggests that we should also begin to focus on factors that lead to positive health.

The simplest multifactoral models take a set of variables, each of which is thought to act independently and perhaps in combination with other factors to 'produce' the result, and combine them in a linear fashion to predict some health outcome. While there may be other factors that contribute to this outcome, they are less important and can be taken account of by a single error term that incorporates them. Most existent research into the determinants of health is based on these relatively simple multifactoral, linear models. More sophisticated models, known as proximate determinant models, group the factors into different levels, based on their 'proximity' to the outcome (Mosley 1989). These complex models are still causal, intending to take into account all the important determinants as well as a staging component, and may contain factors related to susceptibility and resistance.

Several writers have posited an essentially non-linear model of health based on the image of a spider's intricate web. The strands of that web are so interwoven that the identification of an independent effect becomes impossible. Tesh uses this analogy to describe interrelationships among disease agents and hosts and their social, physical, political, psychological, cultural, and economic context. Nájera (Buck *et al.* 1988: 153) calls it a *maraña*, a tangled web. However, Tesh (1988: 79) is frustrated by such models, noting that one gets little guidance from such a complex picture. Where and how should one intervene? Which strands shall be pulled? In her search for fundamental causes of poor health and disease, she ends up opting for a theory that retains a causal hierarchy but goes more deeply into the political realm. She defines the fundamental causes of poor health as unjust social systems, concluding: '[w]hatever makes life better in general also makes it healthier.' In a similar vein, Turshen (1989: 24) describes 'a new theory of disease called "the social production of health and illness."' The way in which society is organized determines health and disease, and while specific etiologies are involved in specific diseases, the vulnerability of a particular group of people is a socially determined historical phenomenon. Marxian analysts see class divisions as intrinsic to this social organization (Laurell 1989).

Thus theories of health and illness include a single cause, multiple discrete causes often identified as risk factors, a distinction between the determinants of illness and those of health, causes or risk factors grouped by their proximity to the outcome in question, with the focus on intervention at the most proximate levels, a concentration on the least proximate causal level (the sociopolitical context), and a tangled web of factors from many different levels of organization that affect both exposure and susceptibility in terms of disease or protection and resistance in terms of health. Decisions on how to study health and how best to intervene to improve it are made in the context of a preferred or implicitly adopted theory.

The Measurement of Health

Perhaps the most important reason to measure health is in order to identify problems. Only if problems are known can solutions be developed, implemented, and evaluated. However, health is an important value not just because it is an end in itself, but because it is also a means to an end – a prerequisite for equal opportunity to participate in the benefits of organized society (Daniels 1985). Thus comparing the health of different populations enables us to evaluate the equitableness of societies. If women, for example, bear a disproportionate burden of poor health and premature mortality, they will have less opportunity than men.

The two indices most commonly used to quantify, and thereby compare, the health of populations are death rates and life expectancy at birth. These measures are relatively easy to collect, they produce rankings that reflect one's intuitive understanding of relative conditions in different locations, and – if one adds age and cause of death information – they provide useful comparative and planning information. If one wishes to compare the health of populations across cultures, then measures must somehow be 'culture-free.' To date, death and life expectancy have been the most widely available culture-free measures at the population level.

Increased life expectancy, however, cannot be equated with increased health. McKinlay, McKinlay, and Beaglehole (1989: 181) point out, for example, that 'the overall health of the American population is not improving.' Using path analytic techniques to predict a combined measure of mortality and morbidity, they found that 'although overall life expectancy has increased over several decades, most of this increase is in years of disability.' If *all* heart disease were eliminated in the USA, life expectancy would increase by only three years; if all cancers were eliminated, it would increase by two years. Our perceptions of our health status, however, would greatly increase.

Other ways to measure health include calculating the amount of new disease each year (disease incidence) or the total number of people with a specific disease at a specific time (disease prevalence). While most countries have in place a system to record births and deaths and cause of death, information about morbidity is available only sporadically, if at all. Perhaps more useful in a comparative sense is measure of disability from disease or illness, an approach that requires information on disease incidence and/or prevalence. Both the World Bank and the World Health Organization are beginning to attempt to generalize from such morbidity and disability data as exist or can be extrapolated in order to rank causes of disability and death, and to do cross-regional and even cross-national comparisons (World Bank 1993, see Chapter 5 below; World Health Organization 1995).

There has been increasing interest in alternative ways to measure health through indicators that take account of the quality as well as the quantity of life, and view disability as only one aspect of health. In keeping with multidimensional conceptualizations of health, Donald Patrick and Pennifer Erickson (1993) presented a comprehensive typology of core concepts of health. These include opportunity, health perceptions, functional status, impairment, and death and duration of life. Within each of these domains are subdomains: impairment, for example, contains the concepts of symptoms and disease. Reduced in scope and closer to being operationalized is a framework developed by Mildred Blaxter, which can be seen as a subset of Patrick and Erickson's typology. Blaxter has defined five 'distinct components' that are tested, measurable indicators of health status: (1) the presence or absence of disease/illness; (2) the frequency of 'feeling ill' or having symptoms; (3) disability as a measure of functional status and the ability to carry out normal activities; (4) physical fitness, including physical well-being, strength, and energy; (5) psychological fitness or psychosocial well-being as opposed to malaise, which includes depression, sleep disturbances, and tiredness.[1]

Each of these dimensions has a negative and a positive pole. Each can be measured and, except for the presence or absence of disease, can take on multiple (more than two) values. Some have clear end points (no illness or symptoms); others do not (physical fitness). Measuring these dimensions on a population from Great Britain, Blaxter (1990) was able to classify individuals into eight non-scaleable categories of health. Using these categories, she has been able to compare age, class, geographic, and gender subgroups. Her comparisons, however, are necessarily much more complex than those based on a single indicator.

Research shows that it may be possible to capture the multi-dimensionality of health in a single question: *In general, how would you say your health has been in the last year: excellent, very good, good, fair, or poor?* This subjective measure of health status, called Self-Perceived Health Status (SPHS) or Self-Rated Health (SRH), has been a better predictor of mortality than physician appraisals, self-reported medical conditions, and health services utilization information (Mossey and Shapiro 1982). This does not imply that health is unidimensional, only that the multi-dimensionality of the concept can be represented by a global rating. While it cannot make distinctions among different dimensions of health, the question seems to capture the well-being described in Blaxter's fifth component.

Blaxter (1985) tested her five measures against the SPHS and found that absence of health problems was always related to a positive self-assessment, but presence of problems did not necessarily relate to a negative self-assessment. People can feel that their health status is excellent or good even if they have a chronic illness, disability, or disease. This is reflected in the finding that physicians may not be the best judges of a person's health – that, as Antonovsky posits, there are dimensions of health status that are somewhat independent of problems such as symptoms, disabilities, and diseases.

The literature on specific factors that have been associated with the production of health and disease (which will be reviewed in later chapters) rarely takes into account such complex, multidimensional approaches to the measurement of health – first because such research has rarely been carried out, and second because it is easier to measure the import of factors when simpler health outcomes, such as mortality or the prevalence of a specific morbidity, are used. Envisioning health as a changing and complex web of interacting factors implies that the measurement of health itself is complex and variable. As we look at the role of empowerment, we shall see how difficult it is to use more complex multidimensional measures of health. For example, empowerment may affect some of the dimensions of health and not others; it may affect quality of life but not quantity.

The Health of Populations

Although health conditions as measured by life expectancy and mortality rates have been dramatically improving throughout the world, the change is far from uniform. There is a broad spectrum of health, both within and between countries. Using language from health transition theory (which will be described later in this chapter), Sally Findley (1989) describes three different groups of developing countries: (1) late-transitional countries (China, Venezuela, some Caribbean countries, and several oil states) have an average infant mortality rate of 41 per 1,000, reduced their rates by an average of 70 percent in the thirty years, and tend to be reducing urban–rural differentials; (2) early-transitional countries (Vietnam, Egypt, Indonesia, Mexico, Colombia, and Thailand) reduced infant mortality by 50 percent between 1950 and 1980 – to an average of 79 per 1,000 – and show some significant urban–rural differences, with urban rates generally 33–50 percent lower than rural; and (3) pre-transitional countries (largely located in sub-Saharan Africa and South Asia) still have a very high infant mortality rate (120 per 1,000 live births or more). The decline in the infant mortality rate in these pre-transitional countries averaged about 36 percent in the thirty years between 1955 and 1985. Regional differences within a country are small.

In pre-transitional societies people are often accused of fatalism, as though that were a psychological trait contributing to their susceptibility to disease and lack of resistance, to be remedied by an injection of modernization. However, such 'fatalism' may in fact reflect a realistic sense of the many health risks that they face. In these countries, as Findley points out, people's lives really are short, and they are more likely than others to be frequently sick with disabling and lingering illnesses. They contract chronic diseases at early ages, and are more likely to die from their illness. They must worry constantly about health and, since the effects of common diseases such as measles and diarrhea seem to vary 'capriciously', they do not feel in control of their health or the health of their children. A major share of their personal resources (both time and money or its substitute) is used in dealing with illness. Investment in the future, either through savings or through education or regular work, as envisioned by the early development theorists, is extremely problematic under these conditions.

About one in ten people throughout the world suffers from at least one tropical disease (D. Brown 1993). The rates in pre-transitional countries are much higher. Recent data from the World Bank (1993) (which I discuss in Chapter 5) indicate that a resident of a developing country is thirteen times more likely to lose a year of healthy life through mortality or disability from communicable disease than a resident of an industrialized country. Moreover, those who live in developing countries also suffer higher rates of injury and of many non-communicable diseases. According to the World Bank's data on years of life lost through mortality or disability from accidents, residents of developing countries lose 2.5 years for every one year lost in industri-alized countries. The burden of chronic illnesses such as coronary disease, obesity, high cholesterol, glucose intolerance, mental disorders, and cancers is also greater in developing countries, whose residents are 1.2 times more likely to suffer from loss of life or disability.

The women about whom I am writing can be found in all societies. A great many of them, however, live in pre-transitional conditions where infant mortality is high. Those who live in early-transitional societies experience great urban–rural disparities and increasing changes in the morbidity and mortality risks that they face. Those in late-transitional and developed societies may live in pre- or early-transitional pockets.

Health in History

Historical information can help us to understand present-day health. In looking at health throughout history, however, we are limited by a lack of data. To compensate for this, current health differences among countries at different levels of development, such as those described in the previous section, have sometimes been used to represent different historical stages. While we can certainly look for patterns and for insights in current data, we must be cautious. There is no reason to think that there is one road to improved health; nor can we assume that all subgroups within a population are represented by such data as we do have. Most importantly, health changes must be looked at in their historical context if we wish to draw conclusions about their determinants – we know enough to know that determinants and their interactions differ depending on many different factors.

Pre- and early history

> All humans lived by hunting and gathering for two million years, 99% of the time that humans have existed. Ninety percent of the humans that have ever lived have been hunter-gatherers, 6% have been agricultural (10,000 years), and only 4% have been industrial (a few hundred years). (Eyer and Sterling 1977: 14)

We know little about the health of this 90 percent of humans, the hunter-gatherers. From studies of contemporary hunter-gatherer societies, whose members probably live more difficult lives than did ancient groups, Mark Nathan Cohen (1989) concludes that infection rates were low, fertility was low, and nutrition was adequate among hunter-gatherers. Joseph Eyer and Pete Sterling (1977) add that among current hunter-gatherer societies, 'degenerative diseases such as coronary heart disease, hypertension and cancer are quite rare, blood pressures are not only low, but show little change with age.'

As societies settled and turned to agriculture, they became stratified and grouped into larger units, population increased, infections spread due to travel and increased density, and intragroup violence increased. Nutrition worsened for a variety of reasons, including separation from the land and its natural resources, increased allocation of food to trade, concentration of resources by elites, and the diversion of energy from meeting individual basic needs to more abstract societal goals (Eyer and Sterling 1977). The domestication of animals meant more exposure to disease for humans, and increasing social complexity caused both environmental and social stresses. Child mortality may have increased. Cohen suggests that the success of modern societies lies in their ability to support larger populations, but that there is a great cost to health from that growth, particularly among those who are exploited or exposed to severe social dislocation.

Although little information is available about health status before the nineteenth century, it seems likely that life expectancy was between thirty and thirty-five years, there was little class difference in health, and disease conditions varied depending upon the natural environment, the domestic animal population, and the level of crowding. Population dynamics were responsible for major epidemics. Delicate balances between infectious organisms and people were upset by migrations and population growth. Plagues carried by traders and invaders devastated populations.

In *Plagues and Peoples* (1976: 61) William H. McNeill describes the major effects of disease on history, attributing the complete domination of Latin America during the conquest to the diseases brought by the invaders. Peru and Mexico lost 90 percent of their population within 120 years, and suffered total cultural dislocation: 'The disruptive effect of such an epidemic is likely to be greater than the mere loss of life, severe as that may be. Often survivors are demoralized, and lose all faith in inherited custom and belief which had not prepared them for such a disaster.' While colonialism is a major explanatory factor in the structure of our world today, Stanley Kunitz (1990: 95), who argues for 'particularism' whenever possible, points out that different forms of colonialism created different health conditions after the initial decimation. The Spanish and the Portuguese 'imposed their authoritarian culture' on their colonies, replicating the semi-feudal conditions at home. They brought 'rural poverty, early and universal marriage, crowded households, inadequate sewerage, and malnutrition [that] increased the risks of early death and, right up to the present, have kept rural mortality higher than urban mortality.' On the other hand, the British, while also bringing early marriage and high fertility, allowed private land ownership and use, which 'resulted in very good nutrition, low density of population and good health,' with lower rural mortality.

Recent history

Mortality data were first regularly collected in the nineteenth century and improvements in health status, as measured by mortality, can be noted from that time. In *The Health of Nations* (1987) Leonard Sagan reviews the steep decline in mortality that began in the eighteenth and nineteenth centuries. It began slowly in Sweden, Great Britain, and the United States, and, as other countries modernized and industrialized, their rates declined even faster. Infant and child mortality rates tended to decrease even faster than overall rates. Kunitz (1990), however, reminds us that conditions were not uniform, even within Europe. Different forms of social organization resulted in different kinds of agriculture. Western Europe was organized into relatively small family farms. Eastern Europe developed large estates devoted to a single exportable crop and farmed by peasants. Rural eastern Europeans were much poorer than westerners and were also more at risk owing to early marriages, more children, reduced opportunities for mothers to breastfeed, since they worked in the fields, and crowded conditions both in the household and in the village.

An even more dramatic example of the importance of culture to health is represented in the following quote from Kunitz (1990: 99). He explains why the Japanese, who were much less developed economically than England and Western Europe in the nineteenth century, had similar health status:

> There was a high degree of government control over social life in Japan which made possible the planning and construction of sophisticated water supplies beginning in the 17th century. Human faeces and urine were regarded as an economic good to be sold as fertilizer, not as waste to be disposed of in unsanitary cesspits or in rivers that also provided drinking water. Because of concern about damage from earthquakes, houses could not be more than one storey tall, so multi-storey tenements such as existed in Western cities were unknown in Japan. Moreover, habits of personal cleanliness deriving from traditional religious values made bathing, hand washing

and laundering common. The custom of drinking tea meant that much of the water consumed had been boiled. Virtually all food was eaten cooked, so contamination from the nightsoil used as fertilizer was reduced. Each member of the household had his or her own eating utensils.

Thus the Japanese did not have to make the major cultural, economic, and behavioral adjustments that Europeans and Americans did to improve health status.

In both developed and developing countries, longevity has increased remarkably over the past forty years: from 66 to 76 (ten years) in more developed countries and from 42 to 63 (21 years) in less developed countries. Developing countries generally began to achieve reduced mortality after World War II, although a few (Argentina, Chile, Uruguay, Costa Rica, Sri Lanka, Taiwan, Singapore, and Mauritius) began earlier. In developing countries, however, unlike developed countries, decreases in child and infant mortality lagged behind overall mortality. Basu (1987) attributes the difference in the relationship between decreases in infant and in overall mortality to two different patterns of declining mortality. Among developed countries, social and economic changes preceded medical and technological development, while in developing countries the technologies (such as immunizations, antibiotics, anti-malaria campaigns) were adopted early, and social and economic changes did not necessarily follow. Infant mortality has been recognized as a sensitive indicator of social and behavioral change. The infant mortality rate is less amenable to reduction through technology than adult mortality and, in the absence of favorable socio-economic conditions, does not decline.

Transitions

Historically, reduction in mortality was followed by a seemingly inevitable increase in population due to increased longevity and larger families (more children surviving childhood). Exponentially increasing population rates and their resultant pressures on land and food distribution are negative outcomes of this change. When fertility rates stabilize at a low enough level to stop this population increase, we have a *demographic transition*. This demographic transition is paralleled by an *epidemiologic transition*: 'a sustained decline in morbidity and mortality rates accompanied by a major alteration in disease patterns – from the acute infectious diseases of childhood to the chronic diseases of old age' (Rockefeller Foundation 1988). Simultaneous improvements in medical care also contribute to the mortality decline.

A third type of transition, called the *health transition*, is also concerned with changes in disease patterns but focuses on non-demographic determinants of health – cultural, social, and behavioral:

> Demographic transition theory was used to highlight the relation between demographic 'regimes' and broader social processes of urbanization, modernization, and industrialization. In this same way, we have adopted the term 'health transition' to call attention to the broader social and developmental processes related to changes in societal health and well-being. (Findley 1989: 61)

A group of researchers, led by John Caldwell at the Australian National University, is investigating the health transition concept, bringing together a variety of approaches and disciplines.

Frenk *et al.* (1991: 34), make an important and often overlooked point about transitions: 'it seems incorrect to assume that change must always occur smoothly and in one direction. In fact, a reversal of trends may occur. The most outstanding example is the emergence of AIDS, a viral disease. Also, there may be relapses of infections that had been previously controlled, such as malaria and dengue fever. In other words, small or large "counter-transitions" may take place.' It is also true that a transition is not the same across an entire society but varies by class; race, ethnic, and age groups; geographic location; and gender.

The future

Is the cup of health half empty or half full? As with other important issues, people's basic outlook on life affects the way they view historical patterns. In fact, we can see parallels to the debates among development theorists taking place among historians of health. One view is that things are getting better and better, owing to socioeconomic development, globalization, and improved health systems (Roemer and Roemer 1990). Murray and Chen (1993: 143) argue convincingly that mortality levels (but not necessarily health status) continue to decline even given severe economic crises, and that in countries recently suffering from famine, war, or natural disasters, there is 'an apparently rapid return of mortality to pre-existing baseline levels.'

Mark Cohen (1989: 141), more interested in the effects of increasing population and social organization and taking a longer look back into history, sees the glass as half empty, arguing that improvements in life expectancy are quite recent, and that technological improvements are often offset by population increases and patterns of consumption:

At best, we see what might be called a partitioning of *stress* by class and location, in which the well-to-do are progressively freed from nutritional stress (although even they did not escape the ravages of epidemics until recently) but under which the poor and urban populations, particularly the urban poor, are subjected to levels of biological stress that are rarely matched in the most primitive of human societies.

Ruzicka and Hansluwka (1982: 567) note the 'deceleration of mortality decline' in South and East Asia with concern. It is leveling off at too high a pitch; subgroup differences have not decreased – indeed, they have increased in some instances; and the worsening economic situation, accompanied by rapid population growth, presents problems that we do not know how to solve.

These are not necessarily diametrically opposed views, since all agree that the last century has brought about great change. The differences are, rather, about where the future will take us. Are we on a course to better health for all or only for some? The Roemers see improvements in the developed world being followed by improvements in the developing world, given proper leadership, while Cohen sees divisions less by nation than by class and location.

Susan Sontag (1989: 92–3), using AIDS as a metaphor for or harbinger of impending international dependency and possible disaster, provides a third prognosis:

> Like the effects of industrial pollution and the new system of global financial markets, the AIDS crisis is evidence of a world in which nothing important is regional, local, limited; in which everything that can circulate does, and every problem is, or is destined to become, world-wide.... From the untrammeled intercontinental air travel for pleasure and business of the privileged to the unprecedented migrations of the underprivileged from villages to cities and, legally and illegally, from country to country – all this physical mobility and interconnectedness (with its consequent dissolving of old taboos, social and sexual) is as vital to the maximum functioning of the advanced, or world, capitalist economy as is the easy transmissibility of goods and images and financial instruments.... AIDS is one of the dystopian harbingers of the global village, that future which is already here and always before us, which no one knows how to refuse.

The interactions between peoples and nations in Sontag's global village are neither those envisioned by the Roemers – developed nations leading underdeveloped ones to a positive, healthful future – nor those predicted by Cohen – pockets of underdevelopment and poverty in every nations. We are now only just beginning to rethink our theories and practices with regard to health in this new global context.

Improving Health

While overall life expectancy has been increasing in most parts of the world, high quality of life and freedom from debilitating morbidities are still only dreams for most of the world's population. Conditions for many people living in poverty in developing countries have been deteriorating for over a decade owing to economic policies that increase income disparity and poverty, unstable governments, political and social violence, increasing environmental problems in both urban and rural habitats, cultural dislocations, emergent virulent infectious diseases, and decreased opportunities to achieve security and stability for most individuals and families.

It has unfortunately become increasingly apparent that many of the well-intentioned efforts of first, second, and third world health and development professionals to mitigate these conditions do not have the desired effect or have unanticipated, damaging side-effects (Goulet 1985; Hancock 1989; R. Schneider *et al.* 1978; Weil *et al.* 1990). In their efforts to improve the health of populations and subpopulations, research, medical, and public health professionals customarily select one or several factors known to affect health and then design, implement, and sometimes evaluate interventions on those factors. While there is a general awareness of the complexities involved in reducing disease and producing health, both an understandable need to have clear, measurable objectives in order to justify large expenditures of scarce resources and valuable time, and the weight of traditional theory and methodology, often impede broader efforts to improve health. However, some broader, more ecological efforts, organized around health programs but responsive to a range of local needs, have been successfully implemented.

In 1940, Sydney and Emily Kark established the first of several community health centers in rural Pholela, South Africa (Tollman 1991). These centers promoted integration – or at least coordination – of curative, rehabilitative, preventative, and promotive care. They fostered a comprehensive approach to health care that took into account behavioral, social, and environmental determinants. Projects used multidisciplinary teams, provided outreach, and considered the entire community to be their domain. Community health programs were seen as including community development and empowerment. This model of health care became the basis of community-oriented primary care, later implemented at community health centers in the USA in the 1970s.

In Jamkhed, India, physicians Mabelle and Rajanikant Arole have worked since 1970 to improve health through community activities:

community kitchens, well digging, communal food growing, water system extension, tree planting, house building, health education, and community and individual empowerment (Arole and Arole 1994; Chakravorty 1983; Christian Medical Commission 1993). They have had spectacular health outcomes in a very poor region of a very poor country. Originally serving seven villages and 10,000 people, by 1992 they worked with 250,000 people in 200 villages. It is reported that infant mortality decreased from 150 to 25 per 1,000, malnourishment decreased from 30 to 4 percent, family planning usage went from one percent to 55 percent, and immunization coverage from 0.5 percent to 80 percent. No diarrhea deaths occurred over a seven-year period during the 1980s.

Such programs are based on multiple, simultaneous interventions that have at their core a recognition that reductionist approaches to improving health are ineffective, and that individuals and communities must play a major role in the selection, design, and implementation of projects if those projects are to succeed. Unfortunately, at this time, health care systems are moving in a different direction – towards privatization and the incorporation of health care into the market economy, cost recovery, and targeted individual-level interventions. When broad community health efforts are attempted, they are likely to take place outside health systems. Many of the activities of women's groups, as described in Chapter 2, are designed as intersectoral and participatory projects to benefit health.

Summary

Health has been perceived as having a single, dominant determinant, multiple determinants, or, more recently, as an intricate, non-linear, tangled web of factors, some of which are sociopolitical. Different models of health lead to different ways of measuring it, and of analyzing its production or destruction. While multidimensional definitions of health reflect our increasing understanding of its complexity and its cultural roots, comparative analyses tend to rely on the traditional outcomes of mortality and life expectancy. While life expectancy has increased a great deal during the last two centuries, we see very different patterns of illness throughout the world, and have identified many general and particular factors that seem to be related to those patterns.

In our concern with modern problems of health and illness, we often use historical data to help us untangle the web, although our industrial societies are indeed very recent. We see that the increasing complexity of society has led both to longer life and to a more strati-fied and inequitable distribution of good health. While global trends have been identified, these are affected by deviations and reversals that often particularly affect the poor – most of whom are women and children. Whatever the scenarios for the future, special attention must be paid to those in greatest need. While they are still rare, there have been innovative and successful health programs that have addressed the needs of these groups. Such programs have been comprehensive, participatory, and multisectoral, based on multifactoral and multi-dimensional conceptualizations of health.

Note

1. Popay *et al.* (1993) argue that tiredness can also be interpreted as a physical symptom, associated with ill health or physical labor.

5

Data on Women's Health

In this chapter we shall look at data on some of the factors that affect health, as well as specific health indicators. Where possible, gender differences will be highlighted. We shall see that women who live in countries that suffer from underdevelopment and poverty are disadvantaged, and they bear a disproportionate burden of that underdevelopment and poverty.

Data on Developing Countries

Tables 5.1 through 5.6 are based on UNICEF's 1995 report on the state of the world's children (Grant 1995) and cover population, income, education, and health. These data are reported using two different country-group comparisons. The first compares 100 developing countries to 30 developed countries and 15 that were formerly members of the USSR, as well as reporting information separately for the 35 least developed countries. The second takes the 100 developing countries and groups them into five regions: sub-Saharan Africa, South Asia, the Middle East and North Africa, Latin America and the Caribbean, and East Asia and the Pacific.[1]

Table 5.1 shows that 78 percent of the world's 5.6 billion people live in developing countries. Ten percent – half a billion people – live in the 35 least developed countries. Two-thirds of those who live in developing countries live in rural areas – a majority or near-majority in every region except Latin America and the Caribbean.

The fertility rate in developing countries is far greater than replacement at 3.6, but the extremely high rate of 5.9 in the least developing countries indicates that the proportion of the world's population living

Table 5.1 Population and demographic data (1993)

	No. of countries	Population (million)			Total fertility rate	Change in annual pop. growth rate*
		Total	Rural	(% Rural)		
Least developed countries (LDCs)	35	550	429	(78)	5.9	−0.1
Developing countries (includes LDCs)	100	4,318	2,764	(64)	3.6	0.3
Industrialized countries	30	941	226	(24)	1.8	0.2
Former USSR	15	293	100	(34)	2.0	n/a
Sub-Saharan Africa	39	547	377	(69)	6.4	−0.2
South Asia	7	1,208	894	(74)	4.2	0.1
Middle East and North Africa	17	350	158	(45)	4.9	−0.1
Latin America and Caribbean	22	459	124	(27)	3.0	0.4
East Asia and Pacific	15	1,754	1,210	(69)	2.5	0.5

* (rate averaged for 1965–1980) minus (rate averaged for 1980–1993).

in the most deprived countries will increase quickly. In fact, even the rate of growth in those least developed countries is increasing, due to increases in sub-Saharan Africa and the Middle East and North Africa.

National income and poverty data, displayed in Table 5.2, clearly indicate how devastating life is in those least developed countries. Two-thirds of the half-billion people living in those countries live below a level of absolute poverty, meaning that their income, given an average GNP per capita of $236 per year, cannot cover the most minimal nutritional requirements. These economies are stagnant on the average, but there is great variation among regions of the developing world, with Asia's economies growing while the rest of the developing world suffers economic decline or stagnation. This is in contrast to data from 1965–80, when the average annual growth rate of GNP per capita was 3.0 in sub-Saharan Africa, 3.2 in the Middle East and North Africa, and 4.1 in Latin America and the Caribbean. Those who live in rural areas – two-thirds of all residents of developing countries – suffer from the greatest poverty.

Table 5.2 GNP and poverty data

	No. of countries	GNP/ capita (US$)[*]	GNP/capita avg. annual growth rate[†]	% pop. below absolute poverty[§] Rural	Urban
Least developed countries	35	236	0.3	70	55
Developing countries	100	918	2.4	31	27
Industrialized countries	30	19,521	2.2	n/a	n/a
Former USSR	15	2,015	1.5	n/a	n/a
Sub-Saharan Africa	39	504	−0.4	62	n/a
South Asia	7	313	3.0	39	33
Middle East and North Africa	17	1,977	−0.7	n/a	n/a
Latin America and Caribbean	22	2,648	0.0	49	18
East Asia and Pacific	15	800	6.5	17	n/a

Notes: [*] 1990; [†] 1980–92; [§] 1980–89.

Data in Table 5.3 show that slightly over half of all women in developing countries are literate, with only 32 percent of women in highly populous South Asia being able to read or write at all. The gender difference in literacy is a key indicator of women's lack of status and opportunity. Women are only 60 percent as likely to be literate in the least developed countries and 75 percent in all developing countries. Asia shows the strongest discrimination, while the situation is most equitable in Latin America.

The data on mortality shown in Table 5.4 demonstrate strikingly both the burden of poverty and the effects of gender discrimination. Given a relatively equitable environment, women live an average of seven years longer than men, with a lifespan 110 percent as long. In the least developed countries that is reduced to 95 percent. In India and China women live on average 94 percent as long as men. Men in the least developed countries can expect to achieve 84 percent of the 'attainable' lifespan in developed countries and women just over 70

Table 5.3 Literacy data (1990)

	No. of countries	Adult literacy rate		
		Female	Male	Female as % of male
Least developed countries	35	32	54	59
Developing countries	100	57	76	75
Industrialized countries	30	n/a	n/a	n/a
Former USSR	15	97	99	98
Sub-Saharan Africa	39	40	61	66
South Asia	7	32	59	54
Middle East and North Africa	17	45	69	65
Latin America and Caribbean	22	83	86	97
East Asia and Pacific	15	71	88	81

percent. People living in developing countries live on average only 80 percent as long as those who live in industrialized countries. This, of course, is related to the child mortality rate. Almost one out of every five children in the least developed countries and in sub-Saharan Africa will die between birth and age five, as compared to one of 100 in industrialized countries.

As Table 5.5 shows, rural areas, where 78 percent of those living in the least developed countries and 64 percent of those living in all developing countries reside, are greatly lacking in available water and adequate sanitation. More than 50 percent of rural residents in the least developed countries lack access to safe water, and almost 75 percent to adequate sanitation. While the urban situation is somewhat better in both cases, 30 to 40 percent of urban residents also lack access to these necessary services. The rates vary by region, with rural Africans lacking water and rural Asians having very little access to sanitation.

Unsurprisingly, contraceptive prevalence is low where the fertility rate is high, as demonstrated in Table 5.6. Only 16 percent of women in the least developed countries use contraceptives. The rates of inocu-

Table 5.4 Life expectancy and child mortality data (1993)

	No. of countries	Life expectancy (LE)*				Under-5 mortality rate
		Total	Female	Male	Female as % of male	
Least developed countries	35	50	58	61	95	173
Developing countries	100	62	n/a	n/a	n/a	102
Industrialized countries	30	76	80	73	110	10
Former USSR	15	69	n/a	n/a	n/a	42
Sub-Saharan Africa	39	51	52	49	106	179
South Asia	7	59	59	59	100	127
Middle East and North Africa	17	64	65	63	103	70
Latin America and Caribbean	22	68	71	65	109	48
East Asia and Pacific	15	68	66	66	100	56

* Female/male breakdown from World Bank (1993). Both the groupings by development level and the region lists differ slightly from UNICEF's. Former USSR countries are included with the industrialized countries.

lation against tetanus, a major preventable cause of infant mortality, are indicative of the lack of health care availability for pregnant women, as are the appalling maternal mortality rates. Only 10 out of 100,000 women living in industrialized countries die on average due to conditions related to childbirth, while that number reaches 616 in sub-Saharan Africa and 607 for all the least developed countries. It is as high as 351 in the entire developing world. It must be emphasized that these maternal deaths have a major impact on the surviving children, greatly increasing their risk for early death. Data on women's non-reproductive health will be provided in the next section.

Thus in many aspects of life, women (and men) in developing countries – and particularly in the least developed countries – suffer in comparison to those in the industrialized world. Recognition of the gap between 'rich' and 'poor' countries has been one reason for the push to increase development throughout the world.

Table 5.5 Water and sanitation data (1988–1993)

	No. of countries	% with access to safe water		% with access to adequate sanitation	
		Rural	Urban	Rural	Urban
Least developed countries	35	46	64	27	62
Developing countries	100	60	88	18	69
Industrialized countries	30	n/a	n/a	n/a	n/a
Former USSR	15	n/a	n/a	n/a	n/a
Sub-Saharan Africa	39	35	73	28	58
South Asia	7	74	84	14	61
Middle East and North Africa	17	61	93	47	94
Latin America and Caribbean	22	55	90	33	79
East Asia and Pacific	15	57	91	13	63

The Health of Third World Women

The health of third world women is becoming a more prominent concern in the fields of international health and maternal and child health. Until recently, the health of these women was considered only in relation to the health of their children, and such programs as existed were restricted to reproductive health matters (Curlin and Tinker 1993; Koblinsky *et al.* 1993a). Because of a confluence of factors – among them an increasing focus on women on the part of both the international health and development communities, an increasing demand from women for comprehensive and lifelong care, recognition that a child's health is determined in large part by a mother's preconceptual health and by the mother's mother's before that, a burgeoning of international women's movements, and a growing dependence on women to take care of the necessities of family and community life – a new emphasis is being given to women's health.

Although accurate data are scarce, it is clear from the tables above that women in impoverished countries suffer greatly in terms of health. Worldwide, each year, over 585,000 women die from causes related to childbirth, and at least 30 million more suffer childbirth-related morbidities (UNICEF 1996). At least one million children lose their

Table 5.6 Women's reproductive health data (1980–1993)

	No. of countries	Contraceptive prevalence	% pregnant women inoculated against tetanus	Maternal mortality rate
Least developed countries	35	16	41	607
Developing countries	100	54	44	351
Industrialized countries	30	72	n/a	10
Former USSR	15	n/a	n/a	n/a
Sub-Saharan Africa	39	12	35	616
South Asia	7	39	70	492
Middle East and North Africa	17	44	48	202
Latin America and Caribbean	22	59	38	189
East Asia and Pacific	15	74	26	159

mothers each year from maternity-related deaths. About 13 percent of those maternal deaths, some 75,000, are the result of self-administered abortions (UNICEF 1996). Overall estimates of the number of maternal deaths due to all abortions are as high as 200,000 per year (Coeytaux *et al.* 1993).

In analyses of women's health status, both the stage of development and the social structure of their communities must be taken into account. Poor women in pre-transitional countries have shorter life expectancies than do non-poor women in these countries; poor and non-poor women in pre-transitional countries have shorter life expectancies than women in early or late transition countries. Diseases, illnesses, and the interactions and importance of determinants change, based not only on the transitional stage and on the distribution of disease clusters among countries but on variations related to gender, race and ethnicity, age, geographical location, and social class.

Gender comparisons

Women are often less advantaged than men in terms of income, nutrition, living conditions, the physical and psychological demands placed on them, and their share of the power and status needed to reduce exposure to and risk from many diseases. While they benefit from the trends towards an increase in longevity, women's health is not improving as fast as men's health in some locations where overall health is improving, and no one's health is improving in areas where social and cultural change has lagged behind technological change, or economic reversals are in effect. Women's health in developing countries remains at an abysmally low level. Many health problems arise because of gender, and they must be addressed with regard to gender. Although in most countries women live longer than men, many suffer greatly from disabilities, diseases, and illnesses that are preventable or whose severity can be mitigated. Recent World Bank (1993) data described below show that in developing countries, women aged between fifteen and forty-four lose only 81 percent of expected years in good health through premature death as compared to men, but they are 25 percent more likely to lose a year through disability.

If only because of differences in female and male endocrinologic and reproductive systems, it is safe to assume that health for women differs from health for men, both presently and historically. Among animals, females generally live longer than males. Among humans, females have better infant survival rates and live longer than males except where they suffer from strong discrimination in infanticide, feeding, caretaking, and medical treatment. Such discrimination currently exists in many parts of the world, particularly in South Asia, where about 15 percent of the world's population lives. Countries in that region average 94 females per 100 males. If they achieved the 'normal' ratio of 105 per 100, there would be an additional 100 million women alive today – 50 million in China alone (Sen 1990). In a recent survey in Madras, India, more than half of the 1,250 women interviewed had killed baby daughters (Anderson and Moore 1993). According to Caldwell (1993: 127), information from the World Fertility Survey shows excess female mortality at ages one to four in 'all of North Africa and the Middle East with the exception of Tunisia, all South Asia, all East and Southeast Asia with the exceptions of Indonesia and Malaysia, and in much of mainland Central America and northern South America, but almost nowhere in Sub-Saharan Africa.'

Elsewhere, as life expectancy for men and women increases, the gap widens and women gain *more* of an advantage over men. In several developed countries, however, there has been some reduction in the excess mortality of men as a result of increased smoking among women and decreased male mortality from ischemic heart disease (Waldron 1993). Kane (1991), using data from developed countries, which have more gender-specific data on health status, reports gender differences in congenital diseases, violence, accidents, mental illness, cancer sites, and disability as well as reproduction-related problems. Some differences in the risks, diseases, and illnesses are biologically based – reproductive illnesses and site-specific cancers – while some are more likely to be completely or partially socially determined – effects of war, mental illness, social violence, domestic violence. Gender differences have also been identified in alcohol and medication effects, cholesterol, high blood pressure effects, blood and sugar levels, and arthritis symptoms (Tavris 1992). While data indicate that men are slightly more likely to suffer from tropical disease than are women (World Bank 1993), there is some indication that women with diseases may be less likely to come under surveillance (Reuben 1993).

Kane finds that the greatest gender differences in illness occur between the ages of forty-five and sixty-four. During this period, women suffer from more minor illnesses – menopausal problems, cystitis, musculoskeletal problems, multiple sclerosis, migraines, pelvic inflammatory disease – and two prevalent major diseases: breast and uterine cancers. Women also spend a greater proportion of their latter years, over the age of sixty-four, with at least one disability (United Nations Information Centre 1992a). The world's over-sixty population is currently 500 million; in thirty years it is expected to reach 1.2 billion (United Nations Information Centre 1992b). As the world's population ages, women will thus be disproportionately affected.

The World Health Organization (WHO) has begun a series of small studies looking at the natural history of disease in women in developing countries, as well as at the meaning and effect of illness on women's lives through their caregiving roles. The WHO is recognizing that women bear a great burden with regard to illness because of gender-related roles. They seek care for themselves belatedly, cannot take time from their work roles for proper recuperation, and provide most of the care to others in their families. Their deaths are particularly damaging to their children.

Historically, there have been only a few efforts to look at women's health as distinct from population health. The United Nations (1991a: 16) reports that life expectancy at birth for women increased from 44 years in 1950 to 61 years in 1980, while the birth rate in developing countries dropped from 5.9 to 4.1. Kane (1991: 188) sees women's increased longevity as due to reduced vulnerability among young girl children and women of reproductive age. Before the health transition in Europe, '[o]nly one in every three women lived long enough to take full advantage of her fertile years: two-thirds had died before age fifty.' In a study of female mortality in twentieth-century Spain, the authors

(Cortés-Majó *et al.* 1990: 327) found that maternal mortality alone was not responsible for high female death rates among women between the ages of fifteen and thirty-four. Higher tuberculosis rates for women than for men accounted for much of the difference. They conclude that 'the analysis of social inequalities with regards to health should begin with the analysis of sexual inequalities...'

Aggregate data about women's health status in underdeveloped countries (and about health status in general) are meager, and difficult to locate in areas other than reproductive health and maternal mortality. However, there have been attempts to estimate certain rates and prevalence levels of some indicators of poor health. Many of these attempts to quantify health are more symbolic than real. One certainly does not know with any precision the nutritional intake of people in Mozambique, or the number of cases of cervical cancer in Latin America. None the less, since it is extremely difficult to arouse the world community to act on no information at all, the international health community – particularly the World Bank, the World Health Organization, the Pan American Health Organization, and UNICEF – has valiantly tried to put together and extrapolate from such information as there is. The information that follows is organized into five sections based on Blaxter's multidimensional model of health status (described in Chapter 4).

Disease/illness

Included in this discussion are chronic communicable diseases of adulthood, conditions related to childbirth, and non-communicable diseases that are often subsumed by the term 'chronic diseases.' We shall see that residents of developing countries are much more likely to experience communicable diseases than those of more developed countries. It is assumed, on the other hand, that non-communicable chronic diseases such as cancers, cardiovascular diseases, and diabetes accompany development, and that populations are subject to them as they become more resistant to infectious diseases. The burden from these diseases, however, is also greater in developing countries (World Bank 1993). Johansson (1991) notes that the existence of chronic disease in developing countries may be underestimated because only when an illness is 'treatable' is it apt to be acknowledged, and single cause-of-death reporting means that little is known about co-morbidities – underlying, undiagnosed chronic diseases. Using a more complicated historical argument, Eyer and Sterling (1977: 22) maintain that chronic illnesses increase at the *same* time as acute diseases among the young do, rather than after a decrease, and that both are attributable to 'the social disruption that is an inextricable part of capitalist development.' Whether non-communicable disease has always been present but underestimated, as Johansson maintains, or is a phenomenon that accompanies modernization, Eyer and Sterling's hypothesis, it accounts for a great deal of ill health in both underdeveloped and developed countries.

Disability-adjusted life years

Until recently, very little information was available on disease burden in the non-industrialized countries. The 1993 World Development Report from the World Bank (1993), however, presents a great deal of data developed jointly by the World Bank and the World Health Organization. These data, further reported and explicated in Murray and Lopez (1994), are based on calculations of disability-adjusted life years (DALYs). Each DALY is an indication of a year lost because of premature death, or a time period – weighted by the severity of the disability and by age so as to be comparable to a year lost to premature death – lived with a disability. While this complex information is based on local studies and a complicated process of evaluation and expert judgment that is still in process, it provides a great deal more information than was previously available.[2]

Worldwide, 46 percent of healthy life loss was due to communicable diseases (which, in the World Bank's typology, include maternal and perinatal causes), 42 percent to non-communicable diseases, and 12 percent to injuries. In sub-Saharan Africa, 71 percent was due to communicable diseases, 19 percent to non-communicable diseases, and 9 percent to injuries. Among the group of 'established market economies,' only 10 percent was due to communicable diseases, 78 percent to non-communicable diseases, and 12 percent to injuries.

The tables below report burden of disease information by gender for the 180 countries grouped as the demographically developing group (DDG), for the 35 countries that are grouped as established market economies (EME), for all 229 countries examined in the World Bank's report (World), and – since the DDG is very broad, and includes every country except the EME and 14 formerly socialist economies of Europe (FSE) – for the 49 countries included in the sub-Saharan Africa (SSA) group. Table 5.7 presents summary information for all age groups by gender across three clusters: (1) communicable, maternal, and perinatal diseases; (2) noncommunicable diseases; and (3) injuries.

Although the meaning of a DALY is complex and mathematically derived, comparisons are informative. Perhaps the most startling

Table 5.7 Burden of disease by gender and economic group (1990)

	DDG		EME		World		SSA	
	F	M	F	M	F	M	F	M
DALYs lost (millions)	582	628	42	52	648	713	140	153
DALYs lost/1000 pop.	288	299	102	133	248	269	542	606
Population (millions)	2,022	2,100	408	391	2,617	2,651	258	252
% world pop. (by gender)	77	79	16	15	100	100	10	10
% world DALYs lost (by gender)	90	88	6	7	100	100	22	21
Excess % (% lost − % pop)	12	9	−9	−7	0	0	12	12
DALYs lost age 15+ (millions)	265	285	38	47	324	362	49	49
% total DALYs lost age 15+	46	45	91	91	50	51	35	32
% DALYs lost due to premature death: all	65	69	47	57	64	68	76	78
% DALYs lost due to disability: all	35	31	53	43	36	32	24	22
% DALYs lost due to premature death: 15+	54	61	47	56	53	61	64	70
% DALYs lost due to disability: 15+	46	39	53	44	47	39	36	30

difference is the DALYs lost per 1,000 population in sub-Saharan Africa as compared to the entire developing world: 542 for females in Africa and 288 in all developing countries. Sub-Saharan Africa has one-tenth of the world's population and more than one-fifth of its disease burden. A large part of that burden is borne by children, with as much as 65 percent of the total DALYs lost to those under fifteen. In that region, however, 46 percent of the population is under age fifteen. Thus within the developing world, there are large variations, indicating that the health of many people is much more precarious than is indicated by summary data as represented by the DDG grouping. Another startling figure is how few DALYs lost in developed countries are to children. This is both because children make up a much smaller proportion of the population – 19 percent as compared to 36 percent on the average

Table 5.8 Burden of disease (%) for selected disease categories by gender and economic group for ages 15+ (1990)

Disease (cluster*)	DDG		EME		World		SSA	
	F	M	F	M	F	M	F	M
Cardiovascular (2)	18.2	17.6	25.7	25.4	20.4	19.7	12.0	9.9
Maternal (1)	10.7	–	1.5	–	9.0	–	16.0	–
Neuropsychiatric (2)	9.8	10.2	15.6	15.7	10.6	10.8	5.6	7.3
Cancers (2)	8.1	9.2	20.7	20.7	10.1	11.3	4.2	3.5
Tuberculosis (1)	5.6	7.6	0.1	0.2	4.6	6.1	9.1	11.9
STDs (1)	5.2	0.9	4.1	0.0	4.9	0.7	7.1	3.4
Unintentional injuries (3)	5.1	13.6	5.1	9.5	5.1	13.2	2.0	12.7
Respiratory (chronic) (2)	4.7	4.9	3.6	4.1	4.5	4.7	2.2	1.6
Intentional injuries (3)	4.0	8.7	2.2	5.7	3.7	8.2	4.5	14.0
HIV (1)	3.9	5.3	0.8	2.6	3.3	4.6	15.6	16.4
Other	3.8	3.0	1.2	1.2	3.5	2.8	4.5	2.3
Digestive (2)	3.5	4.9	3.8	4.9	3.6	4.9	2.5	3.2
Musculoskeletal (2)	3.1	1.3	6.3	2.9	3.6	1.5	0.8	0.3
Nutritional (2)	3.1	2.5	1.7	1.0	2.6	2.1	1.3	1.9
Respiratory (infection) (1)	2.9	2.6	2.5	2.1	2.8	2.4	3.2	2.7
Genito-urinary (2)	2.0	2.1	1.6	1.8	1.9	2.0	1.4	1.2
Sense organ (2)	1.5	1.2	0.1	0.1	1.2	1.0	1.5	1.1
Oral health (2)	1.4	1.3	1.4	1.0	1.6	1.3	0.5	0.5
Diabetes (2)	1.3	0.9	1.9	1.3	1.4	1.0	0.4	0.2
Malaria (1)	1.0	0.8	0.0	0.0	0.8	0.7	3.2	2.8
Tropical cluster (1)	0.8	1.1	0.0	0.0	0.7	0.9	2.2	3.0
Parasites (1)	0.2	0.2	0.0	0.0	0.2	0.2	0.1	0.1
Total DALYs lost (millions)	265	285	38	47	324	362	49	49
% world DALYs lost (by gender)	82	79	12	13	100	100	15	14
Excess % (by gender)	5	–1	–4	–2	0	0	5	4

Notes: * 1: communicable diseases; 2: non-communicable diseases; 3: injuries.

in the DDG – and because they bear less of the overall disease burden. Both men and women in developing countries have a relatively high disease burden, but, as we have already seen, women are more affected by disability than men are – 46 percent of women's DALYs are due to disability as compared to 39 percent of men's (a difference of 7 percent). This is even more true in the developed world, where the difference is 9 percent.

Table 5.8 presents information on specific disease categories for adults (fifteen and over). Disease categories are presented if they were important with regard to adult health and if they accounted for a significant amount of adult disease burden. Residual categories are grouped as Other. The categories have been sorted according to the DALYs lost by women in the DDG (developing countries). The 'winner': 18.2 percent of all DALYs lost to women in the DDG were related to cardiovascular causes.

Again, it is useful to note that there are large differences between sub-Saharan Africa and the entire DDG, particularly with regard to HIV, responsible for 16 percent of male and female DALYs in Africa but only 3 to 4 percent in all developing countries. Maternal conditions for females, tuberculosis for males and females, and intentional accidents for males also account for a higher proportion of disease in SSA countries than in all developing countries. Malaria shows some difference, but is much more important when children are included. The entire disease burden – death and disability – is equally shared between men and women in Africa, but overall in the developing world women bear a slightly greater burden than men do.

For women in developing countries and worldwide, cardiovascular disease accounts for almost 20 percent of DALYs. Cardiovascular disease is primarily composed of cerebrovascular, ischemic heart disease, and peri-, endo-, and myocarditis and cardiomyopathy. Thus, according to these data, a non-communicable chronic disease exacts the greatest cost in both developing and developed countries. Maternal conditions are dominated by sepsis, obstructed labor, hemorrhage, and abortion in that order. Depressive disorders comprise about one-third of the neuropsychiatric group, followed by Alzheimer's, psychoses, epilepsy, post-traumatic stress disorder, alcohol and drug dependency. Breast and cervical cancers account for much of women's cancer, with lung and colon/rectal cancers the next most common. Pelvic inflammatory disease is the major STD. Unintentional injuries are dominated by motor vehicle accidents and falls. Chronic respiratory disease is principally either Chronic Obstructive Pulmonary Disease (COPD) or asthma. Self-inflicted injuries, war, and homicide and violence are

Table 5.9 Female/male ratio and excess burden (%) for selected disease categories by SSA and DDG countries for ages 15+ (1990)

Disease (cluster)	Female/ male ratio DDG	Excess female DDG	Excess female SSA	Excess all DDG	Excess all SSA
Cardiovascular (2)	1.0	−4.0	−1.1	−6.2	−2.2
Maternal (1)	n/a	19.5	16.8	18.5	16.8
Neuropsychiatric (2)	0.9	−1.6	−2.0	−3.0	−1.3
Cancers (2)	0.8	−11.4	−3.7	−13.2	−4.9
Tuberculosis (1)	0.7	22.4	20.2	20.6	18.0
STDs (1)	5.7	10.2	11.9	10.7	18.2
Unintentional injuries (3)	0.3	4.6	−4.2	3.2	1.3
Respiratory (chronic) (2)	0.9	8.9	−2.5	5.5	−4.1
Intentional injuries (3)	0.4	11.5	8.4	7.1	11.9
HIV (1)	0.7	19.9	60.7	15.9	47.6
Other	1.2	11.7	9.6	8.6	5.7
Digestive (2)	0.7	3.7	0.7	1.8	−0.4
Musculoskeletal (2)	2.2	−6.7	−6.9	−7.9	−7.0
Nutritional (2)	1.2	21.1	−2.1	17.5	0.0
Respiratory (infection) (1)	1.0	9.2	7.6	7.4	6.5
Genito-urinary (2)	0.9	7.4	1.1	5.0	−0.5
Sense organ (2)	1.1	20.9	8.5	20.3	6.8
Oral health (2)	1.0	−4.1	−4.9	−3.6	−4.9
Diabetes (2)	1.3	1.9	−5.3	0.1	−5.9
Malaria (1)	1.1	23.0	50.1	22.0	49.0
Tropical cluster (1)	0.7	22.9	40.6	21.9	38.7
Parasites (1)	1.0	23.0	−1.9	22.0	−2.3
Total	0.9	4.7	5.1	2.2	4.3

all important contributors to the intentional injury category. Cirrhosis is the largest component of digestive diseases, while osteoarthritis dominates the musculoskeletal category. Nutritional and endocrine disease includes vitamin A deficiency, protein-energy malnutrition, iodine deficiency, and anemia. Respiratory infections are predominantly in the lower tract. Nephritis and nephrosis dominate the genitourinary illnesses, glaucoma and cataracts the sense organ cluster, periodontal disease dominates within oral health, and shistosomiasis and Chagas'

Table 5.10 Percentage of burden of disease due to disability for selected disease categories by gender and economic group for ages 15+ (1990)

Disease (cluster)	DDG		EME		World		SSA	
	F	M	F	M	F	M	F	M
Cardiovascular (2)	30	30	35	30	31	29	26	26
Maternal (1)	57	–	96	–	58	–	50	–
Neuropsychiatric (2)	91	87	91	89	91	90	91	89
Cancers (2)	21	20	30	29	23	23	14	14
Tuberculosis (1)	15	16	36	28	15	16	9	10
STDs (1)	89	30	100	77	91	30	68	24
Unintentional injuries (3)	42	37	45	26	42	34	40	30
Respiratory (chronic) (2)	48	47	54	48	49	46	64	58
Intentional injuries (3)	19	33	24	26	20	32	30	32
HIV (1)	6	6	9	11	7	6	7	6
Other	44	35	29	31	41	32	44	36
Digestive (2)	39	35	45	41	41	36	38	33
Musculoskeletal (2)	92	93	95	96	93	93	80	85
Nutritional (2)	66	67	69	60	71	66	53	53
Respiratory (infection) (1)	35	38	47	41	37	38	26	29
Genito-urinary (2)	47	61	56	61	48	60	47	65
Sense organ (2)	98	97	97	92	98	97	100	100
Oral health (2)	97	98	100	100	98	98	99	99
Diabetes (2)	19	24	41	40	23	27	19	31
Malaria (1)	26	28	0	0	26	28	29	43
Tropical cluster (1)	49	54	0	0	49	54	32	29
Parasites (1)	79	79	0	0	79	79	87	87
All conditions	47	40	53	43	48	40	37	30

disease the tropical cluster. Among adults, hookworm is the most prevalent parasite. Overall, the results are somewhat unexpected, with common communicable diseases at the bottom of the list.

The next table, 5.9, presents several comparisons for the selected disease categories, again restricted to those aged fifteen and over. The first is the female-to-male ratio for the developing (DDG) countries (men lose 10 percent more DALYs than women do in the DDG countries), the second the percentage of excess among females calculated by subtracting the actual disease burden of women from their expected burden given the female population of the DDG and the SSA (according to the World Bank data, 100 percent of the burden of tuberculosis is in the DDG, which has 78 percent of the world population, indicating an excess of 22 percent), and the third the excess burden of the developing countries and in sub-Saharan Africa.

Women in the DDG are disproportionately affected by STDs and musculoskeletal problems; men by both intentional and intentional injuries. A large part of the overall disproportionate disease burden in developing countries is from malaria, the cluster of tropical diseases, and parasites which, as we have seen, are among the least costly to women in these countries. Among the more costly conditions in terms of DALYs, tuberculosis, nutritional conditions, HIV, and maternal conditions affect women in all developing countries, while HIV overwhelms the other conditions in sub-Saharan Africa. Injuries, both intentional and unintentional, are generally higher in the developing world. There are, in fact, few conditions that are significantly underrepresented among the DDGs, although the cancers and musculoskeletal disorders are less common than expected.

In Table 5.10, I have calculated the percentage of disease burden due to disability for the conditions in Table 5.9. Worldwide, for example, 29 percent of the DALYs lost to men over fifteen because of cardiovascular problems are due to disability, while 71 percent are due to premature death. Keeping in mind the fact that these data are estimated, it is still possible to identify the conditions that most affect the quality of women's lives in developing countries. These include maternal, neuropsychiatric, STDs, unintentional injuries, musculoskeletal, nutritional, genitourinary, sense organ, oral health and parasites. Reproductive conditions, unsurprisingly, show the greatest gender differences. Certain conditions – such as cancers, tuberculosis STDs, respiratory infections, and diabetes – cause less disability in the developing world (particularly in sub-Saharan Africa) than the industrialized, indicating their more fatal effects in the third world.

Finally, since age and stage of life are major factors in health, the data in Table 5.11 from the World Bank report the top ten contributors to disease burden among women for two childhood and three adult age groups for the DDG by gender. This more refined analysis reflects the importance of maternal conditions, HIV, and STDs during the child-bearing years and of chronic conditions, tuberculosis, and dental and vision problems after the child-bearing years. It also points out the dramatic differences between conditions affecting children and adults.

Table 5.11 Top ten causes of disease burden in DDG countries by age for females (1990)

	Age <5	Age 5–14	Age 15–44	Age 45–59	Age 60+
1	Respiratory infections	Parasites	Maternal	Cerebro-vascular	Cerebro-vascular
2	Perinatal	Childhood	STDs	Tuberculosis	Ischemic heart
3	Diarrheal disease	Respiratory infection	Tuberculosis	Ischemic heart	COPD
4	Childhood cluster	Diarrheal disease	HIV	Peri-, endo-, myocarditis	Alzheimer's
5	Congenital	Congenital	Depressive disease	Periodontal	Respiratory infections
6	Malaria	Malaria	Self-inflicted injuries	Cataracts	Peri-, endo-, myocarditis
7	Protein-energy malnutrition	Vitamin A deficiency	Respiratory infections	COPD	Diabetes
8	Vitamin A deficiency	Anemia	Anemia	Diabetes	Tuberculosis
9	Iodine deficiency	Epilepsy	Osteoarthritis	Osteoarthritis	Falls
10	Falls	STDs/HIV	Motor vehicle injuries	Cervical cancer	Cataracts

	DALYs lost (millions)			
250	67	155	49	60

While this first attempt at quantifying the world's disease burden is informative, the technique will prove more useful as it leads to the collection of higher-quality underlying data and more local applications of the findings.

Other data on disease

An additional factor that deserves attention is the effect of co-morbidities on women, who may suffer from malnutrition, STDs, vision problems, backache, malaria, and asthma simultaneously. Particularly insidious here is malnutrition, which increases susceptibility to other diseases. Women suffer from malnutrition when they do not eat enough calories to support the energy they expend. Malnutrition can be measured in several ways: body-fat measurement, calorie intake based on a defined standard, an index of weight for height that may or may not take bone structure into account, or by the prevalence of anemia and other nutrition-related conditions.

Nutritional needs are lifelong, and deficiencies have both immediate and long-term health effects on women and the children to whom they give birth. For example, lack of energy, iron, and vitamin A are related to susceptibility to infection, anemia to hemorrhaging, and stunting to obstructed labor (National Council of International Health 1992).

Among children, malnutrition is visibly manifested by stunted growth. The effects of stunting may be difficult to disentangle, but as Nancy Scheper-Hughes (1992: 156) says in her graphic description of the effects of hunger on a community in Northeast Brazil, '[t]he problem is that stunting from malnutrition is almost invariably accompanied by delayed maturation, reproductive problems (including high risk of miscarriage and low-birth-weight infants), ill health, reduced energy, lowered self-esteem, and adverse effects during childhood on the ability to learn.' Thus nutrition is a lifetime issue for women, with major intergenerational effects (Merchant and Kurz 1993).

While much of the developing world suffers from malnutrition,

> there is ample evidence both in social custom and in surveys that malnutrition occurs disproportionately among girls and women. Food taboos are more commonly imposed on women. Furthermore, in many societies it is customary for the men to eat first, boys next, girls and women last. If protein is scarce, it goes primarily to the men. (Sivard 1985: 25)

UNICEF reports nutritional data for 1988, undifferentiated by gender. On average, Mozambicans get only 70 percent of their required calorie supply, Indians 95 percent, Hondurans 96 percent, and residents of the USA 139 percent (Grant 1992). Given that women often get less than their share in developing countries, these figures probably look better than the reality. Estimates are that from 50 to 83 percent of pregnant women in developing countries are anemic (Jacobson 1991; UNICEF 1996; World Health Organization 1985), as are two-thirds of all Asian women (New Internationalist 1985) and 83 percent of all Indian women (UNICEF 1996). Almost half of the women aged fifteen and older in developing countries are estimated to be stunted as a result of insufficient protein in childhood (Merchant and Kurz 1993).

Besides malnutrition, there are some specific data on other conditions. About five hundred thousand new cases of cervical cancer occur each year in underdeveloped countries (World Health Organization 1985). Cali, Colombia reported a cervical cancer rate of 52.9 compared to 10.7 and 19.5 among white and black women respectively in San Francisco in the 1970s. Breast cancer, though rarer in developing than in developed countries, is increasing, and generally represents the most common cancer among Latin American women (Pan American Health Organization 1985).

The prevalence of hypertension among women ranged from 6.6 percent to 24 percent in nine studies in Latin America (Pan American Health Organization 1985). The US female death rate from cardiovascular disease in 1978 was 110 per 100,000, Cuba's was 128, and Trinidad and Tobago had a rate of 194 (Pan American Health Organization 1985).

Diabetes has a prevalence of 5.5 percent among women in a 1979 study from Argentina, which can be compared to 2.5 percent in the US Framingham study (Pan American Health Organization 1985).

A review of community surveys from 33 countries found prevalence rates of mental disorder and symptoms among women ranging from 5.5 to 34.5 percent (Paltiel 1987). The WHO (1992) estimates that over 50 million people suffer from severe mental illness and that 427 million suffer from less severe illness, neuroses, mental retardation and affective disorders.

Although non-communicable diseases have a devastating effect on third world women, their measurement is often problematic in developing countries. The identification of many of these diseases requires a medical diagnosis. Since so few women receive medical care and so few laboratory tests are done, women are often unaware of diseases from which they suffer. If the chronic disease is not the primary cause of death but, rather, a co-morbidity or precursor, it will not be registered on death forms.

While 'women are not intrinsically more susceptible to malaria than men,' they are particularly vulnerable during pregnancy, when the disease causes abortions, stillbirths, and low-birthweight babies (Reuben 1993: 473).

Women suffer from diseases connected to their reproductive system – particularly from sexually transmitted diseases and reproductive track infections (RTIs). One study in rural India (Bang *et al.* 1989a) found that 92 percent of 650 women examined had at least one RTI, and that these women averaged 3.6 RTIs each. HIV positivity and AIDS are as common for women as for men in developing countries. If half of those infected are females, then from 4.8 to 5.2 million women are suffering and dying from this disease in these countries – countries that have little expectation of being able to afford any of the medical advances that are made against AIDS. The WHO estimates that by the year 2000 there will have been 30 to 40 million individuals infected by HIV and about 12 to 18 million cases of AIDS. About 80 percent of those cases will be in developing countries – particularly southern Africa and Asia (Merson 1992).

Feeling ill/symptoms

Feeling ill and experiencing symptoms are less 'objective' conditions than disease, and are usually measured by self-report. '"Disease" denotes pathology that has some objective manifestation, whereas "illness" refers to malaise or symptoms as experienced by the patient' (Sagan 1987: 6). One can be ill without the presence of a disease, and have a disease without suffering from illness. Defining a condition as an illness is related to cultural norms, and varies according to class, gender, role demands, and personality factors. As for health status, it is the presence or absence of illness over a period of time rather than the current health state that is of interest. Everyone has aches and pains, colds, cuts and bruises much of the time; of interest is greater frequency than 'normal' – indicating greater exposure and/or less resistance.

Although there is little information on illnesses and symptoms among women in developing countries, at the very least they suffer from headaches, joint and muscle pains, back problems, and poor eyesight. Women face problems from the estimated 20 million illegal abortions performed annually – as many as 200,000 women a year die from unsafe abortions (World Health Organization 1985), and clearly the illness and injury rate from abortions is much higher. Women also suffer from the repercussions of the violence inflicted upon them. Estimates of domestic violence vary greatly, with from 20 to 70 percent of women reporting abuse from a partner; as many as one in five US women have been raped at some time in their lives (Heise 1993). Throughout the 1980s, 80 percent of those killed in wars were women and children (InterPress Service 1993a). Thus the preponderance of injured survivors are also women and children – suffering from illness, disability, and impaired functional status.

Illnesses and symptoms play a major role in individuals' appraisals of their own health. There is an enormous variety of potential illnesses and symptoms. Ethnographic work on community norms will be helpful in identifying those that are most important in a given culture. Health surveys in Western industrialized countries often take this dimension as a key indicator of relative health. Its usefulness for women in developing countries will be both in providing information on their health needs and in helping them to be more aware of and to analyze those needs on their own.

Disabilities

Disabilities are defined in relation to functional status – the ability to carry out normal activities, given a woman's age. Disability may be a result of chronic disease or illness; it is usually measured by asking whether or not a person can perform certain common tasks (carry a child or fetch water) and/or to what extent they are affected in their work and social life (not at all, mildly, moderately, severely). The WHO (1992) has distinguished *disability*, a person-level condition, from *impairment*, which exists at the organ level (e.g., poor eyesight that may or may not be disabling), and *handicap*, which occurs when an individual interacts with society (e.g., blindness that restricts one's access to public space). Definitions of disability have a major social and personality component. People are affected differently by similar conditions. Women with few resources may function while suffering from illnesses that would be disabling to women who had assistance available.

Roughly one in every ten people is disabled – more than 500 million people in the world – of whom three-fifths live in developing countries and three-fifths are women and children (Editors 1992a). This means that about 150 million females in developing countries are disabled. The principal cause is malnutrition, while war and other forms of violence leave many disabled from land mines, shelling and bombing, destruction of homes and communities, lack of access to food and health care, and mental disorders. Few facilities exist to care for the disabled in developing countries, and artificial limbs, wheelchairs, hearing and seeing aids are difficult if not impossible to obtain, and often of poor quality.

Disabilities, like symptoms and illnesses, are in part defined through cultural norms. Encouraging discussion among women, through anthropological work and health surveys, will help to increase their consciousness about disabilities and, thereby, to politicize women's health issues.

Fitness

Fitness or the lack thereof is difficult to measure. Mildred Blaxter (1990: 43), unable to disentangle 'mobility or muscular "fitness"' from functional status and individual circumstances, used three objective measures of fitness in her health and lifestyle survey: blood pressure, lung function, and measured weight for height. Less objective conditions are also important. Many women suffer from long-term depletion of energy through multiple births and frequent lactation, and through chronic overwork. They suffer from chronic fatigue because of long hours, hard work, too little sleep, too much responsibility, and too little time, money, and opportunity for those activities that provide respite and can restore energy. Whether this should be considered as lack of fitness, reduced functional status, or reduced psychosocial well-being is not clear. Blaxter's technique of restricting fitness to objective measurements is her way of keeping the dimensions of health distinct. It may, however, be at odds with common understanding of the term.

Fitness is a concept that third world women understand and not one that is restricted to Western women under pressure to be thin, muscular, and cardiovascularly fit. Blaxter's use of lung function, weight, and blood pressure may well correspond to women's needs to be active for many long hours each day, and be useful measures of fitness. It will also be helpful to investigate these women's ideas about fitness in order to develop more easily applied measures based on self-report.

Psychosocial well-being

The final dimension of health that Blaxter describes has malaise at the negative end and psychosocial well-being at the positive end. Blaxter chose not to try to operationalize the positive aspect of psychosocial well-being, but I shall discuss Anton Antonovsky's measure of that concept (Sense of Coherence) in Chapter 6. To ascertain health status on this dimension, Blaxter measures the negative end: tiredness, sleep disturbances, worry, depression, and trouble with nerves. Nerves (*nervios*) is a condition known to many cultures, and may have different meaning within different cultures and age groups. It seems to have a higher prevalence among women, and may be 'a female expression of general social or emotional distress that men express in other somatic forms or with other kinds of behaviors' (Davis and Low 1989b: xiii). Except with respect to nerves, at this time little has been written on the relationship between psychosocial well-being and health from the perspective of third world women.

Again, women everywhere discuss negative facets of well-being such as sleep deprivation, depression, and nerves. Qualitative investigations of well-being are needed if we are to understand its role in women's lives and health, its local variations, and to develop useful measurement strategies.

As women's health gains in importance, both measurement tools and data will be increasingly available. The World Bank's data, speculative though they be, are already providing a basis for policy analyses of women's health issues (M.E. Young 1994). Given research techniques being developed by feminist researchers (see Chapter 8 below), it is also likely that explorations of women's perceptions of the meaning of health and of their health status will be conducted in different locations and among different subgroups of women. The information that is currently available is sparse, but it can provide guidance to further work in this area.

Summary

In this chapter we have examined data on the lives and the health of the women who are the subjects of this book. Three-quarters of the world's population lives in developing countries where the average fertility rate of 3.6 ensures that the proportion will increase in the future. The levels of poverty are extreme, with an average GNP per capita of $918 (1990), and one-third of those in rural areas and one-quarter of those in urban areas living below absolute poverty. Forty-three percent of the women in these countries are illiterate, average life expectancy is sixty-two years, and about one in every ten children dies before the age of five. Many residents do not have access to safe water and adequate sanitation, particularly in rural areas. Among the most disturbing statistics are the high rates of maternal mortality, particularly in sub-Saharan Africa, where it averages 607 deaths per 100,000 births, as compared to 10 in developed countries. Although accurate morbidity and cause-of-death data are difficult to obtain, the 77 percent of the world's women living in developing countries suffer 90 percent of women's worldwide burden of disease. Cardiovascular disease is the most costly, with maternal conditions in second place. An important consideration is co-morbidities among women, particularly those that often accompany malnutrition. There is little extant information on illness and symptoms, fitness, and psychosocial well-being, but it is known that about 150 million women in developing countries are disabled. It is fervently hoped that as concern for women's health and gender awareness increase, more and better data will become available.

Notes

1. These data are the most recent published, and differ from earlier UNICEF reports in that the fifteen countries that previously comprised the USSR are grouped in a separate category.

2. More specifically:

> The duration of time lost due to premature mortality is calculated using standard expected years of life lost where model life-table West with an expectation of life at birth of 82.5 for females and 80 for males has been used. Time lived at different ages has been valued using an exponential function of the form Cxe^{-bx}. Streams of time have been discounted at 3%. A continuous discounting function of the form $e^{-r(x-a)}$ has been used where r is the discount rate and a is the age of onset. Disability is divided into six classes, with each class having a severity weight between 0 and 1. Time lived in each class is multiplied by the disability weight to make it comparable with the years lost due to premature mortality. (Murray 1994: 15)

I should also mention that this volume is somewhat controversial in the international and public health world. Both authors' recommendations and the quality of the data have been criticized. At this stage, however, I feel that we need to be looking at any and all credible data to mitigate our ignorance and to move us forward in gender-based analyses of health status.

6

Factors Affecting Health

There are at least two complementary reasons why scientists and researchers attempt to 'unravel' health: the desire to find ways to improve health and conquer disease and the addictive fascination that puzzle-solving has for them. Health holds out at least the illusion of being understandable and improvable. Decreasing mortality rates indicate progress, providing an incentive to those who seek to make the situation even better. Several approaches have been taken in the search for understanding how health can be improved, including analyses of aggregate data, individual-level studies, historical analyses performed with or without data, and anthropological studies.

Because of the difficulty of defining and understanding health – its relativity, its multidimensional nature, its many possible determinants and their complex interactions, and the fact that, depending on the level of development and health status, determinants differ in the role they play – it is unlikely that there will ever be a definitive model of the 'production' of health. However, there is some consensus on major factors that have led to improved health. From the multiple potential determinants of health, the ones I have selected for review and explication are those that are most commonly found in the literature on health in developing countries (local environmental conditions, national income, modernization, population control, medical technology and medical care, public health and primary care, health education, health behavior, nutrition, and maternal education), certain important factors that are usually taken for granted in discussions of health (geography, germs, and genetics), and several factors that have only recently begun to be discussed in the literature in relation to developing countries but are particularly relevant to women's health (psychosocial and psychoneuroimmunological factors, factors related to the organization of society, violence and sexual abuse, women's status and autonomy, and empowerment).[1] These are not, in an epidemiological sense, all risk factors – measurable and significantly related to outcomes in a testable fashion. Rather, they are vantage points – factors that have received attention because they seem particularly important and informative about health.

I intend to emphasize two sets of particularly complex societal and individual factors that seem to be especially important strands in the web of women's health – the organization of society and the set of psychosocial and psychoneuroimmunological factors. While I shall discuss a relatively comprehensive list of other factors affecting health, the discussions will be brief. My goal in regard to them is to point out possible misapprehensions and innovative findings, as well as connections among all the factors. For convenience I have divided these selected determinants of health into four groups: (1) natural or environmental conditions; (2) societal factors considered principally as sociopolitical and cultural; (3) factors directly related to health and medical care; and (4) individual-level factors. As much of the research to date on determinants of health disregards gender, much of the discussion is not restricted to women's health. I have deferred discussion of those societal factors specific to women – equity, education, and empowerment – to Chapter 7, where my focus returns to women's health.

The organization I have imposed on this material is functional and somewhat misleading, since much of the evidence defies any distinct classification, particularly between factors at the sociopolitical and individual levels. We shall realize that looking factor by factor makes it difficult to pull together a coherent story. Since health is multi-dimensional, both positive and negative, and represented by many diverse indicators, different factors address different aspects. Different factors are analyzed at different levels and studied using a wide variety of methodologies. Evidence as to the lack of clarity about the effect of single factors and continuing indications of apparently weblike interactions among various factors suggest that it may be useful to shift the kaleidoscope: to take a look at the literature from different angles and to recognize that any given configuration is only one of many possible perspectives. Viewed through this kaleidoscope, the literature can help to clarify where we are in our attempts to unravel health and to investigate the role of empowerment in its production.

Environmental Factors

Geography and climate

Geography, being non-manipulable and autonomous (Landers 1993), is frequently ignored in discussions of health, except in considerations of delivery of services (rural versus urban location), locations of disease pockets (environmental or cultural hazards), or the transmission of epidemics. It is, however, an extremely important determinant of health. It is part and parcel of the definition of underdevelopment and a challenge to science, which is always looking for ways to predict and control nature's autonomous behavior. Science has not discovered how to live with and compensate for geography, which is disproportionately problematic in tropical countries, most of which are relatively poor and underdeveloped in part due to their physical location. They suffer from tempest and drought, fluctuating and often insufficient rainfall, eroded topsoil, hostile insects, soil that is low in nitrogen, and a majority of the earth's natural disasters (Harrison 1981). The cost of economic development is therefore higher than it is in more temperate regions. Effects, however, are not limited to the tropics, as it is increasingly apparent that what happens in the tropics has global implications.

Geography and climate are linked to many other determinants of health. They define the local environment in terms of water, soil, and available energy sources; they foster or inhibit the development of germs hostile to humans; they affect GNP by their effect on agriculture and industry; they increase the cost in time and money of development and modernization; they affect nutrition in many ways – by determining what and how much can be grown and distributed, how easily food can be prepared, and by the need to use insecticides and fertilizer. They engender human activities which, while they are directed towards mitigating their negative effects, often themselves have negative side-effects on health. Thus while geography and climate *are* autonomous factors, they are far from discrete. The importance of geography underscores the inappropriateness of theories of health and development that do not take account of local variation.

Germs

Germs are also considered to be an autonomous factor affecting health. Enormous efforts have been made in this century to counter the negative health affects of germs, including eradication, attempts to increase individual resistance, and campaigns to increase immunity through controlled infection of entire populations. Modern medicine is in large part based on the conceptual biomedical model of a host (person, animal) attacked by an agent/germ (virus, bacteria) located in an environment. However, successes in reducing the occurrence of many prevalent and lethal communicable diseases, commonly attributed to the discovery of vaccines that provide immunity, may not be due to biomedical science. McKeown (1976) has painstakingly shown that death rates from infectious diseases were decreasing before the identification of the infectious agents and before the development of vaccines. It can be concluded that other factors reduced the amount of exposure and/or the population's level of susceptibility. Awareness is also increasing that humanity may always be challenged by new (or newly defined) germs – such as the HIV that defines AIDS – and that owing to social conditions, older germs – such as cholera, measles, and malaria – will continue to cause infections.

Much of our focus has turned to more complex explanatory models, addressing questions such as: Why are some exposed people susceptible to a disease while others are not? In the language of mathematics, the agent is a necessary 'cause' of the disease, but not a sufficient one. We see the environment as complicated – not just physical, but cultural, social, political, and economic. The host may not in fact be distinct from the environment. Strategies to reduce exposure and increase resistance require interventions at many levels, from the level of the individual human body to the international, and these strategies must take into account a variety of factors such as historical explanations of disease migration, geographic and climatic conditions that are conducive to the survival and reproduction of certain germs, global development issues, living conditions, nutrition, public health, health education, health behavior, individual resistance, and individual genetic susceptibility.

Local environmental conditions

We shall now focus on the interaction between human behavior and the environment and natural resources as distinct from the autonomous environmental factors – geography and climate – discussed above. Among the environmental conditions that are either implicitly or explicitly linked to behavior and health are land utilization, use of toxic chemicals, air quality, energy sources, waste disposal, and the quantity and quality of water. Somewhat further removed, but receiving increasing attention, are global conditions such as warming, destruction of the ozone layer, and desertification.

Much of the literature decrying the damage to the environment has come from writers on development rather than health, although links to health are commonly assumed. Land utilization policies have led to less nutritional diets, to long-term damage to the soil, and to the devotion of 73 percent of global water to irrigation (Dankelman and Davidson 1988) – most of which is lost to the atmosphere or seeps into the ground before reaching the field (InterPress Service 1992). The use of toxic chemicals in agriculture has affected the health and fertility of agricultural workers and the quality of water. Deterioration of air quality in Mexico City and Los Angeles has led to a disturbing increase in lung diseases and mental retardation resulting from damage to fetuses. Women's health has long been affected by cooking on wood or charcoal fires in closed or poorly ventilated rooms. The loss of traditional energy sources, particularly wood, has caused the use of less efficient sources of fire – animal dung, straw, and crop residues – that were previously useful as natural fertilizers. It becomes more and more difficult to prepare nutritious foods, such as beans, which require long cooking. The work burden on those who travel in search of fuel, generally women and children, is also enormously increased.

Little research has been done on these determinants of health, with the exception of water and sanitation. Sagan (1987: 37), paralleling McKeown's arguments about vaccines, questions assumptions that improved water and sanitation directly caused declining mortality rates. He notes that 'improvements in health preceded rather than followed improvements in environmental sanitation.' He presents a complex but convincing argument that mortality reduction was due largely to a decrease in deaths from common, omnipresent viral diseases (diarrhea and respiratory illnesses) rather than in deaths from water- or food-borne diseases that are amenable to hygienic prevention. There is also research showing that the introduction of sanitation and water improvements are ineffective in improving health outcomes unless they are accompanied by changes in behavior such as hand- and food-washing, food preparation, and household cleanliness (Audibert *et al.* 1993; R. Schneider *et al.* 1978). These behavior changes are not necessarily related to economic development; they are more directly related to individual and community priorities, and to the level of education attained by mothers.

Environmental conditions affect the prevalence and type of germs as well as the quality and amount of nutritious food available. The availability and adequacy of natural resources and the local environment depend on geography and climate, national income, and modernization; type of development, the structure and behavior of society, and the politics of distribution. Medical care can remedy some environmentally related health conditions; public health and health behavior can potentially improve or mitigate conditions. Thus, the relationship between natural resources and the local environment and health is complex and probably more indirect than has been assumed, although their importance to quality of life is indisputable.

Societal Factors

National income

A strong belief in economic determinism went hand in hand with positivist theories of development. The reason for supporting development was not just to increase the GNP but also to provide the concomitant benefits of a bigger GNP – one of which, it was assumed, would be better health. Although it was understood that the relationship between income and health outcomes varied according to historic period, it was assumed until about 1980 that economic development affected health principally through the pathway of increased income. The theory was that as income increased, so did health – on both national and individual levels (Cochrane *et al.* 1980). This was reinforced by studies showing a strong relationship, particularly in class-conscious Great Britain, between social class and all measures of health – morbidity, mortality, and functional status (Macintyre 1986). If a direct relationship between GNP and health existed, it was less important to investigate other proximate or more particular determinants, and reasonable to focus all energy on economic development.

However, studies looking at the relationship between GNP and health outcomes have shown a decreasing correlation over time (Caldwell 1986). Wilkinson (1992) has shown that the relationship between GNP and life expectancy is non-linear, with a strong correlation only until GNP per capita reaches $4,000 to $5,000. Cleland and van Ginneken (1989: 20), reviewing the literature on the relationship between education and income, drew 'the broad conclusion that the economic advantages associated with education (income, water and latrine facilities, clothing, housing quality, etc.) account for about one-half of the overall education mortality association.' Thus 50 percent is unexplained by income. Grosse and Auffrey (1989: 284) state that '[l]iteracy has sometimes been considered a proxy for income or wealth, but the evidence points to literacy being directly linked to better health.' In a study done by Mosley in Kenya (1983), only 14 percent of the decline in child mortality between 1962 and 1979 was due to improvement in the household economic situation, while 85 percent was explained by an increase in maternal education.

One finding is that the distribution of income and the uses to which national wealth are put are more important than GNP, at least when GNP is above some minimal level (Wilkinson 1992). Income level and income distribution are different factors. Another finding is that the importance of national income varies according to the historical period and the culture (Kunitz and Engerman 1993). A third is that poverty, which *is* strongly associated with health, is a much more complex concept than income – one that is tightly woven into the structure of society. If economic determinism is no longer accepted as the primary mechanism for improving health, alternatives that include the role of income within a society must be explored.

National income interacts with geography and climate, as we have seen. It affects and is affected by environmental conditions and natural resources. GNP is tightly entwined with modernization, and often taken to be an indicator of that process. The level of health and/or medical care is in part determined by the level of national income (and in part by its distribution). The availability and sufficiency of food is dependent on national income, particularly with regard to structural adjustment policies that foster exportation and reduce subsidies. The multivariate analyses incorporating the education of women that have been key to the re-evaluation of the relationship between national and individual income indicate that factors related to women are particularly important in the calculus of population health.

Modernization

The term 'modernization' is used to indicate many different kinds of changes that have primarily to do with economic growth. 'As used to describe a society, "modern" generally means a national state characterized by a complex of traits including urbanization, high levels of education, industrialization, extensive mechanization, high rates of social mobility, and the like' (Inkeles 1983: 74). Modernization itself – the intended result of development – affects health. There is a substantial literature connecting changing disease patterns in developing countries to changes in lifestyles that accompany industrialization, urbanization, and other cultural dislocations entailed by development (Cassel *et al.* 1960; Dressler *et al.* 1987a, b; Hanna and Fitzgerald 1993; Labarthe *et al.* 1983; Patrick *et al.* 1983). Marmot and Morris (1984: 107), on the basis of work by Trowell and Burkitt (1981), list some diseases 'that are uncommon in non-western countries and that increase

in incidence during the economic and social development of westernization. These include: hypertension, obesity, diabetes, gall-stones, renal
stones, coronary heart disease, appendicitis, haemarrhoids [*sic*], vari-
cose veins, colorectal cancer, hiatus hernia, and diverticular disease.' In
particular, cardiovascular disease and cancer have been studied as
diseases related to development. It is true, however – as we have seen
in Chapter 5 and as we discussed in Chapter 4 – that the prevalence
of chronic diseases in developing countries has been underestimated.

In one of the rare attempts to link the social and personal effects
of modernization, William Dressler (1987b: 679) describes two possible
and not mutually exclusive explanations for the poor health outcomes
that accompany modernization: (1) 'as individuals accumulate more
traits characteristic of modern life there is greater opportunity for value
conflict and stress, which in turn lead to negative changes in health
status'; (2) modernization is a problem only for those who are locked
into a class structure that is discrepant with lifestyle changes – they are
too poor, too underprivileged, too powerless to attain the status to
which they aspire.

Modernization is an unavoidable and powerful force that affects all
societies. It threatens health and jeopardizes opportunities for improved
health at both the social and the individual level. Since modernization
is such a broad concept, we should look at two particularly important
aspects – urbanization and work – in greater detail. Education, a third
major component, will be discussed in Chapter 7.

Urbanization

Urbanization is increasing, so that half of the world's population will
live in cities by the year 2000 (Yach *et al.* 1990). Latin America is expected
to have more than 75 percent of its population living in urban areas.
By 2000, there will be 28 megacities, each with more than 8 million
inhabitants, 22 of which will be in less developed countries (Rossi-
Espagnet *et al.* 1991). Most of this increase, a result of both migration
and population growth rates, is occuring in developing countries, and
is linked to living conditions that are not conducive to good health. An
average of 50 percent of the urban population in developing countries
live in extreme deprivation; more than one billion urban residents will
be severely deprived by the year 2000 (Rossi-Espagnet *et al.* 1991). As
Yach *et al.* point out, unlike the historical patterns of first world urbanization, economic prosperity does not accompany urbanization and
industrialization in developing countries. Urbanization is, rather, an
indication of the failure of rural development.

The health effects are many. Harpham and Stephens (1991) note that third world urban populations suffer from all disease clusters: infectious, 'man'-made, and chronic lifestyle-related diseases. Yach *et al.* (1990: 512) describe 'the health impacts of social instability': sexually transmitted diseases, violence, crime, and substance abuse. Infectious diseases are prevalent because water and sanitation facilities cannot begin to meet the needs of new neighborhoods; crowding and totally inadequate housing lead to the easy spread of these diseases; nutritious food is difficult to obtain. With westernization come 'man'-made ills. There are few controls over industry. The environment suffers from industrial and vehicular pollution. Workers are exposed to hazardous conditions. 'Lifestyle risks' linked to urbanization are also increased. Third world countries have fewer constraints against tobacco, alcohol, and other known risky substances, and are major markets for multi-national and national tobacco and alcohol corporations. Traffic accidents are now a leading cause of death in many cities. In many developing countries, urbanization and unequally distributed gains from economic development have increased economic crimes, which are more and more frequently associated with violence.

On the other hand, it should be recognized that modernization also provides increased opportunity for earned income, access to education and health care, and increased exposure to health education and family planning, all of which may positively affect health. This is particularly true for women who are often restricted by traditional rural mores.

In their review of the literature on urbanization and health (1991: 63), Harpham and Stephens find that most studies have shown either a link between poverty and mortality, morbidity, and causes of death, or – in the few that looked beyond poverty – a link with the environment, particularly water supply and sanitation facilities. They attribute the paucity of broader research to 'the complexity of the acknowledged synergism of physical, social, economic, political and cultural elements in the urban ecosystem.' Yach *et al.* (1990: 512) argue for 'a broad ecological approach' to research on urban health, since population health will be improved only if social, economic, and political factors are addressed.

Work

Certain types of modern employment are most certainly detrimental to health: exposure to pesticides and other hazardous substances, repetitive motions, eye strain from working with small components. While work has rarely been measured and included in analyses of women's health status (except in research that looks at the relationship between work and birth outcomes), it may be a larger determinant of health status in developing countries than in developed ones, since there are generally fewer protections against the exploitation of workers.

Economic development has changed work patterns for both men and women. First, women have greatly increased their participation in the kinds of work that 'count' – get counted. The percentage of women in developing countries who were counted as being in the work force increased from 37 percent in 1950 to 42 percent in 1985. Most of these women are in what is called the informal economy: 'petty trade, commerce, services, and certain branches of manufacturing, both as entrepreneurs and as dependent workers, whether in family enterprises or as wage workers' (Grown and Sebstad 1989). When they do find employment in the formal sector, their jobs are repetitive and low-skilled. Studies that analyze the complex mix of costs and benefits of these changes in work are beginning to appear (Guendelman and Silberg 1993).

Modernization, including urbanization, industrialization, and work, is closely linked to national income, as well as to many other factors at both the social and the individual level. In this section we have described negative relations with certain environmental factors. At the same time, improved environmental conditions – water, sanitation, energy – are considered to be aspects of modernization, as are population control, improved medical and public health services, and improved nutrition. Health behavior is assumed to improve with modernization. Psychosocial processes have also been associated with modernity. As with development, modernization clearly has differential effects by gender. Since women cannot avoid exposure to the threats to health that accompany modernization, urbanization, and certain work situations, they need protective mechanisms, and equitable access to the services and benefits that accompany modernization.

Population and fertility control

Population control receives a great deal of international attention, as overpopulation is seen as a global threat to health and well-being. Explosive population growth endangers the health of the planet. Exhaustion of water and energy supplies, desertification, pollution, and insufficient food supplies will affect the health and the environment of all. Much like environmental conditions, population control is a determinant that affects and is affected by society at many levels (Rosenfield 1991). Development efforts have been shaped and stymied by continued population growth resulting from declining mortality rates that are not accompanied by decreasing birth rates.

However, an exclusive dependence on population reduction in the third world to ensure global survival may be misplaced. At the global level, it can be argued that it is increased consumption rather than increased population that poses the threat. While the two are related, they are not perfectly correlated. One US birth is the 'ecological equivalent' of 25 births in India (Lane 1994). 'The average [US] American, for example, uses 54 times more resources than the average citizen of a developing country in Latin America, Asia, Africa and the Near East' (Coffin 1991: 2). '[T]he industrialized countries of the North, which collectively account for roughly 25 percent of the world's population, consume 75 percent of the globe's energy, 80 percent of all commercial fuel, 85 percent of all wood products and 72 percent of all steel production' (InterPress Service 1993e).

Population control is achieved through fertility control. However, the two concepts are often far apart in the ends that they seek, and in their effects. Population control has been seen as a punishment for the third world – even as a form of genocide (Lane 1994). Population control may, if it is implemented insensitively, lead to health complications, to a reduction of women's self-determination, and to ineffective interventions. Only recently has the international health community begun to move from the rubric of population control to one of reproductive health.

Clearly, fertility control and reproductive health are issues of vital importance to women. Maternity is a major mortality risk condition for women in developing countries, with the risk as high as 10 percent for some (Rosenfield 1991). Fertility control improves women's health by reducing personal risk. Many women prefer to have fewer children. 'It is estimated that more than one-third of the 140 million women in the developing world who became pregnant in 1988 did not want to have another child' (Program for Appropriate Technology in Health 1989: 7). Contraception is being used by only 23 percent of African women who do not want any more children, 43 percent of Asian women, and 57 percent of Latin American women (Eschen and Whittaker 1993).

If contraception is not available, is unacceptable, or fails, many of these women seek abortions. Some 50 to 60 million abortions occur each year. Somewhere between 8 and 27 million of these are illegal or performed by people without medical training (Program for Appropriate Technology in Health 1989). More than one billion people live in areas of the third world where abortion is either prohibited or severely restricted (Dixon-Mueller 1990). About two-fifths of women's pregnancy-related deaths – some 200,000 deaths per year – are due to botched, usually illegal, abortions (Coeytaux *et al.* 1993). Fewer births would also benefit women's families. Since increased time between births leads to better birth outcomes, infant health can be improved through fewer, better-spaced births (Rosenfield 1991). Since smaller families generally mean more resources per person, family health can also be improved.

Also relevant to women's health is the choice of contraceptives available – both because some have negative side-effects and because protection against reproductive tract infections that are frequently caused or aggravated by unprotected intercourse is also important. A narrow focus on the prevention of pregnancy has led to a concentration on sterilization and the development of hormonal methods that often require medical insertion and removal, and can have undesirable side-effects. These provide long-term protection against pregnancy, but none against infections. The male condom is the principal method that provides both infection prevention and effective contraception. Unfortunately, since it is frequently culturally and personally unacceptable (to both men and women), women may adopt other forms of contraception and forgo infection prevention. Women badly need a combined contraception/infection prevention technique that they can control.

The traditional approach to both population reduction and fertility control is through family planning programs. However, as Bello notes (1992–93: 6), successful fertility decline in Sri Lanka, China, and Kerala, India, was 'part of a more wholistic strategy of fertility control, the centerpiece of which must be efforts to radically improve poor people's access to resources, promote the welfare of women, and bring about a more equitable international economic system.' In each of these locations, a more equitable income distribution and greater income and education opportunities for women contributed to the success of governmental programs, although China's success was certainly also largely due to governmental coercion. Emphasis must be switched from society's control of population through narrowly targeted family planning programs to a woman's control of her own fertility as part of an expansion of her options. Empowerment is increasingly linked to fertility control in discussions of population control, as are increasing women's opportunities for education and work. Women's power and status in relation to the men with whom they have intercourse is key to their ability to use contraception.

Population and fertility control can be seen as determinants of health on different levels: global, regional, familial, and individual. They also have extremely complicated interaction patterns with many other factors. Reduction of population can lead to improvements in local and global environmental conditions and in nutrition levels, although there are many other pathways that also need to be followed, particularly the reduction of consumption in the developed world. GNP is affected by population growth rates. Family planning services and techniques are facets of modernization, made available through medical and health care systems. The means to achieve population control – reduced fertility – is itself a health behavior. Attitudes towards fertility and control of fertility are socioculturally engendered, and have major psychosocial ramifications. Population and fertility control deserve particular attention because they are so directly related to women's situations, and because their very complexity brings into play many of the issues that we need to face with regard to improving health.

Gender-based violence and sexual abuse

When women come together to talk about their health, they often identify violence as their major concern. It is, of course, an entirely negative factor, and one whose roots are very difficult to examine – it is related to the organization of society, psychosocial processes, life situations, geopolitics, and basic biology. It affects men, women and children, but, by and large, discussions about its relations to health have focused on women and on the effects of war. Heise *et al.* (1994) have identified the following health consequences of gender-based violence: fatal outcomes – suicide and homicide; physical health consequences – STDs, injury, pelvic inflammatory disease, unwanted pregnancy, miscarriage, chronic pelvic pain, headaches, gynecological problems, alcohol/drug abuse, asthma, irritable bowel syndrome, injurious health behaviors, partial or permanent disability; and mental health consequences – post-traumatic stress disorder, depression, anxiety, sexual dysfunction, eating disorders, multiple personality disorder, and obsessive-compulsive disorder.

Domestic violence may take the form of physical, mental, and/or sexual abuse. While there are no precise data, the Heise study (1994: 4), using extant data, says that 'in many countries one-quarter to more than half of women report having been physically abused by a present or former partner. An even larger percentage have been subjected to ongoing emotional and psychological abuse...' This violence is often accompanied by enforced isolation. While the most direct health effects result from physical battering, the psychic costs of mental and sexual abuse are very high. Among the recognized causes of domestic violence are structural inequities and discrimination, alcohol and drugs, familial cycles of violence, mental illness, stress, frustration, and unique cultural factors (United Nations 1989). Domestic violence is perpetuated because of values that accord women low status, devaluing their lives and their activities.

Sexual abuse is often related to familial power relations, where male partners (and the culture at large, including many women) see women as passive sexual beings whose role is to be receptive on demand. Relationships that do not allow women's consent, sexual expression, and pleasure are abusive. Sexual abuse by a male partner may result in unwanted and physically dangerous pregnancies, increasing the risk of abortion and maternal morbidity and mortality, and the transmission of STDs, greatly increasing the risk of HIV infection and of cervical cancer. Women are often unable to insist on the use of condoms or to practice birth control, and are accused of promiscuity if they do.

Economic conditions are frequently responsible for many women's exposure to sexual abuse. Women exchange sex for financial support – as prostitutes, as part of a pattern of what has been called sexual networking (multi-partnered sexual relations), or with a 'sugar daddy' who will pay for school supplies or food for their children (Heise and Elias 1995). Women and girls are sold by their families to sex traffickers, or kidnapped. While women's economic dependence on men is not a new phenomenon, the AIDS epidemic has brought it to the attention of the health world. In developing countries (as we saw in Chapter 5), the HIV rates between men and women are about the same, now accounting for about 16 percent of the burden of disease in sub-Saharan Africa. Women, particularly adolescent girls, are exposed by single or multiple, long- or short-term partners who do not use condoms. Men increasingly seek out young virginal girls as sexual partners to reduce their own risk of exposure; susceptibility to the HIV virus is increased by early age at first intercourse, an older sexual partner, and the presence of one or more STDs (Heise and Elias 1995). Unless and until women are powerful enough to negotiate their sexual relationships independent of economic benefit, they are at risk of sexual abuse.

While such 'consensual' sex often involves abuse, rape always does. Its physical and psychological effects are devastating (Doyal 1995). Rape is increasingly acknowledged to be a crime of violence and power, not of sex. It is used as a tool of war (and always has been). As the women's movement began to see it as a health problem and to uncover its shocking prevalence in developed countries, it has moved to the forefront as a symbol of gender inequity and the subordination of women.

Genital mutilation is yet one more form of sexual violence that exists because cultural and social norms denigrate women's sexuality and their right to sexual pleasure. The World Bank estimates that it affects between 85 and 114 million women (Heise *et al.* 1994). It has immediate and long-term health effects, including excruciating pain, danger of multiple infections at the time of execution and after, blockage of urinary and menstrual discharge, pain at intercourse, susceptibility to tears and abrasions that increase risks for STDs and HIV, and innumerable problems related to childbirth, as well as the psychological effects of the reduction in or total loss of sexual pleasure.

War is violence writ large and legal. The devastation that it brings to communities and countries is often beyond the bounds to which our empathetic sensibilities can bring us. Its costs are now principally borne by civilians – by women and children. Twenty-two million people have died in wars since the end of World War II in 1945. Eighty percent of those who died were civilians. Nineteen million people are refugees and 24 million displaced as a result of armed conflict (Judd 1995). War is the ultimate form of social disruption, leading to death, injury, permanent disability, rape, cruelty, torture, psychological trauma, infectious disease, malnutrition, starvation, homelessness, infrastructure destruction, family destruction, disruption of health care systems.

Thus violence exists at multiple levels of society, and is supported by a variety of economic and cultural values. At the level of war, it completely negates the production of health, reducing life to survival. It takes on many forms and is so obviously damaging to health that it is often overlooked as a factor. Yet its prevalence, its relations to women's status, and its complex relationship to the organization of society and to psychosocial processes make it a particularly important factor in any consideration of women's health.

The organization of society

Many health problems in both rich and poor countries are still best explained by multiple weakly sufficient causes, or risk factors. Understanding their incidence, prevalence, and distribution, as well as their prevention and treatment, may require intimate understanding of particular people and settings. This demands a different kind of science, one based upon local knowledge, social organization, cultural beliefs and values, and patterns of behaviour, rather than simply universal knowledge of the behaviour of viruses and GNP per capita. (Kunitz 1990: 106)

George Engel (1977: 130) notes that 'in all societies, ancient and modern, preliterate and literate, the major criteria for identification of disease have always been behavioral, psychological, and social in nature.' Medicine evolved as only one of a number of responses to diseases. Engel describes the biomedical model as *our* folk model, and attributes its current primacy to the 'mind–body dualism firmly established under the imprimatur of the Church,' and to classical science's 'notion of the body as a machine, of disease as the consequence of breakdown of the machine, and of the doctor's task as the repair of the machine.' For the past two or three decades, researchers, practitioners, and patients have been moving towards the reintegration of non-biomedical determinants of health into our medically biased folk model.

Several disciplines took the lead in examining the social determinants of health: social epidemiology, social medicine, medical sociology, medical anthropology, and demography. John Cassel was one of the innovators in the field of social epidemiology. He noted that 'a remarkably similar set of social circumstances characterizes people who develop tuberculosis and schizophrenia, become alcoholics, are victims of multiple accidents, or commit suicide,' and that 'common to all these people is a marginal status in society' (Cassel 1976: 100). Syme and Berkman (1976: 5) argue: '[r]ather than attempting to identify *specific* risk factors for *specific* diseases ... it may be more meaningful to identify those factors that affect *general* susceptibility to disease.'

This emphasis on marginality and susceptibility is highly related to studies showing that social class is a major predictor of health status. According to John Cleland (1990: 416):

> the prolonged experience in the West of examining social class differentials suggests that the search for general factors, guided by social science concepts, may be more fruitful than the search for disease-specific risk factors, guided by the traditions of epidemiology....There is a growing consensus that more attention should be paid to general factors that affect many diseases simultaneously.

Link and Phelan (1995, 1996) describe 'fundamental social causes of disease.' Turshen (1989: 24) claims that 'health and disease are products of the way society is organized,' and describes 'a new theory of disease called "the social production of health and illness."' Tesh (1988: 72) reminds us that these theories are not really new. She notes that for Rudolf Virchow, a pathologist writing in the mid-nineteenth century, 'the sources of disease were poverty and unemployment, political disenfranchisement and lack of education.' Friedrich Engels, writing in England at about the same time, saw capitalism as primarily responsible for poverty and disease. Tesh (1988: 75) says: '[i]n the last fifteen years a group of radical thinkers – intellectual descendants of Virchow and Engels – have argued for a new linear model of disease causality, one that turns the old germ theory-based model upsidedown. In their view, microparticles are the last cause of disease, while first place goes to the social system.'

The final set of societal factors we shall look at in this chapter contains many complex and poorly understood 'general factors that affect many diseases simultaneously,' gathered here under the rubric of the organization of society. It can be shown that they determine the distribution of resources and risks faced by groups of people, as well as affecting individual psyches. Although these factors overlap and are highly interactive, each factor has a distinct literature. There has been little effort to consolidate information on social factors into a coherent framework. The social system factors that have been related to health include aspects of social identity such as class, race, gender, age, ethnicity, religion, residence, and marital status. They include poverty and associated factors such as unemployment and increased environmental exposure to threats to health. Cycles of deprivation that affect the health of individuals, families, and communities have been described. The social disorganization that often accompanies rapid change and modernization affects health. The relative inequality and/or perceptions of inequality that accompany different forms of social organization have also been related to poor health. While traditional analyses do often include some of these factors, they are usually treated 'as if they were characteristics of individuals rather than reflections of patterns of society' (Tesh 1988: 76). They are considered to be either immutable (race, gender), intractable (poverty, social disorganization), or outside the realm of health (poverty, social class). The 'new' theory maintains that the organization of society is in fact mutable, and so intrinsic to the realm of health that it is counterproductive to exclude it from consideration.

Much of the literature that provides the basis for this section comes from the industrialized countries, particularly from Great Britain and the United States. This literature is rarely related to underdeveloped and/or non-westernized countries. When the majority of the population is poor and life expectancy relatively short for all, research is driven less by the need to explain disparities and more by the needs of the entire population – the absolute level of health rather than variations in health. Even among the low-income countries, however, poorer health is associated with societal disparities.

Social disadvantage

A large and important group of variables, classified here as social disadvantage, have each, singly and in numerous combinations, been associated with health status. They include social class, race, age, ethnicity, religion, geographic habitat, and marital status. These variables have usually been conceptualized and statistically treated as individual traits that could be 'controlled for' in statistical analyses. It is becoming clear that they are more usefully considered as contextual variables representing group as well as individual characteristics. They denote a person's social identity, which is formed in large part by societal values and attitudes.

Whenever health outcomes are examined in the UK, people in the lower social classes are found to have poorer health, even though a nationalized health care system has made health care accessible to all (Macintyre 1986). This class mortality differential is increasing (Wilkinson 1986). Beside mortality differences, the lower the social class, the greater the prevalence of chronic and acute illnesses and poor mental health. Average height and average birthweight are directly related to social class, with lower classes having lower averages. Finally, self-perceived health status is positively correlated with social class (Macintyre 1986). The gradient that describes the relationship between socioeconomic status (SES) and health is linear (Adler *et al.* 1994). This gradient provides evidence that poverty is not the only factor contributing to health differences, since health effects are also observable at the high end of the income continuum: among the non-poor, SES still demonstrates a positive correlation with health.

Similarly, there are consistent racial differences in health status in the USA that are reflected in mortality, many morbidities, survival from life-threatening illnesses, receipt of medical care, all birth outcomes, and psychological well-being and quality of life (Cockerham 1990; David and Collins Jr. 1991; Kempe *et al.* 1992; Krieger *et al.* 1993; Schoendorf *et al.* 1992; Woolhandler *et al.* 1985). We discussed gender differences in health outcomes in Chapter 5. Obviously, health status differs with age; however, it is important to recognize that within specific sociocultural contexts, age may be related to other health-related disadvantages. In developing countries little formal care is provided for the elderly, while in the USA children are disadvantaged (Rice 1991). Research on ethnicity in the USA shows differences in birth outcomes (Becerra *et al.* 1991; Cabral *et al.* 1990; Forbes and Frisbie 1991; Scribner and Dwyer 1989; Shiono *et al.* 1986; US Department of Health and Human Services 1985). There are differences among religious groups with respect to deaths from heart disease in Britain (Macintyre 1986). Rural/urban differences in health status and mortality exist both in the USA and in Britain (Macintyre 1986; Schneider and Greenberg 1992). Marital status is associated with differences in birth outcomes and in adult health status (Blaxter 1990; Macintyre 1992; Pratt 1988; Wyke 1992).

In general, the factors that reflect social disadvantage have been studied singly. Macintyre (1986: 399) notes that '[e]mpirically of course any individual simultaneously occupies a position on all of these dimensions, and their interactions may have important consequences.' Research on the relationship between social disadvantage and health is in its infancy, and additional social identities are currently being identified and investigated. Difficulties include subgroup definition, subgroup comparisons, interactions among factors, and the use of limiting models (Adler *et al.* 1994; Cooper and David 1986; Dressler 1991; Dressler *et al.* 1992; Krieger *et al.* 1993; Macintyre 1986; Sheldon and Parker 1992). There is a need for innovative research to help interpret the effects of disadvantage. In the absence of adequate quantitative techniques, the incorporation of qualitative methods may enrich understanding and help to explicate the results of quantitative analyses.

Much work – too extensive to describe in this book – has been done to establish the relationships between the factors of social disadvantage and health. They have been demonstrated without a doubt. The question now being asked is *how* disadvantage leads to poor health. The Black Report on inequalities in health (D. Black *et al.* 1982), which offered a number of explanations for disparities in health related to social class, initiated a discussion that is still ongoing. As reported succinctly by Krieger *et al.* (1993: 94), the Black Report and its 1987 follow-up (M. Whitehead 1987) consider:

> the following four explanations of social inequalities in health: 1) artifact of measurement, 2) natural or social selection, 3) materialist/structural, and 4) cultural/behavioral. Both reports conclude that social inequalities in health are real, that only a small amount can be attributed to social or natural selection, and that material/structural conditions are the fundamental determinant of these inequalities in health, through their direct effects upon health and through their shaping of cultural/behavioral practices that further influence health.

A more recent study of Swedish twins led its authors to conclude that health selection, social causation, *and* childhood experiences are all important in the association between social class and health (Lichtenstein *et al.* 1992).

While it has generally been assumed that social class and race, the most frequently examined forms of social disadvantage, lead to poorer health primarily through the bad living conditions, poor nutrition, lack of education, lack of access to medical care, and 'unhealthy' lifestyles that are associated with poverty (Black *et al.* 1982; Blane 1985), some data conflict with this theory. Certain birth outcomes, such as very low birthweight rate, differ little between educated and middle-class black women and poor black women in the USA (Kleinman and Kessell 1987). A study by Otten *et al.* (1990) showed that about one-third of the difference in black–white mortality among middle-aged adults is *not* attributable to the most obvious risk factors, which include income (explaining 38 percent), smoking, blood pressure, cholesterol, body mass index, alcohol intake, and diabetes. It is becoming clear that racism, classism, and sexism have additional, independent effects on health. As we shall see in a later section on psychosocial determinants of health and their relationship to neurohormonal systems, this is not surprising. Adler *et al.* (1994) identify health behaviors, psychological characteristics, psychological stress, and effects of social ordering as possible explanations for the persistent SES/health gradient that they investigated. Chronic stress, poor self-image, lack of social support, lack of actual and perceived control, are all probable results of external and internalized oppression. Thus it is highly probable that visible effects of poverty are compounded by psychosocial factors.

The linkage between social disadvantage and empowerment is strong – social disadvantage results in part from powerlessness and from structural constraints on the opportunities available to groups of people. Empowerment is a strategy designed to reverse or mitigate this situation, motivated by a recognition of disadvantage and inequity. If it is successful, it should also reverse or mitigate the negative health affects associated with social disadvantage.

Poverty

The existence of findings indicating that discrimination and social disadvantage lead to poor health does not reduce the importance of poverty as a factor affecting health; rather, these findings identify other pathways that act both separately and in conjunction with poverty to affect health. Poverty and class have generally gone hand in hand as control of the economy provides both subsistence and privileges. Poverty is also closely related to other aspects of social disadvantage such as race, ethnicity, gender, age, and residence (Blaxter 1983). Today, in a world with five and a half billion people, more than one billion live in absolute poverty. As with health, poverty has both macro- and micro-level determinants. The economic and social structure of a society interact with the earning potential of a family or an individual. There has been a continuing dialogue in the health literature as to whether poor health leads to poverty (individual focus) or vice versa (social focus). Obviously both can be true. For example, if a society does not provide support for those who are disabled, they will be or become poor. However, as Blaxter states (1983: 1141), poverty itself produces poor health:

> [T]he dangers to health associated with poverty are many and well-known: inadequate or unbalanced nutrition (especially for childbearing women and for children), dangerous or physically exacting work, inadequate or polluted water supply, atmospheric pollution, housing which is overcrowded, damp or insufficiently protective against the climate, absence of convenient household equipment and a domestic situation in which cleanliness and hygiene are difficult, a dangerous environment, especially for children (traffic-filled streets, unclean rivers, a lack of civil order), a lack of education and especially of health knowledge, a lack of social stability, an atmosphere of frustration, hopelessness, anger or conflict.

Given the importance of wage labor as a source of income, unemployment is a major cause of poverty. There is a large literature on the effects of unemployment on health, again mostly from the USA and Great Britain. While it is impossible to disentangle the effects of reduced income, class, status, and security, health effects for unemployed workers (males), their wives, and their children have been documented (Blaxter 1990; Dahl 1993; Marmot and Morris 1984). Income-earning potential is thus one important determinant of poverty; the use of earned income is another. Since the household is traditionally the unit of analysis in economic studies, attention has been paid to household economic behavior. Not surprisingly, when women began to look at issues of income and expenditure, they questioned traditional assumptions that a household is a clearly defined entity, that its members have the same goals and the same behaviors, and that its living conditions automatically improve as income increases. The issue of men's use of at least some of their income for personal pleasures and women's use of all their available resources for immediate family needs – health care, food, clothing, shelter, and education – is complex, and related to cultural values (Bruce 1989). It has been shown, however, that household income is not necessarily correlated to behaviors that improve health. In fact, Bruce (1989) refers to a study from Kenya (Hanger and Moris 1973) showing that when family income increased because women worked for their husbands' income-generating agriculture and no longer grew and marketed their own crops, their personal income decreased, and the nutritional levels of their children fell.

The cycle of deprivation

While immediate poverty has important consequences for health status, much of the research on poverty and health has been more concerned with the internalization and perpetuation of long-term poverty, and with groups identified as 'the poor.' Oscar Lewis first defined a culture of poverty while trying to describe the multigenerational pattern of disadvantage he observed in his anthropological studies of Mexican families (Bullough 1972; Lewis 1983). A concept that parallels the culture of poverty is that of the underclass – a group of people mired in the culture of poverty for more than one generation. This is also principally a US concept. There are several ways of assigning individuals to the underclass: persistent poverty; behaviors and attitudes such as crime, drug use, welfare dependency; neighborhoods; or combinations of these (Mincy *et al.* 1990). Such theses, holding that poverty – and poor health – are somehow self-perpetuating, have been strongly disputed (Blaxter 1983; Foldy 1990). At the bottom of this dispute are questions of cause – Are the poor responsible for their own poverty, or are there other explanations? – and strategies for change – Is individual or structural change more useful? There is much evidence that descriptions of the culture of poverty or of the underclass are simply incorrect – that much of what has been classified as socially pathological behavior is in fact cultural adaptation (Greenstone 1991); that fewer people fit the description of underclass than is commonly believed (Jencks 1991); that economic, political, and social policies have created a no-win situation for ghetto residents (di Leonardo 1992); and that the concept does not help us to find solutions to violence, drug use, and alienation (Foldy 1990). Persistent poverty, however, is undeniably debilitating and in need of remedy.

While the culture of poverty and the underclass were being discussed in the USA, a similar concept called the cycle of deprivation or cycle of disadvantage was under investigation in Britain. It was studied in relation to economic status and living conditions, intellectual performance, occupation, crime and delinquency, psychiatric disorder, and family behaviors (Rutter and Madge 1976). Mildred Blaxter (1981, 1982) extended the research into health. She described three different types of cycles in relation to health. The first (which we discussed in the section on social disadvantage) concerns subgroups of the population – socioeconomic, racial, geographic – who have a disproportionate number of health problems over time; the second, the life cycle of an individual and the likelihood of remaining in a state of disadvantage over that lifetime; and the third, intergenerational effects of disadvantage. Among the factors Blaxter identifies as related to an individual's life cycle are genetically transmitted impairments, prenatal and birth factors; risks from parental characteristics and childhood environment; disadvantages such as race and class as an adult; less access to medical services; and behavioral risk factors. The evidence of intergenerational effects on health has been most commonly studied in relation to birthweight (Baird 1974; Emanuel 1986; Starfield *et al.* 1991: 1167).

Social disorganization

While poverty, unemployment, and cycles of disadvantage are not necessarily related to social disorganization, an association is often found. The concept of social disorganization – the breakdown or lack of a social fabric – seems to have come from social epidemiology. John Cassel (1976) saw social disorganization as chronic stress due to disordered personal relationships and lack of predictability. Using findings from both animal and human research to relate social disorganization to health, he suggested that the way social organization affects one is determined by both personal and social factors. He felt that racial health disparities in the USA could be understood as a result of the social marginalization of blacks – that subservience in and of itself affects health and/or that social disorganization reduces the number of available protective buffers. Oppression and social marginality reduce both one's adaptability and the available social supports, thereby increasing susceptibility in a non-specific manner that leads to many different diseases and illnesses (Cassel 1974). The relationship between oppression, poverty, and social disorganization is reflected in the marginality of those who live in ghettos with high rates of unemployment and few services. Much recent work has focused on the fact that the kind of neighborhood one lives in plays a major part in establishing one's susceptibility (Collins and David 1992; Egolf *et al.* 1992; Haan *et al.* 1987; James and Kleinbaum 1976; Zapata *et al.* 1992).

Income inequality

While poverty, unemployment, cycles of deprivation, and social disorganization have relatively clear and studied relationships to health, there is an additional, less explored social factor that may have an independent effect: income inequality. Richard Wilkinson (1990: 392) has been investigating why GNP is not perfectly related to health, and has found that 'as countries get richer the relationship between life expectancy and average income appears to weaken and be replaced by the growing influence of income distribution.' He argues that in some way, which we do not yet understand, perceptions of equity and of equality directly affect health:

> It looks as if what matters about our physical circumstances is not what they are in themselves, but where they stand in the scale of things in our society. The implication is that our environment and standard of living no longer impact on our health primarily through direct physical causes, regardless of our attitudes and perceptions, but have come to do so mainly through social and cognitively mediated processes.... It seems increasingly that what matters now is the way we are led in modern societies to experience our circumstances and the social and behavioural repercussions which that socially constructed experience has. *In short, it appears that health is now a psychosocially mediated function of the structure of inequality in society.* [emphasis added]

George Davey Smith (1996) describes national-level studies that have shown a correlation between income inequality and infant mortality, life expectancy, height, and morbidity. He and others are now suggesting that income inequality is but one aspect of social inequality that affects health. In a groundbreaking book on the health of populations, Robert Evans *et al.* (1994) identify 'social hierarchies' as the key to the health of populations, and investigate their correlates. Davy Smith warns us that aspects of health such as psychological distress, general well-being, and morbidity may be more rapidly affected than is mortality by the 'increasing inequality and social polarisation' that so many societies are experiencing.

Caldwell (1986: 182) has discussed the role of equity and ideology in the developing-country context. He found

> striking parallels between Sri Lanka, Kerala, and Costa Rica [three countries/states with high health status and relatively low GNPs] ... a substantial degree of female autonomy, a dedication to education, an open political system, a largely civilian society without a rigid class structure, a history of egalitarianism and radicalism and of national consensus arising from political contest with marked elements of populism.

It has been shown that political organization and ideology affect population health outcomes (Cereseto and Waitzkin 1986; Cereseto and Waitzkin 1988; Lena and London 1993; Moon and Dixon 1985). Societies that accord status and education to women have better population health outcomes than those that do not (Caldwell 1986). Racism, regardless of income, negatively affects health (Krieger *et al.* 1993). Thus equality in realms other than income may be equally important to health. Although stratification may be an inevitable concomitant of social organization, there are great variations in the degree, intensity, and stability of social relations. It seems likely that increased equity in any and all realms will positively affect health. If we are to measure and test this thesis, concentrated efforts to gather data on inequalities of all sorts are needed.

Summary and conclusions

Poverty – as measured by income or class, or some other criterion – is widely accepted as a determinant of health. Unemployment, both as a pathway to poverty and as a factor with psychosocial implications, negatively affects health. The distribution of income within a household is an additional factor. Cycles of deprivation have a negative effect on health above and beyond the immediate effects of poverty. Social disorganization also has effects beyond its direct relationship to poverty. Finally, the experience of inequality itself has been implicated in negative health outcomes. How these strands intersect, travel in parallel, or reinforce one another is unexplored. It is not unreasonable, however, to conclude that treating inequity and inequality as fundamental causes of poor health, and striving to remedy them, may be both indirectly effective by helping to reduce poverty, unemployment, and social disorganization, and directly effective by reducing exposure to these pathogens.

All the factors discussed in this section on social organization – oppression and social disadvantage, short- and long-term poverty, inequality, and social disorganization – go hand in hand and lead to poorer health. They present immediate threats to health through exposure to violence, substance abuse, and environmental dangers, as well as their effects on psychosocial processes, which I shall describe below. Historical analyses have indicated that increasing social complexity has brought with it both threats to health through increased density, interactions, and hierarchical structures, and improvements in many different conditions that have led to increased longevity. While the variety of organizational forms is great, the negative factors described in this section are omnipresent. Krieger *et al.* (1993: 109) see inequality as the spider weaving the web of threats to health, and recommend concentrating on the spider: 'Continuing merely to catalog individual risk factors from an amorphous "web of causation" no longer can suffice. If our goal is to alter the web rather than merely break its strands, it is time to look for the spider.' Whether inequality is seen as the spider or as contributing pervasive strands to a spiderless web that are damaging to health, it is suggested here that empowerment may work to strengthen and reinforce salutogenic factors, and weaken some

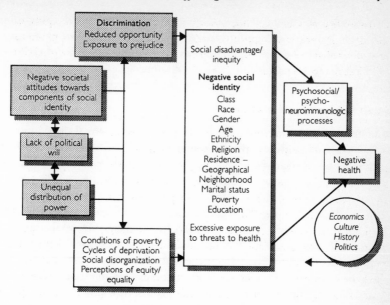

Figure 6.1 The organization of society as it relates to negative health

that are pathogenic. In particular, it is one strategy designed to act at the level of social organization by decreasing the effects of social inequity and increasing protective resources that lead to well-being.

I have developed Figure 6.1 to link together the concepts grouped here under social organization and to place them in a broad model that relates the organization of society to negative health. This model only begins to explore the relations among societal factors, and between these factors and health. The unshaded portions are elements that I will discuss in this section; the shaded elements are intended to fill out the framework. Although not enough is known about how such factors affect either one another or health, the evidence indicates that they are extremely important, and deserve primacy in further research on the determinants of population health.

In this model, social disadvantage is seen as a proximate determinant of health. It consists of an internalized, negative social identity, based on the factors discussed above, which affects health through psychosocial and psychoneuroimmunologic processes. Social disadvantage also directly affects health negatively, by increasing exposure to threats such as violence and through lack of basic resources. Societies act both through straightforward discrimination and through more complex and less direct means such as social disorganization to create and reinforce social identity and life circumstances. These disadvantages can be traced back to attitudes with regard to difference and status, to a lack of the political will needed to remedy recognized structural inequities, and to the unequal distribution of power that is inherent in the organization of all societies. The unequal distribution of power is closely related to 'the reluctance of central authorities to devolve power' (Carr-Hill 1992: 44), and those with power to devolve are not only politicians but others in areas such as health and development policy and practice.

Clearly, by affecting the relationships between individuals, societies, and local and global environments, the many facets of social organization are also interrelated with the other determinants discussed in this chapter. Geography, unhealthy local environmental conditions, the lack or maldistribution of national income, and modernization are factors that can predispose certain groups towards poverty, disadvantage, and social disorganization; while susceptibility to germs, violence, sexual abuse, and lack of access to health and medical care can result – at least in part – from disadvantage and disorganization.

Factors Directly Related to Health and Medicine

Medical technology and medical care

As with economic development, the historical congruence of improvements in population health status with the development of medical technology and the professionalization of medical care led to assumptions about causality. In general, quite naturally, the association of interest was with illness and disease reduction, based primarily on germ theory, rather than on positive aspects of health. For the purposes of this book, medical care is defined as individual care that is predominantly curative and rehabilitative. It is distinguished from primary care/ public health, which is defined as more oriented towards prevention and promotion, and concerned with the health of groups of people.

Medicine's success in the twentieth century has led to rising expectations with regard to its effectiveness in achieving health as well as preventing and curing illness (Ehrenreich and English 1978). In the USA, where more than 10 percent of the GNP goes towards health care, more than 87 percent of that money goes to medical care (Rice

1990). In general, developing countries have followed a similar pattern. However, the effectiveness of medical care and its relationship to health have been questioned (Illich 1976; Sagan 1987). In developed countries, the greatest decreases in mortality preceded medical advances. The development of antibiotics and immunizations, while they have been invaluable in saving individual lives, probably had minimal effects on overall mortality rates, since these were already decreasing at the time of their introduction (Sagan 1987). Studies often show that medical care makes less difference than is generally supposed: age-adjusted cancer death rates are unchanged over the last fifty years; ten-year survival rates for heart patients with and without bypass surgery are similar; and even the value of perinatal care is unproven (Sagan 1987). Moreover, the effect of health services is less in currently underdeveloped countries than in those that developed earlier; and as developed countries mature, the effect of services decreases (Pendleton and Yang 1985).

McKeown (1976: 172) defines the realm of medicine as 'the prevention of sickness and premature death and the care of the sick and disabled,' specifically placing the creation of positive health outside this realm. In addition, even in developed countries most illness is unattended by physicians (Banks *et al.* 1975; Demers *et al.* 1980). While the value of curative medicine as a producer of health is questionable in developed countries, it is more clearly a negative contributor in developing countries: 'For the poor countries of the world, the western approach to health has been a total disaster. It has focused on lavish buildings, imported equipment and drugs, and expensively trained personnel. Its cost has put health care of any kind way beyond the reach of the majority in almost every third world country' (Harrison 1981: 294–5).

On the other hand, one should not thoughtlessly extrapolate from the past to the future. While medical care probably had very little impact before the twentieth century, many 'modern' conditions *are* amenable to medical care. Kunitz (1990) shows large declines in developed countries during the 1960s and 1970s for causes of death that are amenable to medical intervention, such as infant mortality, tuberculosis, chronic rheumatic heart disease, hypertensive disease, appendicitis, and maternal deaths. For women, the prevention of maternal deaths is particularly important, with 585,000 deaths a year and with women in developing countries being twenty times more likely to die from childbirth-related causes than those in developed countries (Boerma 1987). Another condition showing great disparity is survival of cervical cancer, owing to the lack of availability of screening tests and treatment in developing countries (World Health Organization

1992). However, Evans *et al.* (1994: 39) suggest that in modern societies 'we are reaching the limits of medicine.'

McKeown (1976) downplayed the roles of both preventive and curative medicine, but has now become a target for those who feel that health care services have had a greater role in reducing mortality than he acknowledged (Susser 1993). Attention is being paid to different rates and different patterns of the transition from infectious to chronic diseases – among countries that were early to develop, among developing countries, and between developed and developing countries. There has been a great deal of research, of varying quality and some controversy, on the effect of health and medical services in the third world today (Dajer 1991a, 1991b; Garfield 1991; Paul 1991; Sandiford *et al.* 1991).

None the less, medical care probably does not have a major direct role in the production of health, particularly on a population level. It does, however, interact with many other factors. Medical care interacts with germs and diseases related to the environment, even to the extent of causing mutations in infectious agents. Its provision is related to national levels of income and modernization. Population and fertility control come under the domain of medical technology and care. The borders between medical care and public health are fuzzy, with each reinforcing the effectiveness of the other, as we shall see in the next section. At the individual level, health behavior is related to the use of care, and medical care providers attempt to influence health behavior. Genetic factors relate to medical care through disease and susceptibility to disease, and will increasingly come under the control of technology and medical care.

Public health services/primary care

Public health services and primary care also evolved historically at a time when population health was generally improving; researchers have therefore focused on its causal role, often in relation to theories about the lack of effectiveness of medical care. Health care can be defined loosely as services that workers in or adjunct to the health system provide; it can include nutrition programs, immunizations, well-child care, perinatal care programs, water and sanitation improvements, health education, referrals to medical care, treatment of illness, family planning, first aid, and much more. The relation between public health and medical care is not well defined, and shifts over time. Their domains were distinct only until immunizations linked community prevention and individual care (Institute of Medicine 1988).

Much current discussion about public health services revolves around synergistic relationships among health services, parental attitudes, and maternal education. Caldwell (1986) reports on a Nigerian study where mothers' level of schooling and easy access to health care together accounted for 87 percent of gain in life expectancy at birth. Alone, however, access accounted for only 20 percent and education for 33 percent.

The health care system has synergistic relationships with the environmental and societal determinants that have been discussed above. It must deal with environmental hazards and the threats to population health associated with poverty and social disorganization. Along with education, the distribution and quality of public health services indicate how much the government cares to protect the poor. Since governments are responsive to pressures from within as well as without, those countries with a strong egalitarian tradition are more likely to have demands placed on them for public health, and more likely to respond to those demands (Caldwell 1993). Structural adjustment policies are weakening the public health sector, along with education, in much of the third world. The impact is borne primarily by women, who are the principal providers of health care. The health care system is better positioned than the medical care system to reach more – particularly poor – people. None the less, health care, like most of the other factors discussed hitherto, is controversial, or at least poorly understood, as a determinant of health, because its effectiveness has varied depending on cultural, political, and historical circumstances.

Individual-Level Factors

So far in this chapter I have reviewed three groups of factors related to health: environmental conditions, including geography, germs, and local environmental conditions; selected societal factors that act on groups and/or are measured at group levels, including national income, modernization, population and fertility control, gender-based violence and sexual abuse, and the organization and disorganization of society; and factors directly related to health, including medical technology, medical care, and public health. My review is far from comprehensive – it is intended to demonstrate the many connections between what are generally treated as discrete and independent factors, and some of what we do not know about the relationships between these factors and health. I will now discuss another complex set of factors that function primarily at the individual level.

Health education and health behavior

While I have classified health education as a health care factor and health behavior as an individual one, I will discuss them jointly, since health education is specifically designed to effect behavior changes that will improve health. Much poor health has been traced to 'unhealthy' behaviors. Such behaviors may relate to the use of water and sanitation in developing countries or to 'lifestyle' in developed countries. Health educators have put great effort into understanding their determinants. Models that take into account values, attitudes, beliefs, and knowledge as well as intentions, desire, habit, and facilitating conditions have been proposed and tested (Wallston and Wallston 1984). Unsurprisingly, results of research into health behavior vary according to the behavior, the culture, and the model. Much of what 'causes' behavior remains unexplained.

At the simplest level, health behavior models assume individual-level relationships like those represented in Figure 6.2. Each of the links represented in this figure, however, is problematic, with health education not necessarily changing beliefs or behavior, beliefs not necessarily corresponding to behavior (Blaxter 1990), risks not necessarily affected by behavior (G. Rose 1985), and behavior change and decreased risk not necessarily producing the desired health outcomes (Blaxter 1990; G. Rose 1985). Thus each of the arrows in the model is tentative. While health behaviors do have an effect on health outcomes, they are part of a complex set of factors that includes individual susceptibility, risk, and societal and environmental conditions that are often more important determinants of health status than are behaviors.

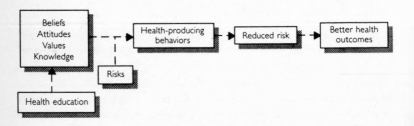

Figure 6.2   Simple model of positive health behavior

Behavior change is difficult, embedded in individual and cultural habits and traditions, and often dependent on the availability of resources and time. Knowledge that cannot be implemented owing to lack of resources, or power, or to competing needs and values, may induce guilt rather than changed behavior.

Societal factors must be added to this model. The emphasis on social as opposed to individual determinants of behavior has been incorporated into health education by Guy Steuart (Steckler *et al.* 1993). For Steuart, health education and other interventions designed to change behaviors should be community public health activities, carried out with the help of professionals but not controlled by them. They should be based on a social analysis and focus on people's strengths rather than weaknesses (Eng *et al.* 1992). He saw the health of the community as integrally related to the health of the individual. The latter cannot be improved without strengthening the former – improving the 'health' or competence of the community will simultaneously reduce risk to and increase resistance of individuals.

Societal norms, often specific to class, race, ethnic, or geographic group, and to gender, play a large role in all known determinants of health behavior. A change in norms may quickly lead to behavior change. Some writers have attributed the powerful effect of women's education on children's health to an unconscious adoption of norms conducive to health, such as cleanliness. Attitudes (and beliefs) 'are widely shared and rooted in social groups.' In fact, 'social and collective phenomenon [*sic*] precede individual phenomenon [*sic*] such as attitudes' (Yach 1992: 608). Blaxter (1990: 243) found that education is an important determinant of health, 'more because better education is associated with general differences in patterns of life than because discrete parts of a lifestyle can be changed.' Rose (1985: 38) states: 'mostly people act for substantial and immediate rewards, and the medical motivation for health education is inherently weak.... Much more powerful as motivators for health education are the social rewards of enhanced self-esteem and social approval.'

Health education and health behavior are frequently the factors that those seeking to improve the health of disadvantaged populations select for intervention. All too often, results are disappointing. It is difficult to disentangle problems with the implementation of an intervention from basic flaws in theory. As we continue to put scarce resources into these areas, we should develop more effective evaluation strategies and uncover relationships between education, behavior, and environmental, societal, and individual factors that will increase the effectiveness of our interventions.

HAROLD BRIDGES LIBRARY
S. MARTIN'S COLLEGE
LANCASTER

Nutrition

The relationship between nutrition and health status is surprisingly complex. While it is true that certain diseases come from or are associated with more or less clearly established nutritional deficiencies – goiter from iodine deficiency, a type of blindness and, more recently, diarrhea from vitamin A deficiency, neural tube defects from insufficient folic acid, rickets from vitamin D deficiency, and scurvy from lack of vitamin C – the general relationship between overall nutrition and health is more problematic.

Much as when research attempts to clarify the relationship between water and infectious disease, the closer one looks, the more elusive, complicated, and confounded is the pattern. McKeown (1976) attributed declines in infectious diseases to improved nutrition, but his argument has since been rebutted (Landers 1993). It is still not clear what nutritional level – beyond that which prevents starvation – is necessary to prevent disease (Hamilton *et al.* 1984; Sagan 1987; Thomson 1959). While breastfeeding infants for one year is one of the best means of reducing infant mortality, the importance of breastfeeding is not the nutritional value of the mother's milk; rather, due to the transmission of immune status and to the avoidance of contaminated containers and liquids, breastfeeding greatly reduces the incidence of infection in infants, particularly diarrheal and respiratory infection. Infection, and the resultant disease, are thought to have a bidirectional relationship with malnutrition: malnutrition reduces resistance to infection, particularly in children, and disease episodes often lead directly to malnutrition. However, two recent reviews of community studies of this relationship question the causal pathway from diarrhea to malnutrition (R.E. Black 1991; Briend 1990).

Whatever the evidence, the provision of an adequate diet (the word *adequate* is poorly defined) is still considered to be necessary for health. And hunger, whether or not it has long-term effects on health, is personally debilitating, greatly affecting the quality of life. Nancy Scheper-Hughes (1992) has vividly described 'the savagery of hunger' in her anthropological study of everyday life in northeast Brazil. As with sanitation and water, however, the mere provision of food is not enough to ensure health. Behavioral and educational factors play a large role in the selection, preparation, and distribution of food within the family.

The interaction of nutrition with multiple factors on multiple levels only complicates the already cloudy relationship between nutrition and health. Nutrition interacts with genetic, developmental, and activity factors, with income, education, and status within the family, with land use and economic organization, and with national and international development strategies, including structural adjustment policies. On a macro-level, nutrition is integrally related to economic and political policies. Hunger and famine result from wars, unjust distributional patterns, and market conditions that favor those who already have resources. Development has not necessarily led to improved nutrition for all (Hernandez *et al.* 1974; Vaughan and Moore 1988).

Genes/genetics

Although genetics is classified here as an individual-level factor, the discussion will be broader than the role played by an individual's genes in her or his health. It also includes the field of genetics which is part of medical care, and therefore a societal-level factor. The genetic contribution to health is difficult to measure, although this is currently one of the areas of greatest scientific activity. Society is right on the edge of a complete unraveling of the mysteries of human genetic structures (Bishop and Waldholz 1990). Some 3,000 conditions, such as sickle cell anemia, Tey Sachs disease, and congenital birth defects, are clearly genetic in origin. Others may or may not be related to genetics – the susceptibility of some children in developing countries who die from common respiratory illnesses while others do not; the propensity of some families or societies to obesity, alcoholism, certain cancers; the possible propensity of blacks to have lower birthweight babies than whites in the USA.

Chromosome-determined differences appear to play a deterministic role in health, at least during the fetal and neonatal stages. Females have a more efficient immune system than do males (Sagan 1987). Although there are strong gender differences in survival at all ages in developed countries, one cannot be sure beyond infancy that the causes are purely genetic, not socially and culturally linked. Thus sex provides a starting point and some basic information about susceptibility, but it is gender – sex as affected by culture – that must be explored if we are to understand women's health.

As the field of genetics accrues more knowledge, we will understand more about the role that genes play in the health and illness of individuals and of genetically related families. It will also be true that geneticists and their practices will have major impacts on the health of population subgroups. As scientific developments in genetic manipulation become part of medical practice, issues of equity and social justice in medical care will gain increasing importance. In the case of genetically caused diseases that are either preventable through genetic manipulation or curable through some intervention, the problem is one of availability and accessibility to all. In the areas of non-preventable genetically caused diseases, disease susceptibility, and undesirable traits that become identifiable but for which there are no treatments, the issue is stigmatization.

We are approaching a time when an individual's genetic composition will be decipherable, and while some important diseases may be eradicable, control over genetics may also lead to even greater population disparities in health and survival. The relationship between genes and health will be redefined as controllable, and the impact of genetics on health may be major. Whether that impact will be positive or negative will be dependent on many other factors – medical and health care, cultural norms, education, power and status relationships, and income.

Psychosocial factors and psychoneuroimmunology

All the factors I have just discussed – health education/health behavior, nutrition, and genes/genetics – have both individual and social components and effects, although they are generally treated as individual-level determinants. The next set of factors is in the same domain. Because of their importance, and the lack of clarity in the very extensive literature that deals with them, I will discuss them in much greater detail, primarily through a review of the literature. This set of factors rivals social organization in its complexity and centrality to health. There is an exceptionally large psychosocial literature on the effects on health of stress, social support, and other coping mechanisms, almost all of which comes from industrialized nations. A relatively new field entitled psychoneuroimmunology provides a framework that can be used to link these concepts. This field concerns itself with the extremely complicated relationships between the immune system, the central nervous system, and the hormonal system. It attempts to answer a major question: by what mechanisms do psychosocial factors cause or otherwise affect health and disease?

The question is motivated by several observations. Certain socially situated groups of people are more likely to get any one of a number of illnesses (Cassel 1976); given the same level of exposure, some people become ill while others do not (Ader 1980); and certain personal experiences are known to be related to illness onset (Locke 1982). The first research efforts designed to address these issues were dedicated to showing that there was in fact a measurable, possibly causal, relationship between psychosocial factors and health. Among the psychosocial factors that have been explored are stress – which serves as a general rubric for all kinds of presumably negative personal and social experiences; the relationship between certain behaviors – such as exercise, nutrition, substance abuse – and stress; and resistance resources/ vulnerability – which include personal coping mechanisms, social support, personality traits such as alienation, sense of coherence, and locus of control, and personality states such as mood, nerves, depression, and loneliness. Among the health outcomes most commonly investigated in relation to psychosocial factors are survival, infection, cancer, birthweight, and blood pressure.

Many psychosocial factors are poorly defined and difficult to measure. Measurement tools proliferate but are difficult to validate, in part because of the imprecision of the concepts. The factors are not all conceptually distinct. Some are thought to be negative (loneliness) and some positive (social support). Some of those may be different poles of a single dimension; some may be independently related only to positive health or only to negative health. Any one may interact with another, and may have different meaning and impact in different cultures and different subgroups within a culture. Clear gender differences have been found with regard to importance and interactions. Thus although there is an enormous accumulation of evidence of an association between many different individual psychosocial factors and health, and some work on the interaction of multiple factors, there is an alarming lack of coherence. The area is diffuse and has generated a lot of research, which has not always produced consistent findings. In fact, research has not demonstrated that established relationships between psychosocial factors and mental illness or depression can be extended to physical health, or that determinants of cancer survival are similar to determinants of high blood pressure.

I have described empowerment as a strategy to modify the psychosocial environment of individuals as well as to effect longer-term changes in structural conditions. If we are to understand the relationship between the empowerment of women and their health, it is necessary to understand the psychosocial factors affecting women both as as individuals and as members of groups. I will begin by presenting a model that helps to relate the many factors in this domain that have been implicated in health and disease processes, then briefly present current research information on many of those factors.

Psychosocial factors and the immune system

If there are relationships between psychosocial factors and health, what are they? For conditions known to be affected by the immune system, such as cancers and infections, the most promising pathway seems to be through the immune system, which in turn is affected by hormonal secretions and by the central nervous system. Since it is possible to measure hormonal levels, nervous system responses, and indicators of immune status, another extensive literature exists on the relationship between the psychosocial factors described above and different aspects of hormonal, central nervous, and immune system behavior. As Howard Kaplan (1991: 911–12) points out, however:

> The literature on the relationships between psychosocial (primarily stress-related) variables and indices of immune system responses is so heterogeneous as to seriously challenge an observer's capacity to find any order at all among these studies. First, diverse measures of a range of psychosocial factors for different populations are related to any of numerous indicators of immune function.... Second, a given psychosocial variable may be associated with some markers of immune functions but not with others.... Third, the same psychosocial variables may have effects on the immune system that are at once interpretable as depressing and enhancing.... Finally a given indicator of immune competence that is ordinarily taken to suggest immunosuppression when evaluated as part of a systemic reaction in fact may indicate immunocompetence.

Even if one could find order in this literature, one would be left with a very important question: Is health affected by these immune reactions that follow psychosocial experiences? Are cancer or cardiovascular disease or headaches 'caused' or exacerbated by immunosuppression that is directly related to psychosocial factors? Research at this level is just beginning, driven in part by a desire to prolong the lives of persons with AIDS and to improve the quality of their lives. One study has shown that academic stress, considered to be a mild form of stress, delayed immune response (Kiecolt-Glaser and Glaser 1992). The authors suggest that this delay could place those feeling more stress at greater risk for more severe illness. However, no matter how clearly one understands that the 'stressor' triggers a response from the brain, the nervous system, and the immune system, it is important to know why the stressor has a negative effect (Vingerhoets and Marcelissen 1988). Interventions will take place at the level of the stressor, not at the biochemical or biophysical level.

While several writers have tried to clarify the morass described above, Howard Kaplan has come closest to that goal. G.A. Kaplan (1985: 239) states: '[p]rogress in psychosocial epidemiology will depend to a great extent on our ability to convert long lists of variables to coherent theories or models.' Howard Kaplan (1991) presents a model,

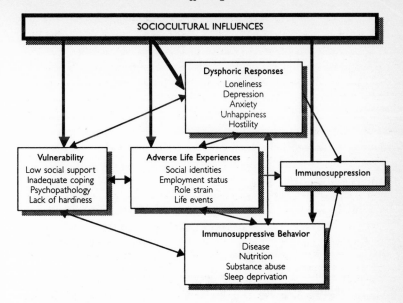

Figure 6.3 Psychosocial influences on immunosuppression

Source: H. Kaplan (1991: 919, slightly modified), reprinted with permission from Elsevier Science Ltd.

which I have slightly simplified in Figure 6.3, that clarifies the pathways from psychosocial influences to immunosuppression.

Some explanations are in order. First, this is a 'negative health' model. It looks at vulnerability rather than resistance, adverse life experiences rather than positive ones, dysphoric[2] rather than euphoric responses, and immunosuppression rather than immunocompetence. Second, the strong presence of sociocultural factors make this more than a model of individual risk. For example, vulnerability varies with sociocultural factors, since 'the opportunities to learn adaptive response patterns and to possess the resources necessary to forestall or assuage distress are provided by the person's cultural and subcultural affiliations and the individual's position in the social structure' (Kaplan 1991: 921). Social and cultural norms determine in part what one defines as adverse life events, and the amount of one's exposure to such events. Both the acceptability of dysphoric responses and the forms they take are affected by sociocultural norms. Finally, immunosuppressive behaviors such as poor diet, lack of exercise, and substance abuse are valued differently by different social classes and cultural groups, and the opportunity to practice positive behaviors is not equally available to all. Thus, although Kaplan models routes to individual illness, very powerful contextual determinants act on those individuals.

The model identifies four latent variables – vulnerability, adverse life experiences, dysphoric responses, and immunosuppressive behavior – that contribute to immunosuppression. All four are interrelated, affecting one another. Latent variables, which represent concepts and cannot themselves be directly measured, can be quantified through the more measurable variables listed in the figure that represent facets of the concept. From the perspective of women's health and empowerment, many of these concepts and variables are crucial. Owing to low status, lack of education, gender oppression, and isolation, women often have low self-esteem, little sense of control, and a lack of effective social support. Owing to the poverty and social disorganization they often face, women suffer from chronic structural, individual, and acute stress. Dysphoric responses are more culturally acceptable for women than anger and confrontation. Finally, women may suffer from disease, poor nutrition, and sleep deprivation due to their status and their workload. Kaplan and others posit that these pathways lead to immunosuppression, and thus to poor health.

Empowerment can be seen as the other side of the coin: as a salutogenic process contributing to immunocompetence. Figure 6.4 recasts Kaplan's model in this mode. In general, research has been concerned with the negative aspects of psychosocial processes – with stress, lack of support, illness. Work being done by Antonovsky and others, however, is intended to move the focus from pathogenesis to salutogenesis. Both processes, of course, occur simultaneously. Empowerment will not eradicate vulnerability, negative experiences, dysphoria, or immunosuppressive behaviors. It may, however, help to counteract, balance, or reduce these pathways to immunosuppression.

I and others have described empowerment as a process that leads to a psychosocial transformation among participants. Many of the factors represented in Kaplan's model, or in extensions of it, are included in lists of components of empowerment. Among these are a sense of coherence (Antonovsky 1979, 1987, 1993), coping skills (Dressler 1985b; Menaghan 1983; Wrubel *et al.* 1981), self-esteem (Rosenberg 1989), a sense of mastery and control (Pearlin *et al.* 1981), adaptive potential (Colby *et al.* 1985), subjective well-being (Zautra and Hempel 1984), alienation and powerlessness (Seeman 1959), social support (Minkler 1987; Turner 1983), companionship (Rook 1987), stress

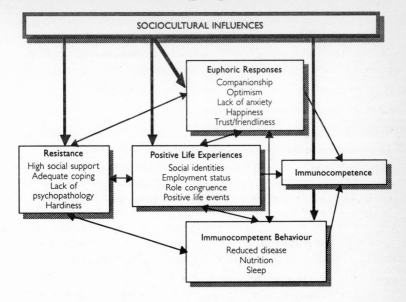

Figure 6.4 Psychosocial influences on immunocompetence

(Dressler 1985a; Pollack 1988; A. Young 1980), and life experiences (Lepore *et al.* 1991; Thoits 1983), all of which will be discussed below.

Figure 6.4 offers an explanation of how women's health is affected by these personal transformations and changes in situation resulting from empowerment. There is evidence from psychosocial studies that psychosocial factors affect health. There is evidence that psychosocial factors affect immune response and that immune system behavior affects health. However, given a lack of knowledge about direct physiological causal links, pathways through the immune system are as yet hypothetical. None the less, it is one possible link between empowerment and health.

Although most scientific efforts are directed towards understanding psychoneuroimmunologic processes within the individual, this work has roots in questions about differences between individuals and between groups of people. There is a dominant underlying theme in the work of Howard Kaplan and others that sociocultural factors strongly affect individual physiology. As psychosocial and psychoneurological processes become demystified, characteristics that have generally been considered as innate or as 'personality traits' may be recast as skills to be learned. The dichotomization of individual/society may be replaced by a more interactive and holistic relationship.

Psychosocial factors and health

The sections below will not be able to do justice to the research that has been done in the area of psychosocial factors and health. There is simply too much of it extant and too little order to it. The material is organized according to the four components described by Kaplan – vulnerability, stress and adverse life experiences, dysphoric responses, and immunosuppressive behaviors.

Vulnerability and resistance resources

This area encompasses positive internal and external factors known collectively as resistance resources – 'personal dispositions and interpersonal resources that are known or hypothesized to prevent the occurrence of, or to reduce the intensity of dysphoria associated with temporally circumscribed or chronic stresses' (Kaplan 1991: 916). The lack of resistance resources thus contributes to one's vulnerability and inability 'to forestall, or to assuage, the distress accompanying adverse life circumstances.'

Anton Antonovsky seems to have coined the term 'resistance resources' – resources that he sees as coming from one's sociocultural and historical context and personal background. These resources include non-psychosocial resources (material, intelligence and knowledge), psychosocial resources (ego identity, coping strategy, social support, commitment), and cultural resources (cultural stability; magic; a stable set of answers derived from religion, philosophy, or art; and a preventative health orientation). The focus in the stress literature has been on psychosocial and cultural resources.

The next five sections discuss some of the major research in this area, grouping the material into the following categories: sense of coherence, coping, self-esteem and other similar constructs, alienation and powerlessness, and social support.

Sense of coherence, hardiness While individuals have different sets of resistance resources, they also have differing capacities for mobilizing those resources, due to personality and life experiences. Antonovsky (1987) has described a global orientation to which he attributes this capacity to mobilize resources. He calls it a *sense of coherence* (SOC) – confidence in the predictability of one's internal and external environment, confidence that things will, by and large, turn out well. A strong SOC reduces one's vulnerability:

> The strong-SOC person will tend to seek to impose structure on the situation, even when to the outside observer there is little structure; will tend to search for what seems to him to be the appropriate [resistance resources] that may facilitate coping with the situation; will tend to consider options within his canon; will tend to believe in self-efficacy; and will tend to accept the challenge of the situation. The weak-SOC person, in contrast, will manifest the tendency to see chaos, to feel hopeless and burdened. (Antonovsky 1987: 186)

Antonovsky has developed a complex model of the production of health, where people with a strong sense of coherence are less likely to see stressors as negative and more willing to confront them. He also sees the SOC as having direct physiological consequences for the immune system. Antonovsky developed his theory partly to explain qualities that led to the survival of prisoners in Nazi concentration camps (Antonovsky 1979, 1987).

Emmy Werner and Ruth Smith (1989: 163), in a book summarizing the results of their groundbreaking longitudinal research on resilient children in Kauai, Hawaii, conclude that '[t]he central component of effective coping with the multiplicity of inevitable life stresses appears to be a sense of coherence, a feeling of confidence that one's internal and external environment is predictable and that things will probably work out as well as can be reasonably expected.' They found that resilient children had a sense of control over events based in their positive coping skills, which contrasted with the 'learned helplessness' of the less resilient children. Werner's focus on resilience as an important resistance resource is increasingly influencing researchers interested in disadvantage, adaptation, and health. In her studies of Mexican women and nerves, Kaja Finkler (1989) has observed that an SOC is protective for women, and that women whose lives are chaotic and unpredictable are particularly susceptible to many illnesses.

Antonovsky has designed an SOC scale whose components are comprehensibility, manageability, and meaningfulness, and published a paper reviewing all known uses of his scale – identifying 42 published studies covering 20 countries and in 14 languages (1993). Few of the groups studied, however, have been poor, non-literate, or from developing countries. Particularly interesting in the context of this book is the fact that when similarly situated men and women were tested for SOC and their results were reported by gender, women scored lower than men in all but one reported case. For example, kibbutz fathers had a higher mean than kibbutz mothers, Finnish adult men scored higher than women. Anson *et al.* (1993) have attempted to explain this finding in a study designed to look at why women with mild hypertension perceive themselves as less healthy than men with the same condition. They traced the difference to unhappiness, distress, and a lower SOC, blaming women's poor socialization for their diminished sense of comprehensibility and manageability. The former is compromised by contradictions between the values accorded by society to personal achievement and paid work, and the emphasis on women's private family responsibilities. The latter is undermined by society's acceptance of women's dependency on men.

Antonovsky himself relates SOC to other orientations that appear in the literature. It is closely related to discussions of *locus of control*, a concept which also maintains that the individual feels that he or she is to a large extent responsible for his or her fate. It differs in so far as Antonovsky recognizes that one can feel in control even though one has ceded control to another, as long as one feels that the other is looking out for his or her best interest. 'It is important to stress that the dimension is not control but participation in decision making.' Rather, one should feel that one has 'appropriate input' in deciding who has control in a given situation. He indicates that while locus of control theories probably make sense in a culture 'based on individualism and free enterprise,' they do not fit more communal cultures (Antonovsky 1987: 37).

Antonovsky also relates his SOC to *hardiness*, a concept put forth by Kobasa (1982) which encompasses the dimensions of commitment, control, and challenge. Commitment lies at the positive end of a dimension having alienation at the other end, control is balanced by powerlessness, and challenge by fear of change and rigidity. Boyce and Schaefer (1985) have developed a theory of *permanence* and *continuity* which, they found, related to pregnancy outcomes. There are five components to this construct: an awareness of a competent and stable self, stable interpersonal relationships, attachment to certain places, daily routines and patterns of behavior, and religious or spiritual conceptions of universal permanence. The sense of permanence is thought to protect against the negative impact of unexpected events and changes.

The SOC concept is intuitively appealing, and is often referred to in literature about stress. However, as Antonovsky notes (1987: 157), an association between a strong SOC orientation and good health does not imply that other goods necessarily flow from it: 'A person with a strong sense of coherence is quite capable of being what many would consider an insensitive, unpleasant, inconsiderate, exploitative bastard.' In our search for good health, we often overlook the danger of optimizing individual health at the cost of other, also important, personal and societal values.

Antonovsky's SOC theory is particularly relevant to a discussion of women and empowerment because he has broadened it to encompass a group sense of coherence, where the group is 'of overriding centrality in the lives of its members. For each, the self and the social identity are deeply interwoven' (Antonovsky 1987: 177). He also recognizes that socially created stresses, such as work-related problems, cannot be resolved on an individual level. Problems that affect a collectivity need to be resolved by the affected group.

Coping For both individuals and groups, a strong SOC facilitates coping:

> Coping can be defined as cognitive and behavioral attempts to change, tolerate or avoid problematic situations (stressors), including attempts to change, tolerate or avoid emotional responses to stressors. Conceptually and operationally coping has been viewed alternately as a personality disposition or trait; a 'style' or set of beliefs about how to approach problematic situations; or, as a set of specific strategies adopted in response to specific events or circumstances. (Dressler 1985b)

Elizabeth Menaghan (1983) further distinguishes between coping styles and coping efforts. Coping *styles* are defined as generalized strategies, such as actively coping by trying to change the situation, or emotionally controlling one's response to the situation by denying it, ignoring it, laughing at it, or blaming others. Coping *efforts* are more situationally dependent – a specific response to a specific problem.

Coping styles have been traced to two unconscious reactions to stress experienced by all animals: either (1) conservation-withdrawal or (2) flight-and-fight. Individuals susceptible to cancer have been described as often exhibiting conservation-withdrawal reactions:

> [T]hey can be described as submissive, non-aggressive, suppressing their perceived needs, adjusting to non-rewarding interpersonal relationships in order to maintain a sense of security and esteem. It is this set of characteristics which predisposes them to be a 'receiver of repression' and thus to be exposed to feelings of helplessness, of giving-up and depression. (Grossarth-Maticek *et al.* 1982: 493)

The authors describe those susceptible to cardiovascular diseases, on the other hand, as responding with flight-and-fight behaviors, exhibiting 'active competitive drive, trying to control possibly threatening situations, expressing their need of approval and self-esteem through visible attempts of performance and achievement.'

There is something intrinsically disturbing about such generalizations, as they imply that one should be able to modify one's behavior and thereby avoid disease. This has led one physician (Angell 1985: 1572) to assert: 'it is time to acknowledge that our belief in disease as a direct reflection of mental state is largely folklore.' It should be clear that the situation is a great deal more complex, and that very little is yet known about the interaction between these so-called styles and more permanent traits and the stressors themselves. It may be more useful to think about these issues in the context Cassel suggested: people have generalized susceptibilities related to both social and psychological factors, and reducing susceptibility is of greater import than unraveling the extremely complex relationship between an individual and a given disease.

Dressler's carefully documented work on interactions between coping styles and social identities emphasizes the importance of evaluating coping styles in the context of race, gender, age, and cultural adaptation or dislocation (1991, 1985b). Coping styles that were beneficial to black males (emotion control and an appearance of unconcern) were not effective for black women, who benefited from an active coping style. However, Menaghan (1983) did not find that such social identity factors were related to specific coping efforts.

Finally, groups have also been described as having coping strategies that act at the group level as well as either reinforcing or inhibiting individual group members' personal coping strategies (Wrubel *et al.* 1981).

Self-esteem, sense of mastery, sense of control, adaptive potential, subjective well-being   Among other resistance resources thought to enhance good health are high *self-esteem* – feeling that one is 'good enough' and that one accepts oneself (Rosenberg 1989)[3] – and a *sense of mastery or control* – feeling in control over 'forces that importantly affect their lives' (Pearlin *et al.* 1981: 340).

Psychosocial researchers have long been interested in generalized *locus of control* and more specific control measures, such as a *health locus of control*. An external locus of control is associated with a belief that one's own efforts cannot determine outcomes; a person with an internal locus of control believes that they can and do control outcomes. As we have seen, Antonovsky questions these concepts because they assume competition – either self-control or control by others –

rather than cooperation – a voluntary ceding of control which is thought to be in one's best interest. Pill and Stott (1985: 989) question another traditional assumption: that working-class people are fatalistic about health because they have an external health locus of control, and that belief prevents them from acting responsibly with regard to health. They found that women understand that their actions affect their health, but that their life situations mitigate against their ability to act as they 'should.' Thus their fatalism and external locus of control may 'be interpreted as a realistic appraisal of the complex variables involved in the aetiology of illness and the improvement of health in general.'

Colby (1985) defines another set of resources which he groups into a concept he calls *adaptive potential*: adaptivity, altruism (affection and prosocial autonomy), and creativity. He theorizes that adaptive potential mediates stress, thereby leading to well-being and the 'maintenance of physical and mental health.' Colby emphasizes the importance of cultural contexts and values to an individual's ability to adapt, and is another spokesperson critical of the narrow individualistic focus of much stress research.

Subjective well-being is another relatively stable trait thought to relate to good health. The concept includes life satisfaction, happiness, and morale (a positive outlook on life). Zautra and Hempel (1984) find evidence of a bidirectional relationship between health and well-being, but few explanations of the underlying mechanisms. One possible pathway is from good health through activity to well-being. They also identify a route from well-being to health through 'a breather from stress,' the restoration of energy, and the sustenance of coping efforts to health.

Luhtanen and Crocker (1992) have begun to investigate the concept of collective self-esteem, and have designed a series of questions to measure it. Although their questions pertain to social groups, the authors have in mind categories such as class, race, and gender. They did find that their measure of collective self-esteem was more highly (negatively) correlated to depression among African-Americans, while among whites the correlation was stronger between personal self-esteem and depression, suggesting the likelihood of cultural differences in mental health. Their scale, however, might pose problems for those who feel one way about one facet of their identity (say gender) and another way about a different facet (class, for example). This scale, however, might be useful in regard to group participation – for example, do empowerment groups engender a higher level of self-esteem than other types of groups?

Alienation and powerlessness   Other concepts and scales have been
designed to measure what may be the negative sides of self-esteem and
sense of control. Seeman (1959) proposed a theory of *alienation* that
included powerlessness, meaninglessness, normlessness, isolation, and
self-estrangement. Bullough (1972) found that alienation reduced the
use of preventative health services and family planning. Meleis (1982)
found that powerlessness and exclusion from household decision-making
was related to increasing psychosomatic complaints among women in
Kuwait. Lack of power translates into lack of material and resistance
resources.

The relationships between a sense of power as a psychosocial
resource and health have generally been examined with regard to negative health. I hope to relate power and a sense of power to positive
health. Power as a component of status will be discussed in the next
chapter.

Social support   While there is neither consensus nor clarity as to any of
the psychosocial factors that effect health, the area of social support is
the most problematic. The concept has been under investigation ever
since Emile Durkheim (1951) showed that lack of a sense of solidarity
predicted suicide. There are at least four different types of social
support:

(1) emotional support, involving empathy, love and trust; (2) instrumental
support, involving behaviors that directly aid the person in need; (3) informational support, composed of information useful in coping with personal
and environmental problems; and (4) appraisal support, involving information relevant to self-evaluation or social comparisons, exclusive of any affect
that might accompany such information. (Turner 1983: 109)

There is the recipient's perception of that support (subjective) and some
actual measure of that support (objective). There is the intensity,
frequency, and durability of support. Who provides the support? How
large a social network does the individual have? Is the support focused
or general? Does the person view the support as positive? Is the person
able to give as well as receive support? Does social support have a
direct effect on health, or does it become important only in certain
situations and among certain groups of people? Clearly one needs a lot
of information to classify a person's social support from all of these
perspectives. None the less, the literature supports both a direct
relationship between social support and health and a stronger effect
for those who are suffering from either structural stress or severe,
adverse, acute events.

There are, however, few suggestions as to the mechanisms by which social support affects health. Meredith Minkler (1987: 4) posits that perceptions of support lead to a more generalized sense of control, and that 'this more global feeling of what Antonovsky described as "sense of coherence" or what Syme has labeled "control over destiny" ... serves as the missing link explaining why social support might be among the factors critically related to health.'

Jay Turner (1983) suggests that we focus on perceived emotional support. Others look at sources of support. Dean and Ensel (1982) maintain that two factors – having a close companion and having enough close friends – may capture the key to social support. Karen Rook (1987) also identifies companionship as a determinant of positive health, noting that the excitement and stimulation of companionship counters loneliness just as other forms of support counter stress. Waxler-Morrison *et al.* (1991) found that friends, not relatives, were related to the survival of women with breast cancer. They saw the ability to select one's friends, and thus to assure positive relationships, as important. American soldiers in Vietnam who had a strong sense of comradeship were shown to have lower levels of stress hormones in combat than they did while they were off duty (Bourne 1970). Jylha and Seppo (1989: 164) found that social participation was highly related to health indicators among the elderly in Finland, but that social contacts were not. They feel that participation may reflect 'an active involvement in society and embeddedness in a social system, a way-of-life which is characterized by social competence and active social interaction in general.'

Franks *et al.* (1992) studied both social support and family functioning – a construct used primarily in mental health. They found that family interaction variables (perceived criticism and emotional involvement) have a more powerful effect on depression as well as on health behaviors than does social support. Traditionally, in developing countries, kinship relationships have provided a lot of social support as well as placing demands upon members of the network. Carol Stack's research into these networks among African-Americans in the United States (1974) provides a model that may also be relevant to changing societies in the third world: a tight combination of instrumental, information, and emotional support. Without other stable means of support, this form of social network may be necessary for basic survival. William Dressler (Dressler *et al.* 1986), however, again emphasizes the complexities. In a Mexican community, he found that males had lower blood pressure with more support from any source; among younger females, support from relatives and friends was related to increased blood pressure; among older women, support from relatives was related to lower blood pressure. Verbrugge (1985a: 165) notes that women tend to look to other people for support (and take medication), while men 'opt more often for quiet brooding or overt behaviors like alcohol, smoking, and illicit drugs.' Thus the processes by which men and women gain social support may be very different. We may therefore expect that the effects of that social support also differ.

Eyer and Sterling (1977: 37) point to a relationship between groups and suicide: 'In the historical statistics of developed countries, the effective kind of community forming process occurs also during mass strikes and popular uprisings, which are accompanied by sharp declines in the suicide rate.' They recommend that medical science concentrate on understanding the effect of community forming, and 'further its practical application.' To that end, one might ask about the health impact of groups as a form of social support, and whether and how empowerment groups enhance a woman's general social support.

In a particularly relevant study, Spiegel *et al.* (1989: 890) reported on an unexpected result of a prospective psychosocial intervention intended to improve the quality (but not length) of life for women with metastatic breast cancer: 'Patients with metastatic breast cancer randomised to weekly group therapy for a year lived significantly longer than did controls, by an average of nearly 18 months.' The authors hypothesize that social support, the provision of 'a place to belong and to express feelings,' and an increased ability to 'mobilise their resources better' may have been the most important factors. They conclude by suggesting that the '[n]euroendocrine and immune system may be a major link between emotional processes and cancer course.' Minkler (1987) also emphasizes the importance of 'macro-level effects' of social support that can be achieved through participation in support groups and community organizations, leading to positive changes in individuals' lives, their communities, and their environments.

Summary   The constructs described here are interrelated and thought to be related to health through reducing vulnerability by increasing resistance resources, or vice versa. Exactly what roles are played by (1) global orientation as represented by the SOC; (2) coping resources, styles and efforts; (3) positive factors such as self-esteem, sense of control, and subjective well-being; (4) negative factors such as alienation, powerlessness, and hopelessness; and (5) the multidimensional construct of social support are unknown.

Particularly important in relation to empowerment is the possibility of increasing resistance through the reduction of vulnerability and the accumulation or strengthening of supportive resources. To that end, the role played by group activities and processes in increasing the availability of resistance resources is an important area to investigate.

Stress/adverse life experiences

Howard Kaplan uses the phrase *adverse life experiences* instead of *stress* to label his second latent variable, perhaps because *stress* is so imprecise. Kristian Pollack (1988: 381) feels that the term is useless – an invention of researchers. She asks:

> While distress of various kinds is assuredly an integral part of the 'human condition', why should it necessarily be considered pathogenic, rather than, for example, as has been the case elsewhere, an act of God, a spur to intense creative activity, a necessary test of moral fibre, or even simply as the norm?

Sterling and Eyer (1981: 35) prefer to talk about arousal, since stress 'signifies so many things' – both external demands and internal responses. Allan Young (1980: 134) gives a physiological definition:

> '[S]tress' is used to distinguish situations in which the organism cannot separate itself from noxious or threatening circumstances and a particular series of neuro-endocrinological and patho-physiological events occurs or can occur. According to some writers, a non-specific hormonal response occurs via increased pituitary–adrenal cortical activity, while according to others particular multi-hormonal patterns are evoked. In either event, the prolonged hormonal activity which results leads to disequilibrating and maladaptive consequences.

Dressler (1985a: 258) suggests that we stop worrying about a precise definition, and view stress and the stress process as phenomena that increase the 'risk of disease by their exposure to or interaction with certain kinds of social occurrences or circumstances.'

Whether we call it stress, adverse life experiences, or arousal, the concept has been tested over and over again for its relationship to health. The literature recognizes several kinds of stress, the two major categories being chronic and acute. Chronic stress is defined as:

> a condition of continuous and manifold changes, demands, threats, or deprivation, frequently small in scale and embedded in daily life events. These forces may be widespread and affect much of the population, or they may be discrete and personal. (Fried 1982: 5)

Chronic stress is of two types: structural and individual. To complicate the issue further, the term 'endemic stress' is used sometimes to

represent all forms of chronic stress, and sometimes only chronic individual stress. Chronic structural stress encompasses low socioeconomic status, geographic mobility, minority group membership,
social marginality, and poor or dangerous living conditions. These social
stressors affect well-defined groups of people. Dressler (1985a: 278)
defines it as 'a function of the macrostructural processes operating on
a community, the unequal distribution of power in the community, and
the symbolic expression of the self-concept.' Makosky (1982) found that
chronic stress had more effect on women's mental health than did
acute stress. Lois Verbrugge (1985a: 165) emphasizes gender differences
in reactions to stress, claiming that women 'tend to be less delighted
about life than men, and this may make them more vulnerable to
stress-related illnesses.'

Chronic individual stress has been defined as 'everyday problems
that occur in individuals' lives and are linked to the major social roles
that these persons perform. For example ... financial stressors, marital
stressors, parental stressors, and job stressors' (Dressler 1985a: 259).
Dressler sees these stressors as 'context dependent' – products of
particular social arrangements – and 'not as individually idiosyncratic
or purely dependent on how individuals perceive problem situations.'

Fried (1982: 16) describes the process by which chronic stress leads
to reduced self-esteem and well-being:

> While anger, resentment, and an altered self-concept are provoked by
> endemic stress, they are easily concealed by feelings of resignation, of
> diminished expectation, and by an awareness of the necessity of living within
> constraint. Frequently, these feelings of resignation are denied, a denial that
> is bolstered by a willing suspension of belief about existential causes and by
> an escape into trivialities.

Dressler (1985a) sees the processes of modernization as producing a
lack of fit between aspirations and status – one suffers from distress
when one's aspirations exceed one's status. There is an entire literature
on the relationship between modernity and illness, begun in the 1960s
and continuing through the 1980s. Cassel and others began the research by analyzing the health effects of rural-to-urban migration and
its concomitant social and cultural dislocation (Cassel *et al.* 1960; King
et al. 1964; Tyroler and Cassel 1961). Relationships between modernization and elevated blood pressure, increased levels of serum lipids,
coronary mortality, and obesity have been shown to exist by Dressler
and others (Dressler *et al.* 1987a, 1987b; Labarthe *et al.* 1983, 1989;
Patrick *et al.* 1983). This research underlies much of the work discussed
in Chapter 5 with regard to social disorganization as a stressor.

Except for looking at modernization, however, very little research around the issue of stress has been done in a developing-country context. One study in India (Lepore *et al.* 1991) found a relationship between chronic strain and psychosomatic symptoms among poor urban men. It is clear that women living in poverty today in urban slums, often as the sole support of their children, are exposed to at least as much dislocation and disorientation as men. Some repercussion on their health can be expected that is above and apart from the environmental and nutritional risks to which they are exposed.

Acute stress consists of supposedly discrete events, such as a death in the family or a job change, which are thought to occur suddenly and affect discrete individuals. It also encompasses *daily hassles*: 'stressors that produce low intensity threats' (Lepore *et al.* 1991: 1029). What is called acute stress is often the result of sociocultural conditions. Although it is customary to think of job loss or a child's failure in school as individual – or at most family – problems, these events can certainly be traced to wider environments. How stress is viewed is important: one can try to reduce the stress and/or increase the individual's power to deal with that stress. Both those things can be done at the level of the individual or family and/or at the societal level. A parent can be retrained and provided with unemployment insurance, and/or a national policy aimed at full, or at least fuller, employment can be the solution. Therapy and remedial education can be provided to the child, and/or the school system can be revamped so as to improve a child's learning environment.

Acute stress is related to change. Is change bad in and of itself? Does it burden our bodies and our psyches, or does it challenge us? Early attempts to answer these questions used a list of *life events*, such as illness, moving, job loss, pregnancy, and vacation, all of which were assumed to unbalance and put stress on an individual. Peggy Thoits (1983) has done a thorough review of the research on life events and psychological distress, which, although representing only one facet of health, can provide guidance in thinking about other dimensions of health. To summarize her findings very briefly: change alone does not seem to be a culprit, although she indicates that physical distress has been shown to be more related to change than has psychological distress. Psychological distress is, rather, related to change through events that are considered undesirable by the person affected (often a socially and culturally determined evaluation), over which they feel they have no control, and which have a compounded damaging effect if they occur close to one another in time.

Acute stressors have been studied in two different ways: (1) people exposed to specific events such as death of a spouse, disasters, plant shutdowns, school examinations, or surgery have been compared to unexposed people; and (2) individuals have indicated which of a set of life events they have experienced, so that people with more events are compared to people with fewer or no events. While there are connections between life events and psychological distress, the statistical association tends to be somewhat weak. However, in one of the clearest studies to date looking at the relationship between stress and infection in the form of the common cold (Cohen *et al.* 1991), researchers did find that stress as measured by negatively perceived life events, negative affect, and perceived inability to cope with current problems was strongly related to infection, after controlling for health habits, health status, personality, demographics, and environmental conditions.

Thoits summarizes some of the problems that may contribute to the weak association found in most studies. Recall of events is inaccurate; interviews seem to elicit better information than self-administered questionnaires; measures do not appear to exhibit high statistical reliability; non-events – 'events that are desired or anticipated but do not occur' (Thoits 1983: 50) – are not measured; lists are highly loaded with events that happen to younger, middle-class, white males; some events are interrelated, such as job loss and reduced income; some events may be the result of the condition they are trying to predict, such as job loss or marital separation resulting from depression or poor health; the common technique of adding events together may not represent the way they interact; events may affect health indirectly, through their consequences – as with widowed men who lose their social connections and do not know how to care for themselves, or recently unemployed or divorced women who lose both self-esteem and a sense of control; there are several categories of life events, and the categories may differentially affect health; and, above all, the impact of events on the individual is dependent on their level of vulnerability. That level is, in turn, dependent on physical, psychological, social, cultural, and structural factors, as well as the amount of endemic stress from which a person suffers.

Dysphoric responses

It can be difficult to distinguish between dysphoric responses and conditions of vulnerability. Kaplan treats dysphoric responses as an outcome of negative life events, compounded by vulnerability and 'unhealthy' behaviors. Among the responses that have been examined in relation to health and health behaviors are loneliness, depression, anxiety, unhappiness, hostility, and nerves (Bullough 1972; Davis and Low 1989a; Johnson-Saylor 1991; Perlman and Peplau 1984; West *et al.* 1986). Other studies link loneliness to immunosuppression (Kiecolt-Glaser *et al.* 1984a, 1984b, 1984c). Short-term dysphoric responses are also linked to poor health. Verbrugge (1985b: 868–9), in ·a study that used health diaries to look at day-to-day health, showed that '[b]ad moods are strongly linked with somatic troubles, both physical malaise and symptom experience.' She observed a complicated interaction between negative events and moods:

> [W]hen negative events occur on *good* mood days, they *increase* the chances of symptoms, medical drug use, medical care, lay consultation and restricted activity. But on *bad* mood days, negative events usually *reduce* the chances of physical malaise, medical drug use, curative drug use, lay consultation and restricted activity. We conclude, first, that proximal factors (bad moods) take precedence as triggers and distant factors (negative events) operate as triggers in their absence. Second, unpleasant events may sometimes draw people's attention away from their low spirits and blunt, but not eliminate, the link between emotional and physical distress.

A common assumption is that 'negative affect' – unhappiness, anger, and hostility – are related to poor health. While this has generally been the case, some research has suggested that anger and hostility are beneficial for cancer patients (Derogatis *et al.* 1979). At the same time, Levy *et al.* (1988) report that joy was predictive of improved survival time among breast cancer patients. This may indicate that 'emotionality and a fighting spirit,' whether positive *or* negative, are beneficial.

Another indicator of dysphoria is nerves, seen by Kaja Finkler (1989) as the embodiment of distress – directly linking adversity and dysphoria, and by Davis and Low (1989b: xiv) as socially induced – '[L]abeling emotional and social distress as nerves often sustains conflictual social relations by medicalizing political and socioeconomic problems, thereby placing the burden for the cure on the individual rather than on society.' In the long run, social change is required if relief is to be more than palliative.

Immunosuppressive behaviors

Immunosuppressive behaviors are behaviors known to contribute to poor health, which interact with vulnerability, life experiences, and dysphoric responses. Kaplan includes behaviors related to disease, nutrition, substance abuse, and sleep deprivation in his model. Many writers have noted that negative life experiences affect these behaviors.

As Kaplan makes clear, however, there are multiple interactions – sleep deprivation affects mood, and vice versa; stress may lead to excessive drinking, and drinking can lead to job loss and family disruption; chronic illness, such as cardiovascular disease, may result from stress, and both illness and medication can affect social support.

Sterling and Eyer (1981: 31) place immunosuppressive behaviors in a sociobiological context, describing the biological process by which 'chronic psychological arousal produces chronic physiological arousal and, in turn, specific biological pathology,' particularly hypertension. They note, for example, that a hormonal reaction to arousal is responsible for a 'strong appetite for salt.' Since lower social class is related to chronic arousal, this appetite for salt may help to explain the prevalence of hypertension among people with fewer resources. They also suggest that a similar process may relate to overeating, too much alcohol, smoking, and lack of exercise. Such evidence can help to explain why behaviors that are known to affect health negatively are so difficult to change. Sterling and Eyer also point out that 'many groups produce and enjoy tobacco, alcohol, and other psychoactive drugs, but as long as their social organization remains undisrupted, they have virtually no problems with chronic abuse.'

Psychosocial factors and empowerment

Psychosocial factors are frequently listed as components of empowerment. They are assumed to be related to health and to one another, but the research is difficult to organize and summarize. Kaplan's model, presented above, begins to provide a framework within which factors and their interactions can be examined. It posits an explicit – albeit poorly understood – pathway between psychosocial factors and health: through neurological and immunological processes. Perhaps most importantly, in the context of this book, Kaplan emphasizes the sociocultural context within which psychosocial factors develop. Problems, needs, and vulnerabilities are not neatly ascribed either to individuals or to society. Individuals are inseparable from society. Empowerment is a strategy derived from these same assumptions. It has psychosocial health as one of its goals, based on a recognition that health and well-being are closely related to psychosocial health. It also sees psychosocial health as a 'weapon' in the 'war' for power and social justice, and sees group activities both as enhancing individual well-being and as necessary to affect change in the sociocultural environment that so often victimizes certain individuals and groups.

Summary and Conclusions

Each of the factors discussed in this chapter has been considered to be a determinant of health, although they are located at different levels of 'proximity' to health outcomes. While there is currently some general agreement on the set of important determinants of health, there is a fair amount of disagreement about their relative importance and level of complexity.

The majority of the women whom I am discussing live in tropical regions where geography and climate make life more difficult than it is in temperate regions, and threats to health are omnipresent. While people living in these regions are particularly susceptible to infectious diseases, there are many outstanding questions about why exposed groups and individuals are differentially susceptible. The traditional germ model of disease does not explain much of the observed variation. Local environmental conditions – such as land utilization, air quality, water quantity and quality, waste disposal, and available energy sources – have well-known impacts on health, and can explain some amount of community variation. They have often been studied one by one, but their interactions and their relationships to social, geographical, cultural, political, and economic factors are poorly understood.

Health researchers have looked increasingly at what societal factors can tell them about health. While it has been assumed that national income, as measured by GNP and modernization, correlates positively with health, it is becoming increasingly obvious that subgroups of populations are differentially affected by this 'progress,' and that it has been accompanied by many negative side-effects. Other societal factors are of particular importance to women. Population control is a top-down policy designed to reduce the number of children women have, and thereby the world's population. It can, if it is applied without regard for women's health and empowerment, have negative effects. Fertility control, through which population control is achieved, is – or should be – more concerned with women's choices and empowerment, and thereby contribute to their positive health. Gender-based violence and sexual abuse, on the other hand, are multi-level problems that negatively affect women's daily lives and their health – over which they have very little control.

Perhaps most promising for an understanding of women's health are the many factors gathered under the rubric of social organization, including social disadvantage, poverty, cycles of deprivation, social disorganization, and income inequality. We are just beginning to under-stand their impact and their relationships to other factors. In part these factors have become significant owing to the realization that traditional assumptions about the importance of medicine and medical technology are questionable with respect to the health of populations – even public health is effective through its interactions with other factors such as education and social organization.

The individual-level factors discussed in this chapter – health behavior, nutrition, genes and genetics – behave and interact in more complicated ways than previously believed. In particular, psychosocial factors and the emerging field of psychoneuroimmunology seem to parallel social organization in their importance and complexity. While many of these factors have been investigated, we are only beginning to put the pieces together into a coherent framework that features socio-cultural influences as an important component. It becomes ever more clear that categorizing factors into sectors and levels is quite artificial, and of limited usefulness in helping us to decide where and how most effectively to intervene to improve women's health.

Thus the tangled-web analogy for health appears suitable, as most people acknowledge without difficulty. The issue, as identified by Tesh, is its usefulness. For those who approach health through the manipulation of individual risk factors, the tangled-web model is problematic. Analytic techniques to capture the dynamic and complex relations among factors do not yet exist, and may never exist (see Chapter 9). However, the complexity of this description of health is not meant to lead to inactivity, paralysis, or hopelessness. Rather, it is intended to move the focus of health-promoting activities and research from an investigation of relatively simple causality to a search for understanding that focuses on synergistic relations and interactions that may be more fundamental and more reflective of reality. Investigating the many connections and interactions is imperative if the relationships between the factors and health are to be better understood, and if that understanding is to lead to successful interventions. As examples of this approach, the broad and successful programs in Pholela and Jamkhed (discussed in Chapter 4) have linked nutrition, public health, and medical care in a context that stresses self-sufficiency, active input from participants, and appropriateness with regard to local social norms and environmental conditions.

Women's status, education, and empowerment remain to be discussed in the next chapter. Empowerment has been presented as a phenomenon that has the potential to restructure development activities so that they are less detrimental to women. We shall see that it is a subtle and complex factor whose effectiveness is dependent on the existence of the tangled web, interacting with the many other determinants in such a way as potentially to improve their relationships to women's health.

Notes

1. While it is possible to treat culture as a separate factor, it is tightly interwoven with other factors, and I have not attempted to separate it out. Other missing factors are spirituality and organized religion – important concepts, but concepts that have not often appeared in the mainstream literature on health.

2. Dysphoria is defined as 'an emotional state characterized by anxiety, depression, and restlessness' (Morris 1973: 407).

3. See also Blascovitch and Tomaka (1990) for a review of measures of self-esteem.

7

The Three Es:
Equity, Education, and Empowerment

In this chapter I shall focus on how aspects of social organization, as reflected in women's status and education, affect women in particular, and how empowerment, a societal- and individual-level tool to reduce inequalities and devolve power, is linked to health. Although little work has been published relating empowerment and health, its relationships to the other factors considered in this study provide fertile ground for speculation.

Equity: Women's Status and Autonomy

Status and autonomy are two related concepts that have been linked to health, albeit more in theory than through scientific evidence. They are none the less important elements that contribute to our understanding of what is needed to improve women's health. After outlining a variety of definitions of these concepts, I will discuss the research that does exist.

Leslie Curtin (1982: 33), describing status as a composite of many different, interdependent, culturally embedded variables studied by a variety of fields, proffers the following definitions of women's status:

> Theoretically, women's status has been defined as 'the degree of women's access to (and control over) *material* resources (including food, income, land, and other forms of wealth) and to *social* resources (including knowledge, power, and prestige) within the family, in the community, and in society at large' (Dixon 1978). It has also been defined as 'the ranking, in terms of prestige, power, or esteem, according to the position of women in comparison with, relative to, the ranking – also in terms of prestige, power, or esteem – given to the position of men.' (Buvinic 1976)

Women's status can be seen as a marker of gender inequity and disadvantage, acting at multiple levels: international, national, community, and family. It has political, economic, social, and cultural dimensions that are both separate and overlapping. Peggy Sanday (1974) has designed a typology for status consisting of a public and a private (domestic) domain, each of which has three parameters: power, prestige, and respect or esteem. There are no given relationships here: power in the public domain need not imply power in the domestic; power in either domain does not necessarily imply respect and prestige.

A lack of power, prestige, and respect implies a lack of autonomy, and vice versa. Karen Mason (1985) suggests that status concerns intersections between gender and class, while autonomy, as it relates to women, is more narrowly restricted to gender. Tim Dyson and Mick Moore (1983: 45) see autonomy as 'decision-making ability with regard to personal affairs.' Evelyn Fox Keller (1985: 97) uses it 'to refer to the psychological sense of being able to act under one's own volition instead of under external control.' Helen Ware (1981: 18) says that 'autonomy is the power of self-government, it is to the individual what independence is to the nation.' Larry Churchill (1987: 54) states: 'autonomy is more an achievement of just communities than a given or natural condition of individuals.' Benjamin Colby (1987) describes two types of autonomy: prosocial and antisocial. The latter is a condition that 'increases autonomy for the self at the expense of autonomy for others.' The former represents a control over one's one life and an independence that are dedicated to socially beneficial behaviors.

Feminists have struggled with the concept of autonomy as part of their attempt to understand the relationship between the individual and the community. Keller (1985: 99), for example, defines a *dynamic* autonomy that reflects 'a sense of self … as both differentiated from and related to others, and a sense of others as subjects with whom one shares enough to allow for a recognition of their independent interests and feelings – in short for a recognition of them as other subjects.' Patricia Hill Collins (1991) distinguishes between *separatism*, which isolates, and *autonomy*, which provides a base of strength from which to work with others.

As I will discuss below, there has been a great deal of research linking women's education to health. John Caldwell (1990: xii), who has carried out much of this research, views education as a more measurable 'subset' of autonomy and autonomy as a subset of egalitarianism, defined as 'greater freedom of choice and action for all.' Empowerment, like education, can be seen as a route to autonomy. According to Ruth Paz (1990: ix):

By definition, empowerment is about working *with* not *for* people; it is participatory and builds on the existing strengths of the individual and the community. It is a process of growth of understanding, skills, knowledge, and self confidence enabling people to manage their own and their children's lives more effectively. It is above all a process of growth into autonomy.

Virginia Seitz (1992: 274) sees empowerment *as* autonomy, defining empowerment as 'social, political, economic, and ideological autonomy; it is both collective and personal rather than individual.' In fact, the four concepts – status, autonomy, education, and empowerment – are all integrally related, each capable of positively affecting the other. Women must have status and autonomy if they are to be empowered; the processes of education and empowerment lead to increased status and autonomy. The question here is how they relate to health. Since research relating female autonomy to health is rare, I can only review data on status and health.

Women's status

Women suffer from low status in comparison to men. A lack of respect for the human rights of women is pervasive, although only very recently have human rights organizations begun to consider women as a group deserving special attention.[1] Particularly in Africa, colonization and development have been associated with a reduction in women's status affecting many health-related conditions, including high fertility rates, family planning, access to abortion, women's increased workload due to the migration of and desertion by men, terrible working conditions in agriculture (whether on their own land or on plantations), increasing alcohol-related physical abuse of women and children, increasing incidence of rape and all other forms of violence against women, increasing malnutrition, and an increase in the number of female-headed households (Raikes 1989).

Shushum Bhatia (1983: 175) describes how 'the low status of women, which is reflected in culturally accepted discriminatory attitudes and behaviour against females, adversely affects the health and well being of women' in South Asia. Female births are unwelcome; inequities exist in care in dressing, in feeding, in the provision of medical care, and in educational opportunities. Marriage at an early age, lack of household power, many pregnancies, and lack of health care negatively affect women's health. Traditional mores concerning dietary practices and childbirth harm child-bearing women. The lack of female health care workers means that women do not get medical treatment. Among poor women, who are often widowed, there is total dependency on male children, due to customs and inheritance laws. Even older women die earlier than men in these countries. Chen *et al.* (1981) showed that in rural Bangladesh, where the mortality of girls between birth and the age of four was 45 percent higher than for boys, girls received 15 percent less protein and calories, and boys were taken for medical treatment 66 percent more frequently. Dyson and Moore (1983: 54), looking at regional differences in India, consider female status to be the major determinant of India's demographic profile, recommending 'a broadly feminist mode of social action – specifically, to increase the autonomous social and political capacity of groups of females – both as an end in itself and as a means to facilitate reduced birth and death rates.'

A literature review that I did in 1991 identified thirty-four articles that specifically relate women's status to health. Some were quantitative studies; others were theoretical. The extant literature reports primarily on individual-level studies, with health outcomes that include women's and children's nutrition, fertility and family planning decisions, and differential mortality by sex. The most important societal-level status outcome variable (apart from education measures) is differential mortality by sex, a clear indicator of the status of women (Bhatia 1983).

Most of the quantitative analyses relating women's status to health have concentrated on looking at gender differences in health outcomes, assuming that low female status was responsible for these differences, but without actually including measures of status in the analyses. Thus a finding that girls are more likely to die than boys, or more likely to suffer from undernutrition, is interpreted as a finding that women's status affects health (Chen *et al.* 1981). Some writers have proposed strategies to quantify women's status (Mason 1985; Powers 1985; Safilios-Rothschild 1982; Sanday 1974). Sanday developed a continuously scaled indicator of female status ranging from 'no positive indicator of status' through female material control, demand for female produce, and female political participation to the existence of female solidarity groups. The Population Crisis Committee (1988) used existing indicators to create national status indices – in the realms of female health, marriage and children, education, employment, and social equality – which they then combined into a single indicator of overall status.

Mayra Buvinic (1976) points out that in the final analysis the determination of which indicators of status are meaningful is dependent upon the members of a society who determine the status of position within that society. If one is to understand and measure women's status, one must understand a society's social structure and how groups gain power, prestige, and esteem in that society. Youssef (1982: 196) notes, in a critique of standard analyses of fertility which disaggregate women's status, that '[c]learly, there is no causal sequence through which the ... different aspects of the role and status of women can separately influence fertility behaviour. All interact in a dynamic way...'

Some research has included specific measures of aspects of status. They include the large body of work that has established the primacy of maternal education (often treated as an indicator of women's status in national comparisons) as a predictor of many health outcomes, including child survival; Chaudhury's work (1984) predicting fertility behavior using three measures that represent aspects of women's status – female education, work experience, and age at marriage; and a study by Schultz (1982) using formal employment and education as independent variables. These analyses involving measures of status, however, have been restricted to within-country or within-region data. To assess the importance of women's status as a factor in child mortality, I did an analysis (Stein 1991) taking advantage of the composite, national-level measure of women's status developed by the Population Crisis Committee (1988). Using national data from 84 countries and standard linear regression techniques, the analysis clearly demonstrated that, controlling for other traditionally important factors – health expenditures, access to water, GNP growth, and GNP per capita – there remains a strong association between women's status and child mortality.

Theoretical work, describing the importance of women's status in determining child survival, fertility, and nutritional status, and hypothesizing about the mechanisms, has been synthesized by Karen Mason (1985) and Priyani Soysa (1987). Other literature is general, as reflected in this quote from the WHO (World Health Organization's Division of Family Health 1980): 'In most parts of the world, women's low social status puts them at an initial disadvantage that aggravates all their other problems. The effort to improve women's health is therefore a complex matter and will necessitate fundamental attitudinal and structural changes in society.' In general, proposals to improve the status of women have a great deal of overlap with those that deal with making development more positive for them. They recognize the need for more resources and more power, through employment, education, and empowerment (Human Rights Coordinator 1993; Wallace 1987).

Conclusion

Women's status is a multidimensional concept, encompassing dimensions of power, prestige, and esteem, relevant in both the public and household domains. It is related to women's autonomy within the household, and to rights and access to resources and power in political, social, and cultural environments. Women's low status is reflected in their treatment as infants, as girls, and as women. Through pathways of discrimination and lack of access to vital resources, it affects their health and well-being. Development has often both reduced their status and served them poorly because of their status. As intense cultural conditioning is required to perpetuate women's position relative to men, it will be difficult to change the status quo. Women's organizations and the empowerment of women at all levels will be necessary if societies are to move towards equity and justice. Although there is little 'hard' research linking status to health – in part because there has been neither agreement on how to define and measure status, nor much gender-specific data – much has been written about the importance of women's status in both the public and the household domains to their health and the health of their children. While the association between status and health has been ascertained, and become part of common wisdom, the mechanisms and pathways from status to health are many and complex; to date, there has been little theoretical work in this area. The evidence presented here, however, indicates that women's health will improve as their status and autonomy improve.

Education

The importance of education – particularly of the mother – has been well established and widely accepted for nearly a decade: better education for women is now a familiar health slogan. Yet understanding of the mechanisms of influence remains no better today than 10 years ago. (Cleland and van Ginneken 1989: 30)

As it became clear to researchers that the panoply of factors associated with economic development – water, sanitation, nutrition, income, work, and medical care – did not sufficiently explain variations in health (mortality and life expectancy) among populations, they began to pay more attention to social factors. In study after study, education or literacy, particularly of females, proved to be an important predictor of health. The first major discussion of the specific impact of maternal education on child mortality was in a paper by John Caldwell (1979). Since that time, four types of analysis have been used to examine the relationship between education and health: historical analyses, cross-sectional national analyses, national case studies, and individual- or household-based research.

Basu (1987: 200) noted that, historically, decreases in child mortality did not necessarily follow decreases in adult mortality, attributing static child mortality to lack of social change 'as measured by female literacy and education.' Using data from many countries and over history, Leonard Sagan (1987: 201) found that 'by far the most consistently powerful predictor of life expectancy was the prevalence of literacy.' Caldwell (1992) points out, however, that maternal education plays a different role in different cultures and historical periods. It appears, for example, to have been less important in England and in the USA than it is in developing countries today.

Most of the aggregate-level research on women's education has been cross-sectional: national data from a given period of time have been used to predict health outcomes. Cochrane *et al.* (1980) reviewed the individual-level evidence on the influence of parental education on child health, since cross-national evidence suggested that education or its proxy, literacy, appeared to be the most important variable involved in studies of infant mortality and life expectancy. Among their conclusions are that each additional year of a mother's schooling reduces infant mortality by 9 per 1,000 live births on the average, and that the effect of mothers' schooling is twice that of fathers.

John Caldwell and his colleagues have performed aggregate, individual, and case studies. In one study aimed at determining which countries performed either much better or much worse in terms of health outcomes than would be expected if health outcomes were linearly related to per capita income, Caldwell (1986) found that poor-achieving countries were mostly Muslim countries, where women were poorly educated and had little autonomy. Those countries that performed better than expected – particularly Sri Lanka, Kerala (an Indian state), and Costa Rica – were all egalitarian societies with a dedication to education and an ideology that encouraged female autonomy. He points out that child mortality is related to the general levels of education as well as the educational level of the individual mother (Caldwell 1989). Uneducated women in developing countries with more general education suffer from fewer child deaths than women in countries with low levels of education.

Studies that consider maternal education and child health using either families, mothers, or children as the unit of analysis abound in the literature, as do review articles (Caldwell 1979; Cleland and van Ginneken 1988; Cochrane *et al.* 1980). Most research, with a few exceptions (Bicego and Boerma 1993; Gürsoy-Tescan 1992), has supported the strong direct association between maternal education and health. Cleland and van Ginneken (1988: 1359) summarize:

The inverse education–mortality relationship is found in all major regions of the developing world; the association is very pronounced, but appreciably closer in childhood than in infancy; and even a modest exposure of the mother to formal schooling is associated with reduced risks of death in most contexts. These are remarkable results in view of the diversity of educational and health standards and of cultural and social systems existing in developing countries today.

Other evidence suggests that the case for the primary role of parental education in child morbidity may be even stronger than previously recognized. Tsui *et al.* (1988) found that educated women identify and report more illness; thus the children of uneducated mothers may have more illness than is being reported. This reporting bias implies that the relationship between education and health may be even stronger than heretofore suggested. As Tsui *et al.* state (1988: 709): 'The influence of maternal education on disease perceptions has unsettling implications for studying morbidity incidence with data from developing country health interview surveys.' Caldwell (1989) also suggests that since breast-feeding declines as education increases, negatively affecting infant health, the effect of education on child health may be underestimated.

Unfortunately, little is known beyond the fact that education (particularly of mothers) is strongly related to health. Research into the mechanisms of education is in its infancy (Joshi 1994). Multivariate analyses have implied a synergistic effect between education and health-promoting activities – as in Caldwell's finding that life expectancy increased much more when both access to care and mothers' education were improved than by either intervention alone (1986). Cleland and van Ginneken (1989: 21) report an 'increased propensity of educated mothers to seek medical care for themselves and their children.' They note, however, that where services are widely available, personal factors, including education, become less important.

Cleland and van Ginneken (1989: 26) write that 'attitudinal, social or cognitive consequences of education may underlie changes in maternal behavior.' Given that very little formal education still has appreciable impact on health outcomes, it seems very unlikely that cognitive consequences, in the form of direct health knowledge, are causing behavior change. Some studies have found little difference in the attribution of disease causality among women with less than secondary-level education. A brief summary of research on the relationships between education and attitudinal, situational, and behavioral change follows, as these factors have been more directly related to improved health.

Education and attitudes

Most of the literature to date has centered on attitudinal changes, in particular on a group of attitudes that are thought to result from the role that schools play in the process of modernization. Education, rather than imparting specific knowledge, imparts skills by a process of modernization, making one feel part of the 'modern system' (Caldwell 1986). Cleland and van Ginneken note that there may be a social effect in that schools may present the first exposure to hand-washing and latrines, and that cleanliness may be imparted as a social norm without its health impact being clear to the students. Caldwell (1989: 106), reporting on studies from Asia, finds:

> [B]ehaviour of school children follows a certain pattern largely because the ex-students know that this is the pattern of behaviour of those who have been to school. They are cleaner because educated people are cleaner; not because the health and hygiene lessons taught them that soap destroyed the bacteria that were the agents of infection. We found in South India that women who had been to school thought of the school as part of the whole modern system, which included independence, five-year plans, government programmes, health centres, modern medicine and themselves. They knew that they were the kind of people who took their children and themselves to health centres....

Education also teaches women

> the rules of navigation. And those rules and understanding of the world's language and symbols give women a power they have never had before.... As Paulo Freire, the revolutionary Brazilian educationalist, declared: 'I can read. Therefore, I can control the world.' (New Internationalist 1985: 79)

Individuals are transformed. Sagan (1987: 181) suggests that education, by providing literacy, 'provides an opportunity to be sensitive to one's own feeling, to communicate and relate with others in a meaningful way, to achieve a sense of competence that the illiterate can rarely gain.' He concludes: 'those who are competent and have confidence in themselves and their ability to control their own lives will experience better health outcomes than those who do not.' The 1989 UNICEF report (Grant 1989: 52) states: 'Education catalyzes ... by replacing resignation with a degree of confidence, acceptance with an awareness of choice.' Simons (1990) relates education to the development of a sense of control that affects all health behaviors. Armer and Isaac (1978), looking at eight different 'modern' behaviors, used complex analytical models to explore key background variables such as rural/urban residence, age, occupational status, income and education level, as well as modern attitudes. They found that each background variable directly affected each behavior except for education, which affected behavior indirectly by changing attitudes. This suggests that education plays a very different role from other 'modernizing' factors, such as employment and urban living – and that Caldwell's thesis that attitudinal changes related to modernization may be responsible for improved health status has validity. Grosse and Auffrey (1989: 294) point out the bidirectionality of the relationship between education and modernity – literacy 'stimulates and facilitates modernization'; while modernization 'increases the demand for literacy and the capacity of a society to meet that demand.'

Education and situational changes

Situational changes resulting from education include having greater decision-making power on health-related and other matters and greater access to resources, including improved marital options (Cleland and van Ginneken 1988; US Bureau of the Census 1980). Actual change in status, increased income, and the independence to change location bring with them the opportunity for better water and sanitation, nutrition, and living conditions. Caldwell (1986) notes that as a society becomes more educated, it demands more and better social services, including health care.

Education and behavior

Although, surprisingly, I have not found any literature that relates a woman's education to her own health, there is a large body of literature that associates her education and health behaviors to her children's health. Cleland and van Ginneken (1989: 25), for example, attribute improved child survival outcomes to better 'domestic child care practices.' They suggest that educated mothers may be 'more knowledgeable about disease prevention and cure,' 'more innovative in the use of remedies,' and 'more likely to adopt new codes of behaviour which improve the health of children though they are not perceived as having direct consequences for health' (Cleland and van Ginneken 1988: 1364).

Mosley and Chen (1984) identified four areas in which behavior affects health: (1) prevention of infection – primarily accomplished through hygiene; (2) reduction of susceptibility to infection – primarily related to nutrition; (3) improved recovery from infection – requiring domestic and external health care; and (4) reduced risk of accidents – requiring supervision. Caldwell (1989: 366) attributes unexpectedly low child mortality in Sri Lanka to 'the awareness of danger, the quickness of identification of illness and consequent action, the appropriateness of the first action, the readiness to change ineffective actions, and the persistence of efforts until success against mortality has been achieved.' While illiterate women may notice that a child is sick, they are less likely to take action on their own:

> Educated women see the whole business as being experimental. The illiterate tend to think in terms of fixed disorders with fixed treatments that either succeed or fail. In addition, they regard the failure as a failure of the healer and any attempt to report it back as being an attack on him or her. Traditional illiterate mothers do not identify all disorders as disease at all but regard many as forms of divine punishment or disfavour and as either immutable or unavoidable.... Educated mothers are much more likely to allow a sick or feverish child to rest, instead of working. Without question, the households of educated women are cleaner and the residents are cleaner. There is more attention to bacteriological pollution and less to ritual pollution. (Caldwell 1989: 106–7)

Caldwell (1986) also identifies the ability to go outside the home for care and to demand treatment by doctors and nurses, reduced fear of medical examination, a more 'trusting and respectful doctor–patient relationship,' adequate feeding of sick children, and cleanliness and hygienic behaviors among health behaviors influenced by education and female autonomy.

Additional explanations

John Simons (1990) sees a set of attitudes, beliefs, and behaviors as responsible for improved outcomes: (1) highly valuing children's survival; (2) a belief that a mother can effectively contribute to her child's health; (3) specific beliefs about specific effective behaviors; (4) the practical skills to apply effective practices appropriately. As to how women develop such a profile, opinions vary widely. In a recent forum on child mortality, Kaufmann and Cleland (1994) suggest that a woman's basic personality accounts for both her school tenure and achievements and her successful parenting, while Douglas Ewbank (1994: 215) attributes the relationship between mother's education and children's health to 'the effects of social interactions and social norms' – focusing on the society rather than the individual. All these formulations remain to be tested, although, as Ewbank warns us, in our attempt to explain rather than just describe, we may oversimplify complex phenomena and, as a result, draw incorrect conclusions.

We may never know exactly how and why the formal education of women has such a strong effect on the health of their families – partly because of complexity and partly because different cultures and different historical patterns produce different pathways. Helen Ware (1983) points out that in one culture education may be a form of assertiveness training, while in another it may confer higher status. The Caldwells (1989) attributed the successful behaviors they identified in Sri Lanka in part to the culture. Stephen Kunitz (1990: 105) also emphasizes the cultural aspects of education:

> [M]aternal education is not a biomedical phenomenon, it is a cultural phenomenon and means something quite different in different cultural contexts. To fail to recognize this creates not understanding but the illusion of understanding.... To think of education as a vaccine that prevents infant mortality the way measles vaccine prevents measles is to ignore the cultural and sociopolitical context within which education occurs and which endows it with significance.

Practical considerations concerning women's education

Throughout the literature on education and health, there is both a recognition of the importance of societal values in creating an environment where women's education is important and a faith in the psychosocial benefits of modernization, however it is arrived at. Nevertheless, fatalism, lack of faith in Western medicine, and the practice of traditions that increase exposure to dangers to health are related to complex cultural patterns and to rational responses to the realities and priorities of women themselves. There is a painfully fine line between blaming the victim for her 'traditional' orientation while imposing Western values upon her, and taking advantage of the research findings reviewed here to help women to improve their situation. The latter requires lay explanations of research findings, recognition of cultural contexts, and encouragement for women to make their own judgments based on information.

But clearly, women's education is one of the winners in the production-of-health contest. If societies could or would put the necessary resources into educating women, many other determinants would be positively affected. As usual, however, change does not necessarily follow understanding. It is neither quick nor easy to educate women formally. As we have seen, the ethos of a society in part determines its willingness to invest in women's education. The barriers are often great (Herz *et al.* 1991). Girls help at home. It costs money to send them to school, and because of discrimination, few opportunities, and marriage outside the family, the family may not recover that cost. Travel to school may be dangerous for girls. There may be few educated female role models; most or all of the teachers may be male. Pregnancy may end schooling for females. Poor countries may find it difficult to institute policies and pay for schooling for girls, although a president of the World Bank (Briscoe 1992) recently estimated the cost of educating as many girls as boys to be $3.2 billion – less than 1 percent of the total investment in new capital goods by governments in the developing world. This money could be raised by 'forgoing construction of one out of 30 power plants planned over the next 10 years.'

None the less, change through this mechanism will be relatively slow. Education levels are falling in many developing countries owing to structural adjustment policies. Alternative related pathways to improved health include intensive health education, which may not be cost-effective; literacy campaigns, which may not have long-term effects; other non-formal education initiatives; and empowerment strategies.

Empowerment

Now cancer isn't something that happens overnight. It must have been secretly growing in her, a thwarted appetite for flesh, for a long time. I've been sitting here thinking and I believe it was hunger that killed Mami. Not the times there wasn't enough to eat, because Mami always found ways to stretch a little bacalao a long way. I think it was the wild dog hunger in her that never had anything to eat but the insults she swallowed, and those English brand names all full of corners, and the vicious retorts she never made to my father's abuse....

The kind of hunger that ate Mami's stomach can't be kept in. It isn't housebroken, tame. It can go years looking like a farm animal, hauling water, carrying wood, cooking and digging and trying to stretch a handful of change into a living. It can even be hit with a stick and cursed for its lameness, but watch out. Sooner or later it gnaws at the rope that binds it, and if that rope is your own life, you die.... If you swallow bitterness, she says, you eat death.

Instead of swallowing bitterness, I've been spitting it up.... I got home from Mami's funeral and that Monday after work I began this book. Now it's done. It's a kind of cookbook I wrote for Mami. A different set of recipes than the ones she lived her life by, those poisonous brews of resignation and regret, those soups and monotony and neighborly malice that only give you gas.... [M]y favorite recipe is the one at the very end. Remedy For Heartburn. This is the most challenging recipe in my book, comadres. The ingredients? You already have them. In your pockets, in your purses, in your bellies and your bedrooms. For this kind of broth, there can't be too many cooks. Get together. Stir the stuff around. Listen to your hunger. Get ready. Get organized. (Morales 1991: 56)

Each of the factors discussed hitherto is part of the literature on health, and is thought to be important to the health of women who live in difficult circumstances. Although they work at multiple levels, there are many recognized interactions and intersections and many unanswered questions about these factors' relationships to aspects of health and to each other. The challenge to puzzle-solvers remains. Given what is known and what is likely, how can current efforts to improve health be facilitated? Chapter 8 will suggest that the tools to study and to understand complex, non-linear, dynamic, dialectical processes do not currently exist; thus progress on understanding and untangling the web will be slow. But we must continue to concentrate on factors that strengthen resistance resources and weaken threats to health. The empowerment of women who have useful expertise and experience but who are usually excluded from planning processes will facilitate the design and use of more sustainable strategies for dealing with the vagaries of geography and climate, and for creating a more healthful local environment (Moser 1993; Shiva 1989). Empowerment also speaks directly to garnering resources – income, food, housing, and other basic needs. Empowerment may be particularly effective because it works at so many levels – affecting, for example, water availability, the effectiveness of medical care, social organization, and psychosocial and psycho-neuroimmunological processes at the individual level.

The evidence on the role of empowerment and health to date is speculative, gathered through informal observations of women who are participating in empowerment projects and from literature descriptive of the process. None the less, it can be seen that many repercussions on both women's and children's health follow from the empowerment process. Informal interviews that I conducted in both Costa Rica and Honduras indicate that women who have benefited from participation in empowerment groups feel that they have more control over their environment, so they take active steps to improve that environment. Their values change, and good hygiene and nutrition become more important. Their increased self-confidence helps them to gain access to health care and to communicate more effectively with health care providers. Through their new or strengthened organizations, they obtain more resources for their community: health care, water, food, sanitation. While they do not escape poverty, they do often increase their income. And – perhaps most importantly – their sense of community, friendship, and mutual support leads to the enhanced psychological and physical well-being that translates into improved health.

Since research and theorizing on empowerment and health are in their infancy, there is little literature to report and review. Nina

Wallerstein, a health educator working in the USA, has been the leading promoter of the importance of empowerment to health. In work that is not specific to women, she has begun to describe that relationship (Wallerstein 1992). Looking at empowerment primarily as an antidote to powerlessness, she traces the history of research into the effects of powerlessness on health. Wallerstein presents two useful theoretical models: one of powerlessness, encompassing many of the social and psychological determinants I have discussed, and a second of empowerment. Her first model is one of negative health – identifying physical and social risk factors associated with disease, and suggesting that they act through powerlessness and a lack of control over one's destiny. Powerlessness and lack of control are indicators of lack of empowerment. Among the risk factors she identifies are poverty, low status, high psychological and physical demands, low control, high chronic stress, low social support, and lack of resources.

Wallerstein (1992: 199) asks: 'Can empowerment as a health-promoting strategy reduce the risk of ill-health due to powerlessness?' Relying on social-psychological theories relating self-concept and world-view to health, and studies of the importance of social support, participation, and the community to health, she proposes a model for health. The process of empowerment, through increasing a sense of community, participation, and empathy, works to reduce social and physical risk factors, thereby increasing both psychological and community empowerment. Those two types of empowerment are linked through the process of critical thinking or conscientization that locates the disempowered individual in a sociopolitical context. She sees the 'act of participating itself in community change' as promoting 'changed perceptions of self-worth and a belief in the mutability of harmful situations, which replaces perceived powerlessness' (Wallerstein 1992: 202). She also recognizes that an organized community can work together to improve health.

Thus Wallerstein sees empowerment as reducing social and physical risk factors, decreasing powerlessness and lack of control and thereby reducing disease. If the health outcomes are broadened to include positive ones such as fitness and well-being, her second model could also be seen as salutogenic. She suggests (1992: 204) that this model is testable, and that her 'findings need to be characterized as preliminary until the concepts can be tested directly.' I argue in my conclusion that this preliminary evidence is strong enough to lead to actions without such tests.

Summary and Conclusions: The Three Es

One can also look at the relationships between equity, education, and empowerment to provide at least theoretical evidence of the positive role of empowerment in health. Empowerment has an increase in women's status and autonomy among its goals. Autonomy, in the sense of making personal decisions and having control over one's activities, occurs at the individual level. It is also possible to consider group autonomy, and look at the independence and sense of control of a women's empowerment group. As I have indicated, however, there has been little work directly linking autonomy to health – it appears in the literature only as a piece of the larger, theoretical picture. If women do not have autonomy, they cannot make the health decisions that they are in the best position to make, they cannot see providers when they need to, they cannot use their family's limited resources in ways most likely to improve health, they cannot keep their own earnings, and they may be unable to obtain formal and informal education. At a societal level, if women's autonomy is not valued, then women will have lower status and suffer from lack of opportunity.

While there is much discussion of the importance of women's status to health in the literature on women's health, again there is little that is not theoretical. Women's status can, however, be directly linked to Wallerstein's model, since, almost by definition, low status implies powerlessness. Low status is a major contextual element in women's lives, relating to needs, strategies and options, and available resources. Will women's empowerment improve their status, and thus be linked to their health through that pathway? That is: will empowerment change the macro-setting so that women's situations are improved? Again, the issue is, at least in part, definitional – almost tautological. For empowerment to occur, activities must address social change. If empowerment brings women increased power, prestige, and esteem, then their status will have been improved. If no change occurs, then empowerment did not occur, although there may have been individual change.

Empowerment and changes in status and autonomy, however, can take place at the family/household, community, or regional/national level. Different women's groups focus on different levels – some, like SEWA, the Indian trade union described above, on all simultaneously. Thus a woman (or a group of women) may improve her (their) position within the household only, within the community only, or only on a national level through legislation or other political action. It is recognized that a route to improved status is through organized activities. If change is to occur on all levels, as is ultimately required, it is most likely to come about through networks or hierarchies of organizations. One can look to local organizations to facilitate change in the house-·hold and the local community. As these groups gain strength, they can make alliances and devote some of their energy and resources to the larger political and economic setting. It is difficult to imagine an improvement in women's status that is not fueled by groups dedicated to their empowerment. Power is not ceded or shared unless those lacking power demand it. Those demands must be backed up by a combination of might, right, and historical openings. This process is going on. The empowerment movement is in its infancy. At this point one can monitor the process, assist it, document its successes and failures, and look to see what health-specific benefits accrue. If the collection of some gender-specific measures that reflect women's status and health is made a priority, long-term trends can be studied.

There is a strong relationship between the benefits of education to women as described in the literature and the goals of empowerment. Education and empowerment can be linked through the psychosocial and behavioral changes that each is thought to effect: increased sense of control, confidence, competence, changed behaviors, increased access to resources, and savvy or an ability to get around in modern society. They are also linked through larger societal effects on women's status and roles. As we have seen, education entered into research on health through the back door. Because it is relatively easy to study, and serves as a marker for social class, it appeared in many projects looking at many different outcomes, and usually showed up as an important predictor. As we have observed, however, there has been little more than speculation about the ways in which education improves health. Much like empowerment, education is multifaceted, varies from place to place, and is related to so many different factors that it is difficult, if not impossible, to sort out its particular role.

The unanswered question is whether empowerment, like education, can be linked to improved health for both children and women. Empowerment, however, is harder to measure. Programs are informal and small, governments have no reason to count them or track participation rates, and programs vary much more than does schooling. Therefore, it may never be possible to test empowerment's relationship to health in the way that education's relationship has been tested. It may be possible, although not necessarily within a reasonable length of time, to examine the pathways from education to health more closely. As measurement tools for such studies are developed, they can also be applied to women who participate in empowerment projects. This would be one way to get at individual changes, although studying enough women to obtain statistically significant results will be extremely costly and difficult. However, empowerment has the additional group component. Individual change is not enough. Groups and communities must also be examined. As Wallerstein suggests, this can be approached by looking for changes in a group's competence and its environment.

To consider empowerment as a supplement to education is in no way to suggest that the education of women need not remain a primary goal of all societies. I have not addressed other known benefits of education, such as improved status, opportunities for employment, and increased information in many domains. The availability of education is an indication of a government's desire and ability to provide essential services to all its citizens. Empowerment is a strategy designed to compensate for societal disadvantage that results in part from the failures of government.

Empowerment is related to both equity and education for women, and these in turn are related to health. Therefore, by rules of logic, empowerment is related to health. But it is not my intention here to lay out neatly a relationship between empowerment and health. This is not feasible at this time, and it may never be possible. The relationships are not linear, not stable, not universal, not independent, not causal, not at all well-behaved in a scientific sense. The point of this book, however, is to establish that the relationship is none the less credible. While some of the relationships are testable, and should and will be tested in the future, what is needed now is a considered look at the whole picture. There is a great risk of overlooking the importance of empowerment and losing this historical opportunity to assist women in activities that can improve both their health and their well-being while we wait for proof. Whatever the scientific evidence, social and political decisions determine the course of policy and of history. Reasoned arguments supporting empowerment, in conjunction with clear evidence of the disadvantaged position of women and its effect on their families and children, and of the increasingly effective organizing efforts on behalf of women and their empowerment, can and should influence policy and history.

Note

1. A Global Tribunal of Violations of Women's Human Rights was held in Vienna in June 1993, in conjunction with the UN's World Conference on Human Rights.

PART III

Scientific Inquiry

8

Theories of Scientific Inquiry

[T]he long course of history has made clear that all secular communities, science as much as any other, are finite and flawed; that reality is complex; and that there are no given, cast-in-stone strategies for confronting and coming to an understanding of reality...

Our science will hit its stride when we understand that our reality is formidably complex, dominated by asymmetries, and forever challenged by the unpredicted. (Bevan 1991: 477, 482)

In this chapter I want to contrast two approaches to scientific inquiry, providing a theoretical framework for the earlier discussion on development, empowerment, and health. The first is the traditional positivist approach that has shaped scientific inquiry for the last three centuries. No work done at this time can avoid being affected by that tradition. I believe, however, that the development of a framework linking development, women's situations, empowerment, and health calls for a less restrictive approach – one that is less reliant on linearity, continuity, emotional distance between observer and observed, and a belief in predictability. Therefore, I will also discuss an evolving set of new constructs that are being developed in response to the identified inadequacies of positivism. These constructs, while they are not integrated and formulated into a single, coherent framework, provide perspectives that are useful for an examination of the issues under investigation here.

Traditional Perspectives on Scientific Inquiry

Science can be defined as the use of systematic study and methods to identify, describe, investigate experimentally, and/or explain theoretically any phenomena (Morris 1973). A certain type of science – interchangeably named positivism, logical positivism, or logical empiricism – has long dominated natural science. This philosophy of science posits the primacy of deductive logic as the method used to establish truth and 'the primacy of observation in assessing the truth of statements of fact' (Morris 1973: 767). First developed and adopted by the natural scientists, it was later incorporated into the fields of social science.

Joyce Nielsen (1990: 4–5) describes five basic assumptions of positivism that pertain to scientific inquiry into diverse phenomena:

1. the natural/social world is knowable through the senses (objectively) and has an objective reality;
2. objective truth cannot be obtained through subjectivity;
3. 'different observers exposed to the same data will come to more or less the same conclusions';
4. 'there is order in the social world,' 'social life is patterned,' and 'this pattern takes a predominantly cause-and-effect form';
5. the deductive method – reasoning from the general, the hypothetical, or the theoretical to the specific – is 'the best, if not the only, legitimate way to ground knowledge.' Inductive methods – reasoning from specific observations to the theoretical, while theoretically valid, are less acceptable.

This philosophy 'emphasizes rationality, impersonality, and prediction and control of events or phenomena studied' (Nielsen 1990: 5). With control come progress, improvement, and development. The implications are that scientific inquiry into health carried out in this framework will continually bring us closer to reality, to objective truths.

Critiques of and Alternatives to Positivism

The framework that engendered this perspective is now being questioned from many sides. In *The Structure of Scientific Revolutions*, originally published in 1962, Thomas Kuhn (1970) was one of the first to question the inevitability of positivist tenets within the natural sciences. Kuhn questioned some of the traditional beliefs of science: the existence of a knowable reality, the goal-orientation of positivism that equates knowledge with improvement, the objectivity of the scientist, and the disparagement of inductive reasoning. However, it is his recognition of the relativity of science – its dependence on history and on the world-view of its participants – that has had such a major impact on current views about scientific inquiry. As a historian of science, Kuhn observed that science itself progresses in a non-linear and sometimes discontinuous fashion. New science does not grow inevitably out of old science, but often comes out of drastic shifts in world-view, revolutions he described as paradigm change. While even Kuhn uses the word *paradigm* in several different senses, the most common understanding of the term is that 'it stands for the entire constellation of beliefs, values, techniques, and so on shared by the members of a given community' (Kuhn 1970: 175). Kuhn observed that several times in the history of modern science, individual scientists – often young and marginal to their profession – picked up on 'phenomena that either do not fit, contradict, or cannot be explained by the existing dominant paradigm' (Nielsen 1990: 12). If they or others also had available or developed an alternative paradigm that could explain these phenomena, and were able to persuade enough others in their field of its usefulness, a revolution or paradigm shift occurred. Among the scientists identified by Kuhn as having contributed to paradigms shifts are Copernicus, Newton, Lavoisier, and Einstein.

Following in Kuhn's footsteps, at least three major attacks on the positivist paradigm have developed over the past several decades. These come from: (1) new sciences that include chaos theory, the science of complexity, and a theory of a dialectical science; (2) feminist research theory; and (3) postmodernism. While each of these newer movements comes from quite different theoretical and disciplinary backgrounds, many of their criticisms and evolving theories overlap. After discussing each of these, I will present a research-specific formulation of the fledgling new paradigm known as New Paradigm Research.

One caveat is in order: the critiques to be presented must be seen in their historical context. At its inception, logical empiricism was a timely reaction to the domination of religious and feudal hierarchies; it was a strategy to democratize knowledge and place it at the service of commerce, capitalism, science, and people's lives. H. T. Wilson (1983) argues that rationality and domination were originally 'distinct, if not opposing notions'; it is modern bureaucracies and meritocracies that have 'fused' them, marshalling rationality to the cause of domination.

The new sciences

Chaos theory

The new sciences formed as natural scientists from several different fields – such as physics, biology, and meteorology – realized that classical scientists had tended to ignore many observations which either complicated or contradicted the assumptions of their disciplines:

Where chaos begins, classical science stops. For as long as the world has had physicists inquiring into the laws of nature, it has suffered a special ignorance about disorder in the atmosphere, in the turbulent sea, in the fluctuations of wildlife populations, in the oscillations of the heart and the brain. The irregular side of nature, the discontinuous and erratic side – these have been puzzles to science, or worse, monstrosities. (Gleick 1987: 3)

According to James Gleick (1987: 304), chaos theory, whose development was contingent on the advent of computers and the development of the field of non-linear mathematics, is based on a few key precepts: 'Simple systems give rise to complex behavior. Complex systems give rise to simple behavior. And most important, the laws of complexity hold universally, caring not at all for the details of a system's constituent atoms.' While patterns do exist, they may be unobservable and disorderly. Objects are pervious, strongly affected by their environment and by what mathematicians call initial conditions: local anomalies which are often too complicated and too random to be measured.

Specifically, chaos theoreticians acknowledge and even welcome non-linearity, lack of continuity, instability, and disorder. Chaos theory, by accepting non-linearity and discontinuity, challenges the concepts of knowability, predictability, controllability, and of quantifiable causes and effects in the natural sciences.

Complexity theory

As chaos theory evolved, an eclectic group of thinkers who accepted its tenets began to seek an explanation of the strong tendencies of systems (organs, computers, the brain, economies, political structures) to increase in complexity – to organize, learn, adapt, and evolve, in seeming contradiction of the law of entropy:

Somehow, the old categories of science were beginning to dissolve. Somehow, a new, unified science was out there waiting to be born. It would be a rigorous science, ... [b]ut instead of being a quest for the ultimate particles, it would be about flux, change, and the forming and dissolving of patterns. Instead of ignoring everything that wasn't uniform and predictable, it would have a place for individuality and the accidents of history. Instead of being about simplicity, it would be about – well, complexity. (Waldrop 1992: 17)

Complexity theory can be seen as an extension or offshoot of chaos theory; it therefore presents similar critiques.[1] Its foci, however, are complexity, connections, interactions, and continual change and motion. This new science involves natural and social scientists: biologists, physicists, computer scientists, chemists, economists, and psychologists.

Among its basic precepts are a world that resembles a kaleidoscope where nothing is fixed, and 'virtually everything and everybody in the world is caught up in a vast, nonlinear web of incentives and constraints and connections' (Waldrop 1992: 65). Complexity develops in an area between stagnation and chaos, stability and fluidity. Systems organize hierarchically from the bottom up into greater levels of complexity, and each level has different properties that do not generalize to other levels. Given this vision of the world, '[t]he crucial skill is insight, the ability to see connections' (Waldrop 1992: 21). Inductive techniques are seen as more useful than deductive ones. The work of science is seen not as prediction but as explanation and understanding – the telling of 'stories that explain what the world is like and how the world came to be as it is' (Waldrop 1992: 318).

This type of science is dramatically different in its implications for policy from one that believes in predicting behavior, isolating components, and intervening based on simplified, stable, linear models. It speaks to careful observation, cautious actions, and lowered expectations:

> What is our relation to a world like that? Well, we are made of the same elemental compositions. So we are a part of this thing that is never changing and always changing. If you think that you're a steamboat and can go up the river, you're kidding yourself. Actually, you're just the captain of a paper boat drifting down the river. If you try to resist, you're not going to get anywhere. On the other hand, if you quietly observe the flow, realizing that you're part of it, realizing that the flow is ever-changing and always leading to new complexities, then every so often you can stick an oar into the river and punt yourself from one eddy to another.... It means that you try to see reality for what it is, and realize that the game you are in keeps changing, so that it's up to you to figure out the current rules of the game as it's being played.... [T]his is *not* a recipe for passivity, or fatalism. You apply available force to the maximum effect.... The idea is to observe, to act courageously, and to pick your timing well.... You go for viability, something that's workable, rather than what's 'optimal.' (Waldrop 1992: 330–31, 333, quoting Brian Arthur)

George Cowen describes it as exercising damage control, iterating day to day and constantly doing some course corrections to make the future a little better (Waldrop 1992).

Barbara McClintock

Barbara McClintock personifies the paradigm-shifting scientist. She is a geneticist who worked alone for thirty years 'doing her own thing.' She has belatedly received recognition, including a Nobel prize, for her work.[2] Although she is not a participant in the complexity movement, she has similarly rejected deductive methods, using induction to discover 'a different approach to genetics, one that recognizes and accepts the complexity of interacting systems, including the interrelationships of observer to observed, cell to organism, and organism to environment: an alternative to the dominance of a simple mechanical order or the dictates of "master" molecules within the cell' (Fee 1986: 48).

Herbert Blalock (1964: 8) stated: 'Put simply, the basic problem faced in all sciences is that of how much to oversimplify reality.' This need to oversimplify led to 'overlooking' the exception, the anomaly. McClintock identified so strongly with the plants she studied, and observed them so intently, that it was the differences between them, the unpredictable lack of predictability, that interested her. 'If [something] doesn't fit, there's a reason and you find out what it is' (Keller 1985: 163). Her now accepted theory of genetic transposition – concerned not only with the form and structure of genes but with their functional and organizational context – was derived through her close observance of differences. Her work represents a shift away from a focus on the isolation and differentiation of objects towards the investigation of connections and relationships, a search for pathways rather than milestones:

> To McClintock, the goal of science is not prediction per se, but understanding; not the power to manipulate, but empowerment – the kind of power that results from an understanding of the world around us, that simultaneously reflects and affirms our connection to that world. (Keller 1985: 166)

Dialecticism

Dialecticism, the third new science to reject positivism, is a perspective that has evolved over time, moving from the realm of philosophy to that of politics and economics and, more recently, to science. While the meaning changed as different philosophers, beginning with Plato, defined and redefined it, Hegel's interpretation, as popularized by Karl Marx, currently holds sway. Hegel saw an endlessly repeating cycle of revealed contradiction, conflict, and attempts at resolution in life and in nature. Development and change are results of these conflicts and attempted resolutions. Denis Goulet (1985: 100) summarizes modern variations on dialectical theory:

> One important trait is common to all these positions: the rejection of an equilibrium model of change based on homeostatic accommodation or

unilinear movement. Basic processes are said to involve if not contradiction, at least opposition, sudden reversals of fortune or position, a degree of unpredictability which escapes purely rational understanding, an element of discontinuity at the very heart of continuity, of new beginnings out of old deaths.

Dialecticism challenges the reductionist assumption that a whole is made up of discrete and harmonious parts and is no more than the sum of those parts. It is also a perspective that is concerned first and foremost with relations and interactions. Sylvia Tesh (1988) presents the mind and the body, or the individual and society, as constructs exemplifying an irreducible and continual interaction. Biologists Richard Levins and Richard Lewontin (1985) have incorporated these concepts into a dialectical framework for science, whose precepts are:

- The whole is a relation of heterogeneous parts that have no prior independent existence as parts.
- Parts have properties that are characteristic of them only as they are parts of wholes.
- The interpenetration of parts and wholes is a consequence of the interchangeability of subject and object, or cause and effect.
- Change is a characteristic of all systems and all aspects of all systems.
- Not only do parameters change in response to changes in the system of which they are a part, but the laws of transformation themselves change.
- Complex systems show spontaneous activity.
- The various levels of organization are partly autonomous and reciprocally interacting.

The new sciences have thus put forth many ideas, many ways of describing a reality that positivism did not capture. Each of the five tenets of positivism described by Nielsen has come under attack. The existence of disorder and constant change argues against a knowable, objective reality. The inevitable interactions and connections between observer and observed undermine the concepts of objectivity and replicability. Non-linearity, discontinuity, chaos, and complexity all contradict rationalism, prediction, and control. Inductive methods, based on careful observation, are considered superior to deductive ones as we try to understand a complex, dynamic, and highly interactive reality.

My presentation of the new sciences here is highly simplified, lacking attention to either the different subject matters or the complex mathematics that both lead to and support much of the theory. None the less, we can identify elements relevant to the study of empowerment and health. These include a concentration on explanation and understanding; the primacy of insight and induction as tools for understanding; the essential nature of connections, interactions, context, change, non-linearity, competition, unpredictability, and the interpenetration of parts and wholes; the complex and non-hierarchical relationships between different levels of organization; and, from dialecticism, an explicit recognition of the relationship between politics and science. Many of these themes have simultaneously emerged from feminism and postmodernism.

Feminist critiques and alternatives

> Metaphors and models that stress context rather than isolated traits and behaviors, interactive rather than linear relations, and democratic rather than authoritarian models of order in both research and nature may enable less partial and distorted descriptions and explanations. These alternative metaphors and models have been associated with womanliness; their use can be thought of as infusing values arising from women's lives into scientific practices and outcomes. (Harding 1991: 301)

The second major challenge to traditional science has a broad base; it emerges from first world feminist movements. Its impetus was the recognition that women were essentially excluded from science: both as scientists within the natural sciences and some of the social sciences, and as subjects or objects of study within the natural and social sciences and humanities. Traditional science developed within patriarchal societies that did not question the assumption that the search for truth benefits everyone impartially – that what was good for men was also good for women. A 'male' science dominates not only nature but women as well. However, feminism, like dialecticism, posits conflict and competition as facets of reality. Like the dialecticians, feminists do not see science and politics as disjoint, but see knowledge and power as closely linked.

Evelyn Fox Keller (1985) has identified a spectrum of feminist critiques of science that corresponds to the spectrum of feminist politics – ranging from liberal to radical. At the more conservative end is what she calls the liberal charge of 'unfair employment practices': women are not proportionally represented among scientists. A slightly more radical criticism is that, owing to the dearth of women in science, men have defined the problems to be studied. Thus, for example, women's health problems have not received the attention they deserve. Yet more radical is a claim that the carrying out of experiments and their interpretations have been biased because women's perspectives have been excluded. Studies supporting these claims have been published in several fields, including primatology (Hrdy 1986), cell biology (The Biology and Gender Study Group 1989), and McClintock's work in genetics. Keller sees as the most radical critique that which questions the very precepts of science, particularly rationality, knowability, and objectivity.

Precepts

These three precepts are closely linked: if the world is organized in a fashion that is reflected by rules of logic, and that organization is observable, then it is knowable. If it is knowable, it is predictable and, given a mechanistic perspective, controllable. Also, if the world is so patterned – independent of who is observing it, where they are located, why they are observing it, and history – then objectivity, as it is traditionally understood, is advantageous. The less of his own idiosyncratic nature the observer brings to science, the 'better' the observation. Feminists, however, see a world that cannot be captured by logic. Ruth Hubbard (1990: 15) states:

> our scientific methodology permits us to examine only those natural phenomena that are repeatable and measurable. It cannot deal with unique occurrences or with systems that flow so smoothly and gradually or are so profoundly interwoven in their complexities that they cannot be broken up into measurable units without losing or changing their fundamental nature.

Joyce Nielsen (1990: 25) suggests that the model of nature preferred by Levins and Lewontin is one in which women actually and inevitably exist – one that more accurately defines their reality:

> [D]ialectical refers to discontinuities, oppositions, contradictions, tensions, and dilemmas that form part of women's concrete experience in patriarchal worlds – dilemmas that are realized only within a feminist consciousness.

Levins and Lewontin explicitly used their political standpoints to envision a better science, one that reflected their world-view. Many feminists follow their example. While there are many different interpretations of feminism and therefore many ways of doing feminist science, the *sine qua nons* of feminist science are: (1) any interpretation includes the perspective of women – as scientists and as subjects; (2) the new science should be for the benefit of women: 'What is common is the commitment to feminism both intellectually and politically, to theorizing and to practices that can help change the lives of women in general' (Bleier 1986: 17). As with the new scientists, it is probably too soon to know whether feminists have formulated an alternative paradigm, and, if so, in what types of science that paradigm will prove useful. Nevertheless, a theory of feminist inquiry *is* being developed through an active dialogue among feminists.

Feminist science acknowledges complexity and context, maintaining that simplification, based on logical positivistic models, distorts the fundamental nature and relationships of phenomena and their social and political context (Bleier 1986). While it embraces a dialectical approach – a search for contradiction and change as part of a process of a constantly evolving understanding – feminist science resists dichotomizations, particularly distinctions between subject and object and between mind and body:

> A feminist epistemology derived from women's labour in the world must represent a more complete materialism, a truer knowledge. It transcends dichotomies, insists on the scientific validity of the subjective, on the need to unite cognitive and affective domains; it emphasizes holism, harmony, and complexity rather than reductionism, domination, and linearity. (H. Rose 1986: 72)

As feminist epistemology evolves, certain concepts have been at the heart of the discussion. These include knowledge itself, power, objectivity, and research methods.

Knowledge and power

Feminist science does not reject the empiricism that underlies positivism; it is in fact based on experiential knowledge. Sandra Harding (1991: 308) suggests that although science is politics, it 'can produce reliable empirical information.' However, feminist empiricism begins with the life of the researcher, not with 'the testing of hypotheses in laboratory situations ... afterward, ... when the "research objects" have been detached from their real-life surroundings and broken down into their constituent parts' (Mies 1991: 66).

Feminists use empirical methods to look for forms of truth and knowledge, but are trying to develop their own definitions of these elusive constructs. Harding maintains that, through science, it is possible at least to move away from falsity and towards a transitory and dynamic truth. In the words of Donna Haraway (1991: 196), feminists are looking for 'better accounts of the world' – not for just any knowledge, but for one that makes sense. Adrienne Rich (1979: 187) argues: 'There is no "the truth," [nor] "a truth" – truth is not one thing, or even a system. It is an increasing complexity.' Gayatri Spivak (1987: 78) talks about 'a weave of knowing and not-knowing which is what knowing is.' Patricia Hill Collins (1991: 208) says that for those without power, knowledge is not enough: 'Knowledge without wisdom is adequate for the powerful, but wisdom is essential to the survival of the subordinate.' Wisdom is knowledge learned from experience, from life, not from books.

Feminists' insistence on the value of particular standpoints and of difference complicates the search for knowledge, for it must be accepting not only of individual differences among subjects but of differences in ways of knowing and in what 'makes sense.' African-American feminists such as Patricia Hill Collins have struggled to define the complex intersections of power relations from the perspective of black women, keeping the issues of differences and similarities in the forefront of feminist analyses. Feminisms of all forms stress the importance of recognizing and accepting differences, but there is an inevitable tension, a dialectical relationship, between 'diversity and difference' and 'integration and commonality' (Tong 1989: 7). What is to prevent feminism, in its efforts to recognize and valorize differences, from slipping into total relativism, giving equal value to everyone's perspective, accepting everything or nothing as true?

The issues of power, control, and domination appear repeatedly in the work of feminist theorists. Elizabeth Fee (1986: 48) sees power as the central issue in critiques of science, with gender being only one of a number of 'dominant/dominated relationships whose intersections must be analysed and placed at the center of a feminist politics.' Sandra Harding (1991) suggests that we need to unlink power and knowledge, using knowledge in order to understand rather than manipulate and control. At the same time, feminist scholarship is geared to changing the status quo, so feminist knowledge must be accompanied by the power to cause change. In the long run, however, feminist standpoint theorists want a socially situated science that has 'democratic, participatory politics,' in both its conduct and its goals.

Finally, feminist knowledge is not an end in itself:

> Neither emotion nor ethics is subordinated to reason. Instead, emotion, ethics, and reason are used as interconnected, essential components in assessing knowledge claims. In an Afrocentric feminist epistemology, values lie at the heart of the knowledge validation process such that inquiry always has an ethical aim. (Collins 1991: 219)

What, then, is scientific knowledge, and how do we gain it, given that 'truth' and 'reality' are neither fixed nor unitary? Feminist knowledge seeks to 'make sense of the world' by recognizing and accepting its complexity, its dynamism, and its ultimate unknowability. The identification of patterns based on connections among unique entities in order to understand and improve the situation of women is a key element of feminist epistemology (Scheman 1991). Knowledge becomes centered around ethics and values. Feminist scientists seek more than equity – they look towards confronting the basic issues of control and domination in order to move towards more egalitarian and participatory ways of knowing and uses of knowledge.

Objectivity

Feminist researchers have struggled with the meaning and usefulness of objectivity, both as part of their assault on domination and exclusivity and because they have found it to be a barrier to understanding. Traditional standards of objectivity – separation between researcher and researched, suppression of the personal characteristics of the scientist, ignorance of the underlying world-view of the scientist and the science – are rejected by many feminist scientists. Revised concepts of objectivity, reliability, and validity have been proposed by feminists and by others (see Chapter 9 below).

There remains, however, a tension between the need to understand and to change women's lives on the one hand, and to be credible on the other. Sandra Harding (1991) resolves this by defining a concept she calls *strong objectivity*, which recognizes the positive effects on research of the incorporation of a feminist standpoint. A feminist standpoint requires a conscious definition of oneself as a feminist and a clear statement that one is located at that standpoint. Feminists must avoid 'various forms of unlocatable, and so irresponsible, knowledge claims. Irresponsible means unable to be called into account' (Haraway 1991: 121). Women, as outsiders, have both a unique perspective and little reason blindly to defend the status quo. Science with women's input is 'less partial and distorted than the picture of nature and social relations that emerges from conventional research' (Harding 1991: 121).

Methods

> [T]he methodological task has become generating and refining more interactive, contextualized methods in the search for pattern and meaning rather than for prediction and control. (Lather 1988: 571)

A final element being addressed by feminist scientists has to do with research methods. Since existing methods have been designed by and for logical positivism, do feminists need new ones that reflect their world-view? While some new methods, mostly qualitative, are being incorporated into women's science, in general, variations of traditional methods are being used (Reinharz 1992). Participatory research, open-ended interviewing, standpoint-derived hypotheses, and an acceptance of the 'validity' of the interaction between researcher and researched are examples of this. It is possible, however – given the overlap be-tween concepts that underlie both feminist research theory and the new sciences of chaos, complexity, and dialecticism – that method-ologies and methods from those areas may, in time, be applicable in feminist research. If so, it may be possible to use quantitative methods in areas where connections, relations, initial conditions, and smallness are crucial – areas that now seem better served by qualitative ones.

Summary

Feminist research has specific goals: the inclusion of women's perspec-tives and the betterment of their lives. Its proponents are looking to understand complex and dynamic situations, rejecting the concepts of universal truths and insisting on the inclusion of the realities of those who have no or little power. This requires a rethinking of the tools and methods of research – focusing on intense observations, involvement, and contextualization. Much of the literature in the field of feminist research is in the form of case studies that focus on actual feminist inquiry rather than on theory. It may be, as is the case with complexity theory, that the evolution of a new research paradigm is proceeding inductively, experientially, and being subjectively observed (or observed with strong objectivity) so that the methodology is thus reflecting the theory itself.

Postmodernism

> Philosophically speaking, the essence of the postmodern argument is that the dualisms which continue to dominate Western thought are inadequate for understanding a world of multiple causes and effects interacting in complex and non-linear ways, all of which are rooted in a limitless array of historical and cultural specificities. (Lather 1991: 21)

The third intellectual movement that has contributed to the assault on traditional science is postmodernism, an exceptionally thorny and abstruse set of loosely related philosophical arguments that are princi-pally and specifically reactions to positivism. These arguments attack formalism – the centrality of rules of logic in science and geometric form in art and architecture; refute the idea of ineluctable progress (modernity) in all intellectual endeavors; and reject the truth of any single perspective.

The movement has had a major impact on academic feminists, many of whom are in disciplines strongly affected by postmodernist theory: literature, culture, arts and architecture, philosophy of thought, and history. In many of these fields, the recognition of the exclusion of women's voices has generated a strong response from feminists. More recently, postmodernism has made inroads into the natural sciences (Rouse 1991). Postmodernists, in so far as they can be discussed as a group, share with feminists a disbelief in universal theories of knowledge, objectivity, and reason, and a rejection of the use of knowledge as a means of domination.

Feminists criticize postmodernism because it has frequently ignored questions of gender, has been accused of 'political naivety' for its decontexualized perspective, and has not resolved issues of relativism – it is unable or unwilling to accord preference to any one voice over another (Fraser and Nicholson 1990). Thus although postmodernism 'supports pluralistic, decentered forms of knowledge' (Jansen 1990: 243), it is not clear that *any* framework remains under its auspices, let alone a new one that can help us to improve women's health. Although feminists also lack a strategy that declares one description or understanding 'better' than another, they are united through the underlying goal of improving life for women.

There is an active dialogue between postmodernists, feminists, and postmodernist feminists as to the relationships between the individual and the community that is relevant to discussions about health. In the current framework, individualism holds the self as the highest value, seeing all others as the same – as recipients of certain rights regardless of who they are – while communalism hopes to smooth away or bury individual differences in some common vision of social interaction. Iris Young (1990: 320) attacks the traditional dichotomization/opposition of those concepts, arguing that what is needed is a 'concept of social relations that embody openness to unassimilated otherness with justice and appreciation.' What Young and others are searching for is some way of living together where individuals are valued for who they are, for their differences and their unique and communal selves. Sylvia Tesh (1988) presents Cuba after its revolution as a possible model. In interviews, she found Cubans describing the State as *we*, not as *they*. Thus individuals saw themselves not as discrete but as a member of a fluid community.

As with many of the critiques of current modes of thought, it is easier to identify the problems and to envision alternatives than to figure out how to operationalize those alternatives. None the less, Linda Nicholson (1990: 12, paraphrasing Haraway) credits postmodernism for moving theory forward: 'what has now become possible is a politics which embraces a recognition of the multiple, pregnant, and contradictory aspects of both our individual and collective identities.'

New paradigm research

It is difficult to synthesize these evolving perspectives into a coherent framework within which to carry out scientific inquiry and research. Nevertheless, a group of British social science researchers, who originally came together in the late 1970s, have attempted to pull together some of these concepts from dialecticism and feminism into a coherent new research paradigm for social science. They developed a *New Paradigm Research Manifesto*, the ninth draft of which states twelve theoretical principles for new paradigm research (Reason and Rowan 1981a):

1. Research can never be neutral.
2. All research enables change.
3. The researcher and the researched co-own the project and share power in the process and product of the research.
4. 'The shared language and praxis of subject and researcher create 'the world' to be studied.'
5. The research is intended to create active knowing that enables self-awareness, autonomous, self-directed action, and power to change the situation of the participants.
6. Human inquiry is 'learning through risk-taking in living.'
7. '[T]here is a new kind of tight and rigorous synthesis of subjectivity and objectivity.'
8. Particularities are celebrated.
9. Generalizations are based on acknowledging particularities and useful as 'general statements about the power, possibilities, and limits of persons acting as agents.'
10. 'Multi-level, multidisciplinary models of understanding' are required 'to do justice to the person-in-context as a whole.'
11. People are not things and the human costs of actions must be evaluated.
12. Research leads to knowledge which leads to power.

New paradigm research incorporates feminist precepts and ethics and postmodernist emphasis on particularities and multiple voices. Its activist perspective encourages the search for new approaches to scientific inquiry.

Summary and Conclusions

In summary, twentieth-century natural and social science has been dominated by a single paradigm, logical positivism, based on assumptions of linearity, continuity, progress, order, and reducibility. It has led to scientific practices that value control and prediction, objectivity, repeatability, and deduction. Certain phenomena are poorly explained within this framework, and women in particular have often been excluded from it. Positivism can be viewed as a framework that is too constricting to support a broad investigation in women's health and women's lives. The dense web of factors and situations will not fit into it without oversimplification.

The newer theories, while they may someday fit together and form a supportive structure, appear at this time as interesting, commingled components without a set of instructions. There may, nonetheless, be an evolving framework, growing out of positivism and moving towards something new, something that is being honed on the edges of the natural and social sciences. This new framework will be intrinsically difficult to elucidate, since it encompasses holism, the particularities of experience and context, complexity, connections and interactions, multiple levels, conflict and dialecticism, democracy, and a desire to contribute to social change. However, in the words of Naomi Scheman (1991: 185): 'While it is uncomfortable to depart from commonly accepted standards when new standards are not yet defined, the evolving framework also incorporates uncertainty and a lack of control over events and relationships.' As we have seen, many people are in the process of weaning themselves away from the very real comforts of certainty and control.

Notes

1. John Casti (1994: 263, 268) presents a different, potentially more useful formulation, grouping under a rubric of *complexification* six 'quite different types of surprise generators' that lead to counterintuitive behaviors with which we must learn to live – logical tangles and self-references lead to paradoxical conclusions, chaotic

motion leads to deterministic randomness, static instability and catastrophes lead to discontinuity from smoothness, uncomputability leads to output that transcends rules, irreducibility to non-decomposible behaviors, and emergence to self-organizing patterns.

2. The information on McClintock is derived primarily from Keller (1985: ch. 9).

9

Methods and Practice
of Scientific Inquiry

In Chapter 8 I described the limitations of traditional scientific and analytic theory, and presented some fledgling alternatives. In this chapter I discuss the limitations of traditional methods and practice with regard to studying the process of empowerment, and introduce some potentially more suitable strategies. The relationship between empowerment and health is not unique in this respect – many other important research questions are also poorly served by the dominant analytic techniques. However, because of their dominance, those of us who frame our questions within newer paradigms must be clear as to why we need new techniques.

For all the variation in content among the fields and subfields of natural and social science, a set of fairly standardized techniques dominates scientific inquiry. In general, one (a) formulates a testable hypothesis based on existent knowledge; (b) designs a study and its instruments, and pretests data collection instruments and procedures; (c) conducts the study, which may be experimental or descriptive, and gathers data; (d) uses well-defined techniques to edit, reduce, and statistically analyze those data; and (e) interprets the information and disseminates the results.

Warning: this chapter is of necessity somewhat technical, and I have tried to cover a lot of ground. But I know of no other place where the many issues related to conducting non-traditional research have been brought together, so I hope that those readers who do or plan to do research, or support research, will find the chapter useful. I have tried to make the issues more explicit through examples of research into empowerment and health; I assume, however, that readers will bring their own areas of interest to the discussion, and thereby expand and extend my arguments.

Hypothesis Testing and Rules of Proof

From early statistical analyses to determine the effect of different fertilizers on the growth of certain crops to recent epidemiological studies of the effects of electromagnetic fields on health, hypotheses have been formulated inductively and subjected to deductive analyses of real-world data. A hypothesis is defined as 'a supposition, arrived at from observation or reflection, that leads to refutable predictions' (Last 1988: 61). These refutable predictions have to do with observable and measurable relationships. Refutability is vital, since within the positivist framework truth is not in fact ascertainable through research alone:

> [I]f the hypothesis is not contradicted it remains a conjectured explanation of the alleged relationship; if the hypothesis is contradicted, in even a single instance, it is rejected. Thus, no amount of experience can confirm an hypothesis; it can never be *verified* or proven to be true by experience. The evidence can, however, reject it decisively. (Kennedy 1983: 15)

Because of the importance of contradictory evidence, hypothesis testing is carried out in a non-intuitive manner. Rather than attempting to prove that a certain relationship exists (an impossibility), a study is designed to prove that it does not exist. Thus the hypothesis to be tested – the null hypothesis – usually posits no relationship. If this hypothesis can be rejected on the basis of some agreed-upon test, then there is an increased 'level of confidence' that the posited relationship does exist.

While it is non-intuitive, such reasoning makes abstract sense. Basic underlying assumptions, however, are that the relationships in question are stable; common, if not universal; and measurable. Questions such as one posed in this study – 'Is empowerment related to the health of women living in difficult circumstances?' – are concerned with relationships that are constantly in flux, deeply embedded in a local environment, and difficult – perhaps impossible – to measure. At the very least, the application of effective hypothetico-deductive methodology to this question will require much preliminary work to develop measurable indicators, many studies to account for local variation, and much time owing to the lengthy process of empowerment and the intrinsic slowness of changes in health. Issues of sample size may be insurmountable; ethical considerations pose additional challenges. Yet the question is urgent, as data on women's health indicate. Decisions as to the best use of scarce resources are made continually, and often with little theoretical or research guidance.

A reliance on hypothesis testing as the acceptable scientific methodology protects researchers from their enthusiasms, narrows the issues they can investigate, provides society with a standard that facilitates decision-making, and reduces the number of voices that must be listened to. While the desire for objective, discriminating standards is understandable, in fact the actual behavior of scientists and decision-makers is more complex:

> In practice, the pressures on researchers to produce 'findings' supporting their hypotheses means that a non-significant result [i.e., acceptance of the null hypothesis] is rarely regarded as a refutation of the research hypothesis – instead the usual conclusion reached is that the study failed to *establish* that the differences were there. (Atkins and Jarrett 1979: 100)

Indeed, the complexities of research based on hypothetico-deductive techniques are such that oversimplification, flaws in design and implementation, and mathematical limitations often lead to very timid and circumscribed conclusions, to a *very* slow accretion of evidence and reduction of uncertainty.

This is the case even though the statistical standards adopted for hypothesis testing are quite high. The accepted standards call for no more than a 1 in 20 or a 1 in 100 chance that a non-existent relationship be considered to exist (Type-1 error). On the other hand, a 1 in 5 chance of not recognizing an existent relationship is acceptable (Type-2 error). It is in this sense that hypothesis testing is conservative, the assumption being that greater harm results from a Type-1 than from a Type-2 error. When we are testing the efficacy of a drug, it may be reasonable to err on the side of conservatism, to be more concerned about false positives than about false negatives. When we are looking to understand or explain social patterns and relationships, using techniques that are often clumsy and ill-suited, it may be more rational to leave the question open when there is significant doubt. It can be argued that for issues that may be life-threatening, such as exposures to environmental hazards, a standard based on the weight of the evidence is more logical. Thus if there was more than a 1 in 2 or 50 percent chance that the hypothesized relationship existed, it should be tentatively accepted. While this standard might seem extreme, there is a large numerical and philosophical gap between it and the accepted standards and therefore room for negotiation and experimentation.

Rothman (1990: 45–6) argues that by adopting such stringent protection against Type-2 errors, we are too likely to attribute an actual relationship to chance. Chance is used to explain results where 'the causal explanations are too intricate, the outcome is too complicated a function of the initial conditions, or the initial conditions are not

known sufficiently well.' He puts forward the following argument, remi-
niscent of a theme from the new sciences, but from within the logic of
positivism:

> Since an empirical scientist presumes that nature follows regular laws, the
> scientist confronted with an extreme observation or association should grasp
> at every opportunity to understand it rather than to ignore it.

Thus traditional hypothesis testing leads to a very restricted set of
comparisons, a conservative standard of support for one's primary
tenet, and a potential confusion of chance and complexity.

Design and Sampling Issues

Within a positivist framework, there are several issues that are problematic at the design stage of many quantitative studies. These have to do
with the definition of the study population, the selection of the study
sample, the type of data to be used, the reliability and validity of the
measures, the validity of the study itself, and the design of data
collection instruments.

Definition of study population

The relationship between empowerment and health is multi-level. The
individual participates in a group process; that process affects the individual, her family, the group, and the community at the very least;
the individual's health is affected by her behavior, the group's activities,
the community, and larger political, social, cultural, and economic
processes. Traditional study designs generally focus on the individual;
if quantitative group data are used, they are generated by the creation
of summary statistics from individual-level information. Questions that
can be answered only at the group level, such as 'Has the group increased the number of its political allies?' or 'Has the organizational
structure become more democratic?' are usually restricted to studies of
organizations. Similar *unit of analysis* problems arise in studies of
physician behavior, where individual patient information is often used
instead of practice-level data (Whiting-O'Keefe *et al.* 1984), and in
studies of the effectiveness of community-based interventions, where
individual-level data are used in place of community-level data (Blum
and Feachem 1983). These distortions are often seen as necessary
because a study must have 'enough' cases for hypothesis testing to take
place, and because techniques of gathering and analyzing individual-

level data are more commonly available and understood than those for other levels.

In the case of empowerment, the issue is further complicated by the need for information at multiple interacting levels and because, as the complexity theorists point out, systems organize at differing but reciprocally interactive levels, each one of which has properties that do not generalize to other levels. While it is possible to study each level separately using positivist methods, techniques for looking at the interactions between levels, or to account for the effects of one level upon another, either do not exist or are in early stages of development. Thus the resulting research greatly oversimplifies the situation and, by effectively partitioning the relationship between empowerment and health among artificially disjoint levels, may mask it.

Another major issue that occurs with any traditional research design concerns the role of the researched as objects of study. Normally, the principal researcher(s) formulates the research question, selects a suitable and feasible design, and then identifies and recruits a suitable study population. Members of the study population serve as providers of information only. The process of empowerment, however, is, in part, one of gaining self-sufficiency and control over the events that affect one's life. While the conflict between enlisting the research participation of women experiencing this process and their needs for decision-making and control may not be insurmountable, it is at the very least time-consuming. Moreover, it is certainly possible that the research process will not be empowering and may interfere with the very process it aims to study. I will argue that alternative forms of research are more applicable to the question, less manipulative, and more likely to contribute positively to the empowerment process.

Both the definition of the sample in terms of unit of analysis and the role of the sample in the research are areas where a study of empowerment and health do not fit comfortably into a traditional study design.

Design and sample selection

Following the most typical resolution of the unit of analysis issue and thus assuming primary reliance on individual-level data for most of the following discussion, the next issues to consider involve study design and sample selection.

Traditional research designs are graded for their stringency, with the strongest designs demanding random assignment to an experimental (empowerment) or a control (no empowerment) group. Only if one is fairly well assured (owing to random assignment) of no pre-existing differences among the groups that are to be compared on the variables of interest can one assert that differences uncovered during analysis, such as women in the empowerment group using birth control methods more effectively, are due to the intervention or activity that is hypothesized to be related to the outcome. However, empowerment projects are necessarily voluntary; women self-select into them. While it is theoretically possible to assign volunteering women randomly to a program or to a control group, in practice it is uncommon to begin a program with too many volunteers. Typically, empowerment groups start with ten to twelve members after extensive recruiting efforts.

If there were enough volunteers, there is no assurance that they would be appropriate controls. If the controls come from the same community as the participants, there will undoubtedly be 'contamination' of the control group, as they will be aware of and participate in community activities generated by the program. If they come from other communities, it may be difficult to ensure that they are similar to the participating women. In general, congruence is measured by simple demographic information such as age, education, number of children, and marital status. This, however, ignores the importance of community-level variables and the distinctive characteristics that neighborhoods develop.[1]

There are also ethical issues in an experimental design that has volunteers serving as controls, in that one is withholding a requested treatment by forming the control group. While this is justified when the effectiveness of a drug (or program) is truly in doubt, or when the resources to serve additional people simply do not exist, in this case the usefulness of the research must be measured against the survival needs of the women. If in fact resources do not exist, the controls can be offered a program at a later date. However, the issues of contamination (same neighborhood) and appropriateness (different neighborhood) are not thereby resolved.

Finally, the number of women to be studied, given an experimental design, remains an issue. Sample size is determined by the research design, the analysis variables, and the desired power of the test. To investigate the relationship between empowerment and health using only one dependent and one independent variable requires the fewest cases. The nominal independent variable in this case would be the group assignment: experimental or control. To select a single outcome variable to represent the health changes that are hypothesized is, of course, extremely difficult. One variable that has been used successfully in some studies (which was discussed in Chapter 4) is self-rated health (SRH): 'How would you say your health has been in the past month – excellent, good, fair, poor, or bad?' This is an ordinal measure, but it can also be treated as continuous or dichotomous. Depending on the assumptions, estimated sample size can range from 12^2 to $2,470^3$.

A reasonable choice in this case would be to treat the variable as continuous and anticipate a .5 expected difference in the mean score for participants and non-participants. The recommended sample size of 154 would then be increased to account for the interval nature of the outcome. Thus 200 might be a reasonable-sized sample to answer this one very narrow question. If one wants to use the data to look within the factors and across the relationship in a more informational manner, or to compare younger women to older women, for example, issues related to multicollinearity, confounding, subgroup analyses, multiple testing, and non-linearity will increase the sample size.

A design with a sample size of 200 would require enlisting from six to eight groups, all of which would need to be started up at about the same time, in neighborhoods as similar as possible. The empowerment process can – and most certainly will – differ among groups; it is in fact many processes, similar in the belief that the participants are learning to make their own decisions and to control the activities of the group. Since it is not prescribed, it will evolve during the process – no single 'intervention' will exist. Thus one might discover, for instance, that three of the groups had an ineffectual program, or did not survive and that participation (the independent variable) was not a good surrogate for empowerment for them. Using this simple design, the null hypothesis would be accepted and little useful information about empowerment would be obtained.

A quasi-experimental design does not require random assignment and is, therefore, accepting of the pre-existence of the study and control groups. In this design, one or more communities selected for a program would be matched with control communities that are as similar as possible. Information on all the women must be collected prior to the inception of the program, since data will be used to assess the comparability of the groups and to control for such differences as are found to exist. Again, self-selection becomes an issue, since ideally the women studied in the control community would select into an empowerment program if one were available. Not infrequently, some such program may in fact exist under a different sponsorship. If members of that group serve as controls, they may well be empowered; if non-members are studied, they may be significantly different from volunteers. It is also common that women in the program community are organized and active to some degree before a program's entry into the community, and that it is because they are organized that they were identified by the program. Thus if no program exists in the control neighborhoods, the neighborhoods themselves may be different. It will also be problematic to identify 'potential' volunteers, as there is usually intensive recruitment at program startup. An additional problem, similar to the one discussed with regard to experimental design, is the sample size required by this design.

In the traditional hierarchy of designs, the least stringent is pre-experimental; no control group is required and information gathered before, during, and after the program is relied on to measure change. While this is feasible, and often used in the natural sciences where neither uncontrollable outside influences nor wide subject variation are common, it has little prestige in traditional social research. It is open to criticism because, using this design, it is impossible to show that a positive effect was due to the program rather than to broader contextual changes, or to show that such change would not have occurred to the women without the existence of the program.

Besides these longitudinal designs which gather information over time but are costly and difficult to implement, a cross-sectional study is a possibility. In this case a (fairly large) number of women who participate in empowerment projects are interviewed, and information is gathered about their participation, their health and empowerment before and after participation. A similar number of non-participating women are interviewed about their health and empowerment. The major problems are again sample size and the need to study multiple projects. Other problems arise because information from the past is gathered retrospectively, a process fraught with unreliability (Blum and Feachem 1983); because participation is not in fact a dichotomous variable and the degree of participation, which is extremely difficult to capture cross-sectionally, may be more important than stated membership; and because women who participate in an empowerment group are encouraged to reflect on their situations, and may be more adept at responding to questions about their past.

On the other hand, longitudinal designs also present both logistic and analytic difficulties. Maintaining contact in order to reinterview subjects may require a lot of resources; study subjects die, move, or drop out; if more than two interviews are conducted, the analysis of change becomes complex – relying on pattern identification rather than simple gain-or-loss (linear) outcomes.

Many of the issues identified as problematic in this section – the units of analysis, role of respondents, sample size, sample selection, and availability of time and resources – frequently plague traditional researchers. There are few studies that do not compromise on design issues, trading off strict adherence to theory for feasibility and useful information. The question is not whether or not a design must be perfect, but whether the compromises are useful or not. Can knowledge be gained that will help to answer the research question and that is worth the great cost, time, and effort that a well-done research project requires?

Methods

Methods are generally classified as either qualitative or quantitative, the latter corresponding to a positivist orientation and the former often related to more inductive strategies (Patton 1990). In general, qualitative methods are 'extremely useful in defining the social process by which problems emerge and for suggesting strategic points of programmatic intervention to deal with particular problems' – increasing understanding at the cost of generalizability (Brewer and Hunter 1989: 187). Quantitative techniques 'are most often useful in understanding the extent and scope of specific problems,' and 'for defining the parameters within which various potential solutions may be debated.' Michael Patton (1990: 14) notes that quantitative methods 'facilitate comparison and statistical aggregation' of data, producing a 'broad, generalizable set of findings presented succinctly and parsimoniously.'

It has been argued that qualitative methods are more suited to the goals of feminist research, while quantitative methods are part and parcel of positivism – leading to oversimplification, overgeneralization, and exploitative methods of data collection. Toby Jayaratne and Abigail Stewart (1991: 101) argue against this dichotomization:

> We believe that the focus of feminist dialogue on 'methods,' and particularly on qualitative versus quantitative methods, obscures the more fundamental challenge of feminism to the traditional 'scientific method.' That challenge really questions the epistemology, or theory of knowledge, underlying traditional science and social science, including the notion that science is, or can be, value free.

They argue for the importance of both types of research, suiting the methods to the questions being asked and to the goal of the research. In the case of empowerment and health, given the present state of knowledge, it seems appropriate to rely heavily on qualitative methods, thereby increasing understanding, defining the social process, and suggesting strategic points of intervention.

Reliability and validity are the traditional standards by which quantitative methods are evaluated. While attempts are being made to reconceptualize these concepts so that they are more suitable to qualitative and 'postpositivist' research (Lather 1986; Reason and Rowan 1981c), some of the difficulties of using traditional quantitative methods for the research in question can be established by considering their traditional definitions.

Reliability in measurement can be thought of as the ability to measure accurately – neither the measurement tool nor the circumstances of data collection should get in the way. Kirk and Miller (1986: 41–2) critically describe three forms of reliability. *Quixotic reliability* concerns 'the circumstances in which a single method of observation continually yields an unvarying measurement'; it is a way of eliciting the 'party line.' *Diachronic reliability* – the stability of an observation over time – 'is only appropriate to measures of features and entities that remain unchanged in a changing world.' *Synchronic reliability* concerns general concurrence within a time period related to 'observations that are consistent with respect to the particular features of interest to the observer.' Wildly varying responses among 'similar' people could indicate either misunderstanding of the question or a highly complex issue. Thus traditional conceptualizations of reliability assume accurately measurable, consistently maintained, and well-defined variables.

While reliable measures of some aspects of health do exist – blood pressure readings, certain medical tests – these must be integrated into a broader health framework if they are to clarify the relationship between empowerment and health. This work remains to be done. As understanding of empowerment is much less advanced than understanding of health, a study of the relationships between these two concepts at this time is unlikely to include many reliable measures.

Validity is a more complicated concept than reliability, since it has many facets and classifications. Donald Patrick (1985) describes three types of validity. *Content validity* concerns the relationship between questions and the concept they are designed to measure; *criterion validity* assumes that a standard exists against which a measure can be tested; *construct validity* tests whether one measure agrees with others thought to measure a similar concept, or is related positively to a concept which is thought to accompany it or negatively to an oppositional concept. Brewer and Hunter (1989) break Patrick's construct validity into *predictive* (positively or negatively related) and *discriminant* (unrelated) validity. (They use the term 'construct validity' to include Patrick's criterion and construct validity.) Reason and Rowan (1981c: 240) define *face validity* – 'whether it "looks right" to the reasonably discriminating observer' – and *contextual validity* – 'how any particular piece of data fits in with the whole picture.'

Again, the concepts of health and empowerment are not, at least at this point, generally measurable by variables that meet these criteria, although specific standards for face and contextual validity do not in fact exist. While certain of the components of psychological, individual-level empowerment do have measures validated on groups from the USA and other industrialized countries, the assumption that those components represent the concept of empowerment sufficiently and generally enough to base a study on them is problematic. Whether or not such culturally based constructs can ever be defined generally enough to be useful in a variety of situations remains to be seen. If not, the effort required to validate scales or other measures of complicated constructs in a traditional manner might better be dedicated to other forms of research. It may be more useful at this time to rely on qualitative investigations into the meaning of the concept to the participants.

Besides issues of measurement, validity is also partitioned into *internal validity*, which addresses the conduct of the research – were biases and confounders controlled? – and *external validity*, which is concerned with the generalizability of the results – to what other groups and situations are the findings applicable? Are the results both believable and useful?

Internal validity assumes that one *can* control for biases and con-founders. Many traditional quantitative methods are designed around these goals. There are innumerable forms of bias; the Dictionary of Epidemiology (Last 1988), based on a definition of bias as 'deviation from the truth,' defines twenty-three – only some of which are relevant here. The following discussion of relevant biases, based on Last, assumes that an experimental design, chosen to minimize biases, has been selected to study the relationship between empowerment and health. Thus it is a best-case situation in the traditional hierarchy.

- *Assumption* or *conceptual bias* occurs when the underlying logical model is faulty, or when a relationship is found but incorrectly explained. While there is no methodological protection against such an error, awareness of the problem speaks to the usefulness of presenting conceptual models for critique before embarking on specific analytic studies.
- *Information bias* results when the two groups have different informa-tion that affects the outcome; in this case the likelihood that partici-pating women have reflected on their health, and view it differently from women who have not participated in an empowerment project, could produce information bias. *Recall bias* is similar, with women

who have reflected on certain events being more likely to remember accurately or, possibly, to have distorted certain memories owing to their conscientization.

- *Interviewer bias* is not likely to be a problem if only one piece of information is collected. This, of course, is an unlikely situation, since once a sample is identified, and the financing and logistics are worked out, researchers and funders would want more data. To discuss issues such as empowerment, health, deprivation, and oppression with women requires sensitive and responsive interviewers. Again, the conscientization of the project women might affect the course of the interview and the interviewers. *Observer bias* results from variation among observers, and is more difficult to control in situations where interviews are not highly structured and responses not narrowly restricted.

- *Response bias* is related to generalizability, since those willing to participate in a research project may be very different from those not willing to participate. In the case of empowerment and women's health, so little is known about women's lives that it will be difficult to compare the sample to the general population, and thereby evaluate its representativeness. *Sampling bias* results from unequal probabilities of selection for members of the sampling universe. In this case, the universe may be difficult to define, particularly if it is composed only of those women 'likely' to participate in empowerment projects.

- *Bias due to withdrawal* usually relates to individuals who withdraw from a longitudinal study. While it is inevitably an issue, in a cross-sectional study women may have begun the empowerment process and have dropped out of the project even before the study begins. This could be from lack of interest, lack of time, group conflicts, or a male partner's forbidding participation because he felt threatened by the participation. These women will not be represented in the study, but would have provided a great deal of useful information about the feasibility of empowerment programs.

- *Confounding* becomes an issue if the questions being asked are more complicated than a relatively simple one like: 'Do women who have participated for two years in an empowerment project have a higher self-reported health status than women who have not participated?' Questions about the process, questions that would lead to an understanding of what empowerment and health mean to the women being studied, or questions about women's empowerment in different locales, require much more complicated analytic models involving more variables. For example, women leaders often report that they have been particularly influenced by one or both parents wanting an education for them and encouraging them to break gender barriers. This influence will be likely to affect whether or not women participate in an empowerment project. Such a variable is described as a confounder, since it may affect health in a way similar to participation but be independent of it. (Of course, confounding makes sense only if the study variables are considered discrete and independent.) While randomization should equally distribute confounders, this is an unlikely design for a study of empowerment and health. It is always an issue in non-randomized designs.

Biases arise in all studies, and a great deal of the effort exerted in designing and conducting traditional research is directed towards minimizing them. The more stringent the design, the more those controls are built in. It is also true that the more stringent the design, the more narrow the questions addressed. At issue is the usefulness of answering a narrow question about concepts that are poorly defined, possibly unmeasurable, and whose relationships are probably non-linear, complex, multi-level, and dynamic.

> It is always possible to establish incontrovertible facts and exact solutions to problems, provided one defines and bounds the domain of experience to which they apply. Positivist science does this implicitly in its search for objective knowledge through the use of research designs and instruments that construct an area in which truth and objectivity can be found. (Morgan 1983a: 395)

External validity is generally handled by finding study subjects who are as representative of the universe in question as possible. Diversity, however, is one key to the empowerment movement. While there are similarities, the large number of organizations, potential incentives, activities, and organizational forms, and the importance of 'local' determination of the activities and goals, makes the identification of 'typical' projects problematic.

In summary, a traditionally designed research study into the relationship between empowerment and health could be costly and time-consuming, but guarantee little in terms of internal and external validity as traditionally interpreted.

Data collection instrument design

A final design issue concerns the development of the data collection instrument(s). While this process will be dependent on the research design – for example, whether it is longitudinal or cross-sectional, or whether randomization has controlled for confounders and group comparability – certain problems arise whatever the design. Among them are: what to include, the length of the instrument, issues of cross-cultural and cross-language suitability, the type of instrument – in this case a structured or a non-structured interview, and the type of questions – open-ended or precoded. It will be assumed in what follows that the information will be collected at the individual level by an in-person interview, since neither written nor telephone surveys are appropriate for the study population.

As usual, there are clearly more factors involved in understanding women's situations, empowerment, and health than could possibly be measured in any single study. These include background variables, demographics, information about a woman's current situation, information about the project and her participation, variables describing internal and external group changes, individual internal and situational changes, health knowledge, health behavior, and health status. Certain elements could be identified as being of key importance, or one small piece of the posited relationships could be investigated. The difficulty with these approaches is that the relationships depend on interaction and dynamism. It is not clear that any one or few variables are necessarily more important or more independent than others. While the possibility of a subset of measurable and meaningful variables must be held open, there is not enough information about the individual concepts, factors, and indicators from the women themselves at this time to make an educated guess as to which these might be.

The length of the instrument will depend on the factors selected for measurement. To meet traditional criteria of validity and reliability, it must contain existent, tested measures. In some areas, particularly those dealing with attitudes and values, the validated scales are very long. In others, where validated measures do not exist, multiple questions should be asked in order to establish reliability. While there are no rules as to the number of questions that can be asked during one interview or a series of interviews, common sense indicates that selection must proceed carefully, and be well justified.

Very few of the validated psychosocial criteria that might be used to measure empowerment were either developed for or validated on women in developing countries. Thus the validation that exists may be irrelevant. Are self-esteem or autonomy concepts that have the same meaning in different cultures? Some work has indicated that the locus of control concept, so useful in US research, is not applicable in cultures that are less individualistic (Antonovsky 1987). No absolute measures of health exist. While blood pressure or iron level can be used in cross-cultural research, the more subjective evaluations of health that relate to health outcomes and definitions of illness are undoubtedly culturally based. The process of developing and validating scales is extremely complicated and time-consuming. While such work may well be justified for research and for understanding, the questions raised in this study about empowerment and health are concerned with situations and activities in many different cultures. An intensive study in one culture would be helpful and desirable, but will not respond to the need for generalizability and timeliness.

The use of measures developed in English and translated into other languages is problematic, even when the concepts are transferable. The recommended process involves translating questions first written in English to the other language, then translating them back into English and evaluating the two English versions on their agreement. The work is repeated until the results are satisfactory. This instrument is then pretested and improved as necessary. This is, of course, a lengthy process.

When information is collected through an interview, structured questionnaires with closed-ended questions are commonly recommended for reasons of validity, reliability, objectivity, and ease of analysis. However, if such an interview cannot elicit 'true' information, the questions may be valid but the study will not. Chris Argyris (1968), discussing first world research, states that we cannot, through rigor, prevent contamination in research, since all social science research is 'contaminated' – the subjects are humans with their own sets of priorities. They may become dependent on and try to please the researcher; they may second-guess the researcher; they may resent and react to a sense of being controlled; they may feel at risk, and thus protect themselves. They may not understand what we are asking.

Women have found that semi- or unstructured interviewing with open-ended questions and researcher self-disclosure 'explores people's views of reality and allows the researcher to generate theory' (Reinharz 1992: 18). This is not necessarily compatible with traditional quantitative methods, but may better help the researcher to uncover 'previously neglected or misunderstood worlds of experience' (Reinharz 1992: 44).

Summary

This section on design and sampling issues raises a number of questions about the possible inappropriateness of traditional strategies for a study of empowerment and health. Most substantive among these questions are the dangers of conducting a narrowly defined inquiry that answers relatively unimportant, or at least overly narrow, questions and the long delays if attempts to find valid and reliable measures of empowerment and health relevant to a study population precede further qualitative investigations. Issues of design, sample size, controlling for bias, and instrumentation are also relevant, and, while they are often problematic in research, the difficulties are compounded here because of the more substantive problems.

Data Collection Issues

Once an instrument is designed, the researcher is confronted by data collection issues. Women in developing countries may have little experience with direct personal questions and fixed response categories. They may be unaccustomed to self-analysis. They may have very little free time. The setting may not be conducive to an interview, and there may be many interruptions. The interviewer may (necessarily) be of a different class; therefore neither woman may be comfortable in the interview situation. The interviewee may feel pressure to give the 'right,' socially acceptable answer. While these problems are not unique to women in developing countries, they are of concern. They clearly affect reliability in that 'accurate measurement' is being obstructed by uncontrollable circumstances.

Again, these are neither insurmountable nor unique difficulties. However, they can be seen as one more reason to consider carefully the framework and the methodology used to study the relationships between empowerment and health.

Analysis/Model-Building Issues

Social scientists, in their attempts to predict or understand complex phenomena, use mathematical models to simplify and organize their thoughts and their data. Generally, these models are used to perform predetermined statistical tests designed to evaluate hypotheses and quantify relationships among factors for which the investigator has collected data. Some problems related to this area have been discussed in the section on hypothesis testing; they include the types of situations – stable and quantifiable – that hypotheses are designed to test, and the stringency of the tests. Other issues arise because of the mathematical laws that are used; these laws are based on certain assumptions that rarely hold – or, at least, cannot be demonstrated to hold –

for much data used to study health and social science (Kreiner 1989). However, because models do provide standardization, carrying with them the prestige of harder sciences that developed some of the design and statistical techniques now used by social scientists, and because researchers are not immune to the normal resistance to change, traditional analytic strategies tightly grip the research community. The kinds of questions raised by the new scientists, feminists, and postmodernists have not, to date, greatly affected research carried out in the biomedical or social sciences.

A relatively simple model for a study of empowerment and health would be a quasi-experimental design where participation or non-participation in an empowerment group is the principal independent variable, some indicator of health is the dependent variable, and some set of other factors that have been determined to be related to the health indicator and also, possibly, to empowerment are secondary independent variables. On the face of it, empowerment resembles other programmatic interventions that are analyzed through quasi-experimental designs. However, it can be difficult to describe women simply as participants or not – owing to contamination, drop out, and differences in communities, and because of the assumption that whoever is in the experimental group received the same treatment (was exposed to the same intervention). The degree of participation, the type of program, and the evolution of the group and its activities are important.

As for the other factors to be included as independent variables, I have presented in Chapter 6 a wide variety of possibilities, while emphasizing their interrelatedness, their relationships to empowerment, the multiple levels on which they might affect health, and their often unexpected behaviors. I have described health as multidimensional, having many potential indicators, few of which are 'well-behaved' in the sense of being normally distributed, continuous variables. An additional problem is that most changes in health take a long time. If empowerment improves health because it facilitates psychosocial, psychoneuroimmunological, environmental, and situational changes, this does not happen quickly, and the longer the process, the more other possible explanatory factors must be taken into account. I am arguing here that empowerment is not like many other interventions, and that more complicated explanatory models might be better suited to analyses of it.

There are several options to explore in looking for a multivariate descriptive model that will do more than test how manipulating empowerment affects health (Cook 1983). The most common alternative model is the General Linear Model (GLM), which evaluates the relative strength of linear relationships between members of a set of independent variables and a dependent variable. Such a model is designed to explore structural relationships and increase understanding about multiple interrelated variables. The abstract GLM posits that a dependent, continuous variable Y can be written as a linear, additive combination of some set of independent variables plus a stochastic disturbance term that accounts for all omitted independent variables.

There are many possible problems with using GLM. Most importantly, such models are difficult to interpret, and misleading if they have not been correctly specified. This means that the model must include all the relevant variables, and that they must be well represented by an additive, linear model. If, in fact, linear assumptions are applied to non-linear data, the estimates of the parameters that indicate the relative importance of each independent variable '(1) have no known distributional properties, (2) are sensitive to the range of the data, (3) may grossly understate the magnitude of the true effects, (4) systematically yield probability predictions outside the range of 0 to 1, and (5) get worse as standard statistical practices for improving the estimates are employed' (Aldrich and Nelson 1984: 30). Given the issues raised by the dialecticians, we must also question assumptions of additivity. Can we conceptualize a concept like health as representable by the sum of some set of variables, even when those variables can themselves be complex? Is not health simultaneously affecting and changing those 'independent' factors?

Since GLM is a correlational model, it suffers from an overriding dependence on sample size and on the 'distribution and range of the component variables' (Rothman 1986: 303). While there is no strict rule, it is generally recommended that a study contain at least ten cases for every independent variable in the model. The greater the deviation from normality and from the assumptions, the larger the number of cases required for reasonably accurate estimation and statistical testing. It would be difficult to obtain a large sample for an empowerment study. It is also true that many of the variables that would be included are not well understood statistically, and that their distribution and range may vary in different contexts. Thirdly, regression is most effective when 'each [independent variable] is strongly correlated with the [dependent variable] and uncorrelated with the other [independents variables]' (Tabachnick and Fidell 1989: 128). I anticipate, however, that some of the independent variables act indirectly to affect health, and that the independent variables are integrally interrelated.

One important assumption of the GLM that may be violated concerns the independence of the subjects, since observations of women who form a close group or community are quite possibly correlated on an individual level, and definitely correlated if the data are about group or community conditions. It is also possible that as women spend more time together, they become more similar in their responses, so that variance will decrease over time, violating a second assumption. On the other hand, the group experience may facilitate individual development, and variance may increase over time.

Several alternative modeling strategies exist, all of which more accurately capture the situation we encounter in studying the relationships between health and empowerment, but all of which are also more complex, require more statistical expertise, and demand relatively large sample sizes. One strategy, confusingly known as Generalized Linear Models (GLM), both subsumes General Linear Models and takes account of non-continuous, non-linear, and non-normal dependent variables. These include binary variables such as diseased/not diseased, ordinal variables such as self-reported health status, and Poisson-distributed variables such as the number of symptoms or conditions that an individual has at a given time. GLM theory assumes that the underlying distribution of the dependent variable is in fact continuous, and that assumptions of the regression are similar to the linear case. Analytic techniques to check for compliance with assumptions are poorly developed, computer programs to perform the analyses are less well developed than for linear regression, and for all but the binary case, few practical examples exist. Issues around the independent variables are essentially the same as in the linear normal case.

Longitudinality poses additional problems when the dependent variable is non-continuous or non-linear (Zeger *et al.* 1988). Since one of the reasons to explore women's empowerment might be to see how it affects women over time, these problems should be taken into account, although very little practical assistance is available. Computer programs are not yet generally available for analyses of how a 'typical individual changes on average over time' (Kleinbaum and Kupper 1992), which is best modeled using a random-effects model (Zeger and Karim 1991).

Structural equation models are an important and useful extension of GLM:

> They are regression equations with less restrictive assumptions that allow measurement error in the explanatory as well as the dependent variables. They consist of factor analyses that permit direct and indirect effects between factors. They routinely include multiple indicators and latent variables. (Bollen 1989: v)

Because the models can include sets of equations, they can be used to capture sequencing. For example, individual and situational changes due to empowerment affect individual behaviors. They and individual behaviors predict health outcomes. Thus one predicted variable predicts another. In structural equations models, these patterns are represented by a path analysis model that incorporates multiple dependent variables.

The techniques of structural equation modeling also capture information on independent latent variables from a variety of indicators, using factor analytic techniques, so that issues of the interdependence of independent variables are less important. On the other hand, factor analyses are highly dependent on the sample selected, on the posited set of indicators, and on the conceptual definition of the latent variable itself. It is often difficult to be explicit about the meaning of such a latent variable, and to generalize from a given study. The solutions to structural equations are also based on assumptions of linearity, additivity, and multivariate normality, although some estimation techniques exist to help correct for deviations from normality. As is the case with factor analysis and linear regression, a relatively large number of cases is required for solutions – since convergence to normality is dependent on the central limit theorem. However, there are no simple standards except that one hundred is thought to be a minimum number of cases, and the number of variables included should be 'as small as possible' given requirements for correct specification of the model.

Finally, there is a technique known as contextual analysis or hierarchical modeling (Bryk and Raudenbush 1992; Findley 1991) that is designed to deal with the issue of multiple levels of analysis, although its use is relatively uncommon and poorly documented. Using this technique, regression equations for the higher-level variables are substituted for the parameters in the first-level regression equations. Standard underlying linear or logistic models are assumed with a minimum of ten different groups – such as empowerment projects or communities. There must be a large number of cases: from ten to twenty per group. Variables from each level are entered into the analysis, along with interaction terms between levels. Deviations from assumptions cause problems similar to those of simple multivariate regression. A three-level model, encompassing individual women, empowerment groups, and communities, could be developed, but the sample size required and the analytic complexities make this only a theoretical possibility at this time.

Thus, although analytic techniques suited to complex situations and variables are being developed, they are still rare. As I mentioned above, social scientists may well be served in the future by models developed by new scientists, since many of the issues are similar.

Interpretation and Dissemination

The final activity in a traditional research project concerns the interpretation and dissemination of the findings. No matter how careful the design, interpretation is an art, not a science. The more complex the model, the more difficult the interpretation of the statistical results, which must often be hand-calculated from abstruse printouts. Efforts to test the data for adherence to assumptions, and to handle missing data and outliers, must be carefully carried out and interpreted. While *a priori* rules about the acceptance or rejection of a hypothesis apply, decisions as to the goodness of fit of the model to the data and the relative importance of the independent variables are much less cut-and-dried, particularly with regard to non-continuous variables, interactions, and transformed variables. It is rare that a study is designed so robustly that a failure to reject the null hypothesis cannot be explained in terms of the design or the sample, leaving the original question open to further research. Given a positive finding, it is also rare that a study cannot be questioned owing to inevitable biases, weaknesses in design, or problems in implementation. Decisions on the importance of the findings are in the end subjective, based on theory, other results, and one's feelings about the quality of the research. Thus traditional techniques, while they provide some standardization and a framework for carrying out research, often have little immediate bearing on our knowledge of the 'truth.'

There is an ethical imperative to disseminate research findings, given the direct costs of research plus the less quantifiable costs to subjects. Dissemination occurs primarily through presentations at conferences and publication in peer-reviewed journals. Since these are discipline-specific, there are few forums for interdisciplinary work. There is also little latitude for speculation, non-traditional methods, theory-building, or inductive approaches to problems. If new paradigms arise from those at the fringes of fields, then peer review can be a deterrent to their publication owing to the mainstream orientation of most reviewers. The large amount of published research also makes it difficult to identify important work, although computerized databases facilitate the identification of relevant articles.

Summary of Critiques

At each stage of the traditional research process, many compromises must be made. Testable hypotheses are selected from a relatively narrow set of alternatives. Sample size and design determinations must balance accuracy and power. Data collection instruments and procedures must balance analysis exigencies and information needs. Analytic techniques inevitably oversimplify complex realities. Biases towards the status quo influence interpretations and dissemination opportunities. There are certainly problems that justify adherence to traditional procedures, and knowledge to be gained from that adherence – selecting the most 'predictive' factors from within a small set in order to design an intervention, identifying the 'extent and scope of specific problems,' or summarizing and evaluating large quantities of data. However, I argue here that the relationships presented in this study of women's empowerment and health reflect many of the critiques presented in Chapter 8 – they are complex, possibly non-linear, dynamic, multilevel, exist in a political and cultural context that is often contradictory and oppositional, and may be unstable, disorderly, and discontinuous. To circumscribe these relationships at this time risks distorting and misunderstanding them:

> [H]ad we to name one key weakness in the analytical approach to research, or in the social sciences in general, it would be that researchers have been bent on testing for simple, circumscribed relationships instead of searching for or constructing rich, insightful patterns. (Miller and Mintzberg 1983: 62)

Descriptions of patterns, connections, and interactions among a large set of indicators are likely to prove more useful at this time than the identification of a few factors that may be highly dependent on the local environment, that represent concepts having complex relationships among the many possible indicators, and that may not behave as expected in an intervention that is narrowly defined to affect those specific factors.

Possible Alternatives

In this section I do not intend to define a research that overcomes or even confronts all the difficulties just considered. Logical positivism evolved over centuries; if some form of new paradigm research does achieve credibility, its methods and techniques will also need time to evolve. At this time, I can only report on the beginnings of that process from the perspective of attempting to increase understanding of the relationship between empowerment and health.

A study of empowerment must be approached thoughtfully, since – unlike much other research – the thing studied will inevitably be affected by the research process, for better or for worse. This is more than a traditional Hawthorne effect, where the researchers' attention may enhance positive benefits of treatment. At the core of empowerment are awareness, control, and participation. Most traditional research, while it shares information about the means and ends of a study with the research subjects through informed consent and publications, is particularly concerned with not effecting change through the research process itself. The research is kept as distinct from the intervention as possible in order to avoid contamination of the intervention and to measure, in so far as possible, its unadulterated effect. This can be disempowering to the subjects who are not part of the decision-making process. But to study the relationship between empowerment and health, one would like to have 'as much' empowerment as possible, and for the research itself to be empowering.

Participatory-action research

Research that is empowering is not a new concept. I have already introduced new paradigm research (in Chapter 8), which incorporates much of what is known as participatory-action research (PAR):

> Grounded in group dynamics, [participatory] action-research uses experiential, or process training to stimulate personal and social change. It begins with the principle that people already know a great deal about their own situations. It builds upon this knowledge, using processes of social interaction to develop a 'critical consciousness' about human behavior and the causes of social phenomena. (Schoepf 1993: 1403)

PAR is a melding of two research traditions: action research and participatory research. Although Brown and Tandon (1983) present a careful analysis of the differences between participatory research and action research, the two are often combined in discussion and in practice (Israel *et al.* 1989). The differences, however, are interesting, as they stem from quite different historical situations – defined by Brown and Tandon (1983: 290) as 'political economies' – and therefore from different ideologies. Action research (AR) has been used in developed countries as a means of achieving change through consensus, primarily in business and industrial situations. Power differences are not emphasized in AR.

Participatory research (PR) has 'emerged from work with oppressed peoples in the Third World' (Brown and Tandon 1983: 279). A key tenet is the right of all to self-determination through knowledge. PR focuses on a societal analysis, rather than one that centers around individuals and groups; based on conflict theory, it assumes that consensus between the *haves* and the *have-nots* is unobtainable, and is concerned with problems of 'equity/self-reliance/oppression' as opposed to problems of 'efficiency/growth' (Brown and Tandon 1983: 283). Rajesh Tandon (1996) describes the multiple roots of PR: debates about the meaning of knowledge, adult education as a form of development, critiques of traditional education; action research, the growth of phenomenology which legitimizes experiential learning, and the emphasis on participation by development activists.

While I accept the historical grounds for the distinction between AR and PR, I use the term *participatory-action research*, as it seems to be the most common descriptor in the literature that is applicable to the study of empowerment and health. This literature is often based on an acute awareness of power differences and conflicts of interest, but it is potentially willing to cooperate with those in power and to employ relatively sophisticated research tools. Empowerment of participants lies at the core of PAR theory. Based on Paulo Freire's theories of conscientization, its 'ultimate goal ... is fundamental structural transformation and the improvement of the lives of those involved' (Hall 1981: 7). It is understood that this goal is achievable only through a process that involves active participation and the empowerment of the participants. Action is a key component – the research must lead to action, not just to additional knowledge.

Action and knowledge, in fact, go hand in hand, with action contributing to, essential to, the production of knowledge:

> Action provides the basic means through which we can come to know the world, since it is through action that we ultimately construct and make contact with our reality. It is in attempting to influence and change that reality that we come to understand it most clearly. (Morgan 1983b: 399)

This is a major departure from concepts of knowledge that value information only if it is produced by an objective, non-participatory observer. PAR also differs from more traditional research in other important ways:

- the steps cannot be carefully laid out ahead of time;
- the community, at the very least, must buy into the researcher's definition of the 'problem'; preferably, it will participate in defining the questions to be studied;
- the professional researcher must have a political commitment to improve the lives of the participants, and to fundamental structural transformation that may produce conflict;
- the entire community, or at least the active participants, become researchers and co-investigators;

- decisions about the meaning and dissemination of the results are shared among all the researchers;
- action, rather than publication, is the final step in the research process.

Ideally, everyone learns together, deriving theory from experience and evaluating experience from a theoretical perspective. Researchers themselves need a different set of skills, one that is rarely learned in school (Meulenberg-Buskens 1996; Tolley and Bentley 1996).

> Generally, traditional paradigm researchers rely on instruments to collect data, whereas in an alternative paradigm, researchers rely much more heavily on human skills such as listening, looking, relating, thinking, feeling, acting, collaborating. In essence, the researcher's awareness is the major instrument and thus must be finely tuned. (Reinharz 1981: 428)

Reinharz adds: '[b]oth paradigms require that researchers have or develop enough political or entrepreneurial skill to move beyond the state of thinking about research, to actually carrying it out, and completing it in some fashion.'

Feminist PAR

Some of the current interest in participatory-action research has been sparked by feminist methodologists. Reacting against the invisibility of women as both practitioners and objects of traditional research, feminists began to define a research that included women and treated then as subjects, not objects, and was deeply committed to the transformation and empowerment of women – helping them to move from being objects of oppression to the sharing of power. They found that traditional methods of data collection obscure rather than elucidate women's truths, and began to question the role and the power of the researcher herself (Nielsen 1990; Quintos Deles and Santiago 1984). Quintos Deles and Santiago (1984: 16) describe a type of research that can reinforce social action in order to 'change the lives of poor women in the grass-roots...' They describe a research that is committed, democratic, leading to deeper insight into issues, pedagological, action-oriented, and feminist: 'expressive of women's nurturing experience and reflective of very deep concern with women's issues.' This type of research has been described as feminist participatory research (Reinharz 1992) and I shall call it feminist participatory-action research. Using feminist PAR, it may be possible both to facilitate the empowerment process and to research it simultaneously.

Practical considerations with regard to PAR
and new paradigm research

As we have discovered, traditional research practice is not always congruent with traditional theory, owing to the exigencies of doing social research and the difficulties in preventing some forms of bias from playing a role. Less is known about the relationship between theory and practice in new paradigm research or PAR (which can be seen as a specific example of new paradigm research), particularly in developing countries. Some informal reports exist, and there is a fair amount of expressed interest in the strategies (Feuerstein 1993; Sanchez *et al.* 1992), but since it does not generally fit into traditional funding and publication formats, projects are neither numerous nor reported in major journals.

As with empowerment, some useful information on participatory-action research comes from descriptions of projects, many of which are from the field of development rather than health (Fals-Borda and Rahman 1991; Feuerstein 1993; Nelson and Wright 1995; Participatory Research Network 1981; Sanchez *et al.* 1992). One particularly useful collection, however, containing both theoretical and descriptive chapters, *is* focused on health (de Koning and Martin 1996). The High-lander Center has been central to applications of this methodology, particularly to environmental issues (Merrifield 1987). Some theoretical work placing participatory-action research in political and intellectual contexts is being done (Park *et al.* 1993; Fals-Borda and Rahman 1991). However, the literature about participatory-action research is still somewhat hard to locate and often specific to individual disciplines – it suffers from obscurity and overuse of jargon.

Environmental PAR often consists of gathering, interpreting, and disseminating epidemiological information on exposure or on incidence. PAR has been useful in developing countries in program evaluations, both process and outcome. There is a great need for more participatory research projects and for dissemination of information about the projects that do exist, so that the field can move from theorizing to the presentation of empirical information and evaluable models. At this point the most that can be said is that PAR will probably be most effective if it is local, related to immediate problems experienced by the participants, relies on qualitative and/or fairly unsophisticated quantitative techniques, and is aimed at problem solving and technical assistance.

One increasing popular research model, known as multimethod research, may be well suited to situations where participatory research is called for. Multimethod research is a composite methodology that uses both quantitative and qualitative methods for the purpose of *triangulation*, a term used to describe how multiple measures try 'to pinpoint the values of a phenomenon more accurately by sighting in on it from different methodological viewpoints' (Brewer and Hunter 1989: 17). One of the early examples in the literature is a project conducted by Israel and her colleagues (1989).

Many questions need to be answered about both the process and the outcomes of participatory research projects. Who represented the 'community'? How were they selected? Was the research actually participatory? Was it democratic? Did the process proceed as intended? Outcome measures must be defined on the basis of the research project's intentions. Was policy regarding pesticides affected by the research? Has the community water system been improved? Is the health post more accessible and responsive to women's needs? Some standards suggested by feminists are value-based, and combine process and outcomes. Does the research accomplish the goal of improving women's situations and lives? As with traditional research, the researcher(s) must constantly critique her or his own performance as well as that of the entire project, on the basis of its objectives. In participatory research, this critique can be part of the research process itself, with the objectives delineated and measures defined by the entire group.

One reality that will always be difficult to deal with is the power relationship between the professionals and the participants:

> The decision to engage in collaborative research does not *de facto* resolve competing interests.... Collaboration and trust do not negate power differentials; rather they create a bond between ... subjects who must then negotiate the power differential between them as they encounter it. (Acker *et al.* 1991: 179–80)

Lather (1986: 265) is also concerned about 'the irony of domination and repression inherent in most of our efforts to free one another,' noting that 'in the name of emancipation, researchers impose meanings on situations rather than constructing meaning through negotiations with research participants.' She suggests the use of 'dialectical practices' that 'require an interactive approach to research that invites reciprocal reflexivity and critique, both of which guard against the central dangers to praxis-oriented empirical work: imposition and reification on the part of the researcher.' This dialectical approach is closely related to the cycle of praxis defined by Freire: listening, dialogue, discussion, self-reflection, critical thought, action, and back to listening.

The most deflating critique comes from Daphne Patai (1991: 144, 145, 150) who, stressing power differentials and a 'spurious identification' of the researcher with the researched that is in fact an 'egregious form of manipulation', says that 'in an unethical world, we cannot do truly ethical research.' She warns against 'assuming that the discourse of feminism itself constitutes a solution to the fact of women's oppression,' and supports total community control of the research process as the only ethical solution.

Evaluating empowering research

The standards used to evaluate traditional research can be codified: power calculations, sample size, p-values and confidence intervals, assurances of objectivity, reliability, and validity. The format is well known and relatively well understood. This is not so for new paradigm research:

> Once one challenges the assumption that it is possible or meaningful to study the social world as a system of objective, empirical regularities that can be neutrally observed, measured, and predicted, the criteria used to evaluate such research become highly problematic. (Morgan 1983a: 394)

In the words of Celia Kitzinger (1987: 189): 'Lacking criteria of truth and falsehood, and deprived of a priori reliance on empiricist methodologies, how can we judge the adequacy of our social constructionist methods and theories?' Not only must researchers be able to evaluate their own work, but – if policy is to be affected, and change encouraged – the credibility of the research must be established. Objectivity, reliability, and validity must be considered, and possibly redefined. As Jayaratne and Stewart (1991: 100) point out, 'the greatest benefit of apparent objectivity lies in its power to change political opinion.' Thus, given the goal of social change, the tension between new paradigm research and traditional concepts of objectivity must be resolved.

Reason and Rowan (1981b: xiii) see new paradigm research as 'objectively subjective,' neither narrowly objective like old paradigm research nor overly subjective like what they call 'naive inquiry.' The feminists, as we have seen, call for a similar standard, naming it strong objectivity. How might such a standard be established? Jerome Kirk and Marc Miller (1986: 20) provide useful definitions of objectivity, reliability, and validity:

> Objectivity is the simultaneous realization of as much reliability and validity as possible. Reliability is the degree to which the finding is independent of

accidental circumstances of the research, and validity is the degree to which the finding is interpreted in a correct way.

This description moves the burden of definition on to the more methodological terms of reliability and validity.

While there is no presumed identity between empowering research and qualitative research, it is not unreasonable to assume that much new paradigm research will be qualitative. Qualitative methodologies have been struggling with issues of credibility and objectivity for some time, so much of what follows comes from that domain. With regard to reliability, Kirk and Miller (1986: 52) state: 'the contemporary search for reliability in qualitative observation revolves around detailing the relevant context of observation.' This context is much more complex than in traditional research situations, where the research is structured so as to reduce the impact of the context. The observer – not a questionnaire or an instrument – is the tool, and the situation is 'natural' – not controlled or contrived. It is unrealistic in qualitative observations to expect quixotic reliability – unvarying measurement over time – since the observer is not a machine. Neither is diachronic reliability – stability over time – likely to be applicable to many of the traits and entities related to empowerment and health. How, then, should reliability be interpreted? Kirk and Miller's synchronic reliability – a reasonable distribution of responses that indicates a similar perception of a concept or understanding of a particular question – appears to be relevant to qualitative research. Cook (1983: 83) discusses a critical reliability that is less concerned with 'the infallible measurement of external objects' than with a reliability that assumes measurement bias but attempts to make 'sure that biases are involved that operate in all conceivable directions.' Most important, as a means of ensuring that the findings are grounded in high-quality research, in research that is neither sloppy nor idiosyncratic, the research process must be well documented and sensitive to the 'accidental circumstances' in which it is carried out – that is to say, the relevant context must be detailed:

> Qualitative researchers can no longer afford to beg the issue of reliability.... For reliability to be calculated, it is incumbent on the scientific investigator to document his or her procedure. This must be accomplished at such a level of abstraction that the loci of decisions internal to the research project are made apparent. (Kirk and Miller 1986: 72)

Standards for this type of reliability will presumably evolve as qualitative research and new paradigm research gain acceptance.

If validity is defined as the correct interpretation of findings, surely new paradigm research must find ways of incorporating it into research designs. There is no reason for PAR, or other forms of new paradigm research, to reject measurement validity in its many forms. While criterion and construct validity may be difficult to achieve, content, face, and contextual validity are all relevant and can be built into projects. Internal validity, the control of the many potential biases and confounders, is an area challenged by the active cooperation between researcher and researched, and by the probable deviation from traditional experimental and quasi-experimental designs. However, not all biases will be increased. Assumption or conceptual biases may be reduced; subject withdrawal may be reduced; confounding will be expected and actively incorporated into theory. Other forms of bias, such as information, recall, and response, are also problems in more traditional social research, and need to be taken into account. It is important to recognize that the tradeoff between traditional designs and PAR is quite possibly more accurate and useful information, better representing the conditions that exist. Better data may also result because of close relationships between interviewer and interviewee.

What is fundamental is new paradigm research's goal of increasing understanding. It is incumbent on the researcher to ensure that the research process accomplishes this, and that information above and beyond the 'accidental circumstances' of the research is gathered and correctly interpreted. Reason and Rowan (1981c: 244) argue that

> validity in new paradigm research lies in the skills and sensitivities of the researcher, in how he or she uses herself as a knower, as an inquirer. Validity is more personal and interpersonal, rather than methodological.

They emphasize that since knowledge is a relationship between the knower and what is to be known, and since reality is a process, not an object, '[v]alid research rests above all on high-quality awareness on the part of the co-researchers.'

Patti Lather (1986: 270), in discussing validity in relation to praxis-oriented research, reiterates the importance of 'self-corrective techniques' that check the credibility of data and minimize the distorting effect of personal bias upon the logic of evidence. She calls for the conscious use of designs that seek 'counterpatterns,' a constant interaction between theory and data to evaluate construct validity, a greater emphasis on face validity that 'provides a "click of recognition" and a "yes, of course" instead of "yes, but" experience,' and attention to what she calls catalytic validity – 'the degree to which the research process reorients, focuses, and energizes participants toward knowing

reality in order to transform it, a process Freire terms conscientization.'
Derek Yach (1992) also proposes that a standard of credibility be substituted for internal validity as a means of evaluating 'truth.'

Acker *et al.* (1991: 145–7) interpret validity as both 'adequacy of
interpretation' – which has to do with the selection, organization, and
interpretation of findings as buttressed by social theory – and 'adequacy of ... findings' – that research results fairly and accurately reflect
what they purport to represent. Adequacy of interpretation requires
that 'the active voice of the subject should be heard in the account,'
that the investigator is accounted for as well as the investigated, and
that research accounts satisfactorily relate the thing studied to daily
life. Adequacy of interpretation can be verified in part through feedback from those studied, as long as the importance and 'reality' of
change over time is recognized. It will also be evaluated by those
apprised of the research.

The final form of validity to be considered is external validity, or
generalizability. New paradigm research, in recognizing diversity and
grounding research in a concept of active knowledge developed as part
of the research process itself, questions the usefulness of this concept.
The goal of generalizability may be unachievable, or may excessively
distort the research.

There is an urgent need for practical applications of the theories
presented by new paradigm researchers and proponents of PAR. How
much contextual detail is enough to establish reliability? How much
effort should be expended on process documentation, which often takes
resources away from project activity? How can power relationships be
evaluated? Whose 'yes, of course' response is important? How, in
practice, do researchers allow for counterpatterns and biases in all
conceivable directions? At this time, since activities are taking place in
so many different fields and disciplines, those who are interested in
PAR and in new paradigm research will have to read widely and to
evaluate thoughtfully innovative techniques in their own research.

Summary

PAR has been introduced as an antidote to traditional methods for
studies of issues such as empowerment and health. PAR does not,
however, substitute for that research. It may well take on similar forms
and use similar techniques. It is not a license for sloppy research. It is,
none the less, very different from traditional research in its goals, in
the questions addressed, in the role of the study population and the
researcher, and in the evaluation of its successes. Most important in

the context of this book is that empowerment is central to the process of PAR. If I succeed in demonstrating that empowerment contributes to health, it follows that PAR may also have on impact on health. Looking for connections and interactions may well open new vistas at many levels.

Summary and Conclusion

As I said in the introduction to this book, I am trying to build a framework that 'makes sense' and elucidates patterns. It is one phase of a cycle; it must be followed by critiques and by real-world tests of its usefulness. These tests may well be in the form of research. In this chapter, I have addressed both traditional research methods and practice, and some variations and alternatives. These alternatives are designed to overcome anti-women biases, broaden narrow foci, and move past assumptions that the factors of interest are independent, discrete, linearly related, and free of local and historical context.

Neither theorizing nor empowering research alone will elucidate subtle and complex patterns. Rather, their interplay is needed. It has been shown that women's lives, their health, and their empowerment are affected by theory. Theory is being affected by women's lives, as we saw in Chapter 8. Research serves as a link between daily life and theory. Empowering research may serve to gather more useful, realistic information, and simultaneously contribute to the development of theory dedicated to social change. However, there are many practical questions about such research that need to be answered. As with the theory, the practice of post-positivist research is at a nascent stage. There are many loose ends, and the hard work of linking new perceptions, new paradigms, and new or modified methodologies remains a challenge.

Notes

1. Susan Eckstein (1988), in a historical analysis of neighborhood organizations in Mexico City, describes the relevance and the complexity of such information.

2. In this case the assumptions are: $\alpha = .05$, $\beta = .2$, one-tailed test, normal distribution, standard deviation $= 1$, mean SRH for participants is 4 and for non-participants is 2, which indicates a large difference.

3. In this case the assumptions are: $\alpha = .05$, $\beta = .2$, one-tailed test, dichotomous distribution with excellent/good versus fair/poor/bad, proportion of participants in excellent/good health is .5 and of non-participants is .45, which indicates a smaller difference.

PART IV

Finale

10

Conclusions

In earlier chapters I have presented information on development and women's situations, empowerment, and health. In the main, these have been treated as different domains, each with its own theory, literature, and practice. It is my intent here to bring the information from those chapters together into a coherent theoretical and practical framework, based on the emerging new paradigms of science and research described in Chapter 8. I have organized this synthesis into eight key points (P1–P8), extracted from or designed to synthesize the information.

P1
The policies derived from development and structural adjustment theories have frequently had a negative impact on women's situations and their situations in turn have negatively affected their health and well-being. Poor health has simultaneously made their lives more difficult.

Figure 10.1 is a simple model designed to show relationships described in P1. The situations of women living in developing countries in difficult circumstances have been related to the theories and practices of development and structural adjustment in Chapter 2. Data documenting their situations and their health status appear in Chapter 5. A women-centered analysis of development shows that gender discrimination plays a major role in explaining why women are particularly disadvantaged in countries where relative disadvantage often places them on the edge of survival. For example, agricultural development policies, designed to produce export crops that will improve the balance of trade and earn foreign currency that can be used to help pay off the national debt, often deprive women of easily accessible, high-

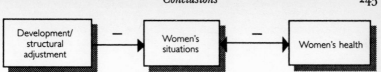

Figure 10.1 Negative relationships between development, women's situations, and women's health

quality land on which to grow traditional subsistence foods. They either stop growing and eating such foods – which negatively affects their health, since nutritional substitutes are either non-existent or un-affordable – or they travel great distances to farm poor-quality land, which negatively affects both the quality of the food grown and their own nutritional stores. They have less time available for child care and the multitude of other chores that fill their very long work-days. Thus both their situations and their health are negatively affected by this policy. If their health deteriorates, their situations are immediately affected, since often only their efforts and their energy sustain entire families and communities.

P2
Empowerment is a strategy designed to reduce inequity and redistribute power, which women, in particular, are using to improve their situations.

Empowerment was described in Chapters 2 and 3 as an international phenomenon based in a variety of movements, all of which are dedicated to social justice and self-determination. While many factors are thought to compose the phenomenon, at its core are an increase in political and social awareness, a sense of possibilities and change, improved interpersonal and organizational skills, the development of communal feelings, and political and social activism. It is an individual, group, and community process that requires active participation and local decision-making.

In the struggle for their families' survival, women have used traditional forms of working together and developed new forms that have produced a fledgling women's empowerment movement, as described in Chapter 3. Throughout the third world, organizations dedicated to improving women's situations have been created, taking on many organizational forms and with many different immediate goals. Most of the recognition of and support for empowerment strategies have come from the field of development and have focused on economic and educational benefits.

P3

Empowerment may – by reducing inequity and increasing the power and status of women – prevent or mitigate the negative impact of development on women.

P3 indicates that the negative relationships represented in Figure 10.1 can be changed – can be positively affected by the processes and outcomes of empowerment that improve women's situations, which, in turn, improve their health, as depicted in Figure 10.2.

Continuing the example described above, a group of women, who through their group activities have identified the loss of their garden plots as a problem that they wish to remedy, can take action (education, confrontation, negotiation, squatting) to regain their land or to gain access to other land that they can farm communally. In response to their deteriorated situation, through a process of empowerment, they can improve that situation. With less expenditure of energy and with available nutritious foods, they may be in a better position to maintain and/or improve their health. Thus organizing in response to situations negatively affected by development is one pathway to empowerment. A second pathway is that positive forms of development can lead directly to empowerment. That is to say: empowerment can be, and sometimes is, an expressed goal of development projects, thereby avoiding negative outcomes from development. In such a case,

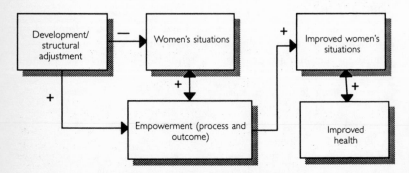

Figure 10.2 Relationships between development, women's situations, and women's health as modified by empowerment

land use decisions would include women in the decision-making process, and be designed with their needs in mind.

P4
Women's health is a poorly understood phenomenon only recently receiving attention.

Health has been linked to development in theory and in rhetoric. It has been seen as a by-product and indicator of successful development, and as something that is particularly vulnerable to negative aspects of development. As women are distinctly affected by development, so is their health. As part of the new focus on women internationally and in recognition of the importance of women's health to the health of children, the subject of women's health has recently gained prominence. However, little attention has been paid to how to define and measure the health of women in developing countries. In international health, commonly used measures are mortality and life expectancy. While differential and early mortality clearly indicate disadvantage, such indicators do not provide sufficient information on the health of the living. During life, women suffer from many disabilities, and as they usually live longer than men, spend a larger proportion of their lives with disabilities. Data show that women in developing countries suffer from cardiovascular disease, maternal morbidity and mortality, neuropsychiatric problems, cancers, TB, STDs, unintentional injuries, chronic respiratory diseases, intentional injuries and, increasingly, from HIV. Women have stressed the impacts of violence, malnutrition, and illegal abortions on their health. As women's health gains in importance, there is a growing need for additional and better data on their health status, and for information from women on their needs and perceptions with respect to health.

P5
Health can be seen as a complicated web of factors, all of which are interdependent and no one of which can be understood in isolation.

Current theories of health (reviewed in Chapter 4) recognize that it is a multidimensional phenomenon affected by many different, interactive factors that function in different domains and at different levels. Mildred Blaxter has measured five components in the course of her research: diagnosable illness and disease, self-perceived illness and symptoms, disabilities, fitness, and psychosocial well-being. Factors affecting health may affect any one, some, or all of these components. However, research rarely takes such broad conceptualizations into account. Whether the focus has been on more proximate factors affecting health such as nutrition, water, medical care, exposure to germs, or on less proximate factors such as income/poverty, education, and societal organization, little attention has been paid to synthesis and the development of theoretical frameworks. Historical analyses, based primarily on mortality data, have often provided the broadest picture, revealing in particular the importance of both social and cultural factors in the health of populations.

In the 'real' world, where interventions to improve health take place, this complexity is often resolved by intervening on one or several factors, such as access to medical care or improved nutrition. The assumption is that a piecemeal approach to health is effective to some degree, and at least feasible. The literature on health is splintered in a similar fashion, and rarely synthesized. However, the discussion in Chapter 6, based on what are generally considered to be important determinants, shows that the factors are far from isolated; that their relationship to health is complex, both positive and negative, and not always clear; and that all are greatly affected by social, political, economic, cultural, and historical circumstances.

P6
Inequity is integrally related to health through its relationship to all other factors, particularly those directly related to the organization of society and psychosocial factors.

An outstanding question, then, is whether there is another approach – differing from intervention on one or several 'risk' factors – to improving health that takes into account the complexity described in Chapter 6. Two sets of factors discussed in that chapter are particularly important in that regard. The first, psychosocial factors and psychoneuroimmunological processes, is primarily concerned with individual susceptibility and resistance in a social context – addressing questions rising from differential responses to all the factors that affect health. The second, the organization of society, provides a contrasting vantage point, while addressing similar questions. It serves as a framework for identifying those groups at greatest psychosocial and psychoneuroimmunological risk, and for investigating why they are at particular risk. Lack of equity and of formal education are the aspects of societal organization that have been investigated in regard to women's health. While little is known about how and why they affect

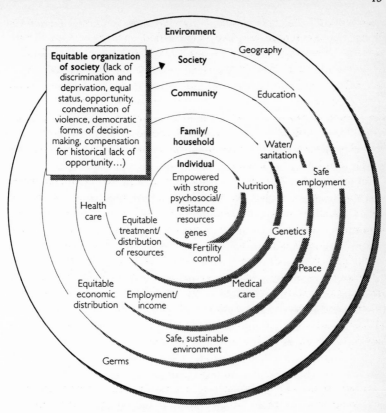

Figure 10.3 Utopian model of health

women's health so strongly, their dominant place in the international health literature serves to identify social organization as a key factor.

If there were a single spider weaving a web of negative health, it would seem to be inequity, as reflected in psychosocial vulnerability and social organization, and maintained by cultural, political, economic, and social relations. Women, and all others who are oppressed by discrimination and gross social inequity, need to work to reduce discrimination and inequity, and to increase their resistance resources, in order to improve their health and the health of their families.

Another way to evaluate the importance of equity and social organization to health is to shake the kaleidoscope of factors and arrange the pieces so that societies are organized in such a way as to support those who are weak or who have previously suffered from discrimination. Figure 10.3 is such an arrangement.

It becomes much easier to organize factors affecting health under a supposition of equitably organized societies. Different levels are synergistic – with the individual, the household, the community, and the society in concert, not conflict. For example, nutrition can be seen as being particularly important at the household level, where, in Utopia, women and children are not discriminated against, but it is influenced by individual behavior, community norms, and societal distribution and equity, as well as by environmental and geographical settings. While threats to health continue to exist, they are fewer. In an equitably organized, utopian society, the mediable factors of disadvantage – racism, sexism, classism, unequal distribution of resources leading to extremes of poverty, and the social disorganization resulting from all the previous factors – disappear from the picture. Society would be working with, not against, women; it would be an extension of them, not the frequently described dichotomous 'other.' If such a society were attainable, empowerment as a process would be superfluous. Empowerment of peoples would be part of the definition of an equitably organized society.

Much, of course, is missing from this picture: history, economics, cultural differences – whatever it is in human nature that makes this utopian and not real. Unfortunately, this utopian model does not make much sense when the surrounding environments are not supportive of the individual or of one another. Under those conditions, any and all the factors and layers can become threats to health, and the interactions are complex, as we saw in Chapter 6. One cannot discuss nutrition without considering that females are more deprived than males, and why; that communities often cannot provide the food they need; that the distribution of food nationally and internationally favors some and not others; or that lack of education and resources hinders the adoption of healthful nutrition practices. The lack of social justice, the inequitable organization of society, is not a separate layer, or separate strands of the web that somehow undergird other strands, but, rather, an integral, controlling, fundamental part of all of the tangled strands.

P7

Empowerment can – by improving women's situations, by positively interacting with other factors that affect health, and by reducing inequity – improve women's health.

P7 is concerned with direct relationships between empowerment and health as reflected in the interaction between empowerment and the

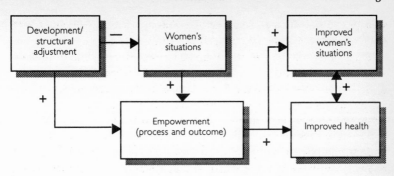

Figure 10.4 Relationships between development, women's situations, and women's health as further modified by empowerment

other factors affecting health. Figure 10.4 extends Figure 10.2 by representing that direct link. A brief review of the relationship of other factors to health and to empowerment follows.

Geography and climate are exogenous factors that tend to have more negative effects on health in tropical, third world countries. There is a growing awareness that local knowledge and experience are important components of efforts – such as developing sustainable agriculture and making the best use of available water – designed to mitigate those negative effects, as well as the negative side-effects of some technological approaches developed and instituted without regard for local conditions. Empowerment of women is considered to be an important element in designing and implementing improved strategies to mitigate natural hazards.

Germs are another exogenous factor negatively affecting health. While their role is not contested, the effectiveness of fighting germs as the primary strategy to reduce disease and improve health has been increasingly questioned. An accumulation of research indicating the important interactions between germs and social conditions, and psychosocial/psychoneuroimmunological factors, suggests a need to look towards reducing susceptibility and increasing resistance to germs in a non-biomedical context as well as seeking, through biomedical activities, to eradicate or inoculate against these threats to health. Empowerment is intended to improve social conditions, and is integrally related to those psychosocial and psychoneuroimmunological factors that are thought to relate to susceptibility and resistance.

The local environment – water, sanitation, energy sources, land quality, and air quality – affects health in many ways, but research indicates important links to other factors, such as public health and health behavior. Empowerment often expresses itself in activities designed to preserve or improve the local environment and to mitigate dangerous conditions. It also plays a major role in behavior change.

It has often been thought that national income strongly affects the health of populations because of its role as an indicator of development level. It has been shown that this assumption, based on theories of development and modernization, is faulty except in very low-income countries. In other countries the distribution of income and social policy on public expenditures may be more important. When the relationship between GNP and social progress was shown to be weaker than had been supposed, investigations into determinants of health broadened their focus, leading in particular to findings about the importance of women's education.

Modernization, while it is thought to be reflected by GNP, has specific characteristics that have been linked to health: the use of wage labor, increased use of technology, urbanization, and industrialization, as well as improved education, which is considered separately here. The research on modernization shows both positive and negative effects on health, and reveals gender differences related to development policies. Since empowerment has been developed as a strategy to reduce the negative impacts of development and modernization, it can serve to improve health.

Population and fertility control are linked to the health of individual women through the high rates of maternal mortality and morbidity in the third world, and to the health of populations through the effects of overpopulation on food and land availability. While government policies have often fostered programs that are top-down and separated from other health activities, it is becoming clear that effective programs involve women and focus on women's empowerment. Ecological data indicate that as opportunities for women and their status increase, fertility rates decline.

Violence and sexual abuse have only a negative relationship to health. At the level of domestic violence, both changes in societal norms with regard to the human rights of women and the treatment of violence as unacceptable are needed to improve women's lives and their health. Empowerment of women at the household and community level, the changing of laws and enforcement policies at the urging of women, and the increasing call by women for their human rights are the pathways currently being taken. Empowerment serves to bring women together, reducing their isolation and increasing their ability to recognize and deal with the violence perpetrated against them.

Empowerment is also related to strategies to attain economic independence for women, and thereby to free them of the need to sell their
bodies. Rape and genital mutilation are indicators of women's low
status, which empowerment is designed to counter. As for war, the
ultimate form of violence, the most that can be hoped is that society
will finally recognize how often and how brutally it is waged against
women.

There are many different factors ascribed to the organization of
society here. Some, such as poverty and social disorganization, have
long been identified as related to poor health outcomes; others, such
as belonging to socially disadvantaged groups, are currently under
extensive study; and, most recently, conditions of inequality, which
subsume the other factors, have been identified on a societal level as
negatively affecting population health. There is still a great need for
research into why and how inequality acts on health, but surely one
pathway is through psychosocial and psychoneuroimmunological routes.
Empowerment links psychosocial/psychoneuroimmunological factors to
factors related to social organization. It is designed to produce
psychosocial changes, while it is dedicated to equalizing power and
resources. A second pathway from empowerment to health would be
through increased access to needed resources, many of which appear
here as separate factors: sanitation and energy sources, health and
medical care, nutritional food, and income. Empowerment, by seeking
to redress social imbalance, seeks to redistribute such resources.

While medical technology and medical care have been credited with
global improvements in health in the last century, the down side of
modern medicine must be acknowledged. Evidence is emerging that
medicine is effective for certain conditions in certain historical contexts, but that overemphasis on Western medicine often causes neglect
of public health so that the health of subpopulations, particularly those
living in poverty and/or in rural areas, suffers. Recognition of the
limitations of modern medicine has increased the search for other
determinants of health. However, medical care must also be viewed as
one of the resources of society that should be equitably distributed.
Women are calling for access to these services for all their health
problems, not only those that are reproductive. An empowered population will inevitably affect the distribution and content of medical
care and the use of medical technology.

Public health has often been credited as a major contributor to
global health improvements. Although there is controversy as to the
relative importance of public health in improving health in different
historical situations, its potential is recognized. Along with education,

support for public health is seen as an indicator of social development. While it requires governmental support, public health is also implemented through community support. This generally means women's support, and women are now speaking to the need for empowerment as a means of developing more responsive and relevant public health systems.

Both health education and health behavior are considered to be important factors in and of themselves and in relation to many other determinants. However, the relationship between individual behaviors and individual health is not straightforward; resistance and susceptibility vary among individuals, affecting that relationship. It is also probable that disadvantaged people are more affected by their circumstances than by their behavior. As research often points up how difficult it is to understand and modify behavior at the individual level, attention is being paid to changing norms, which in turn affect behavior at the social level. Empowerment is thought to facilitate such normative changes.

While some links between vitamin deficiencies and health are very clear, the relationship between overall nutritional levels and health, morbidity, and mortality is cloudy. Malnutrition has long-term debilitating effects, and increases susceptibility to infection; chronic hunger reduces the quality of life at the very least. Programs and policies to improve nutritional levels, like those to reduce population, depend on women for successful implementation. Frequently, such programs are developed by women. Empowerment is both a component that improves such programs and an outcome of successful programs.

Attention has been paid in this book to the role of genes and genetics in health, although this area is usually considered to be in the exclusive domain of biomedicine and other hard sciences. As the ability to manipulate genetic composition increases and becomes more diffused, the importance of genes moves from the individual level to the societal level. Many societal decisions will be made in the very near future that will have direct and long-term population health effects, and if women are to contribute to the decision-making process, they will need to have power in the domains where these decisions will be made.

Along with the emergence of important social questions in the field of genetics, psychosocial and psychoneuroimmunological factors and processes are being investigated in broad social contexts. This set of factors also links innermost individual states with conditions considered to be more distant from the individual. Some variables investigated in these fields are the same as, or closely related to, those defined as components of empowerment. Information unfolding about psychosocial and psychoneuroimmunological processes provides insight into how empowerment might act to improve health. It is important, however, to recognize that empowerment is social as well as psychosocial, affecting not only the person but also the individual's situation and the individual's relationship to that situation.

All the above factors have been studied with regard to the health of populations and are not specific to women, although women may be disproportionately affected by some, such as local environmental conditions, population control, violence, and nutrition. However, the remaining factors – women's status and women's education – are specific to women, and can best be viewed as indicators of social inequity based on gender.

The fact that women's status has so frequently been associated with their health, despite the paucity of research into the relationship, is perhaps an indicator of the general recognition of the importance of equality and equity to good health. It is also, however, an indication of the intransigence of the problem, since even those organizations most vocal about the need for equity, such as the United Nations and the World Health Organization, have not gone far towards achieving it in their own leadership. Empowerment, intended to increase both power and status, is clearly a pathway to change.

Finally, women's education has been identified as possibly the most important determinant of children's health, and must surely also have a major impact on women's health. However, education is an indicator; what it stands for is as yet unclear. It does not always represent the same thing in all cultures. Its effectiveness may lie more in the way in which it changes norms, values, behaviors, and psychosocial orientation than in the knowledge and skills it teaches and the economic advantages it bestows. While this is of great interest, the means by which education affects health may be less important than knowledge of its effects. It provides a straightforward, available route to improved health. Empowerment may act in similar ways. Unfortunately, empowerment is less easy to measure and evaluate. However, it seems rational to put resources and energy into strategies like empowerment that parallel or reinforce formal education, which has been clearly shown to be effective.

P8
Linking together development and women's situation, empowerment, and health; placing them in a context that includes historical, political, economic, cultural, social, and local circumstances; and adopting a non-reductionist, non-linear, dialectical approach to understanding complex issues,

provides a framework to reorient our thinking about health
from pathogenic to salutogenic.

Much of the material presented in this book has been concrete, based
on descriptions of how women live and the organizations they form.
This material is useful in fleshing out the theoretical model presented
in Figure 10.4. Figure 10.5, entitled the Women's Empowerment Model,
adds detail and context to the earlier model, representing the described
pathways to improved health for women. It is intended to depict the
framework described in P8. The model is based on observations and
reports on women's activities and strategies in the 1980s and 1990s; it
links those activities and strategies with the results of empirical investigations into health and with health, and empowerment theory.

It may be seen that the Women's Empowerment Model incorporates
the three broad concepts presented in this book, with development as
a contextual factor but one that specifically has impact on the circumstances within which women live and on their needs, as depicted in the
first two columns. Empowerment, encompassing the four central columns of the model, grows out of groups organized in response to those
needs, and is thought to lead to a wide variety of outcomes affecting
the women, their situations, and the groups in which they participate.
The final two columns of the model concern health.

I have discussed the difficult circumstances and basic needs of the
women who are the subjects of this book throughout. Chapter 2
describes how some of these women are organized, or organize themselves, into projects that use the process of empowerment described in
Chapter 3. The potential outcomes for participants in empowerment
projects are many and varied, and occur on both group and individual levels. At group level, positive changes within the project or
organization itself and within the community can be anticipated.
These, of course, interact. Individuals may also experience internal
and situational changes. The positive internal changes have been
described both theoretically and as observed. Changes in the living
situations of women have also been both theorized and observed.
Finally, potential negative changes in women's situations must also be
anticipated. Again, there will be interactions among these different
individual components. Two pathways have been posited between these
outcomes of empowerment and improved health. The first is through
changes in factors as detailed in P7 above, particularly in those directly
relating to women's health knowledge, practices, behaviors, and relations to the health and medical care systems. The second is through
beneficial psychoneuroimmunological changes that may result from

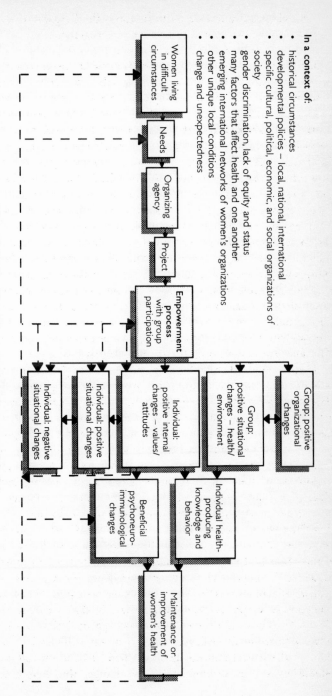

Figure 10.5   The Women's Empowerment Model

internal psychosocial and situational changes. Together, these will act on the multiple dimensions of women's health described in Chapter 5. While there is no claim that all the dimensions of health will be positively affected, the model is salutogenic because it suggests that health will be improved. The focus here is on positive health, although negative health (illness, disease, disability) may be reduced as well.

This temporal pathway takes place in both a real-world and a theoretical context. I have described the importance of the specific historical and geopolitical situation, development practices, the societal/political/cultural/economic structures, discrimination due to gender, the multiple factors affecting health and each other, and the emerging women's empowerment movement. The theoretical framework described in Chapter 8 reinforces the importance of the local situation to events and relationships, and emphasizes the roles of change and unexpectedness and the dynamism of the situation and the relationships. This dynamism is partially represented in the diagram through feedback loops (dotted lines) that only begin to indicate the complex interrelationships between situation, strategies, individual and group changes, and health and those factors that affect health. The theoretical framework also emphasizes interactivity, non-linearity, lack of clear distinction between whole and parts, conflict, and complexity, aspects of the context that are not represented in Figure 10.5.

The model represented in Figure 10.5 is a micro-level model, tracing individual women and groups of women through cycles of change. Macro-level, contextual effects, represented here as external to and surrounding the micro-level process, have a major impact on health. Women can and will improve their situations and their health through their own efforts, but, as the review of factors affecting health has shown, they cannot completely compensate for a damaging contextual environment. The use of empowerment strategies has evolved in large part in response to negative stimuli: the increasing needs and responsibilities of women, environmental dangers, exclusion from the benefits of development, cultural disregard of women's needs. If such negative stimuli do not change, or if conditions worsen, women will continue to suffer disproportionately from preventable illness and disease.

The potential for empowerment groups and programs to affect the macro-level context positively – leading to changes in societal structures, cultural, political, and economic patterns, and development policies – is not represented in the Women's Empowerment Model, and I have only briefly addressed it in Chapter 2. If such changes do occur, they will be due in large part to the emerging networks of organizations that are providing technical assistance, financial support, and visibility to the many different locally based activities, while simultaneously presenting and representing women's empowerment groups to a world-wide audience.

Summary and Conclusions

In this chapter I have presented eight key points that seem to me to synthesize the information from the earlier chapters. I hope that the reader sees them as sensible and self-evident, and is accepting of a framework that draws together many aspects of women's lives and relates them to their health; my goal is that we begin to develop common understanding and terminology. Recognizing where we are and what is what is only a stepping stone. The important questions about how and why must now be addressed.

Can we move away from pathogenesis and towards salutogenesis, and if so, how? While a better road to improved health is not clearly delineated, there are traces of evidence – light footprints – which indicate that a focus on development and empowerment, on social organization and equity, will have a greater impact on women's health than a concentration on factors thought to be more directly related to health. The effects on health of attempts to follow single strands in the tangled web formed by the determinants of health, while ignoring or 'controlling for' intersecting ones, is unpredictable. It has been proved that nutrition supplementation programs for infants contribute to producing bigger children who need more food – which is unavailable – in adolescence. Better, perhaps, to strengthen the whole fabric by concentrating on the strands that provide the major support. It is social justice and equity – as envisioned by Sen and Grown and by others – that will lead to positive health. The empowerment of women is one of the clearest roads to social justice in these times.

However, empowerment is not to be seen as a cure-all. It is applicable only where it is willingly adopted, when historical openings allow for its emergence, and for as long as it serves those in need. Many questions remain. If there is an effect on health from empowerment, does it endure? Can it protect against temporary adversity? Will resistance to women's empowerment increase as the movement becomes more organized and devoted to larger issues of equity? Can men be brought into this movement and both share its benefits and increase its effectiveness, while resisting the temptation to dominate? And – perhaps the biggest question of all – is the present women's empowerment movement going to bring us closer to those visions of an equitable and just world where '[e]ach person will have the opportunity to develop her or his full potential and creativity, and women's values of nurturance and solidarity will characterize human relationships' (Sen and Grown 1987: 81)? In such a world, illness, disease, and death will not disappear, but health will be less constricted by social and cultural barriers. Although Utopia is out of reach, its image can provide guidance to those who seek to make things just a little better now.

No simple conclusions can be drawn from the material presented, or from the eight points that I have emphasized in this chapter. Important hints, insights, and recognitions about the health of all, and of women in particular, are contained in them. They represent a world-view: a belief that relationships – whether structural ones based on power or personal ones based on a myriad of social, cultural, and personality factors – are extremely important to health. I am both cynical and hopeful. While there has been an undeniable improvement in health throughout the world, there are many places and peoples who either remain untouched or who have benefited less than expected. To date, we have placed too much of the burden of correcting the wrongs and finding ways to survive in difficult or worsening situations on women. On the other hand, it is impossible not to be moved and inspired by what *is* being done – by concerned advocates, researchers, and practitioners, and by almost infinitely creative and resilient women who suffer from poverty and oppression.

II

What Now?

In this final chapter, I want to discuss practical implications of the preceding discussion on development, empowerment, health, and research alternatives. I hope that this will be useful to those who are involved in efforts to improve women's health, and that it will enhance the effectiveness of the women's empowerment movement, since there is a unique historical opportunity to foster the movement that may not come again. That opportunity results from several factors. Policy-makers are relying more on women to carry out policies for which governments are unwilling or unable to pay. An increasing amount of literature is pointing out the interrelatedness of health and development, and there is a growing recognition that empowerment and self-determination have a relationship to health. Finally, there is growing pressure from women for control over their lives, and for their share of power. My recommendations are offered in the spirit of the evolving theoretical framework presented in Chapter 9 – as guides intended to stimulate thought, not as answers or prescriptions. They are based on a salutogenic, holistic perspective grounded in the everyday realities of women confronting underdevelopment. They are derived from conclusions suggesting that a focus on positive development and empowerment, on social organization and equity, will have a greater impact on women's health and well-being than will a concentration on factors generally thought to be more directly related to health. In particular, they support empowerment as a strategy for confronting under-development and improving health.

I also recognize, however, a real-world tension between competing visions of empowerment – as a means of pacification and cooptation, as a way to improve the lives of some individuals, as a strategy to accomplish needed community work, as a process to improve the lives

261

of organized groups of people, or as a pathway to the creation of more socially just societies. My perspective is that empowerment, by definition, must lead to meaningful changes in power and access to resources for groups of people. If it also contributes to a reduction of the roles of inequity and discrimination, so much the better. However, even if it does not move us towards more salutogenic societies, the evidence reported here indicates that improvements in the health and well-being of those women fortunate enough to have opportunities for empowerment can still be anticipated.

My recommendations also take into account the fact that empowerment is about power, and therefore about conflict and change, so that many will resist efforts truly to empower women. Realistically, *power* is and should be at the root of empowerment. If empowerment is to succeed, a devolution of power is required: from those who benefit from current power arrangements to those who want to support women's activities. Individuals may both benefit from current arrangements and support women's activities, a fact that increases the complexity of the situation. (I speak personally here as a middle-class, white citizen of the USA.) Since power is generally viewed as a scarce commodity, I do not expect the recommendations about to be presented, intended to lead to radical changes in the distribution of power, to be adopted immediately and willingly.

At this time, it is probable that those in power, if they are confronted with the framework I present, are more likely to call for research into the relationships presented, and to exhibit a 'wait and see' attitude, than to recommend action. There are conservative biases in the fields of both health and development, and inherent difficulties in deviating from the status quo. Policies and practices are designed and implemented within positivist frameworks by members of immense, entrenched bureaucracies. Health and development practitioners have accumulated power and a history of working autonomously. However, a 'wait and see' strategy is unlikely to cast much light on the relationships owing to previously discussed factors such as:

- the complexity and multidirectionality of the relationships among the many factors involved in development, empowerment, and health;
- the different units of analysis – individual, family, household, community, program, and organization;
- the importance of historical, social, cultural, and politico-economic contexts;
- the necessarily small size of empowerment projects;

- the timespan required for the fruition of the process of empowerment;
- the dynamism of international affairs; and
- the problem of measuring concepts that have different meanings to different people at different times.

All these issues make research into empowerment and health complicated, as indicated in Chapter 9. The search for strong associations between empowerment and health, causal or otherwise, may not only take many years owing to the nature of the empowerment process, but may be futile, if, as has been suggested, current methods can never capture the relationships and connections represented in the models presented in Chapter 10.

I do not argue, however, that empowerment and health should not be researched. Rather, I argue that policy modifications should not be deferred in the interim. It is my hope that the circumstantial, associational, and theoretical evidence I have presented is convincing enough to encourage those who are in a position to support women's own initiatives to improve their health and well-being to do so now and to study the impact of these initiatives. While evidence is important as argument and helpful as justification, decisions regarding support for empowerment are also a question of world-view. Who can best make decisions about people's needs? Who can best implement programs designed to meet those needs? Is self-determination fundamental to quality of life? Is equity a right and an important social goal? Empowerment is a natural strategy for those who see self-determination and equity either as important ideals or as pragmatic principles that make things work better. For those who see a greater need for expertise, for control, for centralized decision-making, it can be seen as anarchic and inefficient. In general, those in positions of power are those who feel entitled and qualified to make decisions, like to make decisions, and have much to gain from maintaining the status quo. Given that I have described empowerment as a successful strategy for improving women's lives, as embodying a world-view, and as a threat to the status quo, change will have to be negotiated. Such negotiations will evolve if the women's empowerment movement continues to gain strength. Out of the inevitable power struggles, in due time, will come new policies, new forms of practice, and relevant research.

In this chapter I directly address several different heterogeneous and overlapping groups of people who affect women's situations and their lives, and can and will play a role in encouraging or discouraging change:

- those who develop and implement programs and projects that do or might incorporate empowerment;
- the emerging networks of women's organizations that begin to bridge the gap between the projects and the policy-makers;
- the activists and scholars whom I have described as moving back and forth between their personal realities, the realities of the third world, and academia;
- those who frame policy and those who in fact define policy through funding and through implementation;
- those who provide health and medical care, and organize medical and public health practice; and
- researchers who have an interest in one or another aspect of the complex domains of development, empowerment, and health, or study women in developing countries.

Several other groups should be mentioned as influential. Among these are local and national political and military leaders, religious leaders, and men (husbands, sons) in the community. These groups are, of course, extremely important to the success of women's efforts. However, owing to the enormous variation in their roles, relationships, and behaviors, and to the paucity of information on their interactions with women's groups, they will not be addressed in what follows.

Also not directly addressed are those who have led me during this research process and are making their own way: the women who were, are now, or will be members of a local group hoping to make life a little easier and to get enough resources to ensure the survival of their families. My only 'advice' to them is to keep on keepin' on, and to 'Get together. Stir the stuff around. Listen to your hunger. Get ready. Get organized' (Morales 1991: 56).

Considerations for Programs and Projects

Among those groups most able to foster empowerment (and thereby improve health) are the programs and projects that already support empowerment and the women's empowerment movement. The increasing popularity of empowerment strategies among NGOs, grass-roots organizations, and other groups is surely an indication of their success. With the accumulation of projects and the growth of networks of projects, a new stage is approaching. With success, however, will come both external and internal threats to the integrity and effectiveness of an organization.

Dangers of excessive structure and cooptation

One of the most immediate problems facing programs is an inevitable conflict: how to remain local, flexible, and responsive to participants and, at the same time, increase the number of women who can participate and expand activities, as funders and policy-makers are encouraging them to do. As the following quotation indicates, when empowerment becomes more acceptable, pressures to formalize and quantify the construct increase:

> Anonuevo said governments, multilateral agencies and funding agencies were now taking up women's issues, but were enshrining them in words like empowerment, democracy and the phrase 'women in development'.
> Anonuevo is critical of the excessive structure imposed by many development bodies. 'We who have evolved the practice are now, in turn, shaped by the development language that has emerged. We are asked to come up with indicators of empowerment, or to quantify our work, or worse, to fit into logical analytical frameworks.'
> According to Anonuevo, such frameworks put issues into boxes where they can be reproduced and institutionalised. 'As agents of change, we have the opportunity to push these rigid structures. But how? I still have to find out.' (Miers [1993] quoting Carol Anonuevo, Executive Director of the Centre for Women's Resources, Manila, the Philippines)

Thus women have to devise ways of encouraging empowerment, democracy, and positive development that avoid 'excessive structure.' For surely excessive structure is the antithesis of empowerment. Programs must, therefore, consider their options carefully and monitor their effectiveness continually, recognizing that there are no known short cuts to empowerment.

Success can also lead to cooptation. Governments, multilateral agencies and funding agencies may so reshape programs, consciously or unconsciously, that they are no longer empowering. Academics can play an important watchguard role by identifying the strategies used to undermine or coopt women's activities. Such monitoring is easier (and safer) from a distance.

Need to maintain honesty

There are other risks associated with success and recognition. One risk is honesty – acknowledging problems, wrong-turns, and weaknesses. Empowerment groups ideally reflect and act cyclically, making decisions based on conditions that are not fixed and on a consciousness that is constantly evolving. Clearly, honesty must be a part of this process. However, funders and those in power can mistake this for failure, leading organizations to less honest reporting and possible suppression of disagreement. While there are no obvious solutions to this tension, it is vitally important to the health of an organization that it remain realistic and cognizant of weaknesses as well as strengths. Continuing dialogue with powerful outsiders on the importance of the flexibility of the empowerment process and the importance of honest evaluation may help to change traditional perceptions of success and failure.

Need for creative leadership

Another risk stemming from success is the enshrinement of leaders. Sen and Grown (1987) have noted the excessive reliance by women's groups on charismatic leaders. These leaders may be trapped into seeing themselves as irreplaceable because of their acceptance by power-brokers. They may become accustomed to the perquisites that accompany such acceptance: travel, access to information, increased opportunities for income. Others may hold back criticism and independent activity for fear of undermining current successes. The greatest protection against debilitating institutionalization will be the constant production of new and creative leaders. Over and over again, one individual or a few individuals are identified as having been the moving force in the creation of an empowerment or a community development project. These individuals are caring, creative, optimistic, resilient, and enduring. On the basis of frameworks emphasizing hierarchy, domination, and control, we have few models to help produce these kinds of leaders. They are often seen as unusual and the product of lucky circumstances. However, experience has shown that there are many such potential leaders, that empowerment activities identify such leaders, and that non-hierarchical organizational structures can allow for multiple leaders and reduce the burden that accompanies the leadership role in hierarchical organizations.

Programs should take to heart the advice from Sen and Grown and others to confront this and other internal organizational problems that have been noticed with some frequency, such as the avoidance of clear assignment of responsibilities, reluctance to participate in interorganizational activities, and an inability to gain meaningful political representation.

Need to foster active participation and empowerment

Most important, organizations fostering empowerment must continue to be democratic and empowering, never forgetting that the process is really what matters. Without a participatory process, the change they manage to stimulate is likely to be short-term and superficial. As women have indicated repeatedly, it is the experience of decision-making and the opportunities for self-determination that lead to enduring change and an unwillingness to go back to what was. Empowerment is subtle. It is more than participation, more than exposure to information designed to increase consciousness of social barriers, more than increased comradeship. It is an end as well as a process. Actual change must occur at both a personal and a societal level.

Considerations for Supporters

As we have seen, the women's empowerment movement has been facilitated by a heterogeneous group of supporters – networks of organizations, funding groups such as the Global Fund for Women, networks of activists and academics, and independent activists and scholars. There is not, and need not be, a clear division of labor among these supporters. Depending upon situation, resources, audience, and talents, any one of these players can take on any number of support activities. A major part of their efforts should be to look at what is, not what they think should be. The important questions are often asked by those at or close to the grass roots. The environment is dynamic and unpredictable, so insights will be more useful than answers. The considerations that follow cross disciplinary and organizational lines and, as always, are focused on supporting the women's empowerment movement.

Need for a variety of networks and outreach activities

If empowerment projects must remain local and flexible, it is counter-productive to talk about large projects; yet a goal must be to enable as many women as possible to participate. The Nicaraguan model of networks of organizations described in Chapter 2 presents an attempt to meet both those goals. Projects group themselves by focus – education, health, sexuality, and so on. However, they are also attempting to form non-hierarchical, non-bureaucratic networks that can work at a national (and international) level to affect policy and carry out strategic planning related to long-term needs. Other such networks have been formed on a regional basis. Funders such as the Global Fund for Women or certain NGOs provide services aimed at bringing their grantees into a network. Service organizations such as ISIS and WAND also serve to create and maintain networks. Meetings such as the 1995 women's conference in China contribute to these efforts.

These amorphous networks must continue to build power bases of local, national, and international supporters while serving their constituent organizations. Their strategies to date have been very successful, involving outreach and communication through media and technologies such as video, radio, theater, art, newsletters, and computer networks such as the Association for Progressive Communications and the Internet. Efforts to organize conferences such as the United Nations conferences on the environment, population, social development, human rights, and women have been massive. These efforts are dedicated to grass-roots representation, and are powerful forces bringing women together, organizing data, and telling women's stories. They are accompanied by continued activities designed to increase the visibility of women's organizations at all levels, to increase access to policy-makers at all levels, and to increase the role of women in policy development and funding decisions. As visibility increases, much of what may seem threatening and revolutionary may come to be seen as a positive and hope-generating strategy for all those who seek to reduce misery and create more equitable societies.

Need for process and outcome information

At this stage of the movement there is a great need to collect and organize process and outcome information useful to projects, to policy-makers and funders, and to those academics and scholars who are studying the movement. Information is not only a means to resources and power. According to Margaret Wheatley (1994: 102), 'It is information that gives order, that prompts growth, that defines what is alive. It is both the underlying structure and the dynamic process that ensure life.' Women's networks have understood the importance of information, both for women at the grass roots and for those who need to understand women's situations. Traditional sources of academic information are not always suitable for these organizations. Standard peer-reviewed articles are often full of jargon and void of the real-world difficulties that projects experience. Negative results, so important to practitioners, often go unpublished for fear of funding repercussions, although problems and 'failures' provide at least as much information as successes.

Policy analysts and scholars who study women's activities need to share their findings and their theories with the women themselves, on whom they are building their careers. The generation of short, readable résumés of research activities and of final results in the language of the country should be a prerequisite of funding. Other useful information includes informal internal self-studies, grant applications, evaluations done with the help of academics or other trained evaluators, and academic studies. Such information can be fed into repositories in a somewhat standardized format. Abbreviated or complete versions can be available by computer. Women's organizations such as ISIS do now and can continue to serve as repositories for these documents, while increasing their efforts to computerize the information. These organizations also confront language problems, often maintaining multiple databases with duplicated information in at least English, Spanish, French, and German.

Need for studies of the devolution of power

Power does not redistribute on its own. The political roots of policy must be analyzed, so that issues of power distribution are seen for what they are. This analysis needs to take into account the complex relations between gender and power. Besides their own efforts, those who support the empowerment movement can make use of trained professionals and academics who are committed to bettering conditions for women. The intricacies of national and international policies towards health and development, and the responsiveness of those policies to economic conditions and pressures and to political instability, make efforts to affect policy extremely difficult. The need for simultaneous efforts to increase the ability of organizations to meet women's practical and strategic needs and to develop effective ways to 'apply available force to the maximum effect' at national and international levels suggests that collaboration with those who have studied policy will be helpful. To that end, honest appraisals of the methods and the effects of devolving power must be undertaken. Fields dedicated to policy studies, such as political science and health policy, need to democratize themselves – to make their analyses accessible, to train others to analyze local situations, and to incorporate standpoints not traditionally included in analysis. Those with the most at stake need to know potential entry points and leverage points in the policy-making process.

Need for organizational studies

Appropriate organizational structures also need further theoretical and practical development. Studies that look at organizations dedicated to social change in the context of new science, feminism, participation, and empowerment can provide information to organizers and funders. Of course they can also be used by those who wish to undermine or coopt organizations seeking change. That risk cannot be avoided, and all who are involved in the movement must be aware that they are in a struggle, and that their guard must be up at all times. Information on how best to use information and to protect against its misuse is also a continuing need.

Considerations for Health and Development Policy, Funding, and Implementation

C. Arden Miller (1987: 15) defines health policy as 'the aggregate of principles, stated or unstated, that more or less consistently characterize the distribution of resources, services, and political influence that impact on the health of the population of concern.' These principles evolve from interactions between politics and ideology. There are many players producing health and development policy through policy statements, implementation of policy, and allocation of funds.

At the global level are (1) international organizations such as the United Nations and its agencies, including UNICEF, the World Health Organization, and its regional branches; (2) bi- and multilateral aid agencies such as USAID, Canada's CIDA and IDRC, and Denmark's DANIDA; (3) non-governmental organizations run by religious or other ideological or philanthropic groups; (4) private foundations that fund in the area of health and development such as Ford, Rockefeller, Carnegie, and Kellogg; (5) international financial agencies such as the World Bank and the International Monetary Fund; (6) multinational corporations; (7) academics and practitioners who generally participate through other organizations; and, more recently, (8) women's networks and funders such as DAWN and the Global Fund for Women.

At the national level, the players include (1) ministries of health; (2) the executive and legislative branches of national governments; (3) educational and service institutions; (4) academics and practitioners and their organizations; (5) NGOs; (6) economic elites; and (7) organized forms of public pressure. At more regional or local levels, many of these groups have representatives in addition to other locally based organizations. The point to be made here is that all these policy-makers are acting from different perspectives and from specific paradigmatic standpoints, making the 'aggregation of principles' described by Miller an extremely complicated and often mysterious process.

Decisions on resource allocation among competing needs, training, equity in access, and responsiveness to local conditions are made at a national level. However, international pressures and economic support play a very large role in decision-making. Also, much national-level policy is implemented at local level, where effectiveness becomes a major factor. Some international NGOs and WHO programs avoid national-level politics and go directly to the local level. Often the interaction among levels is as important as the levels themselves – a reflection of the newer paradigms.

Need to focus on inequity

One consideration applies to all the various policy-makers and funders: decisions about policy and funding should be made with an emphasis on reducing or avoiding inequity and inequality. Inequity and inequality have been implicated as negatively affecting social, political, cultural, ecological, and psychosocial factors that are known to affect health. My conclusions suggest that they are central, fundamental, and particularly pervasive determinants. Many groups of people suffer as a result of inequities. Women are affected because of their gender and often also because of their race, their ethnicity, their poverty. All policies – health-specific or not – should be formulated and implemented in light of the information regarding the central role of inequality as a factor affecting health and well-being.

One immediate need in regard to inequity is relief from the disproportionate effects of current policies of development and structural adjustment. Women are increasingly being forced, due to international and national economic policies and their effects on family and community structures, to take on the struggle for basic needs – for food, health care, child care, housing, income – and for what is literally a fight for the survival of the next generation. Health systems everywhere are in a process of change, with increasing privatization, cost-cutting, and attention to prevention. Reports of the negative effects on nutrition, disease, and access to care of structural adjustment and privatization are beginning to appear in the literature (Loewenson 1993). The effects of these policies on women should be acknowledged, and policies to relieve this inequitably distributed burden should be developed.

Need to focus on violence and sexual abuse

A second immediate need is for a continuation and intensification of discussions around issues of violence and sexual abuse against women. Violence is an important health issue and a key indicator of women's status. Violence goes hand in hand with social disorganization. Time and time again women have identified freedom from threats of violence as a major need. While interventions against violence are not yet well developed, policy statements from above can establish a political climate where violence and sexual abuse against women are seen as unacceptable, thereby speeding up or reinforcing other efforts to deal with this endemic threat to health.

Need for support of and resources for empowerment

Another important recommendation that applies equally to all policy-making and funding organizations is that support and resources for women's organizations should be provided as a part of health and development programs. Those working in the area of health should join forces with those working in development and, as part of their strategy to improve women's status, health, and well-being, should base their activities in what women are doing to achieve those same goals.

It may be, unfortunately, that the capacity or likelihood of policy-makers, funders, and project implementers to cause harm is greater than their capacity to help in the areas of health and development programs and research. Harm can result from reinforcing or worsening existing inequities; from instilling dependency while undermining functional local traditions; or from disrupting communities by injecting money, outside experts, and sophisticated technologies and then pulling out – declaring the project to be a failure, no longer a priority, or well on the road to self-sufficiency. Often such outcomes are a result of overcentralized decision-making and emphasis on the needs of the policy-making or funding organization over the needs of the program recipients. Concentrating on helping women to stay or become healthy will encourage empirical decision-making that is primarily focused on such helping. While the exigencies of funding and policy agencies will always exist, and will not necessarily correlate with the needs of recipients, looking to the recipients for ideas and focusing on strengthening what has already been shown to work may prove less harmful than some current strategies.

What is called for from those who work internationally is something quite different from what currently exists. Key to the reorientation is working with and not for, acting with and not on, doing with and not to. Most important is that the women involved determine their own strategies. Support for women's organizations or for organizations working with women should be provided, with as little conscious or unconscious control as possible. Donors, sponsors, networks of organizations, and the organizations themselves will have to develop methods which, while making available knowledge, the experience of others, technical assistance, and other forms of support, ensure that decisions are in fact made at the participant level. This is, of course, implicit in the meaning of empowerment, but not easily achieved. It is difficult to be patient and to allow for personal and group development rather than to impose a structure that worked somewhere else, or 'ought' to work.

How can organizations accustomed to top-down decision-making, power, and control adapt to an environment where a large part of the decision-making, power, and control belong to those at the bottom? The process will be slow and tentative. Lip service comes first, and some of that already occurs. Small projects follow, and some already exist, most frequently sponsored by NGOs. More specifically, program funders – be they international health organizations, aid agencies, NGOs, private foundations or international financial organizations – can provide technical assistance, startup financing, leadership training, and supplies to empowerment projects and networks. They can also provide opportunities for sharing information about strategies, successes, and failures, and for networking through the support of travel to international forums, publications, and further development and support of computer communication.

Such aid need not cost a great deal. One major problem with aid funding has been the large amounts of money that suddenly appear in a community or country, breeding dependency, competition, and economic stratification. Rather than undermining independence, equity, and sustainability through an influx of financial and technical support, a sensitive response to expressed needs is required:

> Unemployed, with no hope of finding work in the midst of civil war, a group of women in the small Nicaraguan town of Estelí *began meeting two years ago to find ways to survive*. After many discussions, the group decided to take control of their situation by working cooperatively, teaching each other such income-generating skills as sewing, silk-screening, and making piñatas. Calling themselves the *Movimiento de Mujeres Desempleadas de Estelí* (Movement of Unemployed Women of Estelí), they also talked about forming consciousness-raising workshops to discuss female human rights. They only needed money to get started.
>
> In the rarefied world of philanthropy, a group like this is usually out of the loop. But a foundation called the Global Fund for Women, based in Menlo Park, California, heard of the efforts of the Movimiento de Mujeres and gave the group a $7,500 grant in 1992. Unlike most other funders, *the Global Fund doesn't dictate the use of the money. The women themselves defined their needs*; they decided to buy yarn and other supplies to start their enterprises, and to open a small cafetería. (Zia 1993: 20; emphasis added)

According to Anne Firth Murray (Zia 1993: 21), past president of the Global Fund for Women: 'Women on the ground level say that the best funders give them money and leave them alone.' Although few funders are likely to take that stance, their assistance and advice can be positive, and can reinforce rather than undermine or coopt women's groups:

> We have learned much from the many women's groups we work with. Our experience shows, for example, that plans, programs, and organizations initiated locally have a much greater chance of surviving and being useful than plans, programs, and organizations that are initiated 'from the outside.' We see again and again that commitment, vision, and initiative are far more important than money to the success of a program. We have also learned that the key to progress is individual empowerment. Some women have even said that such empowerment can be impeded by too much money being imposed upon groups from the outside. (Murray 1994a)

The $7,500 startup money given without strings to the Movimiento de Mujeres in Estelí avoids destructive disruption. In another innovative program, the Global Fund for Women took $50,000 and distributed it to ten previously funded organizations. These ten groups then each awarded five $1,000 grants to other organizations. The closer the grantors are to the grantees, the more likely the selection of the grantee is based on more than an ability to write proposals.

In Bangladesh – one of the world's poorest countries and one in which women's status is particularly low – the eighteen-year-old Grameen Bank has extended credit to 1.5 million landless people, of whom 93 percent are women. The average loan is 60 dollars, with an interest rate of 16 percent, and the repayment rate is about 95 percent. It is serving as a model for programs in both developed and underdeveloped countries (InterPress Service 1993c, 1993d; Khandker 1994).

Funders must be willing to take chances, to fund innovation, and to fund those in the greatest need. Proposal writing should not be the only standard used to award funding. While good proposal writing does indeed indicate that an organization can produce results in a timely fashion, and can clearly explain its goals and methods, it can also indicate centralized skills that do not necessarily lead to effective field work. First-hand knowledge of the situation can provide at least useful supplementary information.

NGOs have been and will continue to be particularly important funding sources for the kinds of activities that women want and need. The 1993 Human Development Report of the UN Development Programme says that there are now over 50,000 major NGOs in the developing world, providing grants of over $5 billion a year, benefiting more than 250 million people. Important as these are, they reach only 20 percent of the people living in absolute poverty, and account for only 13 percent of official aid and 2.5 percent of total resource flow to developing countries (InterPress Service 1993b). However, much of this aid is suited to its purpose – not overwhelming, and with fewer strings attached than governmental or non-NGO international aid. As other NGOs develop successful models, it will be important that they publicize both their successes and their failures so that funders and recipients can see what might be adaptable to their own environments. NGOs can link up with scholars, researchers, and women's information networks to encourage and distribute findings from descriptive and analytical evaluations that serve both their programs and the broader policy community.

Need to foster intersectoral programs

While I have not produced a universal model of health, but, rather, argued that the roles of history, culture, geography, and other similar factors are such that universal models are improbable, I have shown that interactions among factors both inside and outside the traditional domain of health are many, multidirectional, and dependent on the historical and social context. To treat these factors as independent in the hope that the complexity can be ignored distorts reality to the point where much effort, energy, and resources are wasted. Walls between sectors must be broken through – water, health, education, environmental protection, and economic opportunity are not independent, and should not compete for turf and power. Intersectoral approaches to health receive verbal acknowledgment, but are rare in practice. Even given a commitment, it is difficult to achieve from the top down. However, as Pholela and Jamkhed indicate, services can be coordinated when the initiative comes from the grass roots, where distinctions between sectors are easily seen as artificial. Both by supporting grass-roots efforts and by continually struggling at the higher levels of policy development and implementation to overcome artificial barriers, policy-makers and funders can incorporate broad approaches to improving health in their activities.

Need for salutogenic policies that focus on 'health stocks'

Empowerment at the psychosocial/psychoneuroimmunological level can be seen as increasing an individual's long-term capacity for health. In keeping with the long-term goals of empowerment, both policy-makers and funders should switch their social focus from short-term crisis-oriented interventions to what Murray and Chen (1993: 151) have called 'longer-term cumulative processes related to the build-up or depletion of a society's "health stocks."' These societal stocks may be physical – health care and education facilities, transportation, housing, water supply, and sanitation; social – education, health status, health perceptions and behaviors; or institutional – social, political, and cultural institutions. The authors suggest that social assets, unlike physical assets, do not necessarily depreciate over time, and may contribute to a society's ability to withstand short-term negative events. They recommend evaluation strategies that measure asset accumulation, such as 'improving primary school completion rates, extending the health infrastructure, or improving the quality of housing and water supplies,' and the use of relevant indicators such as 'the capacity and quality of the health care system, the household environment, and most importantly broad-based literacy, education, enhanced status of women, health perception and health tastes' (Murray and Chen 1993: 151, 153).

Need for new paradigms for policy research and evaluation

Much as revised indicators of general progress are required, new techniques to evaluate the viability and usefulness of specific activities are called for. Funders of policy research and program evaluation can, for their part, support innovative methodologies that capture complexity, focus on long-term effects, and contribute to empowerment, such as participatory-action research. They should reconsider and reframe some traditional scientific values, such as objectivity and generalizability. The large sample sizes and lack of room for re-evaluation and program modification required by traditional research's goal of generalizability restrict the kinds of programs that receive funding for research and evaluation. Many of the research issues being grappled with in attempts to develop new paradigms relate to policy research and program evaluation.

Need to expand the role of women in organizations

A particularly blatant indicator of inequality is the paucity of women in leadership roles in policy-making agencies at all levels. It is discouraging to see how long many agencies have been making strong statements about the health and status of women and the importance of self-determination, and how little change there has been in their own structures or programs. However, given the increasing scale of women's activities locally and globally in terms of their status, their human rights as women, and their unique needs, organizations will be increasingly pressured to 'walk their talk.' All international policy groups can make sure that their own houses are clean – that they have an equitable and meaningful inclusion of women at all levels within their organizations. Since the accumulation of documents and statements has helped to fuel changing consciousness, it is also important that policy agencies continue to put out strong statements backing equity for women, support the collection of gender-specific data, and publish studies evaluating progress towards equity and equality.

Considerations for Health Services, Practice, and Education

There are also a varied group of individuals who are specifically concerned about women's health, as health system administrators, providers, or educators. Again, my recommendations for these individuals focus on salutogenesis and on support for empowerment.

Need for health care systems that emphasize salutogenesis

The majority of health professionals work within national health/ medical care systems. There is obviously an enormous variety of these systems in the developing world, ranging from those that provide care primarily for the rich and do essentially nothing for the majority of their people, through those that serve both rich and poor but are heavily tilted towards tertiary care in urban areas, to those that try to put the principles of primary health care into practice. Most health care systems, however, are in a period of major change at the moment, retracting and privatizing. At the same time, there are calls for broader, more salutogenic types of health programs. The confusion engendered by these competing policies is reflected in the following statement from an informal report by the World Bank Office on Population, Health, and Nutrition (1994). The World Bank has been playing and will continue to play a major role in structural adjustment and in the system modifications that they euphemistically call health reform:

> We know WHAT needs to be done. But we need to understand the HOW: how people 'produce' health; how to ensure technical efficiency of health care systems; how to change corporate culture in bureaucracies dealing with health; how to adapt health policy making to the momentous changes that have swept the globe.

We need to develop our understanding of the determinants of health. We agree that health is broader than health care. Yet, we find ourselves confined to discussing only health care reform. We agree that people, not health services, produce health. But beyond that statement the mystery remains: how do people's interactions within the household and the community, with service providers, and with their physical, biological, cultural, economic and political environment determine their health? We have yet to develop a common language that would allow us to analyze and act upon micro, meso and macro determinants of health....

Why don't people utilize cost-effective interventions such as EPI and ORT? The major reason is probably that providers don't care. And providers don't care because they have no incentive to do so. Too often, Ministry of Health staff care more about their powers than about the quality and equity of health services – a flaw shared by international multi- and bilateral agencies.

Here is a picture of uncaring providers, who do not understand health, offering ineffective treatments and services. While, as noted above, there is often a great distance between Ministry of Health staff, policy-makers, and providers and those needing medical or health care, there is also, as reflected in this report, a frustration at the well-recognized ineffectiveness of many programs and services. There is a call for a 'common language that would allow us to analyze and act upon micro, meso and macro determinants of health.' As women become more visible proponents for their own health, and as their responsibility for their family's health is more widely recognized, opportunities may open for professionals to consider appropriate, effective, and empowering systems of care.

Need to broaden understanding about health

The long-term implications of a salutogenic approach to health would certainly include an adjustment in the relationship between public health and medicine, strengthening the former and democratizing the latter. As Hertzman *et al.* (1994: 82) point out, our emphasis on medically diagnosable causes of disease and death does not represent a very sensible definition of health-related research activity, given that these causes are 'extremely rare events for all but the very elderly, in whom they are more or less inevitable and nonspecific.' If salutogenesis were the goal, the kinds of broad, intersectoral programs described in Chapter 4 would be the norm. If health programs will be made more effective by moving away from narrow biomedical interventions and towards broad developmental ones, how can practitioners of public health and medicine assist this effort? As a start, they can educate themselves about health and illness in a fuller context than has been usual. I have presented one such context. While there are many possible alternative formulations of the meaning of health and the factors affecting health, increased emphasis on the cultural relativity of health, the historical influences, the changing needs throughout the life span, and the complexity of the construct and of its production should be part of the education of both public health and medical care providers.[1] Whether or not providers decide that issues such as social organization and power are within their purview, they need to factor them into their frameworks for understanding, treating, and preventing illness and disease. If they choose also to affect positive health, they will probably have to expand the purview of their activities.

Need to recognize the roles of power and powerlessness in health and health care

Others propose more drastic remedies. John McKnight (1985: 37), in an article entitled 'Health and Empowerment,' argues that 'many modern maladies are caused by powerlessness,' but 'there is no effective treatment that can be administered to the powerless.... This has resulted in a dismal array of abandoned programs, palliative remnants and "burned out" health workers.' In their desire to help or in response to political pressures – as Nancy Scheper-Hughes (1992: 202) points out – health workers all too often exacerbate powerlessness by medicalizing and individualizing conditions that result from 'acts of violence and malicious neglect practiced against the poor in the economic and political spheres.' McKnight notes that by taking unto themselves so much of the resources available to the poor, the health and medical care systems have become part of the problem they are trying to solve.

McKnight (1985: 37) presents four guidelines for medical/health policy, all of which would have a major impact on providers. He would require all therapeutic services to prove that they produce more health than if their money were given directly to the poor and their organizations, or used for prevention. All health activities should 'strengthen local authority and legitimize the competence of the local community' with decisions made by the community. Medical techniques should be empowering, not 'mystifying, mega-scale, manipulative devices and methods that necessarily require outside dominance to achieve their "healthful" effect.' Health should be seen as an outcome, 'a condition and not an intervention ... [that] measures the power, competence and justice of a people.' His prescription is drastic:

transfer 'tools, authority, budgets and income to those with the malady of powerlessness.'

McKnight, dramatically, gets to the heart of the issue: *can* health and medicine move from a pathogenic to a salutogenic orientation? If so, what does the role of providers become? The changes he describes are so fundamental that we cannot begin to answer those questions. And it is hard to imagine any profession, let alone the medical profession, giving away the store – tools, authority, budgets, and income. But the congruence between the power of the provider and the powerlessness of the patient, and the effect of that relationship on health, must be wrestled with by providers. It has been faced by community social workers and psychologists, and by community organizers, but less frequently by medical providers. Jamkhed, the Pholela experiment, and community health programs being conducted in Pakistan by the Aga Khan Medical School (Bryant 1991) are among the few programs that are dedicated to the transfer of power from professionals to the community. Right now, perhaps the best we can do is to learn from existing programs and attempt to broaden the primary and continuing education of health providers.

Need to provide comprehensive, appropriate, and effective care for women's health

Public health in third world countries, when available, is often limited to primary care programs that focus on maternal and child health, and on family planning. Where subdisciplines of public health exist, these public health activities have often been in the domain of the field known as Maternal and Child Health (MCH). Existing projects care for women as reproducers only – providing prenatal, delivery, and postnatal services that are focused on child survival (Timyan *et al.* 1993). Many existing public health programs are neither women-centered nor culturally appropriate (Mensch 1992). Women are asking for a more responsive, suitable system of care that provides for them as women and not just as mothers. I (and many others) have identified the health needs of women throughout their lives and in all their roles as needing attention. In a developed world context, but entirely relevant to the third world, Helen Rodriguez-Trias (1992: 664) describes a type of public health that is more responsive to women's needs – one in which women participate in decision-making at all levels:

> Perhaps public health workers are now beginning to understand two delim-
> iting concepts that the women's movement has long espoused, namely,

centrality and totality. *The term 'centrality,' as used in this context, defines health problems as women themselves experience those problems.* Centrality casts women as active decision makers in their own lives. This is to reject and reshape the all too common view of women as passive recipients of health care and public health action. Rape, abortion, abuse by husbands or lovers, sense of powerlessness, oppression in terms of gender, race, culture, and economics are all frequent experiences for women. Health interventions from a public health perspective that involve women must address these issues as defined by women. *The term 'totality,' as used here, defines the health problems of women as deeply implanted in the statuses that derive from their multiple social relations.* Thus totality sees women as inextricably involved with their families and communities. Women cannot separate their roles as workers, caretakers, mothers, sisters, and wives. [emphasis added]

Health professionals can, in the process of broadening their conceptualization of health and health care, incorporate the concepts of centrality (the need for self-definition of health and illness) and totality (the 'embeddedness' of health in all of life) described by Rodriguez-Trias. For example, women doctors in Nigeria have been going out to women in the markets, and to women's gatherings, to provide cancer education, screening, and counseling (Okusanya 1993). In their current roles, health professionals can take advantage of their prestige, power, and resources to garner support for what women are doing for themselves. They can strengthen the community through their support for groups of women. They can contribute to women's self-sufficiency by teaching, training, and empowering women to provide as much care as possible, recognizing that women provide the majority of all health care (MacCormack 1992). However, while women are aware of and proud of their major roles as givers of health care, they value and feel entitled to professional care.

It is also important that practice be designed with an eye towards long-term effectiveness. Particularly in the areas of AIDS and STD prevention and contraceptive use, research shows that little progress can be made without the empowerment of women (McCurdy 1992; Schoepf 1993; Ulin 1992; World Health Organization 1985).

A health care system that is responsive to and effective for women does not yet exist. We do not yet know what such a health care system would look like from women's perspectives. Therefore, to develop guidelines, providers should listen acutely to women's groups as those groups gain strength, experience, power, and confidence. At the very least, providers have been asked for available, accessible holistic care, for gender-sensitive and culturally appropriate care, and for affordable services. Providers should work with groups of women to define systems of care that are equitable and effective. In this time of ferment, when public services and supports are being reduced, both providers and populations will need to contribute to ensuring the provision of care.

Considerations for Research and Evaluation

The final set of considerations presented in this chapter affect those professionals, usually academics, who, through their research and evaluation, play a role in the development of programs and projects, in the development and implementation of policy, and in the training of practitioners and the design of systems. The theoretical framework adopted for this book and proposed for further studies has quite drastic implications for researchers in the area of health and development, although many of the issues that affect the ability of research to demonstrate a clear relationship between empowerment and health are not unique. They arise whenever broad models of health are considered and whenever evaluation of small, flexible, self-determined projects is undertaken.

As I said in Chapter 8, I have no prescience on how social science will incorporate aspects of the 'new' reality such as non-linearity, complexity, and feminist perspectives. At this time, however, with regard to women's situations, empowerment, and health, certain implications can be drawn and recommendations made.

Research about empowerment should contribute to empowerment

In studies of empowerment, both the context of research and the roles of researcher and researched need to be redefined. Empowerment is not an abstract concept; it is both a process and a goal that comes from groups of people – women in this case – who are in need and who, with or without external help, develop ways of supporting one another and changing their lives. If it is to be researched, it should be done with these women, in such a way as to answer questions that they might have and to help them in their activities, not as a purely academic study for 'the advancement of knowledge' or for career advancement alone. 'Our greatest challenge lies not in how to effectively research empowerment but how to participate in it and encourage it,' conclude Chavis and Wandersman (1990: 77). They ask whether *we* – the professionals – are really ready to commit ourselves to change and struggle, and 'the social conflict that will occur in the process of helping the powerless to become empowered.' We must not gloss over the fact that empowerment *is* about social conflict.

Need for methods for empowering research

In Chapter 9 I discussed in detail the difficulties of applying traditional research methods based on logical positivism to complex situations viewed through a framework that incorporates new science, feminist, and postmodernist perspectives. I presented multimethod research as a protection against the weaknesses of any single method, and participatory-action research as a form of research that is congruent with empowerment – that is actually a form of empowerment. However, little systematic, empirical information is available on empowering research. Shulamit Reinharz (1981: 428) has said that it requires different skills, 'human' skills such as 'listening, looking, relating, thinking, feeling, acting, collaborating,' and entrepreneurial skills. In general, research training neither emphasizes nor encourages these skills, leading to a chicken–egg problem. Who is 'qualified' to conduct and teach such research? Clearly, there is a need for research and reflection on research itself. It is likely that the evolution and 'formalization' of empowering research will evolve much as empowerment has evolved – in response to felt needs, done on a small scale, localized, participatory, and ad hoc. The existence of networks that encourage and disseminate empowerment findings will facilitate access to information about empowering research. Since some of those networks are particularly oriented to activist scholars, they may choose to study issues related to the evaluation and research of empowerment.

Empowering research is not restricted to issues such as empowerment and participation. In a particularly important study whose results played a major role in the recognition of the prevalence of STDs in rural women, Bang *et al.* (1989b) conducted participatory-action research. Their work included four components:

1. participatory research on women's reproductive health;
2. participatory mass education on sexual, reproductive, and social issues;
3. village-based women's health care services; and
4. referral services.

This study is exemplary, and provides an example of how feminist participatory-action research can be carried out on a specific health issue that the community finds important. Their study, however, is well-known for its finding, not its methodology. The keywords assigned to the article cited above are *rural*, *India*, *reproductive health*, *gynecology*, *abortion*, and *STDs* and do not include methodological references. It is quite probable that other such work is being conducted around a variety of health issues without results being published or, as with the Bang article, without an emphasis on methodology.

Suggested research strategies

The tension between flexibility and institutionalization that programs experience extends to researchers as well. It is possible to constrict activities so that they fit a predefined model – to box in empowerment so that money is given to support a well-defined process where the results are easily measured. If research proceeds too quickly in the area of empowerment, that is a probable result. If, however, we take time to explore this amoeba-like process in a qualitative fashion, and if we look to incorporate relevant concepts from the new sciences, the study of empowerment may be groundbreaking in the social sciences. The phenomenon of empowerment is well suited to innovative research strategies, given its focus on relations and connections, its focus on power and dialectics, its localness and unexpectedness, its small scale and long time frame, and its multilevel domain. This provides researchers with an exciting future agenda, but also demands patience and experimentation. Thus there will be additional tension between an eagerness to explore an exciting phenomenon and potential damage to the movement that can result from conducting improperly designed research.

Within the traditional research paradigm, efforts towards measurement definition, hypothesis generation, suggestions of association, and descriptive studies can be carried out. There is an immediate need to explore the concepts of health and empowerment with groups of women in different locations who have different cultural, political, social, and economic experiences. With them, existing measures can be validated or new ones that are meaningful in specific environments can be developed. In working with groups concerned about empowerment and health, questions can be developed which they consider to be important and/or to provide them with useful information. Some of these may fit into a traditional program evaluation framework; others may be concerned with longer-term individual outcomes. This work, designed to generate hypotheses or questions that can be researched, can be conducted with a secondary goal of documenting and possibly codifying empowerment activities.

Not all women will respond to empowerment as a strategy to reduce need. Therefore, another researchable issue, whatever the paradigm, is differential responsiveness to programs and experiences:

We need to identify the elements in individual and group experience that lead some women to an involvement in and a desire for change, while others eschew, reject, and even organize against it. To examine these issues is to avoid, from the onset, the common pitfalls of treating women as an undifferentiated group; treating gender as if it were always the primary determinant of behavior; and treating change as if it were inherently good or evil. (Bourque and Divine 1985: 2)

Wallerstein (1992: 202–3) describes three testable assumptions about the relationship between empowerment and health. Her assumptions, based on the relationship between powerlessness and poor health, cover individual change, and group internal and external effects:

1. [T]he act of participating itself in community change promotes changed perceptions of self-worth and a belief in the mutability of harmful situations, which replaces perceived powerlessness.
2. [T]he experience of mobilizing people in community groups strengthens social networks between individuals and enhances the community's or organization's competence to collaborate and solve health problems.
3. [E]mpowerment education interventions promote actual improvement in environmental or health conditions.

As a means of establishing the hypothesized link between empowerment and health, tests of such assumptions would be a big step forward. Rather than actually measuring health itself, one can begin – as Wallerstein suggests – to establish the relationship by relying on some more easily measured and shorter-term outcomes that have themselves been accepted as determinants of health: improved self-esteem, social networks, community competence, and local environmental/health conditions.

More generally, any of the hypothesized relationships in the Women's Empowerment Model can be investigated, as long as the important concepts of context, interdependence, change, and variability are incorporated. As my final illustration, I expand the framework presented in Figure 10.5 to include potential research variables, many of which I have specifically discussed. This model is not a recipe for research. Its complexity and multifacetedness indicate that the entire model is not researchable as such. The reason for presenting this level of detail, however, is twofold. First, I have suggested that research on women's empowerment and health can begin with small questions and specific portions of this model. Therefore, the items indicated in Figure 11.1 can serve as a starting point for future research. Second, I have emphasized throughout the importance of a holistic perspective on women's lives and activities, and Figure 11.1 graphically represents the many different elements that such a perspective must take into account.

Figure 11.1 The Women's Empowerment Model – research version

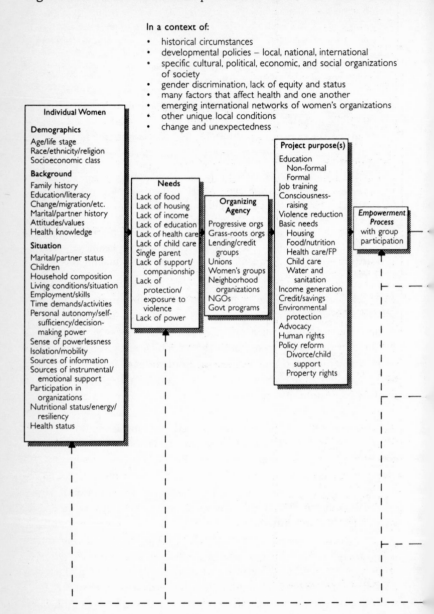

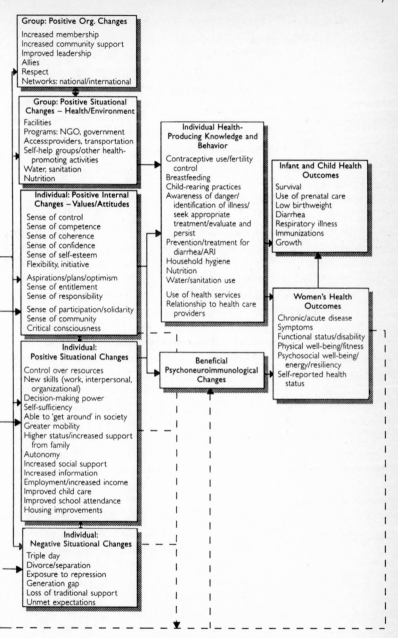

Group: Positive Org. Changes

Increased membership
Increased community support
Improved leadership
Allies
Respect
Networks: national/international

Group: Positive Situational Changes – Health/Environment

Facilities
Programs: NGO, government
Access:providers, transportation
Self-help groups/other health-
  promoting activities
Water, sanitation
Nutrition

Individual: Positive Internal Changes – Values/Attitudes

Sense of control
Sense of competence
Sense of coherence
Sense of confidence
Sense of self-esteem
Flexibility, initiative

Aspirations/plans/optimism
Sense of entitlement
Sense of responsibility

Sense of participation/solidarity
Sense of community
Critical consciousness

Individual: Positive Situational Changes

Control over resources
New skills (work, interpersonal,
  organizational)
Decision-making power
Self-sufficiency
Able to 'get around' in society
Greater mobility
Higher status/increased support
  from family
Autonomy
Increased social support
Increased information
Employment/increased income
Improved child care
Improved school attendance
Housing improvements

Individual: Negative Situational Changes

Triple day
Divorce/separation
Exposure to repression
Generation gap
Loss of traditional support
Unmet expectations

Individual Health-Producing Knowledge and Behavior

Contraceptive use/fertility
  control
Breastfeeding
Child-rearing practices
Awareness of danger/
  identification of illness/
  seek appropriate
  treatment/evaluate and
  persist
Prevention/treatment for
  diarrhea/ARI
Household hygiene
Nutrition
Water/sanitation use

Use of health services
Relationship to health care
  providers

Beneficial Psychoneuroimmunological Changes

Infant and Child Health Outcomes

Survival
Use of prenatal care
Low birthweight
Diarrhea
Respiratory illness
Immunizations
Growth

Women's Health Outcomes

Chronic/acute disease
Symptoms
Functional status/disability
Physical well-being/fitness
Psychosocial well-being/
  energy/resiliency
Self-reported health
  status

The research version of the Women's Empowerment Model begins with a set of items which together give a fairly complete picture of a woman's background and situation. While the population of women considered here share structurally based disadvantages, individuals are at varied life stages with varied health problems; they have their own histories; and there are many configurations of family relationships, work, community participation, and psychosocial/psychoneuroimmuno-logical status. Whether certain women are more likely to participate in and benefit from the empowerment process is not known. Thus, while generalization is useful and necessary, women cannot be treated as interchangeable. The empowerment process works by responding to individual as well as group needs. The group dynamic is determined by its members.

However, the women are all confronted by gender discrimination, economic deprivation, and social disorganization. Thus they and their families often have a similar set of needs that may include food, housing, income, education, health care, child care, support and companionship, protection from violence, and power in some or all the spheres in which the women carry out their activities.

There is a large variety of organizations including progressive political groups, lending and credit groups, community-based or more broadly composed women's groups, unions, and both governmental and non-governmental organizations which attempt to address these needs. These organizations may have one or a number of goals, among which are the provision of formal or non-formal education, job training, consciousness-raising, violence reduction, the meeting of basic needs such as food or housing, income generation and the provision of credit, environmental protection, advocacy of women's rights or human rights, or policy reform with regard to gender. Often explicitly included in the goals of such organizations is the empowerment of the women who belong to them.

Empowerment is, as I have discussed it, a group process which, if successful, can lead to many positive group and individual changes. The group itself is strengthened, with improved internal and external relations. It may increase its membership or spin off additional projects. The community may accord it more prestige and support. The members may achieve a respect that they had not previously been accorded. Allies may be enlisted from other organizations, from people in political positions, and from others working on similar issues. All this can work to increase the power of the groups and its members. In addition, the organization can learn from its experience, improving the quality of leadership and the opportunities for suitable participation.

Finally, the group may become part of those national and international networks that provide support, visibility, opportunities for the interchange of ideas and for creative reflection on the processes of empowerment and improving women's situations.

If the group is effective, it is likely to take on projects related to health and the environment, whatever its primary goal. The access to health care facilities or to convenient, clean water may be increased. Sanitation may improve; nutrition or food provision programs may be instituted. A health center or a health promoter may locate in the community. The group may take on community-wide health education responsibilities. Other governmental and non-governmental programs may seek out a well-organized group to help to implement additional health-related programs.

The discussion in Chapter 3 of the conceptualization of empowerment has described both positive individual changes in values and attitudes as well as changes in women's personal situations thought to result from the process. Among the potential internal changes are increased sense of control, competence, coherence, confidence and self-esteem. With those changes come greater flexibility and an increased willingness to take initiative. A more optimistic view of the future is accompanied by a sense of entitlement, and increased personal and community responsibility. The group experience leads to a sense of solidarity, friendship, and community.

Situational changes are equally important. As a result of successful organizing, women gain skills and control over resources. Their role and status within the household, the family, and the community may improve, so that they will be better able to make decisions, act independently, and feel comfortable in a variety of situations. They will have more sources of information available to them. From the friendships they establish, they will receive increased social support and companionship. Some of their needs – such as for income, credit, child care, or improved housing – may be met through activities taken on by the organization.

It is also possible that empowerment is accompanied by negative changes in a woman's situation. The additional time demands and community responsibilities are added to an already overburdened day. Relationships with a partner and with older women on whom they were previously dependent may be negatively affected as women seek to increase their independence and change old patterns of behavior. In some political situations, organizations of women are perceived as threatening, and organizations seeking social change are considered revolutionary. Thus participants may be exposed to repressive tactics designed to disrupt their organization. Finally, women who experience personal change but encounter resistance to situational and social changes may be left with unmet expectations, which may dampen some of their earlier psychosocial gains.

In the Women's Empowerment Model, two routes linking the empowerment pathway and health are represented – one through changing knowledge and behavior, needed to take advantage of improvements in women's situations; the other through posited psychoneuroimmunological responses to psychosocial and situational improvements. Among the potential behaviors/knowledge variables are contraceptive use, breastfeeding and child-rearing practices, illness recognition and treatment behavior, hygiene, nutrition, water and sanitation, and health service use. These pathways are related to women's health outcomes which have earlier been described as providing a relatively practical and multidimensional picture of both positive and negative health. They are also related to the health of these women's children – to their survival, to birth outcomes, to resistance to and immunization against common childhood diseases, and to the achievability of normal growth.

The designation of specific contexts would lead to a further particularization of this model. Thus in some locations, some variables will dominate; in others, some may be irrelevant. The relative importance of specific factors and their patterns of interaction vary between individuals, between cultures, between geographic locations, at different points in time, between socioeconomic classes, and so on. Because of historical change, and the pace at which women are organizing to improve their lives, new factors will emerge that play a role in the empowerment process. The selection of factors included in this model is meant to be representative and fairly comprehensive, but not definitive.

Other potential research activities include the collection and organization of the literature and research that exists on women's activities – from life stories to national surveys. Researchers can design research projects that follow groups of women over time, examining the process of empowerment in greater detail. They can apply some of the techniques of organizational research to women's groups, with an eye towards learning useful lessons that can be shared. They can help groups to design and implement evaluations that meet programs' needs as well as the needs of funders. They can continue, as I have tried to do here, to look at what research within narrower domains tells us about health, about empowerment, and about the situations and strategies of women struggling to survive. If a framework for linking these fields is adopted, researchers can continue to investigate how evidence from different fields supports or brings into question the factors and their interrelationships, continually refining and improving the framework.

Some Final Words

We are coming to recognize that what women do in their attempts to change power relationships is politics:

> Women all over the world, both in the past and the present, have been involved in what [Margaret] Randall refers to as 'less conventional' politics.
> [Their strategies include] interpersonal networking, grass-roots economic development projects, protests of many kinds, use of traditional women's activities in the cause of national liberation, and involvement in non-governmental and informal women's groups and organizations. (Bystydzienski [1992: 3] quoting Randall [1987])

I do not know how an increasing number of women come to offer an alternative to governance by dominance and stratification. I only know that many women, acting from their daily lives – their needs, their relationships, their responsibilities – have been looking for ways to obtain their fair share of power that are in concert with values of equity and democracy. I hope that this book will encourage others to support these women. However, dangers accompany advocacy. It is easy to overstate one's cause, to understate difficulties and opposition, and to ignore discordant information. While I advocate that we should encourage immediate policy changes to support the women's empowerment movement, in no way do I wish to imply that empowerment is a panacea that will work for all women everywhere, or that it will be easy to support those women for whom it is a positive strategy.

Neither do I suggest that empowerment projects, however prevalent and successful, can completely counter the macroeconomic, political, and social trends that are leading the world towards ever greater income and social disparities. I do not know whether significant change 'from below' leading to a reallocation of power is feasible. There is always a danger of romanticizing what is in large part a struggle for survival – for *existence* rather than *resistance*, in the words of Nancy Scheper-Hughes (1992: 533). So I cannot say where the women's empowerment movement will take us or if it will in fact gain enough adherents to have a lasting impact. I believe, however, that if we support women in their attempts to solve their own problems, large numbers will be able to improve their lives, their families' lives, and the life of their communities. Moreover, through their politics, they may just possibly facilitate deeper social change.

We are in yet one more era where uncertainty, social, economic, and political inequity, violence, and desperation define the environment of so many – those who were born in a place where resources are unavailable, or where war and violence dominate all else; born with a skin color or into a class that is a target of discrimination; or born female in a world where males are advantaged by their gender alone. It is also, however, an exciting time to be listening, writing, and thinking. Feminists, along with biologists, physicists, mathematicians, and others, sense that we may have come to see facets of reality that cannot be accounted for by rational positivism and the methodology it has spawned. The fact that women have been outside traditional science and traditional power structures is structural, not accidental. Therefore, when women gain inclusion and start to view history and the present from female standpoints, they alter the structure and rules of the game. They declare that the paradigm centered around the prediction and control of natural events and human behavior is no longer suitable. Their reality encompasses complexity, unexpectedness, connectedness, and diversity – that is, unpredictability and an inability to control through domination.

I wish here to repeat, for all who seek to help women to improve their situations and their health, Brian Arthur's wise advice:

> If you think that you're a steamboat and can go up the river, you're kidding yourself. Actually, you're just the captain of a paper boat drifting down the river. If you try to resist, you're not going to get anywhere. On the other hand, if you quietly observe the flow, realizing that you're part of it, realizing that the flow is ever-changing and always leading to new complexities, then every so often you can stick an oar into the river and punt yourself from one eddy to another.... It means that you try to see reality for what it is, and realize that the game you are in keeps changing, so that it's up to you to figure out the current rules of the game as it's being played.... [T]his is *not* a recipe for passivity, or fatalism. You apply available force to the maximum effect.... The idea is to observe, to act courageously, and to pick your timing well.... You go for viability, something that's workable, rather than what's 'optimal.' (Waldrop 1992: 330–31, 333)

In Margaret Wheatley's words (1994: 111):

> The intent becomes one of understanding movement based on a deep respect for the web of activity and relationship that comprise the system. Physicist David Peat terms this 'gentle action ... involving extremely subtle actions that are widely distributed over the whole system.' The intent is not to push or pull, but rather to give form to what is unfolding.

I feel as though I *am* giving form to something positive that is unfolding. If the theoretical framework presented in Chapter 8 represents the perception of reality that makes the most sense in these times, as I believe it does, the effects on our ways of thinking, doing, and being are fundamental. It may seem simple to talk about 'punting from one eddy to another' or 'giving form to what is unfolding,' but we have been trained and socialized to reduce, to disconnect, to simplify, and to intervene – to do *for* on the basis of our perceptions of need and solution. We are much less comfortable merging, sensing, listening, participating, and 'going with the flow.' This book is a result and reflection of the tension between the old and the new. It is an attempt to describe the river down which we are drifting in a paper boat, but the words, the images, the structure, and the evidence come from the age when the steamboat was trying to go upstream.

If complexity is the edge between chaos and stagnation, then that is where this book aspires to be. But this is new territory, so the exploration is tentative. Undoubtedly the reader has been frustrated by some of the trails untaken, and questioned the direction of some of the paths that were followed. Since what is sought is increased understanding and not 'right' answers, that is a positive outcome. To quote Wheatley again (1994: 150–51):

> In our past explorations, the tradition was to discover something and then formulate it into answers and solutions that could be widely transferred. But now we are on a journey of mutual and simultaneous exploration. In my view, all we can expect from one another is new and interesting information. We can *not* expect answers. Solutions, as quantum reality teaches, are a temporary event, specific to a context, developed through the relationship of persons and circumstances....
>
> In this new world, you and I make it up as we go along, not because we lack expertise or planning skills, but because that is in the nature of reality. Reality changes shape and meaning because of our activity. And it is constantly new. We are required to be there, as active participants. It can't happen without us and nobody can do it for us.

What I hope I have shown through this exploratory journey is that empowerment has an important role in the 'production' of health, and that it is integrally related to all we know about that process. I hope that the injustice and oppression confronted by women has been once again documented in a convincing manner, and that I have fairly presented the creativity, endurance, and toughness of so many. Surely we will all be enriched by including in our frameworks and our worldviews a feminist perspective, one that values women's contributions and helps to sustain the survival strategies that women are constructing.

Note

1. Other useful formulations include Lesley Doyal's *What Makes Women Sick* (1995), organized around the activities and roles of women; the life stage approach taken by the Office of Research on Women's Health (1993); and the aging-plus-cohort approach proposed by Matilda Riley (1993).

References

Acker, J., K. Barry, and J. Esseveld (1991) 'Objectivity and truth: problems in doing feminist research.' In *Beyond Methodology: Feminist Scholarship as Lived Research*, Fonow, M.M. and J.A. Cook (eds) pp. 133–53. Indiana University Press, Bloomington, IN.

Ader, R. (1980) 'Psychosomatic and psychoimmunologic research', *Psychosomatic Medicine*, vol. 42, no. 3, 307–21.

Adler, N.E., T. Boyce, M.A. Chesney, S. Cohen, S. Folkman, R.L. Kahn, and S.L. Syme (1994) 'Socioeconomic status and health: the challenge of the gradient', *American Psychologist*, vol. 49, no. 1, 15–24.

Aldrich, J.H. and F.D. Nelson (1984) *Linear Probability, Logit, and Probit Models.* vol. 45. Quantitative Applications in the Social Sciences, Lewis-Beck, M.S. (ed.). Sage, Newbury Park, CA.

Alemán, V. and C. Miranda (1993) 'The Nicaraguan women's movement: networking to solve their problems.' *Barricada Internacional*, June, 23–5.

Alexander, G.R. and D.A. Cornely (1987) 'Racial disparities in pregnancy outcomes: the role of prenatal care utilization and maternal risk status', *The American Journal of Preventive Medicine*, vol. 3, no. 5, 254–61.

Allen, J.A. and D.J. Barr (1990) 'Experiencing the empowerment process: women and development', *Networking Bulletin, Cornell Empowerment Project*, September, 1–17.

Almond, F. (1990) 'Preface.' In *Tinker, Tiller, Technical Change*, Gamser, M.S., H. Appleton, and N. Carter (eds) pp. vii–viii. Intermediate Technology Publications, London.

Anderson, J. (1989) 'Women's community service and child welfare in urban Peru.' In *Women, Work, and Child Welfare in the Third World*, Leslie, J. and M. Paolisso (eds) pp. 237–55. Westview Press, Boulder, CO.

Anderson, J.W. and M. Moore (1993) 'Born oppressed: women in the developing world face cradle-to-grave discrimination, poverty', *The Washington Post*, 14 February, A1.

Angell, M. (1985) 'Disease as a reflection of the psyche', *New England Journal of Medicine*, vol. 312, no. 24, 1570–72.

Anson, O., E. Paran, L. Neumann, and D. Chernichovsky (1993) 'Gender differences in health perceptions and their predictors', *Social Science & Medicine*, vol. 36, no. 4, 419–27.

Antonovsky, A. (1979) *Health, Stress, and Coping.* Jossey-Bass, San Francisco.

Antonovsky, A. (1987) *Unraveling the Mystery of Health: How People Manage Stress and Stay Well.* Jossey-Bass, San Francisco.

Antonovsky, A. (1993) 'The structure and properties of the sense of coherence scale', *Social Science & Medicine*, vol. 36, no. 6, 725–33.

Antrobus, P. (1989) 'The empowerment of women.' In *The Women and International Development Annual*, Gallin, R.S., M. Aronoff, and F. Anne (eds) pp. 189–207. vol. 1. Westview Press, Boulder, CO.

295

Anyadike, O. (1991) 'Zambia: women's self-help takes off', online *Peacenet, InterPress Service*, 3 August.

Aptheker, B. (1989) *Tapestries of Life: Women's Work, Women's Consciousness, and the Meaning of Daily Life*. University of Massachusetts Press, Amherst, MA.

Archer, D. and P. Costello (1990) *Literacy and Power: The Latin American Battleground*. Earthscan, London.

Argyris, C. (1968) 'Some unintended consequences of rigorous research', *Psychological Bulletin*, vol. 70, no. 3, 185–97.

Armer, M. and L. Isaac (1978) 'Determinants and behavioral consequences of psychological modernity: empirical evidence from Costa Rica', *American Sociologic Review*, vol. 43, 316–34.

Arnstein, S.R. (1969) 'A ladder of citizen participation', *Journal of the American Institute of Planning*, vol. 35, no. 4, 216–24.

Arole, M. and R. Arole (1994) *Jamkhed: A Comprehensive Rural Health Project*. Macmillan, London.

Atkins, L. and D. Jarrett (1979) 'The significance of "significance tests".' In *Demystifying Social Statistics*, Irvine, J., I. Miles, and J. Evans (eds) pp. 87–109. Pluto Press, London.

Audibert, M., D. Coulibaly, O. Doumbo, B. Kodio, G. Soula, and S. Traore (1993) 'Social and epidemiological aspects of guinea worm control', *Social Science & Medicine*, vol. 36, no. 4, 463–74.

Baird, D. (1974) 'The epidemiology of low birth weight: changes in incidence in Aberdeen, 1948–1972', *Journal of Biosocial Science*, vol. 6, 323–41.

Bandura, A. (1982) 'Self-efficacy mechanism in human agency', *American Psychologist*, vol. 37, no. 2, 122–47.

Bang, R., A. Bang, M. Baitule, Y. Choudhary, S. Sarmukaddam, and O. Tale (1989a) 'High prevalence of gynaecological diseases in rural Indian women', *The Lancet*, vol. 1, no. 8629, 85–8.

Bang, R., A. Bang, and SEARCH Team (1989b) 'Commentary on a community-based approach to reproductive health care', *International Journal of Gynecology and Obstetrics*, suppl. 3, 125–9.

Banks, M.H., S.A.A. Beresford, D.C. Morrell, J.J. Waller, and C.J. Watkins (1975) 'Factors influencing demand for primary medical care in women aged 20–44 years: a preliminary report', *International Journal of Epidemiology*, vol. 4, no. 3, 189–95.

Basu, A.M. (1987) 'Household influences on childhood mortality: evidence from historical and recent mortality trends', *Social Biology*, vol. 34, no. 3, 187–205.

Batt, R. (1992) 'Women's unequal burden: economic restructuring hits women hardest', *Dollars & Sense*, June, 12–13.

Becerra, J.E., C.J.R. Hogue, H.K. Atrash, and N. Pérez (1991) 'Infant mortality among hispanics: a portrait of heterogeneity', *Journal of the American Medical Association*, vol. 265, no. 2, 217–21.

Bello, W. (1992–93) *Population and the Environment: The Food First Perspective*. Food First. Action Alert.

Beneria, L. and S. Feldman, (eds) (1992) *Unequal Burden: Economic Crisis, Persistent Poverty, and Women's Work*, Westview Press, Boulder, CO.

Bevan, W. (1991) 'A tour inside the onion', *American Psychologist*, vol. 46, no. 5, 475–83.

Bhatia, S. (1983) 'Traditional practices affecting female health and survival: evidence from countries of South Asia.' In *Sex Differentials in Mortality: Trends, Determinants and Consequences*, Lopez, A.D. and L.T. Ruzica (eds) pp. 165–77. Department of Demography, Australian National University, Canberra.

Bhatt, E. (1989) 'Toward empowerment', *World Development*, vol. 17, no. 7, 1059–65.

Bicego, G.T. and J.T. Boerma (1993) 'Maternal education and child survival: a comparative study of survey data from 17 countries', *Social Science & Medicine*, vol. 36, no. 9, 1207–27.

Biology and Gender Study Group (1989) 'The importance of feminist critique for contemporary cell biology.' In *Feminism and Science*, Tuana, N. (ed.) pp. 172–87. Indiana University Press, Bloomington, IN.

Bishop, J.E. and M. Waldholz (1990) *Genome: The Story of the Most Astonishing Scientific*

Adventure of Our Time – The Attempt to Map All the Genes in the Human Body. Simon & Schuster, New York.

Black, D., J. N. Morris, C. Smith, and P. Townshend (1982) *Inequalities in Health: The Black Report.* Penguin, Harmondsworth.

Black, J.K. (1991a) *Development in Theory and Practice: Bridging the Gap.* Westview Press, Boulder, CO.

Black, R.E. (1991b) 'Would control of childhood infectious diseases reduce malnutrition?', *Acta Paediatr Scand.*, vol. 374, Supplement, 133–40.

Blalock, H.M. (1964) *Causal Inferences in Non-Experimental Research.* University of North Carolina Press, Chapel Hill, NC.

Blane, D. (1985) 'An assessment of the Black Report's explanations of health inequalities', *Sociology of Health and Illness*, vol. 7, no. 3, 423–45.

Blascovitch, J. and J. Tomaka (1990) 'Measures of self-esteem.' In *Measures of Social Psychological Attitudes*, Robinson, J.P., P.R. Shaver, and L.M. Wrightsman (eds) pp. 115–21. 3rd edn, Academic Press, Orlando, FL.

Blaxter, M. (1981) *The Health of Children: A Review of Research on the Place of Health in Cycles of Disadvantage.* Heinemann Educational Books, London.

Blaxter, M. (1983) 'Health services as a defense against the consequences of poverty in industrialized societies', *Social Science & Medicine*, vol. 17, no. 16, 1139–48.

Blaxter, M. (1985) 'Self-definition of health status and consulting rates in primary care', *The Quarterly Journal of Social Affairs*, vol. 1, no. 2, 131–71.

Blaxter, M. (1990) *Health and Lifestyles.* Tavistock/Routledge, London.

Blaxter, M. and E. Paterson (1982) *Mothers and Daughters: A Three-Generational Study of Health Attitudes and Behaviors.* Heinemann Educational Books, London.

Bleier, R. (1986) 'Introduction.' In *Feminist Approaches to Science*, Bleier, R. (ed.) pp. 1–17. Pergamon Press, New York.

Blum, D. and R.G. Feachem (1983) 'Measuring the impact of water supply and sanitation investments on diarrhoeal diseases: problems of methodology', *International Journal of Epidemiology*, vol. 12, no. 3, 357–65.

Boerma, J.T. (1987) 'Levels of maternal mortality in developing countries', *Studies in Family Planning*, vol. 18, no. 4, 213–21.

Bollen, K.A. (1989) *Structural Equations with Latent Variables.* John Wiley and Sons, New York.

Boserup, E. (1970) *Women's Role in Economic Development.* St. Martin's Press, New York.

Bourne, P.G. (1970) *Men, Stress and Vietnam.* Little Brown, Boston, MA.

Bourque, S.C. and D.R. Divine (1985) 'Introduction.' In *Women Living Change*, Bourque, S. and D. Divine (eds) pp. 1–21. Temple University Press, Philadelphia.

Boyce, W.T. and C. Schaefer (1985) 'Permanence and change: social and psychological factors in the outcomes of adolescent pregnancy.' Unpublished paper.

Branch, T. (1988) *Parting the Waters: America in the King Years 1954–63.* Simon & Schuster, New York.

Brewer, J. and A. Hunter (1989) *Multimethod Research: A Synthesis of Styles.* Sage, Newbury Park, CA.

Briend, A. (1990) 'Is diarrhoea a major cause of malnutrition among the under-fives in developing countries? A review of available evidence', *European Journal of Clinical Nutrition*, vol. 44, 611–28.

Briscoe, D. (1992) 'Education women: great cost–benefit', online *Peacenet, Associated Press*, 22 September.

Brown, D. (1993) 'From focus on women, useful insights on society and illness', *The Washington Post*, April 12, A3.

Brown, L.D. and R. Tandon (1983) 'Ideology and political economy in inquiry: action research and participatory research', *Journal of Applied Behavioral Science*, vol. 19, no. 3, 277–94.

Bruce, J. (1989) 'Homes divided', *World Development*, vol. 17, no. 7, 979–91.

Brusco, E. (1986) 'The Household Basis of Evangelical Religion and the Reformation of Machismo in Colombia.' PhD Dissertation, City University of New York.

Bryant, J.H. (1991) 'The role of third world universities in health development', *Asia-*

Pacific Journal of Public Health, vol. 5, no. 2, 123–30.

Bryk, A.S. and S.W. Raudenbush (1992) *Hierarchical Linear Models*. Sage, Newbury Park, CA.

Buck, C., A. Llopis, E. Nájera, and M. Terris (1988) *The Challenge of Epidemiology: Issues and Selected Readings*. Pan American Health Organization, Washington, DC.

Bullough, B. (1972) 'Poverty, ethnic identity and preventive health care', *Journal of Health and Social Behavior*, vol. 13, 347–59.

Buvinic, M. (1976) *Women and World Development: An Annotated Bibliography*. American Association for the Advancement of Science and The Overseas Development Council, Washington, DC.

Buvinic, M. and M.A. Lycette (1988) 'Women, poverty, and development in the Third World.' In *Strengthening the Poor: What Have We Learned?*, Lewis, J.P. (ed.) pp. 149–62. Overseas Development Council, Washington, DC.

Bystydzienski, J.M. (1992) 'Introduction.' In *Women Transforming Politics: Worldwide Strategies for Empowerment*, Bystydzienski, J.M. (ed.) pp. 1–8. Indiana University Press, Bloomington, In.

Cabral, H., L.E. Fried, S. Levenson, H. Amaro, and B. Zuckerman (1990) 'Foreign-born and US-born black women: differences in health behaviors and birth outcomes', *American Journal of Public Health*, vol. 81, no. 1, 70–72.

Caipora Women's Group (1993) *Women in Brazil*. Monthly Review Press, New York.

Caldwell, J.C. (1979) 'Education as a factor in mortality decline: an examination of Nigerian data', *Population Studies*, vol. 33, no. 3, 395–413.

Caldwell, J.C. (1986) 'Routes to low mortality in poor countries', *Population and Development Review*, vol. 12, no. 2, 171–220.

Caldwell, J.C. (1989) 'Mass education as a determinant of mortality decline.' In *Selected Readings in The Cultural, Social and Behavioural Determinants of Health*, Caldwell, J.C. and G. Santow (eds) pp. 101–11. Health Transition Centre, The Australian National University, Canberra.

Caldwell, J.C. (1990) 'Introductory thoughts on health transition.' In *What We Know About Health Transition: The Cultural, Social and Behavioural Determinants of Health*, Caldwell, J., S. Findley, P. Caldwell, G. Santow, W. Cosford, J. Braid, and D. Broers-Freeman (eds) pp. xi–xiii. vol. 1. Health Transition Centre, The Australian National University, Canberra.

Caldwell, J.C. (1992) 'Old and new factors in health transitions', *Health Transition Review*, vol. 2, Supplement, 205–216.

Caldwell, J.C. (1993) 'Health transition: the cultural, social and behavioural determinants of health in the third world', *Social Science & Medicine*, vol. 36, no. 2, 125–35.

Caldwell, J.C., I. Gajanayake, P. Caldwell, and I. Peiris (1989) 'Sensitization to illness and the risk of death: an explanation for Sri Lanka's approach to good health for all', *Social Science & Medicine*, vol. 28, no. 4, 365–79.

Carr-Hill, R.A. (1992) *From Health for Some to Health for All*. University of York, England. Draft Report to the World Health Organization, Office of Health Services Research.

Cassel, J. (1974) 'An epidemiological perspective of psychosocial factors in disease etiology', *American Journal of Public Health*, vol. 64, no. 11, 1040–1043.

Cassel, J. (1976) 'The contribution of the social environment to host resistance', *American Journal of Epidemiology*, vol. 104, no. 2, 107–23.

Cassel, J., R. Patrick, and D. Jenkins (1960) 'Epidemiological analysis of the health implications of culture change: a conceptual model', *Annals of the New York Academy of Sciences*, vol. 84, no. 17, 938–49.

Casti, J.L. (1994) *Complexification: Explaining a Paradoxical World Through the Science of Surprise*. HarperCollins, New York.

Cereseto, S. and H. Waitzkin (1986) 'Capitalism, socialism, and the physical quality of life', *International Journal of Health Services*, vol. 16, 643–58.

Cereseto, S. and H. Waitzkin (1988) 'Economic development, political-economic system, and the physical quality of life', *Journal of Public Health Policy*, Spring, 104–120.

Chakravorty, U.N. (1983) 'A health project that works – progress in Jamkhed', *World Health Forum*, vol. 4, 38–40.

Charlton, S.E. (1984) *Women in Third World Development*. Westview Press, Boulder, CO.

Chaudhury, R.H. (1984) 'The influence of female education, labor force participation, and age at marriage on fertility behavior in Bangladesh', *Social Biology*, vol. 31, no. 1–2, 59–74.

Chavis, D.M. and A. Wandersman (1990) 'Sense of community in the urban environment: a catalyst for participation and community development', *American Journal of Community Psychology*, vol. 18, no. 1, 55–81.

Chen, L.C., E. Huq, and S. D'Souza (1981) 'Sex bias in the family allocation of food and health care in rural Bangladesh', *Population and Development Review*, vol. 7, no. 1, 55–70.

Chossudovsky, M. (1992) *Structural Adjustment, Health and the Social Dimension: A Review*. Canadian International Development Agency. Report.

Christian Medical Commission of the World Council of Churches (1993) 'The comprehensive rural health project, Jamkhed, India', *Contact*, February, 1–14.

Churchill, L.R. (1987) *Rationing Health Care in America: Perceptions and Principles of Justice*. University of Notre Dame Press, Notre Dame, IN.

Cleland, J.G. (1990) 'Maternal education and child survival: further evidence and explanations.' In *What We Know about Health Transition: The Cultural, Social, Behavioural Determinants of Health*, Caldwell, J., S. Findley, P. Caldwell, G. Santow, W. Cosford, J. Braid, and D. Broers-Freeman (eds) pp. 400–19. vol. 1. Health Transition Centre, The Australian National University, Canberra.

Cleland, J.G. and J.K. van Ginneken (1988) 'Maternal education and child survival in developing countries: the search for pathways of influence', *Social Science & Medicine*, vol. 27, no. 12, 1357–68.

Cleland, J.G. and J.K. van Ginneken (1989) 'Maternal schooling and childhood mortality', *Journal of Biosocial Science*, vol. 10, Supplement, 13–34.

Cochrane, S.H., D.J. O'Hara, and J. Leslie (1980) *The Effects of Education on Health*. World Bank. Staff Working Paper no. 405.

Cockerham, W.C. (1990) 'A test of the relationship between race, socioeconomic status, and psychological distress', *Social Science & Medicine*, vol. 31, no. 12, 1321–26.

Coeytaux, F.M., A.H. Leonard, and C.M. Bloomer (1993) 'Abortion.' In *The Health of Women: A Global Perspective*, Koblinsky, M., J. Timyan, and J. Gay (eds) pp. 133–46. Westview Press, Boulder, CO.

Coffin, T. (1991) 'Earth, the crowded planet', *The Washington Spectator*, 15 August, 1–3.

Cohen, M.N. (1989) *Health and the Rise of Civilization*. Yale University Press, New Haven, CT.

Cohen, S., D.A. Tyrrell, and A.P. Smith (1991) 'Psychological stress and susceptibility to the common cold', *New England Journal of Medicine*, vol. 325, no. 9, 606–12.

Colby, B.N. (1987) 'Well-being: a theoretical program', *American Anthropologist*, vol. 89, 879–95.

Colby, B.N., C.M. Aldwin, L. Price, C. Stegemann, and S. Mishra (1985) 'Adaptive potential, stress, and illness in the elderly', *Medical Anthropology*, vol. 9, no. 4, 283–95.

Collins, J.W.J. and R.J. David (1990) 'The differential effect of traditional risk factors on infant birthweight among Blacks and Whites in Chicago', *American Journal of Public Health*, vol. 80, no. 6, 679–81.

Collins, J.W.J. and R.J. David (1992) 'Differences in neonatal mortality by race, income, and prenatal care', *Ethnicity & Disease*, vol. 2, no. 1, 18–26.

Collins, P.H. (1991) *Black Feminist Thought: Knowledge, Consciousness, and the Politics of Empowerment*. Routledge, Chapman & Hall, New York.

Cook, T.D. (1983) 'Quasi-experimentation: its ontology, epistemology, and methodology.' In *Beyond Method: Strategies for Social Research*, Morgan, G. (ed.) pp. 74–94. Sage, Newbury Park, CA.

Cooper, R. and R. David (1986) 'The biological concept of race and its application to public health and epidemiology', *Journal of Health Politics, Policy and Law*, vol. 11, no. 1, 97–117.

Cornia, G.A., R. Jolly, and F. Stewart, (eds) (1987a) *Adjustment with a Human Face: Protecting* the Vulnerable and Promoting Growth, Oxford University Press, Oxford.

Cornia, G.A., R. Jolly, and F. Stewart (1987b) 'Introduction.' In *Adjustment with a Human Face: Protecting the Vulnerable and Promoting Growth*, Cornia, G.A., R. Jolly, and F. Stewart (eds) pp. 1–8. Oxford University Press, Oxford.

Cortés-Majó, M., C. García-Gil, and F. Viciana (1990) 'The role of the social condition of women in the decline of maternal and female mortality', *International Journal of Health Services*, vol. 20, no. 2, 315–28.

Cuadra, S., G. Fernández, and F.L. Ubeda (1992) 'Nicaraguan women's conference: seeking unity in diversity', *Barricada Internacional*, March, 22–31.

Curlin, P. and A. Tinker (1993) 'Introduction.' In *The Health of Women: A Global Perspective*, Koblinsky, M., J. Timyan, and J. Gay (eds) pp. 1–2. Westview Press, Boulder, CO.

Curtin, L.B. (1982) *Status of Women: A Comparative Analysis of Twenty Developing Countries*. Population Reference Bureau. Reports of the World Fertility Survey no. 5.

Dahl, E. (1993) 'Social inequality in health – the role of the healthy worker effect', *Social Science & Medicine*, vol. 36, no. 8, 1077–86.

Dajer, T. (1991a) 'On information and ideology', *Links*, Winter, 12–13.

Dajer, T. (1991b) 'Why Nicaraguan children survive', *Links*, Spring, 12–14.

Daniels, N. (1985) *Just Health Care*. Cambridge University Press, Cambridge.

Dankelman, I. and J. Davidson (1988) *Women and Environment in the Third World: Alliance for the Future*. Earthscan, London.

David, R.J. and J.W. Collins Jr (1991) 'Bad outcomes in black babies: race or racism?', *Ethnicity and Disease*, vol. 1, no. 3, 236–44.

Davis, D.L. and S.M. Low (1989a) *Gender, Health, and Illness: The Case of Nerves*. Hemisphere Publishing Corporation, New York.

Davis, D.L. and S.M. Low (1989b) 'Preface.' In *Gender, Health, and Illness: the Case of Nerves*, Davis, D.L. and S.M. Low (eds) pp. xi–xv. Hemisphere Publishing Corporation, New York.

Dean, A. and W.M. Ensel (1982) 'Modelling social support, life events, competence and depression in the context of age and sex', *Journal of Community Psychology*, vol. 10, 392–408.

de Koning, K. & M. Martin. (1996) *Participatory Research in Health: Issues and Experiences*. Zed Books, London.

Demers, R.Y., R. Altamore, H. Mustin, A. Kleinman, and D. Leonardi (1980) 'An exploration of the dimensions of illness behavior', *The Journal of Family Practice*, vol. 11, no. 7, 1085–92.

Derogatis, L., M. Abeloff, and N. Melisaratos (1979) 'Psychological coping mechanisms and survival time in metastatic breast cancer', *Journal of the American Medical Association*, vol. 242, 1504–09.

di Leonardo, M. (1992) 'White lies, black myths: rape, race, and the black "underclass"', *The Village Voice*, 22 September.

Dixon, R.B. (1978) *Rural Women at Work*. Johns Hopkins University Press, Baltimore, MD.

Dixon-Mueller, R. (1990) 'Abortion policy and women's health in developing countries', *International Journal of Health Services*, vol. 20, no. 2, 297–314.

Doyal, L. (1995) *What Makes Women Sick: Gender and the Political Economy of Health*. Rutgers University Press, New Brunswick, NJ.

Dressler, W.W. (1985a) 'Psychosomatic symptoms, stress, and modernization: a model', *Culture, Medicine and Psychiatry*, vol. 9, 257–86.

Dressler, W.W. (1985b) 'The social and cultural context of coping: action, gender and symptoms in a southern black community', *Social Science & Medicine*, vol. 21, no. 5, 499–506.

Dressler, W.W. (1991) *Stress and Adaptation in the Context of Culture: Depression in a Southern Black Community*. State University of New York Press, Albany, NY.

Dressler, W.W., J.E. Dos Santos, P.N. Gallagher Jr, and F.E. Viteri (1987a) 'Arterial blood pressure and modernization in Brazil', *American Anthropologist*, vol. 89, 398–409.

Dressler, W.W., G.A.C. Grell, P.N. Gallagher Jr., and F.E. Viteri (1992) 'Social factors mediating social class differences in blood pressure in a Jamaican community', *Social Science & Medicine*, vol. 35, no. 10, 1233–44.

Dressler, W.W., A. Mata, A. Chavez, F. Viteri, and P. Gallagher (1986) 'Social support and arterial pressure in a central Mexican community', *Psychosomatic Medicine*, vol. 48, no. 5, 338–49.

Dressler, W.W., A. Mata, A. Chavez, and F.E. Viteri (1987b) 'Arterial blood pressure and individual modernization in a Mexican community', *Social Science & Medicine*, vol. 24, no. 8, 679–87.

Dubos, R. (1965) *Man Adapting*. Yale University Press, New Haven, CT.

Durkheim, E. (1951) *Suicide: A Study in Sociology*. The Free Press, New York.

Dyson, T. and M. Moore. (1983) 'On kinship structure, female autonomy, and demographic behavior in India', *Population and Development Review*, vol. 9, no. 1, 35–60.

Eastman, P.C. (1973) 'Consciousness-raising as a resocialization process for women', *Smith College Studies in Social Work*, vol. 43, no. 3, 153–83.

Eckstein, S. (1988) *The Poverty of Revolution: The State and the Urban Poor in Mexico*. Princeton University Press, Princeton, NJ.

Editors (1990) 'Aid Monstrosities.' *New Internationalist*, June, 24.

Editors (1991) 'The short run', *Dollars & Sense*, January–February, 4.

Editors (1992a) 'Liberty, equality, and disability: the facts', *New Internationalist*, September, 18–19

Editors (1992b) 'Undoing the damage: author Lourdes Beneria on women and economic development', *Dollars & Sense*, June, 14–15.

Editors (1993) 'African Women's Health: Overview from the 7th IWHM', *Women's Health Journal*, 58–60.

Edwards, M. (1993) 'How relevant is development studies?' In *Beyond the Impasse: New Directions in Development Theory*, Schuurman, F.J. (ed.) pp. 77–92. Zed Books, London and Atlantic Highlands, NJ.

Egolf, B., J. Lasker, S. Wolf, and L. Potvin (1992) 'The Roseto effect: a 50–year comparison of mortality rates', *American Journal of Public Health*, vol. 82, no. 8, 1089–92.

Ehrenreich, B. and D. English (1978) *For Her Own Good: 150 Years of the Experts' Advice to Women*. Doubleday, New York.

Emanuel, I. (1986) 'Maternal health during childhood and later reproductive performance', *Annals of the New York Academy of Science*, no. 477, 27–39.

Eng, E., M. Salmon, and F. Mullan (1992) 'Community empowerment: the critical base for primary care', *Journal of Family and Community Health*, vol. 15, no. 1, 1–12.

Engel, G.L. (1977) 'The need for a new medical model: a challenge for biomedicine', *Science*, vol. 196, no. 4286, 129–36.

Eschen, A. and M. Whittaker (1993) 'Family planning: a base to build on for women's reproductive health services.' In *The Health of Women: A Global Perspective*, Koblensky, M., J. Timyan, and J. Gay (eds) pp. 105–131. Westview Press, Boulder, CO.

Evans, R.G., M.L. Barer, and T.R. Marmor (1994) *Why Are Some People Healthy and Others Not? The Determinants of Health of Populations*. Aldine de Gruyter, New York.

Evans, S.M. (1979) *Personal Politics: The Roots of Women's Liberation in the Civil Rights Movement and the New Left*. Vintage Books, New York.

Evans, S.M. and H.C. Boyte (1986) *Free Spaces: The Sources of Democratic Change in America*. Harper & Row, New York.

Ewbank, D.C. (1994) 'Maternal education and theories of health behaviour: a cautionary note', *Health Transition Review*, vol. 4, no. 2, 215–23.

Eyer, J. and P. Sterling (1977) 'Stress-related mortality and social organization', *The Review of Radical Political Economics*, vol. 9, no. 1, 1–44.

Fals-Borda, O. and M.A. Rahman, (eds) (1991) *Action and Knowledge: Breaking the Monopoly with Participatory Action-Research*, The Apex Press, New York.

Fanon, F. (1963) *The Wretched of the Earth*. Grove Press, New York.

Fee, E. (1986) 'Critiques of modern science: the relationship of feminism to other radical epistemologies.' In *Feminist Approaches to Science*, Bleier, R. (ed.) pp. 42–56. Pergamon Press, New York.

Ferguson, K.E. (1990) 'Women, feminism, and development.' In *Women, International Development, and Politics: The Bureaucratic Mire*, Staudt, K. (ed.) pp. 291–303. Temple University Press, Philadelphia, PA.

Feuerstein, M.-T. (1993) 'Participatory Evaluation: The Patna Experience', *Contact*, August, 1–15.

Findley, S.E. (1989) *Community, Social Structure and Health: Alternative Pathways of Influence.* Rockefeller Foundation Health Transition Workshop. Unpublished paper.

Findley, S.E. (1991) 'Towards a contextual model of the health transition.' In *The Health Transition: Methods and Measures*, Cleland, J. and A.G. Hill (eds) pp. 381–406. Health Transition Centre, The Australian National University, Canberra.

Finkler, K. (1989) 'The universality of nerves.' In *Gender, Health and Illness: The Case of Nerves*, Davis, D.L. and S.M. Low (eds) pp. 79–101. Hemisphere Publishing Corporation, New York.

Fisher, J. (1993) *Out of the Shadows.* Latin America Bureau, London.

Fishman, P.M. (1990) 'Interaction: the work women do.' In *Feminist Research Methods: Exemplary Readings in the Social Sciences*, Nielsen, J.M. (ed.) pp. 224–37. Westview Press, Boulder, CO.

Foldy, S. (1990) *Metaphor as Illness: The Underclass Concept and Medical Care.* Presentation at American Public Health Association, New York City.

Foner, N. (1989) 'Older women in nonindustrial cultures: consequences of power and privilege.' In *Women in the Later Years: Health, Social, and Cultural Perspectives*, Grau, L. (ed.) pp. 227–37. Haworth Press, New York.

Forbes, D. and W.P. Frisbie (1991) 'Spanish surname and anglo infant mortality: differentials over a half-century', *Demography*, vol. 28, no. 4, 639–60.

Ford Foundation (1992) *Reproductive Health and Population Programming Workshop.* Ford Foundation. Report.

Forum on Women and Politics (1992) 'Open letter to Dr. Manmohansingh, Finance Minister', online *Peacenet, Women.news*, 27 February.

Franks, P., T.L. Campbell, and C.G. Shields (1992) 'Social relationships and health: the relative roles of family functioning and social support', *Social Science & Medicine*, vol. 34, no. 7, 779–88.

Fraser, N. and L. Nicholson (1990) 'Social criticism without philosophy: an encounter between feminism and postmodernism.' In *Feminism/Postmodernism*, Nicholson, L. (ed.) pp. 19–38. Routledge, New York.

Freire, P. (1970) *Pedagogy of the Oppressed.* The Seabury Press, New York.

Freire, P. (1974) *Education for Critical Consciousness.* The Seabury Press, New York.

Freire, P. (1990) *Pedagogy of the Oppressed.* Continuum, New York.

Frenk, J., J.L. Bobadilla, C. Stern, T. Frejka, and R. Lozano (1991) 'Elements for a theory of the health transition', *Health Transition Review*, vol. 1, no. 1, 21–38.

Fried, M. (1982) 'Endemic stress: the psychology of resignation and the politics of scarcity', *American Journal of Orthopsychiatry*, vol. 52, no. 1, 4–19.

Garfield, R. (1991) 'Informational malpractice', *Links*, Fall, 13–14.

George, S. (1977) *How the Other Half Dies: The Real Reasons for World Hunger.* Penguin, Harmondsworth.

Gereffi, G. (1989) 'Rethinking development theory: insights from East Asia and Latin America', *Sociological Forum*, vol. 4, no. 4, 505–33.

Gleick, J. (1987) *Chaos: Making of a New Science.* Penguin Books, New York.

Gottschalk, J. and L. Teymour (1993) 'Third world women call for a balanced perspective on women's health', *Health Care for Women International*, vol. 14, 111–16.

Goulet, D. (1985) *The Cruel Choice: A New Concept in the Theory of Development.* University Press of America, Lanham, MD.

Gourlay, C. (1992) 'Development: "Invisible women" bear brunt of poverty', *InterPress Service*, December 6.

Grant, J. (1989) *The State of the World's Children 1989.* Oxford University Press for UNICEF, New York.

Grant, J. (1992) *The State of the World's Children 1992.* Oxford University Press for UNICEF, New York.

Grant, J. (1993) *The State of the World's Children 1993.* Oxford University Press for UNICEF, New York.

Grant, J. (1995) *The State of the World's Children 1995.* Oxford University Press for UNICEF, New York.

Greenstone, J.D. (1991) 'Culture, rationality, and the Underclass.' In *The Urban Underclass*, Jencks, C. and P.E. Peterson (eds) pp. 399–408. The Brookings Institution, Washington, DC.

Grossarth-Maticek, R., J. Siegrist, and H. Vetter (1982) 'Interpersonal ·repression as a predictor of cancer', *Social Science & Medicine*, vol. 16, 493–8.

Grosse, R.N. and C. Auffrey (1989) 'Literacy and health status in developing countries', *Annual Review of Public Health*, vol. 10, 281–97.

Grown, C.A. and J. Sebstad (1989) 'Introduction: toward a wider perspective on women's employment', *World Development*, vol. 17, no. 7, 937–52.

Guendelman, S. and M.J. Silberg (1993) 'The health consequences of maquiladora work: women on the US–Mexican border', *American Journal of Public Health*, vol. 83, no. 1, 37–44.

Gürsoy-Tescan, A. (1992) 'Infant mortality: a Turkish puzzle?', *Health Transition Review*, vol. 2, no. 2, 131–49.

Gutiérrez, L.M. (1990) 'Working with women of color: an empowerment perspective', *Social Work*, vol. 35, no. 2, 149–53.

Guy, J. (1992) 'Querer es Poder.' Masters of Public Health Thesis, Department of Health Behavior and Health Education, University of North Carolina's School of Public Health.

Haan, M., G.A. Kaplan, and T. Camacho (1987) 'Poverty and health: prospective evidence from the Alameda County study', *American Journal of Epidemiology*, vol. 125, no. 6, 989–98.

Hall, B.L. (1981) 'Participatory research, popular knowledge and power: a personal reflection', *Convergence*, vol. 14, no. 3, 6–17.

Hamilton, S., B. Popkin, and D. Spicer (1984) *Women and Nutrition in Third World Countries*. Praeger, New York.

Hancock, G. (1989) *Lords of Poverty: the Power, Prestige, and Corruption of the International Aid Business*. Atlantic Monthly Press, New York.

Hanger, J. and J. Moris (1973) 'Women in the household economy.' In *MEWA: An Irrigated Rice Settlement Scheme in Kenya*, Chambers, R. and J. Moris (eds) pp. 209–44. Welfforum Verlag Afrikastudien, Munich.

Hanna, J.M. and M.H. Fitzgerald (1993) 'Acculturation and symptoms: a comparative study of reported health symptoms in three Samoan communities', *Social Science & Medicine*, vol. 36, no. 9, 1169–80.

Haraway, D.J. (1991) *Simians, Cyborgs, and Women: The Reinvention of Nature*. Routledge, New York.

Harding, S. (1991) *Whose Science? Whose Knowledge? Thinking from Women's Lives*. Cornell University Press, Ithaca, NY.

Harpham, T. and C. Stephens (1991) 'Urbanization and health in developing countries', *World Health Statistics Quarterly*, vol. 44, 62–69.

Harrison, P. (1981) *Inside the Third World*. Penguin, New York.

Heise, L.L. (1993) 'Violence against women: the missing agenda.' In *The Health of Women: A Global Perspective*, Koblinsky, M., J. Timyan, and J. Gay (eds) pp. 171–95. Westview Press, Boulder, CO.

Heise, L.L. and C. Elias (1995) 'Transforming AIDS prevention to meet women's needs: a focus on developing countries', *Social Science & Medicine*, vol. 40, no. 7, 931–43.

Heise, L.L., J. Pitanguy, and A. Germain (1994) *Violence Against Women: The Hidden Health Burden*. World Bank Discussion Paper 255.

Heisel, M.A. (1989) 'Older women in developing countries.' In *Women in the Later Years: Health, Social, and Cultural Perspectives*, Grau, L. (eds) pp. 253–72. Haworth Press, New York.

Helmore, K. (1985) 'The neglected resource: women in the developing world', *The Christian Science Monitor*, December 20.

Hernandez, M., C.P. Hidalgo, J.R. Hernandez, H. Madrigal, and A. Cháves (1974) 'Effect of economic growth on nutrition in a tropical community', *Ecology of Food and Nutrition*, vol. 3, 283–91.

Hertzman, C., J. Frank, and R.G. Evans (1994) 'Heterogeneities in health status and the determinants of population health.' In *Why Are Some People Healthy and Others Not? The*

Determinants of Health of Populations, Evans, R.G., M.L. Barer, and T.R. Marmor (eds), pp. 67–92, Aldine de Gruyter, New York.

Herz, B., K. Subbarao, M. Habib, and L. Raney (1991) *Letting Girls Learn: Promising Approaches in Primary and Secondary Education*. The World Bank, Washington, DC. Discussion Paper no. 133.

Hess, R. (1984) 'Thoughts on empowerment.' In *Studies in Empowerment: Steps Toward Understanding and Action*, Rappaport, J. (ed.) pp. 227–30. Haworth Press, New York.

Hirschman, A.O. (1984) *Getting Ahead Collectively: Grassroots Experiences in Latin America*. Pergamon Press, New York.

hooks, b. (1989) *Talking Back: Thinking Feminist, Thinking Black*. South End Press, Boston, MA.

Hope, A. and S. Timmel (1990) *Training for Transformation: A Handbook for Community Workers*. vol. 1–3. Mambo Press, Harare, Zimbabwe.

Horton, M., P. Freire, B. Bell, J. Gaventa, and J. Peters (1990) *We Make the Road by Walking: Conversations on Education and Social Change*. Temple University Press, Philadelphia, PA.

Hrdy, S.B. (1986) 'Empathy, polyandry and the myth of the coy female.' In *Feminist Approaches to Science*, Bleier, R. (ed.) pp. 119–46. Pergamon Press, New York.

Hubbard, R. (1990) *The Politics of Women's Biology*. Rutgers University Press, New Brunswick, NJ.

Human Resources Development and Operations Policy (1993) 'Alcohol-related problems: an obstacle to human capital development?' *HRO Dissemination Notes*, 12 October.

Human Rights Coordinator (1993) 'Empowering women: the call for equal rights', online *Peacenet, Women.news*, 17 March.

Illich, I. (1976) *Medical Nemesis: The Expropriation of Health*. Bantam Books, New York.

Inkeles, A. (1983) *Exploring Individual Modernity*. Columbia University Press, New York.

Inkeles, A. and D.H. Smith (1974) *Becoming Modern: Individual Change in Six Developing Countries*. Harvard University Press, Cambridge, MA.

Institute of Medicine (1988) *The Future of Public Health*. National Academy Press, Washington, DC.

InterPress Service (1992) 'Population: water supplies strained by high growth rates', online *Peacenet*, 18 December.

InterPress Service (1993a) 'Children: big crises stealing spotlight from silent', online *Peacenet*, 6 March.

InterPress Service (1993b) 'Development: donors opt for NGOs more and more', online *Peacenet*, 20 May.

InterPress Service (1993c) 'Development: Grameen banker urges donors to set clear targets', online *Peacenet*, 26 May.

InterPress Service (1993d) 'Development: South Asian NGOs are teaching governments', online *Peacenet*, 22 May.

InterPress Service (1993e) 'Population: third world NGOs throw punches at rich north', online *Peacenet*, 21 May.

InterPress Service (1994) 'Development: Focus on Africa', online *Peacenet*, 1 February.

Isbister, J. (1991) *Promises Not Kept: The Betrayal of Social Change in the Third World*. Kumarian Press, West Hartford, CT.

Isis International and Development Alternatives With Women for a New Era (1988) *Confronting the Crisis in Latin America: Women Organizing for Change*. ISIS International, Santiago, Chile.

Israel, B.A., B. Checkoway, A. Schultz, and M. Zimmerman (1994) 'Health education and community empowerment: conceptualizing and measuring perceptions of individual, organizational, and community control', *Health Education Quarterly*, vol. 21, no. 2, 149–70.

Israel, B.A., S.J. Schurman, and J.S. House (1989) 'Action research on occupational stress: involving workers as researchers', *International Journal of Health Services*, vol. 9, no. 1, 135–55.

Jacobson, J.L. (1991) *Women's Reproductive Health: The Silent Emergency*. Worldwatch Institute, Washington, DC. Worldwatch Paper no. 102.

James, S. and D. Kleinbaum (1976) 'Socioecologic stress and hypertension related mortality rates in North Carolina', *American Journal of Public Health*, vol. 66, no. 4, 354–8.

Jansen, S.C. (1990) 'Is science a man? New feminist epistemologies and reconstructions of knowledge', *Theory and Society*, vol. 19, 235–46.

Jaquette, J.S. (1982) 'Women and modernization theory: a decade of feminist criticism', *World Politics*, vol. 82, 267–84.

Jayaratne, T.E. and A.J. Stewart (1991) 'Quantitative and qualitative methods in the social sciences: current feminist issues and practical strategies.' In *Beyond Methodology: Feminist Scholarship as Lived Research*, Fonow, M.M. and J.A. Cook (eds) pp. 85–106. Indiana University Press, Bloomington, IN.

Jayawardena, K. (1986) *Feminism and Nationalism in the Third World*. Zed Books, London.

Jencks, C. (1991) 'Is the American underclass growing?' In *The Urban Underclass*, Jencks, C. and P.E. Peterson (eds) pp. 28–100. The Brookings Institution, Washington, DC.

Johansson, S.R. (1991) 'The health transition: the cultural inflation of morbidity during decline of mortality', *Health Transition Review*, vol. 1, no. 1, 39–68.

Johnson-Saylor, M.T. (1991) 'Psychosocial predictors of healthy behaviors in women', *Journal of Advanced Nursing*, vol. 16, 1164–71.

Joll, J. (1977) *Gramsci*. William Collins Sons and Co., Glasgow.

Joshi, A.R. (1994) 'Maternal schooling and child health: preliminary analysis of the intervening mechanisms in rural Nepal', *Health Transition Review*, vol. 4, no. 1, 1–28.

Judd, F. (1995) 'Conflict, famine and the arms trade', *Medicine and War*, vol. 11, no. 2, 99–104.

Jylha, M. and A. Seppo (1989) 'Social ties and survival among the elderly in Tampere, Finland', *International Journal of Epidemiology*, vol. 18, no. 1, 158–64.

Kak, L.P. and S. Narasimhan (1992) *The Impact of Family Planning Employment on Field Workers' Lives: A Strategy for Measuring Empowerment*. The Centre for Development and Population Activities, Washington, DC. Working Paper no. 1.

Kane, P. (1991) *Women's Health: From Womb to Tomb*. St. Martin's Press, New York.

Kanji, N., N. Kanji, and F. Manji (1991) 'From development to sustained crisis: structural adjustment, equity and health', *Social Science & Medicine*, vol. 33, no. 9, 985–93.

Kaplan, G.A. (1985) 'Psychosocial aspects of chronic illness: direct and indirect associations with Ischemic Heart Disease mortality'. In *Behavioral Epidemiology and Disease Prevention*, Kaplan, R.M. and M.H. Criqui (eds), pp. 237–69. Plenum, New York.

Kaplan, H.B. (1991) 'Social psychology of the immune system: a conceptual framework and review of the literature', *Social Science & Medicine*, vol. 33, no. 8, 909–23.

Karl, M. (1995) *Women and Empowerment: Participation and Decision Making*. Zed Books, London.

Katz, A.H. and E.I. Bender (1990) *Helping One Another: Self-Help Groups in a Changing World*. Third Party Publishing Company, Oakland, CA.

Kaufmann, G. and J. Cleland (1994) 'Maternal education and child survival: anthropological responses to demographic evidence', *Health Transition Review*, vol. 4, no. 2, 196–9.

Keller, E.F. (1985) *Reflections on Gender and Science*. Yale University Press, New Haven, CT.

Kempe, A., P.H. Wise, S. Barkan, W.M. Sappenfield, B. Sachs, S.L. Gortmaker, A.M. Sobol, L.R. First, D. Pursley, H. Rinehart, M. Kotelchuck, S. Cole, N. Gunter, and J.W. Stockbauer (1992) 'Clinical determinants of the racial disparity in very low birth weight', *The New England Journal of Medicine*, vol. 327, no. 14, 969–73.

Kennedy, G. (1983) *Invitation to Statistics*. Basil Blackwell, Oxford, England.

Khandker, S.R. (1994) *Poverty Reduction Strategy: The Grameen Bank Experience*. World Bank. HRO Dissemination Notes Number 23.

Kiecolt-Glaser, J.K., W. Garner, C. Speicher, et al. (1984a) 'Psychosocial modifiers of immunocompetency in medical students', *Psychosomatic Medicine*, vol. 46, 7–14.

Kiecolt-Glaser, J.K., D. Ricker, J. George et al. (1984b) 'Urinary cortisol levels, cellular immunocompetency, and loneliness in psychiatric inpatients', *Psychosomatic Medicine*, vol. 46, 15–23.

Kiecolt-Glaser, J.K. and R. Glaser (1992) 'Psychoneuroimmunology: can psychological interventions modulate immunity?', *Journal of Consulting and Clinical Psychology*, vol. 60, no. 4, 569–75.

Kiecolt-Glaser, J.K., C.E. Speicher, J.E. Holliday et al. (1984c) 'Stress and the transformation of lymphocytes by Epstein-Barr virus', *The Journal of Behavioral Medicine*, vol. 7, 1–11.

Kindervatter, S. (1979) *Nonformal Education as an Empowering Process.* Center for International Education, Amherst, MA.

Kindervatter, S. (1986) *Las Mujeres Trabajan Unidas.* Overseas Education Fund, Washington, DC.

Kindervatter, S. (1987a) *Femmes, Travaillons Ensemble!* Overseas Education Fund, Washington, DC.

Kindervatter, S. (1987b) *Women Working Together for Personal, Economic, and Community Development.* 2nd edn, Overseas Education Fund, Washington, DC.

King, H., C.A. M., H.A. Tyroler, and J. Cassel (1964) 'Health consequences of culture change – II: the effect of urbanization on coronary heart mortality in rural residents', *Journal of Chronic Disease*, vol. 17, 167–77.

Kirk, J. and M.L. Miller (1986) *Reliability and Validity in Qualitative Research.* vol. 1. Qualitative Research Methods, Sage Publications, Newbury Park, CA.

Kitzinger, C. (1987) *The Social Construction of Lesbianism.* Sage, London.

Kleinbaum, D.G. and L.L. Kupper (1992) *Specialized methods for the analysis of epidemiologic data.* Unpublished notes for Epidemiology 141, School of Public Health, University of North Carolina.

Kleinman, J.C. and S.S. Kessell (1987) 'Racial differences in low birth weight: trends and risk factors', *New England Journal of Medicine*, vol. 317, no. 12, 749–53.

Kneerim, J. (1989) 'Village women organize: the Mraru, Kenya bus service.' In *Seeds: Supporting Women's Work in the Third World*, Leonard, A. (ed.) pp. 15–30. The Feminist Press at the City University of New York, New York.

Kobasa, S.C. (1982) 'The hardy personality: toward a social psychology of stress and health.' In *Social Psychology of Health and Illness*, Sanders, G.S. and J. Suls (eds) Erlbaum, Hillsdale, NJ.

Koblinsky, M., O.M.R. Campbell, and S.D. Harlow (1993a) 'Mother and more: a broader perspective on women's health.' In *The Health of Women: A Global Perspective*, Koblinsky, M., J. Timyan, and J. Gay (eds) pp. 33–62. Westview Press, Boulder, CO.

Koblinsky, M., J. Timyan, and J. Gay, (eds) (1993b) *The Health of Women: A Global Perspective*, Westview Press, Boulder, CO.

Kreiner, S. (1989) 'Statistical analysis of complex health and social data', *Social Science & Medicine*, vol. 29, no. 2, 253–8.

Krieger, N., D. Rowley, A.A. Herman, B. Avery, and M.T. Phillips (1993) 'Racism, sexism, and social class: implications for studies of health disease, and well-being', *American Journal of Preventive Medicine*, vol. 9, no. 6 (Supplement), 82–122.

Kuhn, T.S. (1970) *The Structure of Scientific Revolutions.* 2nd edn, University of Chicago Press, Chicago.

Kunitz, S.J. (1990) 'The value of particularism in the study of cultural, social and behavioural determinants of mortality.' In *What We Know about Health Transition: The Cultural, Social, Behavioural Determinants of Health*, Caldwell, J., S. Findley, P. Caldwell, G. Santow, W. Cosford, J. Braid, and D. Broers-Freeman (eds) pp. 92–109. vol. 1. Health Transition Centre, The Australian National University, Canberra.

Kunitz, S.J. and S.L. Engerman (1993) 'The ranks of death: secular trends in income and mortality', *Health Transition Review*, Supplement to Volume 2, 1992, 29–46.

Küppers, G., (eds) (1994) *Compañeras: Voices from the Latin American Women's Movement*, Latin American Bureau, London.

Labarthe, D., D. Reed, J. Brody, and R. Stallones (1983) 'Health effects of modernization in Palau', *American Journal of Epidemiology*, vol. 98, no. 3.

Labarthe, D., D. Reed, J. Brody, and R. Stallones (1989) 'A modernity score for individuals in Melanesian society', *Papua New Guinea Medical Journal*, vol. 32, 11–22.

Landers, J. (1993) 'Introduction', *Health Transition Review*, Supplement to Volume 2, 1992, 1–27.

Lane, S.D. (1994) 'From population control to reproductive health: an emerging policy agenda', *Social Science & Medicine*, vol. 39, no. 9, 1303–14.

Last, J.M., (ed.) (1988) *A Dictionary of Epidemiology*, 2nd edn, Oxford University Press, New York.

Lather, P. (1986) 'Research as praxis', *Harvard Educational Review*, vol. 56, no. 3, 257–77.

Lather, P. (1988) 'Feminist perspectives on empowering research methodologies', *Women's Studies International Forum*, vol. 11, no. 6, 569–81.

Lather, P. (1991) *Getting Smart: Feminist Research and Pedagogy With/in the Postmodern*. Routledge, New York.

Laurell, A.C. (1989) 'Social analysis of collected health in Latin America', *Social Science & Medicine*, vol. 28, no. 11, 1183–91.

Lemann, N. (1991) *The Promised Land: The Great Black Migration and How it Changed America*. Vintage Books, New York.

Lena, H.F. and B. London (1993) 'The political and economic determinants of health outcomes: a cross-national analysis', *International Journal of Health Services*, vol. 23, no. 3, 585–602.

Leonard, A., (eds) (1989) *Seeds: Supporting Women's Work in the Third World*, The Feminist Press, New York.

Lepore, S.J., M.N. Palsane, and G.W. Evans (1991) 'Daily hassles and chronic strains: a hierarchy of stressors', *Social Science & Medicine*, vol. 33, no. 9, 1029–36.

Levins, R. and R. Lewontin (1985) *The Dialectical Biologist*. Harvard University Press, Cambridge, MA.

Levy, M.F. (1988) *Each in Her Own Way: Five Women Leaders of the Developing World*. Lynne Rienner Publishers, Boulder, CO.

Levy, S.M., J. Lee, C. Bagley, and M. Lippman (1988) 'Survival hazards analysis in first recurrent breast cancer patients: seven-year follow-up', *Psychosomatic Medicine*, vol. 50, 520–28.

Lewis, O. (1983) *La Vida*. Editorial Grijalbo, S.A., México, DF.

Lichtenstein, P., J.R. Harris, N.L. Pedersen, and G.E. McClearn (1992) 'Socioeconomic status and physical health, how are they related? An empirical study based on twins reared apart and twins reared together', *Social Science & Medicine*, vol. 36, no. 4, 441–50.

Link, B.G. and J.C. Phelan (1995) 'Social conditions as fundamental causes of disease', *Journal of Health and Social Behavior*, extra issue, 80–94.

Link, B.G. and J.C. Phelan (1996) 'Editorial: understanding sociodemographic differences in health – the role of fundamental social causes', *American Journal of Public Health*, vol. 86, no. 4, 471–3.

Locke, S.E. (1982) 'Stress, adaptation, and immunity: studies in humans', *General Hospital Psychiatry*, vol. 4, 49–58.

Loewenson, R. (1993) 'Structural adjustment and health policy in Africa', *International Journal of Health Services*, vol. 24, no. 4, 717–70.

Longino, H.E. (1989) 'Can there be a feminist science?' In *Feminism & Science*, Tuana, N. (ed.) pp. 45–57. Indiana University Press, Bloomington, IN.

Luhtanen, R. and J. Crocker (1992) 'A collective self-esteem scale: self-evaluation of one's social identity', *Personality and Social Psychology Bulletin*, vol. 18, no. 3, 302–18.

MacCormack, C. (1992) 'Planning and evaluating women's participation in primary health care', *Social Science & Medicine*, vol. 35, no. 6, 831–7.

Macintyre, S. (1986) 'The patterning of health by social position in contemporary Britain: directions for sociological research', *Social Science & Medicine*, vol. 23, no. 4, 393–415.

Macintyre, S. (1992) 'The effects of family position and status on health', *Social Science & Medicine*, vol. 35, no. 4, 453–64.

McCurdy, S. (1992) 'Colonialist Concepts of AIDS.' *Links*, Fall, 4.

McKee, K. (1989) 'Microlevel strategies for supporting livelihoods, employment, and income generation of poor women in the third world: the challenge of significance', *World Development*, vol. 17, no. 7, 993–1006.

McKeown, T. (1976) *The Modern Rise of Population*. Edward Arnold, London.

McKinlay, J.B., S.M. McKinlay, and R. Beaglehole (1989) 'A review of the evidence concerning the impact of medical measures on recent mortality and morbidity in the United States', *International Journal of Health Services*, vol. 19, no. 2, 181–208.

McKnight, J.L. (1985) 'Health and empowerment', *Canadian Journal of Public Health*, vol. 76, Supplement, 37–38.

McNeill, W.H. (1976) *Plagues and Peoples*. Anchor Books, New York.

Makosky, V.P. (1982) 'Sources of stress: events or conditions?' In *Lives in Stress: Women and Depression*, Belle, D. (ed.) pp. 35–53. Sage, Beverly Hills.

Marmot, M.G. and J.N. Morris (1984) 'The social environment.' In *The Oxford Textbook of Public Health*, Holand, W.W. and K. Detels (ed.) pp. 97–118. Oxford University Press, Oxford.

Mason, K.O. (1985) *The Status of Women: A Review of its Relationships to Fertility and Mortality*. Population Sciences Division of the Rockefeller Foundation. Unpublished paper.

Meleis, A.I. (1982) 'Effect of modernization on Kuwaiti women', *Social Science & Medicine*, vol. 16, 965–70.

Menaghan, E. (1983) 'Individual coping efforts: moderators of the relationship between life stress and mental health outcomes.' In *Psychosocial Stress: Trends in Theory and Research*, Kaplan, H.B. (ed.) pp. 157–91. Academic Press, Orlando, FL.

Mencher, J.P. and A. Okongwu, (eds) (1993) *Where Did All the Men Go?*, Westview Press, Boulder, CO.

Mensch, B. (1992) 'Quality of care: a neglected dimension.' In *The Health of Women: A Global Perspective*, Koblinsky, M., J. Timyan, and J. Gay (eds) pp. 235–53. Westview Press, Boulder, CO.

Merchant, K.M. and K.M. Kurz (1993) 'Women's nutrition through the life cycle: social and biological vulnerabilities.' In *The Health of Women: A Global Perspective*, Koblinsky, M., J. Timyan, and J. Gay (eds) pp. 63–90. Westview Press, Boulder, CO.

Merrifield, J. (1987) 'Putting scientists in their place: participatory research in environmental and occupational health.' Highlander Research and Education Center, New Market, TN. Unpublished paper.

Merson, M.J. (1992) 'AIDS: the world situation', *Journal of Public Health Policy*, vol. 14, no. 1, 18–26.

Meulenberg-Buskens, I. (1996) 'Critical awareness in participatory research: an approach towards teaching and learning.' In *Participatory Research in Health: Issues and Experiences*, de Koning, K. and M. Martin (eds), pp. 40–49. Zed Books, London.

Miers, H. (1993) 'Women: seminar speakers challenge development assumptions', online *Peacenet, InterPress Service*, 16 June.

Mies, M. (1991) 'Women's research or feminist research? The debate surrounding feminist science and methodology.' In *Beyond Methodology: Feminist Scholarship as Lived Research*, Fonow, M.M. and J.A. Cook (eds) pp. 60–84. Indiana University Press, Bloomington, IN.

Miller, C.A. (1987) 'Child health.' In *Epidemiology and Health Policy*, Levine, S. and A.M. Lilienfeld (eds) pp. 15–54. Tavistock Publications, New York.

Miller, D. and H. Mintzberg (1983) 'The case for configuration.' In *Beyond Method: Strategies for Social Research*, Morgan, G. (ed.) pp. 57–73. Sage, Newbury Park, CA.

Mincy, R.B., I.V. Sawhill, and D.A. Worl (1990) 'The underclass: definition and measurement', *Science*, vol. 248, 450–53.

Minkler, M. (1987) *Update on Social Support Theory*. Presentation at the annual meeting of the American Public Health Association.

Moghadam, V.M. (1990) *Gender, Development, and Policy: Toward Equity and Empowerment*. World Institute for Development Economics Research, Helsinki. Report.

Mohanty, C.T. (1991) 'Under western eyes: feminist scholarship and colonial discourses.' In *Third World Women and the Politics of Feminism*, Mohanty, C.T., A. Russo, and L. Torres (eds) pp. 51–80. Indiana University Press, Bloomington, IN.

Moon, B.E. and W.J. Dixon (1985) 'Politics, the state, and basic human needs: a cross-national study', *American Journal of Political Science*, vol. 29, 661–94.

Moore, M. and J.W. Anderson (1993) 'Women, Fed Up and Fighting Back', *Washington Post*, February 18, A1.

Morales, A.L. (1991) 'A remedy for heartburn: in memory of Dona Gina Torres of Bartolo.' *Ms.*, 52–6.

Morgan, G. (1983a) 'Exploring choice: reframing the process of evaluation.' In *Beyond*

Method: Strategies for Social Research, Morgan, G. (ed.) pp. 392–440. Sage, Newbury Park, CA.

Morgan, G. (1983b) 'Research strategies: modes of engagement.' In *Beyond Method: Strategies for Social Research*, Morgan, G. (ed.) pp. 19–42. Sage, Beverly Hills, CA.

Moriz, C. (1991) *Pentecostalism, Gender, and Alcoholism.* Presentation at the biennial meeting of the Latin American Studies Association in Crystal City, VA.

Morris, W., (ed.) (1973) *The American Heritage Dictionary of the English Language*, Houghton-Mifflin, Boston, MA.

Moser, C.O.N. (1989) 'Gender planning in the Third World: meeting practical and strategic gender needs', *World Development*, vol. 17, no. 11, 1799–825.

Moser, C.O.N. (1993) *Gender Planning and Development: Theory, Practice & Training.* Routledge, New York.

Mosley, W.H. (1983) *Will Primary Health Care Reduce Infant and Child Mortality? A Critique of Some Current Strategies with Special Reference to Africa and Asia.* Presentation at the International Conference of Population. Paris, France.

Mosley, W.H. (1989) 'Will primary health care reduce infant and child mortality? A critique of some current strategies with special reference to Africa and Asia.' In *Selected Readings in the Cultural, Social and Behavioural Determinants of Health*, Caldwell, J.C. and G. Santow (eds) pp. 261–94. Health Transition Centre, The Australian National University, Canberra.

Mosley, W.H. and L. Chen (1984) 'An analytical framework for the study of child survival in developing countries', *Population and Development Review*, vol. 10, no. 25, supplement, 25–45.

Mossey, J.M. and E. Shapiro (1982) 'Self-rated health: a predictor of mortality among the elderly', *American Journal of Public Health*, vol. 72, no. 8, 800–08.

Muller, M.S. and D. Plantenga (1990) *Women and Habitat: Urban Management, Empowerment and Women's Strategies.* Royal Tropical Institute, Amsterdam. Bulletin no. 321.

Munyakho, D. (1992) 'Kenya: community takes charge of health services', online *Peacenet, InterPress Service*, 3 August.

Murray, A.F. (1994) 'Annual International Women's Day Letter to Supporters.'

Murray, C.J.L. and L.C. Chen (1993) 'In search of a contemporary theory for understanding mortality change', *Social Science & Medicine*, vol. 36, no. 2, 143–55.

Murray, C.J.L. (1994) 'Quantifying the burden of disease: the technical basis for disability-adjusted life years.' In *Global Comparative Assessments in the Health Sector: Disease Burden, Expenditures and Intervention Packages*, Murray, C.J.L. and A.D. Lopez (eds) pp. 3–19. World Health Organization, Geneva.

Murray, C.J.L. and A.D. Lopez, (eds) (1994) *Global Comparative Assessments in the Health Sector: Disease Burden, Expenditures and Intervention Packages*, World Health Organization, Geneva.

National Council for International Health (1992) 'International Health News.' *Healthlink*, 8 November.

National Council for International Health (1992) *Women's Health – The Action Agenda.* Statement of the 18th Annual International Health Conference of the NCIH. Washington, DC. Report.

Navarro, M. (1989) 'The personal is political: las Madres de Plaza de Mayo.' In *Power and Popular Protest: Latin American Social Movements*, Eckstein, S. (ed.) pp. 241–58. University of California Press, Berkeley, CA.

NCAHRN. (1991) 'Philippines: one woman's liberation', *Links*, Spring, 19–22.

Nelson, N. and S. Wright (eds) (1995) *Power and Participatory Development*, Intermediate Technology Publications, London.

New Internationalist (1985) *Women: A World Report.* Oxford University Press, New York.

Nicholson, L. (1990) 'Introduction.' In *Feminism/Postmodernism*, Nicholson, L. (ed.) pp. 1–16. Routledge, New York.

Nielsen, J.M. (1990) 'Introduction.' In *Feminist Research Methods: Exemplary Readings in the Social Sciences*, Nielsen, J. (ed.) pp. 1–37. Westview Press, Boulder, CO.

Office of Research on Women's Health (1993) *Report of the National Institutes of Health: Opportunities for Research on Women's Health.* NIH. Report.

Okusanya, E. (1993) 'Nigeria: women doctors start cancer education campaign', online *Peacenet, InterPress Service*, 24 May.

Otten, M.W., S.M. Teutsch, D.F. Williamson, and J.S. Marks (1990) 'The effect of known risk factors on the excess mortality of black adults in the United States', *Journal of the American Medical Association*, vol. 263, no. 6, 845–50.

Pacific News Service (1991) 'Latin women filling political void left by men', online *Peacenet*, 18 April.

Paltiel, F.L. (1987) 'Women and mental health: a post-Nairobi perspective', *World Health Statistics Quarterly*, no. 40, 233–66.

Pan American Health Organization (1985) *Health of Women in the Americas*. Pan American Health Organization, Washington, DC.

Pan American Health Organization (1992) *International Health: A North–South Debate*. Pan American Health Organization, Washington, DC.

Papanek, H. (1990) 'To each less than she needs, from each more than she can do: allocations, entitlements, and value.' In *Persistent Inequalities: Women and World Development*, Tinker, I. (ed.) pp. 162–81. Oxford University Press, Oxford.

Park, P., M. Brydon-Miller, B. Hall, and T. Jackson (1993) *Voices of Change: Participatory Research in the U.S. and Canada*. Ontario Institute for Studies in Education, Ontario.

Participatory Research Network (1981) 'A selective bibliography on participatory research', *Convergence*, vol. 14, no. 3, 74–9.

Patai, D. (1991) 'U.S. academics and third world women: is ethical research possible?' In *Women's Words: The Feminist Practice of Oral History*, Gluck, S.B. and D. Patai (eds) pp. 137–53. Routledge, New York.

Patrick, D.L. (1985) 'Measurement issues: reliability and validity.' *Baseline* (Health Services Research Center, UNC-CH).

Patrick, D.L. and P. Erickson (1993) *Health Status and Health Policy: Allocating Resources to Health Care*. Oxford University Press, New York.

Patrick, R.C., I.A.M. Prior, J.C. Smith, and A.H. Smith (1983) 'Relationship between blood pressure and modernity among Ponapeans', *International Journal of Epidemiology*, vol. 12, no. 1, 36–44.

Patton, M.Q. (1990) *Qualitative Evaluation and Research Methods*. 2nd edn, Sage, Newbury Park, CA.

Paul, B.K. (1991) 'Health service resources as determinants of infant death in rural Bangladesh: an empirical study', *Social Science & Medicine*, vol. 32, no. 1, 43–9.

Paz, R. (1990) *Paths to Empowerment: Ten Years of Early Childhood Work in Israel*. Bernard van Leer Foundation, The Hague.

Pearlin, L.I., M.A. Lieberman, E.G. Menaghan, and J.T. Mullan (1981) 'The stress process', *Journal of Health and Social Behavior*, vol. 22, 337–56.

Pendleton, B.F. and S.W. Yang (1985) 'Socioeconomic and health effects on mortality declines in developing countries', *Social Science & Medicine*, vol. 20, no. 5, 453–60.

Perlman, D. and L.A. Peplau (1984) 'Loneliness research: a survey of empirical findings.' In *Preventing the Harmful Consequences of Severe and Persistent Loneliness*, Peplau, L.A. and S.E. Goldstein (eds) pp. 13–46. National Institute of Mental Health, MD.

Pill, R. and N.C.H. Stott (1985) 'Choice or chance: further evidence on ideas of illness and responsibility for health', *Social Science & Medicine*, vol. 20, no. 10, 981–91.

Pollack, K. (1988) 'On the nature of social stress: production of a modern mythology', *Social Science & Medicine*, vol. 26, no. 3, 381–92.

Popay, J., M. Bartley, and C. Owen (1993) 'Gender inequalities in health: social position, affective disorders and minor physical morbidity', *Social Science & Medicine*, vol. 36, no. 1, 21–32.

Population Crisis Committee (1988) *Country Rankings of the Status of Women: Poor, Powerless and Pregnant*. Population Crisis Committee. Population Briefing Paper no. 20.

Powers, M.G. (1985) *Measures and Indicators of Women's Status: Some Recent Developments*. Women and International Development, Joint Harvard/MIT Group. WID Working Paper no. 8.

Pratt, M.W. (1988) 'The changing maternal and child health population: demographic parameters.' In *Maternal and Child Health Practices*, Wallace, H.M., G.M. Ryan, and

A.C. Oglesby (eds) pp. 47–77. 3rd edition, Third Party Publishing Company, Oakland, CA.

Program for Appropriate Technology in Health (1989) 'The impact of unsafe abortion in the developing world', *OutLook*, vol. 7, no. 3, 2–7.

Programa Educativa para la Mujer (1990) *Conociéndome a mí misma*. Programa Educativo para la Mujer, Honduras.

Quintos Deles, T. and I.M. Santiago (1984) 'Connecting research with social action: the feminist challenge', *Women's Studies Quarterly*, vol. 3, Women's Studies International Supplement, 15–16.

Raikes, A. (1989) 'Women's health in East Africa', *Social Science & Medicine*, vol. 28, no. 5, 447–59.

Randall, V. (1987) *Women and Politics: An International Perspective*. University of Chicago Press, Chicago, IL.

Rappaport, J. (1981) 'In praise of paradox: a social policy of empowerment over prevention', *American Journal of Community Psychology*, vol. 9, no. 1, 1–25.

Rappaport, J., (eds) (1984) *Studies in Empowerment: Steps Toward Understanding and Action*, Haworth Press, New York.

Rappaport, J. (1986) 'Collaborating for empowerment: creating the language of mutual help.' In *The New Populism: The Politics of Empowerment*, Boyte, H.C. and F. Fiessman (eds) pp. 64–79. Temple University Press, Philadelphia, PA.

Rappaport, J. (1987) 'Terms of empowerment/exemplars of prevention: toward a theory for community psychology', *American Journal of Community Psychology*, vol. 15, no. 2, 121–48.

Rathgeber, E.M. (1990) 'WID, WAD, GAD: trends in research and practice', *The Journal of Developing Areas*, vol. 24, 489–502.

Reason, P. and J. Rowan (1981a) 'Afterword.' In *Human Inquiry: A Sourcebook of New Paradigm Research*, Reason, P. and J. Rowan (eds) pp. 485–92. John Wiley and Sons, Chichester.

Reason, P. and J. Rowan (1981b) 'Foreword.' In *Human Inquiry: A Sourcebook of New Paradigm Research*, Reason, P. and J. Rowan (eds) pp. xi–xxiv. John Wiley and Sons, Chichester.

Reason, P. and J. Rowan (1981c) 'Issues of validity in new paradigm research.' In *Human Inquiry*, Reason, P. and J. Rowan (eds) pp. 239–50. John Wiley and Sons, Chichester.

Reinharz, S. (1981) 'Implementing new paradigm research: a model for training and practice.' In *Human Inquiry: A Sourcebook of New Paradigm Research*, Reason, P. and J. Rowan (eds) pp. 415–35. John Wiley and Sons, Chichester.

Reinharz, S. (1992) *Feminist Methods in Social Research*. Oxford University Press, New York.

Reuben, R. (1993) 'Women and malaria – special risks and appropriate control strategy', *Social Science & Medicine*, vol. 37, no. 4, 472–80.

Rice, D.P. (1991) 'The medical care system: past trends and future projections.' In *The Nation's Health*, Lee, P.R. and C.L. Estes (eds) pp. 72–93. 3rd edn, Jones and Bartlett, Boston.

Rich, A. (1979) *On Lies, Secrets, and Silence: Selected Prose, 1966–1978*. Norton, New York.

Richters, A. (1992) 'Introduction', *Social Science & Medicine*, vol. 35, no. 6, 747–51.

Riley, M.W. (1993) 'A theoretical basis for research on health.' In *Population Health Research: Linking Theory and Methods*, Dean, K. (ed.) pp. 37–53. Sage, London.

Rockefeller Foundation Staff (1988) 'Memo to the Board.' New York: Rockfeller Foundation. Unpublished statement.

Rodriguez-García, R. and A. Goldman, (eds) (1994) *The Health–Development Link*, Pan American Health Organization, Washington, DC.

Rodriguez-Trias, H. (1992) 'Women's health, women's lives, women's rights', *American Journal of Public Health*, vol. 82, no. 5, 663–4.

Roemer, M.J. and R. Roemer (1990) 'Global health, national development, and the role of government', *American Journal of Public Health*, vol. 80, no. 10, 1188–92.

Rook, K.S. (1987) 'Social support versus companionship: effects on life stress, loneliness, and evaluations by others', *Journal of Personality and Social Psychology*, vol. 52, no. 6, 1132–47.

Rose, G. (1985) 'Sick individuals and sick populations', *International Journal of Epidemiology*, vol. 14, no. 1, 32–8.

Rose, H. (1986) 'Beyond masculinist realities: a feminist epistemology for the sciences.' In *Feminist Approaches to Science*, Bleier, R. (ed.) pp. 57–76. Pergamon Press, New York.

Rosenberg, M. (1989) *Society and the Adolescent Self-Image*. Wesleyan University Press, Middletown, CT.

Rosenfield, A. (1991) 'Population growth: implications and problems', *Infectious Disease Clinics of North America*, vol. 5, no. 2, 277–96.

Rossi-Espagnet, A., G.B. Goldstein, and I. Tabibzadeh (1991) 'Urbanization and health in developing countries: a challenge for health for all', *World Health Statistics Quarterly*, vol. 44, no. 4, 186–244.

Rothman, K.J. (1986) *Modern Epidemiology*. Little, Brown, Boston, MA.

Rothman, K.J. (1990) 'No adjustments are needed for multiple comparisons', *Epidemiology*, vol. 1, no. 1, 43–6.

Rouse, J. (1991) 'The politics of postmodern philosophy of science', *Philosophy of Science*, vol. 58, 607–27.

Rutter, M. and N. Madge (1976) *Cycles of Disadvantage: A Review of Research*. Heinemann Educational Books, London.

Ruzicka, L.T. and H. Hansluwka (1982) ' Mortality transition in South and East Asia: technology confronts poverty', *Population and Development Review*, vol. 8, no. 3, 567–88.

Sachs, W. (ed.) (1993) *The Development Dictionary: A Guide to Knowledge as Power*, Zed Books, London.

Safa, H.I. (1990) 'Women's social movements in Latin America', *Gender and Society*, vol. 4, no. 3, 354–69.

Safilios-Rothschild, C. (1982) 'Female power, autonomy and demographic change in the Third World.' In *Women's Roles and Population Trends in the Third World*, Anker, R., M. Buvinic, and N.H. Youssef (eds) pp. 117–132. Croom Helm, London.

Sagan, L. (1987) *The Health of Nations: True Causes of Sickness and Well-being*. Basic Books, New York.

Sanchez, E., L. Howard-Grabman, D.L. Rogers, and A. Bartlett (1992) *Researching Women's Health Problems Using Epidemiological and Participatory Methods to Plan the Inquisivi Mothercare Project*. Save the Children, Westport, CT. Report.

Sanday, P.R. (1974) 'Female status in the public domain.' In *Woman, Culture, and Society*, Rosaldo, M.Z. and L. Lamphere (eds) pp. 189–206. Stanford University Press, Stanford, CA.

Sandiford, P., P. Morales, A. Gorter, E. Coyle, and G. Davey Smith (1991) 'Why do child mortality rates fall? An analysis of the Nicaraguan experience', *American Journal of Public Health*, vol. 81, no. 1, 30–37.

Scheman, N. (1991) 'Who wants to know?: the epistemological value of values.' In *(En)Gendering Knowledge: Feminists in Academe*, Hartman, J.E. and E. Messer-Davidow (eds) pp. 179–200. University of Tennessee Press, Knoxville, TN.

Scheper-Hughes, N. (1992) *Death Without Weeping: The Violence of Everyday Life in Brazil*. University of California Press, Berkeley, CA.

Schneider, D. and M.R. Greenberg (1992) 'Death rates in rural America 1939–1981: convergence and poverty.' In *Health in Rural North America: The Geography of Health Care Services and Delivery*, Gesler, W.M. and T.C. Ricketts (eds) pp. 55–68. Rutgers University Press, New Brunswick, NJ.

Schneider, R., M. Schiffman, and J. Faigenblum (1978) 'The potential effect of water on gastrointestinal infections prevalent in developing countries', *American Journal of Clinical Nutrition*, vol. 31, 2089–99.

Schoendorf, K.C., C.J.R. Hogue, J.C. Kleinman, and D. Rowley (1992) 'Mortality among infants of black as compared to white college-educated parents', *The New England Journal of Medicine*, vol. 326, no. 23, 1522–26.

Schoepf, B.G. (1993) 'AIDS action-research with women in Kinshasa, Zaire', *Social Science & Medicine*, vol. 37, no. 11, 1401–13.

Schuler, S.R. and S.M. Hashemi (1993) *Defining and Studying Empowerment of Women: A Research Note from Bangladesh*. John Snow, Arlington, VA. JSI Working Paper no. 3.

Schultz, T.P. (1982) 'Women's work and their status: rural Indian evidence of labour market and environment effects on sex differences in childhood mortality.' In *Women's Roles and Population Trends in the Third World*, Anker, R., M. Buvinic, and N.H. Youssef (eds) pp. 202–36. Croom Helm, London.

Schuurman, F.J. (1993) 'Introduction: Development Theory in the 1990s.' In *Beyond the Impasse: New Directions in Development Theory*, Schuurman, F.J. (ed.) pp. 1–48. Zed Books, London and Atlantic Highlands, NJ.

Scribner, R. and J.H. Dwyer. (1989) 'Acculturation and low birthweight among Latinos in the Hispanic HANES', *American Journal of Public Health*, vol. 79, no. 9, 1263–67.

Seager, J. and A. Olson (1986) *Women in the World: An International Atlas*. Simon & Schuster, New York.

Sebstad, J. (1984) 'Struggle and success: building a strong, independent union for poor women workers in India', *Women's Studies International*, vol. 3, 7–11.

Seeman, M. (1959) 'On the meaning of alienation', *American Sociological Review*, vol. 24, 783–91.

Seitz, V.R. (1992) 'Women, Development, and Communities for Empowerment: Grassroots Associations for Change in Southwest Virginia.' PhD Dissertation, Virginia Polytechnic Institute and State University.

Sen, A. (1990) 'More than 100 million women are missing.' *New York Review of Books*, 20 December, 61–6.

Sen, G. and C. Grown (1987) *Development, Crises, and Alternative Visions: Third World Women's Perspectives*. Monthly Review Press, New York.

Serrano-García, I. (1984) 'The illusion of empowerment: community development within a colonial context.' In *Studies in Empowerment: Steps Toward Understanding and Action*, Rappaport, J. (ed.) pp. 173–99. Haworth Press, New York.

Sheldon, T.A. and H. Parker (1992) 'Race and ethnicity in health research', *Journal of Public Health Medicine*, vol. 14, no. 2, 104–10.

Shiono, P.H., M.A. Klebanoff, B.I. Graubard, H.W. Berendes, and G.G. Rhoads (1986) 'Birth weight among women of different ethnic groups', *Journal of the American Medical Association*, vol. 255, no. 1, 48–52.

Shiva, V. (1989) *Staying Alive: Women, Ecology and Development*. Zed Books, London.

Sigerist, H. (1941) *Medicine and Human Welfare*. Yale University Press, New Haven, CT.

Simon, B.L. (1990) 'Rethinking empowerment', *Journal of Progressive Human Services*, vol. 1, no. 1, 27–39.

Simons, J. (1990) 'Cultural dimensions of the mother's contribution to child survival.' In *Selected Readings in The Cultural, Social and Behavioural Determinants of Health*, Caldwell, J.C. and G. Santow (eds) pp. 132–145. Health Transition Centre, The Australian National University, Canberra.

Sivard, R.L. (1985) *WOMEN ... A World Survey*. World Priorities, Box 25140, Washington, DC 20007.

Small, C. (1990) 'Planning social change: a misdirected vision.' In *Women, International Development, and Politics: The Bureaucratic Mire*, Staudt, K. (ed.) pp. 265–288. Temple University Press, Philadelphia, PA.

Smith, G.D. (1996) 'Income inequality and mortality: why are they related?', Editorial, *British Medical Journal*, vol. 312.

So, A.Y. (1990) *Social Change and Development: Modernization, Dependency, and World-System Theories*. Library of Social Research 178, Sage, Newbury Park, CA.

Soethe, F. (1993) 'Final document on the women's human rights session at the Asian NGO conference on human rights', online *Peacenet, dh.mujer*, 14 May.

Solomon, B. (1976) *Black Empowerment*. Columbia University Press, New York.

Sontag, S. (1989) *AIDS and its Metaphors*. Farrar, Straus & Giroux, New York.

Soysa, P. (1987) 'Women and nutrition', *World Review of Nutrition and Dietics*, vol. 52, 1–70.

Spiegel, D., H.C. Kraemer, J.R. Bloom, and E. Gottheil (1989) 'Effect of psychosocial treatment on survival of patients with metastatic breast cancer', *The Lancet*, 14 October, 888–91.

Spivak, G. (1987) *In Other Worlds: Essays in Cultural Politics*. Methuen, New York.

Stack, C. (1974) *All Our Kin: Strategies for Survival in the Black Community*. Harper & Row, New York.

Stamp, P. (1990) *Technology, Gender, and Power in Africa*. The International Development

Research Centre, Ottawa, Ontario, Canada.

Staples, L.H. (1990) 'Powerful ideas about empowerment', *Administration and Social Work*, vol. 14, no. 2, 29–42.

Starfield, B., S. Shapiro, J. Weiss, K.-Y. Liang, K. Ra, D. Paige, and X. Wang (1991) 'Race, family income, and low birth weight', *American Journal of Epidemiology*, vol. 134, 1167–74.

Steckler, A.B., B.A. Israel, L. Dawson, and E. Eng (1993) 'Community Health Development: An Anthology of the Works of Guy W. Steuart', *Health Education Quarterly*, Supplement 1.

Stein, J. (1989) Unpublished interviews.

Stein, J. (1991) 'Back to basics: the relationship between women's status and child mortality.' Unpublished paper.

Sterling, P. and J. Eyer (1981) 'Biological basis of stress-related mortality', *Social Science & Medicine*, vol. 15E, 3–42.

Sultana, M. (1988) 'Participation, Empowerment and Variation in Development Projects for Rural Bangladeshi Women.' PhD Dissertation, Department of Sociology, Northeastern University.

Susser, M. (1993) 'Health as a human right: an epidemiologist's perspective on the public health', *American Journal of Public Health*, vol. 83, no. 3, 418–26.

Syme, S.L. and L.F. Berkman (1976) 'Social class, susceptibility and sickness', *American Journal of Epidemiology*, vol. 104, no. 1, 1–8.

Tabachnick, B.G. and L.S. Fidell (1989) *Using Multivariate Statistics*. 2nd edn, Harper & Row, New York.

Tandon, R. (1996) 'The historical roots and contemporary tendencies in participatory research: implications for health care.' In *Participatory Research in Health: Issues and Experiences*, de Koning, K. and M. Martin (eds) Zed Books, London.

Tavris, C. (1992) *The Mismeasure of Woman*. Touchstone, New York.

Tesh, S.N. (1988) *Hidden Arguments: Political Ideology and Disease Prevention Policy*. Rutgers University Press, New Brunswick, NJ.

Thoits, P.A. (1983) 'Dimensions of life events that influence psychological distress: an evaluation and synthesis of the literature.' In *Psychosocial Stress: Trends in Theory and Research*, Kaplan, H.B. (ed.) pp. 33–103. Academic Press, Orlando, FL.

Thomson, A.M. (1959) 'Diet in pregnancy', *British Journal of Nutrition*, vol. 13, 509–25.

Timyan, J., S.J.G. Brechin, D.M. Measham, and B. Ogunleye (1993) 'Access to care: more than a problem of distance.' In *The Health of Women: A Global Perspective*, Koblinsky, M., J. Timyan, and J. Gay (eds) pp. 217–34. Westview Press, Boulder, CO.

Tinker, I. (1976) 'The adverse impact of development on women.' In *Women and World Development*, Tinker, I. and M.B. Bramsen (ed.) pp. 22–34. Praeger, New York.

Tinker, I. (1990) 'The making of a field: advocates, practitioners, and scholars.' In *Persistent Inequalities: Women and World Development*, Tinker, I. (eds) pp. 27–53. Oxford University Press, New York.

Tolley, E.E. and M.E. Bentley (1996) 'Training issues for the use of participatory research methods in health.' In *Participatory Research in Health: Issues and Experiences*, de Koning, K. and M. Martin (eds), pp. 50–71. Zed Books, London.

Tollman, S. (1991) 'Community oriented primary care: origins, evolution, applications', *Social Science & Medicine*, vol. 32, no. 6, 633–42.

Tong, R. (1989) 'Introduction: the varieties of feminist thinking.' In *Feminist Thought: A Comprehensive Introduction*, Tong, R. (ed.) pp. 1–9. Westview Press, Boulder, CO.

Trowell, H.C. and D.P. Burkitt (1981) *Western Diseases*. Edward Arnold, London.

Tsui, A., J. DeClerque, and N. Mangani (1988) 'Maternal and sociodemographic correlates of child morbidity in Bas Zaire: the effects of maternal reporting', *Social Science & Medicine*, vol. 26, no. 7, 701–13.

Tuana, N., (eds) (1989) *Feminism & Science*, Indiana University Press, Bloomington, IN.

Turner, R.J. (1983) 'Direct, indirect, and moderating effects of social support on psychological distress and associated conditions.' In *Psychosocial Stress: Trends in Theory and Research*, Kaplan, H.B. (ed.) pp. 105–55. Academic Press, Orlando, FL.

Turshen, M. (1989) *The Politics of Public Health*. Rutgers University Press, New Brunswick, NJ.

Tyroler, H.A. and J. Cassel (1961) 'Health consequences of culture change – I: health status and recency of industrialization', *Archives of Environmental Health*, vol. 3, no. 25, 167–77.

Ulin, R. (1992) 'African women and AIDS: negotiating behavioral change', *Social Science & Medicine*, vol. 34, no. 1, 63–73.

UNICEF (July 1996) *The Progress of Nations*. Online http://www.unicef.org/pon96.

Unidad de Servicios de Apoyo para la Participación de la Mujer Hondureña (1991) Personal interview conducted by the author.

United Nations (1989) *Violence Against Women in the Family*. United Nations, New York.

United Nations (1991a) *Women: Challenges to the Year 2000*. United Nations, New York.

United Nations (1991b) *The World's Women 1970–1990: Trends and Statistics*. United Nations, New York.

United Nations Information Centre (1992a) 'Aging, disability and gender', online *Peacenet*, 17 September.

United Nations Information Centre (1992b) 'Aging, health and disability', online *Peacenet*, 17 September.

US Bureau of the Census (1980) *Illustrative Statistics on Women in Selected Developing Countries*. US Bureau of the Census, Washington, DC.

US Department of Health and Human Services (1985) *Report of the Secretary's Task Force on Black and Minority Health*. US Department of Health and Human Services, Washington, DC. Report.

Urribarri, R. (1991) 'Venezuela: the regeneration of a nation', *Women's Feature Service*, 1 August.

Vaughan, M. and H. Moore (1988) 'Health, nutrition and agricultural development in northern Zambia', *Social Science & Medicine*, vol. 27, no. 7, 743–5.

Vella, J. (1989) *Learning to Teach: Training of Trainers for Community Development*. Save The Children, Overseas Education Fund International, Westport, CT, Washington, DC.

Verbrugge, L.M. (1985a) 'Gender and health: an update on hypotheses and evidence', *Journal of Health and Social Behavior*, vol. 26, 156–82.

Verbrugge, L.M. (1985b) 'Triggers of symptoms and health care', *Social Science & Medicine*, vol. 9, no. 2, 855–76.

Vindhya, U. and V. Kalpana (1989) 'Voluntary organisations and women's struggle for change: experience with BCT', *Indian Journal of Social Work*, vol. 50, no. 2, 183–97.

Vingerhoets, A.J.J.M. and F.H.G. Marcelissen (1988) 'Stress research: its present status and issues for future developments', *Social Science & Medicine*, vol. 26, no. 3, 279–91.

Wahid, A.N.M., (ed.) (1993) *The Grameen Bank: Poverty Relief in Bangladesh*. Westview Press. Boulder, CO.

Waldron, I. (1993) 'Recent trends in sex mortality ratios for adults in developed countries', *Social Science & Medicine*, vol. 36, no. 4, 451–62.

Waldrop, M.M. (1992) *Complexity: The Emerging Science at the Edge of Order and Chaos*. Simon & Schuster, New York.

Wallace, H.M. (1987) 'The health status of women in developing countries of the world', *Journal of Tropical Pediatrics*, vol. 33, 239–42.

Wallerstein, N. (1992) 'Powerlessness, empowerment, and health: implications for health promotion programs', *American Journal of Health Promotion*, vol. 6, no. 3, 197–205.

Wallerstein, N. and E. Bernstein (1988) 'Empowerment education: Freire's ideas adapted to health education', *Health Education Quarterly*, vol. 15, no. 4, 379–94.

Wallston, B.S. and K.A. Wallston (1984) 'Social psychological models of health behavior: an examination and integration.' In *Handbook of Psychology and Health*, Baum, A., S.E. Taylor, and J.E. Singer (eds) pp. 23–56. vol. IV. Lawrence Erlbaum Associates, Hillsdale, NJ.

Ware, H. (1981) *Women, Demography and Development*. The Australian National University, Canberra.

Ware, H. (1983) 'Effects of maternal education, women's roles, and child care on child mortality', *Population and Development Review*, vol. 10, Supplement, 191–214.

Waxler-Morrison, N., T.G. Hislop, B. Mears, and L. Kan (1991) 'Effects of relationships on survival for women with breast cancer: a prospective study', *Social Science & Medicine*, vol. 33, no. 2, 177–83.

Wedeen, L. and E. Weiss (1993) *Women's Empowerment and Reproductive Health Programs: An Evaluation Paradigm*. Center for Population and Family Health, Columbia University, NY. Presentation at the Annual Meeting of the Population Association of America. Cincinnati, OH.

Weil, D.E.C., A.P. Alicbusan, J.F. Wilson, M.R. Reich, and D.J. Bradley (1990) *The Impact of Development Policies on Health: A Review of the Literature*. World Health Organization, Geneva.

Werner, D. and B. Bower (1982) *Helping Health Workers Learn*. The Hesperian Foundation, Palo Alto, CA.

Werner, D. and B. Bower (1984) *Aprendiendo a Promover la Salud*. The Hesperian Foundation, Palo Alto, CA.

Werner, E.E. and R.S. Smith (1989) *Vulnerable but Invincible: A Longitudinal Study of Resilient Children and Youth*. Adams, Bannister, Cox, New York.

West, D.A., R. Kellner, and M. Moore-West (1986) 'The effects of loneliness: a review of the literature', *Comprehensive Psychiatry*, vol. 27, no. 4, 351–63.

Wheatley, M.J. (1994) *Leadership and the New Science: Learning about Organization from an Orderly Universe*. Berrett-Koehler Publishers, San Francisco, CA.

Whitehead, M. (1987) *The Health Divide*. Penguin, Harmondsworth.

Whitehead, T.L. (1986) 'Breakdown, resolution, and coherence: the fieldwork experiences of a big, brown, pretty-talking man in a West Indian community.' In *Self, Sex, and Gender in Cross-Cultural Fieldwork*, Whitehead, T.L. and M.E. Conaway (eds) pp. 213–39. University of Illinois Press, Urbana, IL.

Whiting-O'Keefe, Q.E., C. Henke, and D.W. Simborg (1984) 'Choosing the correct unit of analysis in medical care experiments', *Medical Care*, vol. 22, no. 12, 1101–13.

Wignaraja, P. (1990) *Women, Poverty and Resources*. Sage Publications Inc., Newbury Park, CA.

Wilkinson, R.G. (1986) 'Socio-economic differences in mortality: interpreting the data on their size and trends.' In *Class and Health: Research and Longitudinal Data*, Wilkinson, R.G. (ed.) pp. 1–20. Tavistock Publications, London.

Wilkinson, R.G. (1990) 'Income distribution and mortality: a "natural" experiment', *Sociology of Health & Illness*, vol. 12, no. 4, 391–412.

Wilkinson, R.G. (1992) 'National mortality rates: the impact of inequality', *American Journal of Public Health*, vol. 82, no. 8, 1082–4.

Wilson, H.T. (1983) 'Anti-method as a counterstructure in social research practice.' In *Beyond Method: Strategies for Social Research*, Morgan, G. (ed.) pp. 247–59. Sage, Newbury Park, CA.

Wipper, A. (1984) 'Women's voluntary associations.' In *African Women South of the Sahara*, Hay, M.J. and S. Stichter (eds) pp. 69–86. Longman, London.

Women's Feature Service (1993) *The Power to Change: Women in the Third World Redefine Their Environment*. Zed Books, London.

Woolhandler, S., D.U. Himmelstein, R. Silber, M. Bader, M. Harnly, and A.A. Jones (1985) 'Medical care and mortality: racial differences in preventable deaths', *International Journal of Health Services*, vol. 15, no. 1, 1–22.

World Bank (1993) *World Development Report 1993: Investing in Health*. Oxford University Press, New York.

World Bank Office of Population; Health; and Nutrition (1994) *The How-To of Health Reform*. PHN Flash 11.

World Health Organization, Division of Family Health (1980) *Health and the Status of Women*. World Health Organization, Geneva. Report R 181-781-981-982.

World Health Organization (1985) *Women, Health and Development*. World Health Organization, Geneva.

World Health Organization (1992) *Women's Health: Across Age and Frontier*. World Health Organization, Geneva.

World Health Organization (1995) *The World Health Report 1995: Bridging the Gaps*. World Health Organization, Geneva.

Wrubel, J., P. Benner, and R.S. Lazarus (1981) 'Social competence from the perspective of stress and coping.' In *Social Competence*, Wine, J.D. and M.D. Smye (eds) pp. 61–99. Guilford Press, New York.

Wyke, S. and G. Graeme (1992) 'Competing explanations for associations between marital status and health', *Social Science & Medicine*, vol. 34, no. 5, 523–32.

Yach, D. (1992) 'The use and value of qualitative methods in health research in developing countries', *Social Science & Medicine*, vol. 35, no. 4, 603–12.

Yach, D., C. Mathews, and E. Buch (1990) 'Urbanisation and health: methodological difficulties in undertaking epidemiological research in developing countries', *Social Science & Medicine*, vol. 39, no. 4, 507–14.

Young, A. (1980) 'The discourse on stress and the reproduction of conventional knowledge', *Social Science & Medicine*, vol. 14B, 133–46.

Young, I.M. (1990) 'The ideal of community and the politics of difference.' In *Feminism/ Postmodernism*, Nicholson, L. (ed.) pp. 300–323. Routledge, New York.

Young, M.E. (1994) *Health Problems and Policies for Older Women: An Emerging Issue in Developing Countries*. World Bank. Informal Report.

Youssef, N.H. (1982) 'The interrelationship between the division of labour in the household, women's roles and their impact on fertility.' In *Women's Roles and Population Trends in the Third World*, Anker, R., M. Buvinic, and N.H. Youssef (eds) pp. 173–200. Croom Helm, London.

Yudelman, S.W. (1987) *Hopeful Openings: A Study of Five Women's Development Organizations in Latin America and the Caribbean*. Kumarian, West Hartford, CT.

Zapata, B.C., A. Rebolledo, E. Atalah, G. Newman, and M.-C. King (1992) 'The influence of social and political violence on the risk of pregnancy complications', *American Journal of Public Health*, vol. 82, no. 5, 685–90.

Zautra, A. and A. Hempel (1984) 'Subjective well-being and physical health: a narrative literature review with suggestions for future research', *International Journal of Aging and Human Development*, vol. 19, no. 2, 95–110.

Zeger, S.L. and M.C. Karim (1991) 'Generalized linear models with random effects: a Gibbs sampling approach', *Journal of the American Statistical Association*, vol. 86, no. 413, 79–86.

Zeger, S.L., K.Y. Liang, and P.S. Albert (1988) 'Models for longitudinal data: a generalized estimating equation approach', *Biometrics*, vol. 44, 1049–60.

Zia, H. (1993) 'The Global Fund for Women – Money with a Mission.' *Ms.*, 10–21.

Zimmerman, M.A. (1985) 'Empowerment, Perceived Control, and Citizen Participation: A Dissertation Proposal.' PhD Proposal, University of Illinois Psychology Department.

Zimmerman, M.A. (1990a) 'Taking aim on empowerment research: on the distinction between individual and psychological conceptions', *American Journal of Community Psychology*, vol. 18, no. 1, 169–77.

Zimmerman, M.A. (1990b) 'Toward a theory of learned hopefulness: a structural model analysis of participation and empowerment', *Journal of Research in Personality*, vol. 24, 71–86.

Zimmerman, M.A. and J. Rappaport (1988) 'Citizen participation, perceived control, and psychological empowerment', *American Journal of Community Psychology*, vol. 16, no. 5, 725–50.

Index